Journey to the End of an Era

AN INFORMAL AUTOBIOGRAPHY BY

MELVIN HALL

NEW YORK
CHARLES SCRIBNER'S SONS
1947

TO JOSEPHINE

I am a part of all that I have met;
Yet all experience is an arch wherethro'
Gleams that untravell'd world whose margin fades
For ever and for ever when I move.

Contents

ix

IV. SOUTH PERSIAN WANDERINGS

V. EUROPA INFELIX

1–I Hitch My Wagon to a Restless Star

On the Fortuity of Things

That the current of one's life should often be diverted into new and untried channels is not in itself a matter of wonderment, even though its major deviations have sprung from beginnings so casual as chance meetings over club bars. Yet I am led sometimes to reflect on the fortuity of things, and occasionally on the disproportion between causes and effect.

I was born on the Connecticut River at Bellows Falls, Vermont, for the customary reason that my mother was there at the time. Not being able to show four generations or so of Vermont ancestors back to the days when Vermont was an independent republic, and having spent only about twelve years there, I am not recognized by Vermonters as a true Vermonter. My ancestry on both sides of the family for many generations sprang from Massachusetts. But having neither been born nor ever having lived in that State I am not recognized there at all.

Bellows Falls, the part of it wrought by man, was an ugly little town located in a splendid natural setting. Even the setting has been gravely damaged by rugged individualism in the exploitation of natural resources. Fall Mountain, a shapely but stark prominence once covered with pines, which faced my birthplace from across the river, was denuded of every tree. The falls themselves, dropping fifty-two feet in less than half a mile, where the Connecticut River breaks through a narrow defile between the foothills of the Green and the White Mountains, are now a sorry tangle of dry and pot-holed rocks, the water having been led off for power of a hydro-electric plant. But the hinterland remains unspoiled and delightful.

The Great Falls, as they were earlier called, were the reason for the first canal built in America, begun in 1792 and opened ten years later. Shortly after 1830 a canal-boat named *William Hall* made an experimental trip up the Connecticut River. It was a side-wheeler, and whether its builders forgot to include the paddles in their calculations of its beam I do not know, but it could not pass through the canal. It was pulled by oxen over the streets of Bellows Falls, around one of the few places on American inland waters then designed for the convenient passage of river traffic. The boat appears to have been named for a

3

William Hall Jr., appointed in 1816 as joint manager of the canal. My father's name was William Hall, but he was born some thirty-six years after the canal-boat venture and was not, as far as I know, related very closely, if at all, to the one for whom the boat had been named. Yet that throw-back of my parent's name, at Bellows Falls, seemed an entertaining coincidence.

My father was an interesting though not a typical product of long New England background. He was a human dynamo of energy, a restless and ingenious individualist, and a keen sportsman along many lines. He made a multitude of friends in all walks of life. At the age of twenty-one he graduated from Massachusetts Institute of Technology and was promptly placed by his uncle, William A. Russell, to superintend the latter's Fall Mountain Paper Company mill at Bellows Falls— the first mill in the world, I believe, to manufacture paper from wood pulp. There for a short while he was referred to by the men who worked under him, all older than he, as the "silk-stocking kid."

Any one with a collegiate education was a silk-stocking kid to a two-fisted workman in those days, and my father was extremely young for his responsibilities. Also, his uncle owned the mill, as well as the canal company and other properties. (The mill was subsequently merged at a high valuation, at least partly as a result of my father's efforts, in the International Paper Company which William A. Russell founded.)

Youthful though he was, my father was capable, enthusiastic and— perhaps the most valuable asset of all at that time—a first-class amateur boxer. After he knocked out four or five of the toughest bruisers of the paper mill and log driving crews, under modified Marquess of Queensberry rules (one mustn't bash the other fellow over the head with a cant-dog or gouge out his eyes), often ceding up to fifty pounds in weight, they ceased to call him the silk-stocking kid.

(At the age of seventy he was still sparring three rounds twice a week with young French sailors in the port of Toulon.)

He ran one of the most efficient and toughest log drives in America. This started on the Wild Ammonoosuc and other rivers that debouch into the Connecticut from the White Mountains of New Hampshire, where the pulp-logs were cut in winter and poised on skids to be rolled into the spate as soon as the freshet started in spring. There were few rougher gangs in America than the lumberjacks—many of them French-

Canadian Indian half-breeds—who annually tooled those spruce logs through the freshet and down the Connecticut, booming off the millions of board feet earmarked for the Bellows Falls mill before the logs should go over the dam. On one occasion in medium high water a few particularly lusty jacks, probably well primed with raw red whisky, ran the dam and the narrow, turbulent chute below in their high-prowed bateau, a highly speculative as well as spectacular feat.

The rapids were formidable in those days. I remember hearing with native pride that Captain Paul Boyton who negotiated them in an inflated suit in 1879 (and was very nearly drowned) stated, after he revived, that they were far more dangerous than those of Niagara.

The rapids are among my earliest recollections—they and the whistled *whooo—whooo—who-o—who-o* of the locomotive echoing between Fall Mountain and the bluff on the Vermont side as the afternoon train puffed up the grade along the terraced slopes of the river valley. My father was an expert canoeman. Under his guidance I learned at a tender age to wield a paddle properly and handle the frail craft in rough water. Sometimes, disregarding his specific injunctions, I would sneak up alone into the eddy of the rapids, to be swung suddenly around and then try desperately to keep the tricky cockle-shell right side up.

The eddy formerly had been famous for salmon, which managed to fight their way up the falls; and for shad, which could proceed no farther.

My father had several Old Town canoes which he used to send to the headwaters of various Eastern rivers, and when he could get away we would go to one of these and run the river until it became too tame, camping along the banks by night. Nothing in my early life do I remember with so much pleasure as those canoe trips from the headwaters of our New England rivers. We ran the Fifteen Mile Falls of the Connecticut in the height of the spring flood (long before they were dammed and flattened out), and that was "putty wild watter" as a venerable inhabitant informed us just before we took off. But we made it, and only on one short stretch had recourse to sluicing the canoe, covered over with an apron, on the end of a cord down through an impossible turbulence.

It was just as well that we were good swimmers, though we very rarely upset. But once I went down a tearing rapid without visible means of support, and knew enough to relax my whole body so that it flowed around the rocks without concussion.

I was an only child, my father was an only child and his father was an only child. That sequence may doubtless have some bearing on one's character. But at least we were not descended from a long line of maiden aunts.

I learned to swim in an "old swimming hole" in Saxton's River, which drops into the Connecticut on the edge of Bellows Falls, and never missed a day in summer. It was an ideal hole. The water was clear and fresh, but not too cold. The pool was screened by trees, a sheer cliff, and a wide basin where I also learned to ride. There was a round rock on one side, and a ledge high up the cliff on the other from which one could dive.

After an absence of thirty-five years I returned to that swimming hole. I drove around the top of the basin, curiously terraced by the river, and down into it; then along the willow-studded banks of the little river to the hole. It was just as secluded as ever. Leaving my clothes in the car I pulled on a pair of trunks and walked up onto the round rock. I could feel the same grips beneath my feet on the surface of the rock that in days gone by I had used for diving. I dived, and having in one motion sloughed off thirty-five years, swam across to the far side, stepped on an invisible shelf eight inches below the surface and swarmed up the sheer side of the cliff by scarcely visible hand- and toe-holds—not one of which I missed—to the narrow diving-ledge about twelve feet overhead. I dived in again, quite sure of the depth. It was an extraordinary feeling. Not a thing about that swimming hole or its aspect had changed in thirty-five years, nor had I lost a single touch in my recollection of it. There are not very many spots in the built-up United States where that could happen.

My mother was an Adams from Massachusetts. She was small, with tiny feet, and was extremely good-looking in her youth. She was just twenty-one when I was born; my father was a year older. Both of them were keen riders and we always had horses, including a diminutive Shetland pony for me when I was about five. We kept them in the stable of Mrs. Hetty Green, America's richest and meanest woman, who practically starved and froze her ailing husband—"Old Green" she called him—to death in a dingy though once-fine grey brick house a few hundred yards from ours.

Rudyard Kipling lived for a time at Brattleboro, twenty-five miles south of us. My father knew him, and I remember sometimes staring with the wide-eyed curiosity of youth at that moth-eaten-looking, irascible, brilliant little man. He had married a Balestier girl of Brattleboro and started a house there overlooking one of the loveliest reaches of the Connecticut River. But he faced the house the wrong way round because people kept driving out on the communal road to look at it; and he quit Brattleboro and America forever after a row with his brother-in-law, "Batty" Balestier, over the building of it.

Batty had been left in charge of construction while the Kiplings were away in the South. Rudyard returned unexpectedly and was informed by one of Brattleboro's ancient hackmen that Batty had not drawn a sober breath all the time the Kiplings were away, and had committed some prime stupidities in the building of the new house, such as laying the drainpipes with their flanges uphill so that they all froze and burst in the Vermont winter. Rudyard Kipling was not in a very amiable frame of mind when he reached the property and found Batty reeling about gurgling happily to himself. He blasted Batty in searing terms with having ill requited his trust.

"Rudzh'd," said Batty thickly, "'f you talk t'me tha' way I'll have t' knock yu down!"

If Kipling, small though he was, had pushed Batty with one hand the latter probably would have gone over backwards and stayed there. Instead, Rudyard went to Brattleboro and swore out a warrant against his brother-in-law for attempted assault. The trial brought to that small town the best journalistic talent in the United States, and the publicity was not flattering to Kipling. He pulled up stakes at the end of it, never to set foot in America again.

My father had been an enthusiast at bicycling when that was a sport which afforded many of the thrills of flying in the early days of the Wright brothers. The contrivance he proudly manipulated around about the end of his school days had a backbone and forks of solid iron on which he perched above an enormously high, solid-tired wheel, with a little trailer-wheel behind. It was impossible to pedal the thing up a hill. It had no brake, and any toe-braking on that great wheel tended to catapult the rider clean off his elevated perch. On descents my parent would put his legs over the handlebars in the hope that when he met an irregularity in the road and the cycle turned over he would have some chance of landing on his feet. Yet he rode it 108 miles in a single day.

I never actually saw him on that cycle. By the time I was old enough to notice things, or it may have been before I was born, he had acquired one of the first "safety" bicycles with two wheels of the same size. This, as I remember, was a Remington, a "marvel of lightness" according to the manufacturers, which weighed seventy pounds. It had single-tube pneumatic tires, among the earliest of their kind. As soon as I was old enough I had one too, smaller and not so heavy, and split my head open one evening on a bad spill when I ran over a concealed dog.

It was quite natural, of course, that my father should have gone in for motorcars, or "horseless carriages" as they were called, in the very earliest days of their introduction. He bought the seventh car, I believe it was, that Alexander Winton sold commercially. It was the first automobile ever brought into the State of Vermont, and, I think, was the first introduced into New Hampshire and Maine as well. That was in 1898. The first car sold in America antedated it only by a few weeks.

The Winton was a horseless carriage in all senses, including the lack of a horse to drag one home when it broke down. Oddly enough this did not occur very often, though our returns were sometimes rather limping. It had a sloping dashboard—without a whip-socket—and steered by a tiller. It had two kerosene side-lamps in case we were caught out after dark, and a folding leather hood against the rain. It did not boast, as I recall it, a single instrument.

Under the seat was a one-cylinder horizontal engine. This had an enormous spark-plug in the head, so arranged that to remove it for cleaning one had first to undo the body-bolts and lift the body. The wheels had single-tube tires cemented to the rims. There was no spare, nor even a repair kit provided in the event of a puncture.

My father, having had experience with his "safety" bicycles equipped with such tires, wrote to Mr. Winton. Unfortunately the correspondence was lost, but as I recall it the interchange went roughly as follows:

"Dear Mr. Winton: I am now in possession of my horseless carriage which is giving me fine service. There is one feature, however, which disturbs me, and that is the question of repair of the tires in case of a puncture. I am familiar with the repair of pneumatic bicycle tires, but these of your horseless carriage are much thicker than bicycle tires and there is no one here who knows how to repair them. I would appreciate your advice in this matter."

"Dear Mr. Hall: I am glad to hear that your horseless carriage is giving you the satisfaction that I felt sure it would. As to the tires, you need have no concern. They are made of real rubber and are five-eighths of an inch thick. You will have no punctures . . ." Actually the tires were of practically pure rubber, so that if one pulled out a fragment from a cut it became translucent and would snap back like an elastic band. But my father was not satisfied.

"Dear Mr. Winton: I appreciate that the tires are made of real rubber five-eighths of an inch thick and that a puncture is highly improbable. But I might run over a railway spike or something else that would pierce even their tough resistance. In such case, what should I do? No one here can suggest how a repair might be effected."

"Dear Mr. Hall: In the highly improbable event that you will ever have a puncture in one of your tires, I can only suggest that you remove the wheel and send it back to our factory at Cleveland, Ohio. We will then get the manufacturer of the tires to make the repair and will return the wheel and tire, duly restored, to you." Not a completely satisfactory way of repairing punctures, since Cleveland, Ohio, was somewhat remote from Bellows Falls, Vermont. But Mr. Winton was right. I do not recall that we ever had a puncture. We made up for this in later models.

My father's automotive pioneering in that noisy, horse-frightening contraption attained a local though temporary odium that might well have deterred any less buoyant spirit. (Mount Desert Island was closed to motor vehicles for some twenty years after an exploratory tour of the Halls' Winton.) I thus gained considerable early knowledge of the behavior of frightened horses, and with my father developed a special technique in handling them. Yet this did not solve the problem. Among my recollections is one of walking seventy-five yards ahead of our "benzine buggy" armed with a red flag, leading it temporarily out of the State across the covered wooden toll-bridge over the Connecticut, when unsympathetic horse-owning township elders were seeking to restrain its activities under decrees framed for itinerant steam-rollers.

I remember also a day when the muffler blew out and the spiral baffleplate stuffed with asbestos-wool uncoiled and trailed out behind. My father was driving, my mother beside him with a parasol up and a dust-veil draped from her large-brimmed hat. I was sitting on the floor. A wide-eyed gamin suddenly stopped shrieking the usual hail of the day, "Git a horse! Git a horse!" and pointed at my mother. "Hey, Missis," he yelled, "yer guts is coming out!"

The Winton was followed in due course by other motor vehicles, some of which were rare and wonderful specimens. One of these was a shrimp-pink, eight-horsepower, two-cylinder Panhard with rear wheels half again as large as the front. It had a basket-type tonneau with a rear entrance, where two passengers could sit facing quarteringly inward. Its ignition came from hot platinum tubes heated by pilot-lights affixed below the cylinder jackets. The system worked reasonably well until one met a starboard cross-wind strong enough to douse the naked flames. Then the engine would sputter and die.

"Those damn pilot-lights!" my father would grunt. "They've blown out again!" And I would clamber down the step to unstrap the bonnet while he fumbled with matches in the driving wind.

Each night after we extinguished the pilot-lights we waited for the tubes to cool, then removed and carried them off in our pockets lest some bright chauffeur with knowledge of their value should remove them permanently to other ends.

My father loved the water and was fond of sailing-canoes and small boats. He kept a launch called the *Widgeon* on the Connecticut above the Bellows Falls dam at a time when I think there were extremely few pleasure launches throughout the length of the river. Later, when we summered at York Harbor, he had the *Iole,* the fastest motorboat on the Atlantic coast north of Boston—once one got it started. He also acquired a large motor houseboat named the *Ruffhouse* which he took down to Florida, but sold her to Harry Payne Whitney after one season.

He worked hard and made a substantial amount of money through his restless inventive genius. He developed several highly successful processes and formed companies to exploit them, including the Casein Company of America, and pulled out from these as soon as they were firmly established. He was very generous, spent his money freely and enjoyed himself in doing so, which perhaps was all for the best, as in the end he lost everything he had. He was, of course, the prime mover in the fortuity of early environment, exploratory proclivities and keen interest in the foreign scene that served to shape my ends.

When I was about twelve my family moved to New York. As a young boy accustomed to the country and the outdoors, I hated it. But we spent the summers in Maine, first at Winter Harbor and later at York Harbor; and when I could get away from school I would sometimes go with my father to shoot wild boar and other game in the Blue Mountain Forest Park in New Hampshire. This 25,000-acre estate, which included the fair-sized Croydon Mountain, had been stocked by Austin Corbin Sr. with Bavarian and Russian boar, elk, bison and many other alien beasts in addition to its deer, beaver, wildcats, black bears, foxes and such native fauna. Often when clambering around the mountain I ran almost head-on into a bearded Siberian goat that regarded me with grave disfavor. For me that park was the most fascinating place in America.

I took up motorcycling with vigor and had one of the first two-cylinder machines in America. It was a French Peugeot and was the cause of my being arrested in York Harbor on the complaint of Thomas Nelson Page, who charged that I was a public menace. Probably I was.

I attended Princeton University and there distinguished myself more for extracurricular activities than for the excellence of my grading, though I had no particular trouble with my studies when I applied myself to them. But there were so many other things to do!

One beautiful sunny day I was looking out of a window from a lecture room on the top floor of Nassau Hall a little before the lecture started. I noticed that someone had left an extension ladder reaching almost, but not quite, to the window, and thought that if I should hang out the window I could drop right onto the upper rungs of the ladder. I was not especially interested in the lecture and my seat happened to be on the aisle, opposite the window. So when the monitor had marked the absentees by checking the numbers on the empty seats, and the lecturer (I think it was Henry van Dyke) turned his back for an instant, I leaped for the window, swung out and dropped onto the ladder. My classmates who observed this move were a bit startled, not knowing about the ladder. I scurried down it and when I touched ground looked around to see Woodrow Wilson, then President of the University, standing at the foot surveying the performance. He did not appear unduly disapproving, but I felt a mild shock of confusion.

"Was the lecture very boring, Mr. Hall?" he asked with a twinkle.

"Very, sir," I said. He gave a slight smile and walked away. I never heard anything more about that incident.

One of my classmates, Harry Cannon, had a Stoddard-Dayton runabout. I think no others in my class had cars, which were still a rarity on the bumpy trails that connected even the principal cities. He was not especially keen on driving; I was, so usually I acted as chauffeur. Some of our cruises in that clattering piece of mechanism were weird and wonderful, often with seven or eight highly irresponsible class-mates hanging on to odd projections. More than one of these supernu-meraries had his behind well cooked while riding on one of the loose mudguards, which the weight of a body caused to drag against the tire until it became red-hot from the friction and the postilion rider howled in agony. This was esteemed a prime joke.

We did many rather outrageous things, but a merciful Providence which looks after children and lunatics saved us somehow from just retribution. In this matter a brace of completely irrelevant license plates also helped. On occasion they inspired constructive suggestions to unmounted policemen as to what they might do with the numerals they had noted down.

"I've got your number!" they would shout. Some of our crew always had apt though inelegant proposals for the guidance of the "cops" in such cases.

At certain grade crossings the single-bar barriers were usually down at night, their guardians asleep in obscure places. We found it tiresome to halt each time to raise the barriers, especially as the car would seldom stop within some two hundred yards under the illusory appli-cation of its brakes. Harry, sitting astride the motor hood, developed considerable skill in throwing up the bars with his hands as we ap-proached at about twenty miles an hour. The probability of decapita-tion of us both, had he missed, added a sporting zest to the procedure.

There was a night when the two of us got lost in a snowstorm. We could see nothing through the flakes save an occasional reflected glint from our feeble acetylene lights off some car-tracks I had straddled as the only clew to direction. The road was so remarkably rough that we scarcely noticed, though moving then quite slowly, a sudden acute bumping, until the regularity of it induced suspicion that all was not well.

"God in heaven!" yelled Harry, now wide awake. "Where on earth do you suppose we are?"

We were not on earth. I undertook a reconnaissance, first feeling down with my foot before stepping out of the car. The foot touched nothing directly below.

"I'll bite!" I responded. "Where do *you* suppose we are?"

Further exploration with an electric flashlight which carried less than a yard through the driven snowflakes revealed that we were out on a single-track trolley trestle, without guard-rails. Its widely spaced ties were there some forty feet above running water. We measured this by lowering a wrench tied to the end of a rope.

I backed the car for nearly half an hour off that trestle, one tie at a time. And as always we got home intact, at some unseemly hour the next day, which was the usual outcome of our binges.

In the summer of 1902, then a callow child of twelve, I made my first trip to Europe with my parents. In Paris my father rented a cumbrous two-cylinder, twelve-horsepower Panhard with a high roof over it on top of which, just above the front seat, was perched a large coil radiator that leaked hot, rusty water at every jounce in the road, so that wherever the surface was at all rough we had to travel with open umbrellas over our heads. A chauffeur named Henri went with it (nearly all French chauffeurs of that decade were named Henri). He earned his pay, for the lumbering vehicle had a phenomenal ability for picking up nails in its tires that took two hours to change, including hand pumping up to eighty-five pounds pressure. Yet with it we covered a sizable area of France, Belgium, Holland and Germany. Motor touring, even over the well-maintained highroads of western Europe, counted as pretty much of a sporting venture in the crude, under-powered benzine-wagons of that epoch.

That was the first of a number of such trips, my father continually seeking new territories to explore. We were towed out of difficulties by man-power and woman-power, by horse- and cow- and even dog-power, variously aided and abetted, sheltered, patched up and sent on our way by a steadily increasing number of races whose languages were often beyond our grasp.

I went over in 1908, with Penn Harvey as a guest and partly to supervise my irregularities (he had, I suspect, a fairly tall order there). This time we brought a Packard and struck into southern France and Italy. Again in 1910 we went as far as Warsaw, and from that now devastated city my mother and I continued on around the world—the first of four circumnavigations all by different media of transport—across the Trans-Siberian Railway and through China and Japan.

From each of those trips I returned with growing question whether the demarkation of human behavior essentially followed international frontiers.

DD-1532

In the early autumn of 1911 I accompanied my father and mother to India for the Coronation Durbar of King George V. During that summer we had motored across Europe and through the land of the Black Mountains—the Montenegrin fastnesses whose sturdy farmers presented spades in salute as we passed their small plots of terraced field, since only the Royal Family had motorcars. After various difficulties due to the Italo-Turkish war we brought the car to Bombay, and thence in due course reached Delhi.

The Coronation Durbar of King George was the only occasion when a British sovereign has held Durbar in India in person. It was also probably the last ceremonial of its kind to be staged in the full splendor of Oriental pageantry. Already the motorcar was displacing the elephant as a processional vehicle. This made for a somewhat faster moving procession (the King-Emperor and his entourage rode on horseback in the State Entry) and slightly reduced the extravagance of the parade. But the *mise en scène* was lavish enough without the processional elephants, and it is unlikely that it will ever be repeated.

There were twenty-five square miles of tents comprising one hundred eighty-four separate camps of every size and shape. The largest and most dignified, as was fitting, was the great *shamiana* of the King-Emperor in its setting of gardens and green lawns, where had been only the dun-colored Delhi plain a few short months before. The camps of the Ruling Princes were extremely colorful, resplendent with hanging embroideries and paintings of weird and fearsome animals on the sides of the *shamianas,* with entries through elaborate gateways flanked by fanciful guardians of the gates. The smallest, I believe, was the neat row of bachelors' tents of Curzon House Visitors' Camp, one of which I occupied. At dusk, from the slight rise of the Ridge when the fragrant smokes of evening wisped languidly overhead and the myriad lights—those of a hundred miles of lighted roads being but a modest part—picked out that vast expanse of canvas and decorative effects, the tented city of a quarter million souls was an unforgettable thing.

There were fifty thousand troops of all arms. The massed bands of forty-eight regiments played with three thousand pieces, along with the Governor General's orchestra and seven Dohl and Sirenai bands of native music. The troops and the bands were the vanguard and background of every performance, the whole show, of course, at the great Military Review. They were immensely picturesque in the variety and color of their uniforms and the trappings of their animals. Every morning I would be wakened, just before my bearer slipped barefooted through the tent-flaps with early tea, to the fife-strains of "British Grenadiers" or skirling bagpipes that might be Scotch or Himalayan, as unit after unit swung smartly down the road past my tent on the way to their early stations.

The State Entry was lent a fantastic touch by the Ruling Princes who followed after the King and Queen, surrounded by their ancient forms. There were Rajas in silver and gold carriages flanked by footmen bearing golden staves and silver hatchets. Other Rajas rode in phaetons and barouches guarded by escorts in chain mail, by macebearers and spearmen, by barefooted hillmen in green smocks and kilts armed with battle-axes, swords and shields, or matchlocks and silver powder horns. There were Rajas attended by state bards chanting their masters' titles, by bearers of embroidered umbrellas and peacock fans, by bearers of jeweled processional weapons and honorific symbols defying Western description.

I was bedazed by the phantasmagoria of costumes on Durbar Day, and the jewels that were a part of them, as the Ruling Princes and principal dignitaries of all India advanced in order of their rank up the golden carpet to salaam in their different fashions to their Imperial Overlord. The King and Queen were seated in full regalia on the Durbar thrones beneath a red-and-gold *shamiana* stretched on gilded poles against the Eastern sun. The salaaming lasted for several hours. I observed His Majesty now and again furtively mopping his brow under the ermine band of his heavy crown.

There came Princes in pink brocade, in robes of peacock blue broidered with gold and pearls, in skirted robes of fine white muslin with gold and emerald accoutrements. There were Princes in long black gowns hung with necklaces of diamonds and ropes and ropes of pearls. The Nizam of Hyderabad made his obeisance in a frock coat, unadorned save for the Nizami diamond of 277 carats on his black, brimless hat. There were Princes in cloth of silver and of gold with emeralds and rubies and diamonds strung uncut, wrought into floral patterns, encrusting their sabers, belts and buckles. The Maharaja of

Indore wore a dog collar of gigantic pearls and several ropes of emeralds the size of walnuts around his neck; the Maharaja of Cooch Behar was the glamour-boy of the lot in a peach-colored gown all emblazoned with pearls in flowery patterns simulating bunches of grapes from his turban to his waist. There were Princes in black velvet with gold lace and golden headdresses; in white silk with gold embroidery, with bird-of-paradise plumes and hawsers of emeralds; in blue satin over primrose brocade all embroidered with pearls and diamonds.

They were variously topped off by splendid jewelled turbans with gold and pearl egrets, golden hats set with emeralds, plumed hats bordered with pearls, hats like inverted flower-pots surmounted by peacock feathers. The Shan Chiefs and Sawbwas of Burma wore stiff golden capes flaming upwards at the edges, with lacquered hats or hats like multi-staged pagodas of beaten gold.

Many bore marvelous styles and names, running often to four or five full printed lines. Even the shorter ones possessed a quaint flavor, such as the repetitious flow—rather like a bird call—of Maharaja Sri Sri Sri Sri Sri Sir Ugyen Wangchuck.

Some of the Rajas sported magnificent beards dyed glossy black or red or pink, parted in the center and brushed fiercely upwards at the sides. There were Judges resplendent in grey wigs and scarlet robes, youthful Maharajas in the gorgeous light-blue uniform of the Imperial Cadet Corps, with littler ones in the pale blue and gold of princely pages sitting on the steps around the throne, alongside the towering *chobdars* in gold and red who held the Imperial golden maces.

Together they reflected the splendor of the Eastern sky through the mauve shadows of the *shamianas*.

At Delhi our car was assigned a special registration number for the duration of the ceremonies that officially lasted ten days—DD (Delhi Durbar) 1532. Under that license I drove eastwards, shipping here and there across the intervening seas, until I came to New York more than a year later.

We first struck south into Rajputana and for several days *en route* to Jaipur and Udaipur followed desert trails unknown to motorcars. One day of laborious effort and the aid of a span of bullocks advanced us fourteen and three-quarter miles. We ran the length of the Grand

Trunk Road, frightening horses and zebu, donkeys, camels and elephants in the ceaseless flow of pedestrian and wheeled traffic through
which Kim used to slip unobserved on his special occasions. We raced
the great grey apes that loped easily alongside, and startled solemn
adjutant birds three feet tall into loud clacking of their beaks. As we
progressed eastward the crowds on the road became ever denser, until
I could barely push a way through the plodding masses; easterly
plodding masses, carrying their shoes in their hands.

"They going Magh-Mela," said our bearer Anthony, a Christian
from the south who regarded such things with disapproval. "They going
wash in River Ganga." And so we crept along with the Hindu pilgrims
converging on Allahabad, intent on saving themselves an infinity of
rebirths through bathing in the confluence of the 'three' sacred rivers
during the holy month of Magh.

Throughout Hindustan there is no spot so sacred as the Prayaga,
the Place of Sacrifice at Allahabad, where the blue waters of the Jumna
wed the yellow waters of the Ganges, and the lost Saraswati that van-
ishes in the sands of Sirhind four hundred miles away unites—so devout
Hindus believe—with the other two from underground.

Each year in the Hindu month of Magh there is held a vast festival
called a Mela, that draws the pious in their hundreds of thousands from
all over India. Every sixth and twelfth year, when the Sun and Jupiter
are in a certain relationship, this becomes an Adh-Kumbh or a Kumbh
Mela—an Extraordinary Mela—which they attend in their millions.
Millions of devout, practising the outward forms of their faith, coming
from great distances afoot to wash away their sins in one of the greatest
mass manifestations of religious fervor on our globe.

Then also the various sects of ascetics foregather from their monas-
teries and mendicant wanderings to bathe in formal procession at the
junction of the sacred rivers, and the devotees of Siva go in their 'official'
state of nakedness which they are not permitted to assume at any other
time in the year.

It so happened that we came to Allahabad in an Adh-Kumbh year,
during the holy month of Magh.

There were two million souls on the sandy spit of land between the
two rivers, at whose confluence the third and lost one allegedly springs
forth.

"Maybe you think there are no headaches in keeping 'em in order,
these simple, peaceful pilgrims bent on their religious observances,"

remarked one of the British officers from the Allahabad Fort who were responsible for the maintenance of the peace. "Well, the hell there aren't! The different sects cordially despise one another, they're desperately jealous of their positions and prerogatives, and some of 'em are damn fanatical. If a couple of the *akharas*—the bodies of parading fakirs—should happen to run afoul of each other there's no telling *what* might result. I can assure you that marshalling 'em in that mess of two million-odd excitable souls is no sweet job!" Religious observance is not always carried out in a spirit of humility and loving thought.

The confluence was commanded by the guns of Allahabad Fort. "And those guns are loaded, old boy," said my British friend, "and manned day and night during the whole of the show. Wouldn't want to use cannon, of course, unless we damn well have to; but with millions of inflammable people—including most of the permanent population of Allahabad itself—ready to go off at a spark, one has to be prepared."

Anthony, our Christian bearer, looked upon the whole performance not only with disapproval but concern. "You are my father and my mother," said he, "yet I thinking it not good to go down there." I did go 'down there', of course, and often: I would not have missed that sight on the Tirathraj, the "Chiefest Place of Pilgrimage," for many rebirths, potential or to be remitted.

For two miles or more the sandy spit was a solid mass of humanity. The mass spread out onto densely packed boats and barges idling along the water's edge, where the bathers were so thick that the beach at Coney Island in a heat wave would have seemed like an underpopulated atoll. An endless, varicolored overturn of devotees determined on washing away their sins, pouring their hopeful gifts of milk and flowers upon the restless breast of Mother Ganga.

At the upper end stood a great multitude of little shops, huts, preaching booths, places of entertainment and police commissariats; and quantities of open shaving serais where the ground was covered inches deep with the hair of more than a million heads. That hair would all be packed up before the moon had waned, and be dumped into the river, for every hair above the chin that finds its way into the Ganges during the month of Magh secures the release of its former owner from the small matter of ten thousand rebirths.

Through the middle of the human mass packed beneath the guns of the Fort ran a roped way leading to the *Tirbeni,* the junction of the 'three' rivers. This was the processional way by which, on the three holiest days of Magh, the various fakir sects paraded with pomp and music and elephants to bathe at the rivers' confluence. Along its fringes on either side there lay or squatted or hung in unreposeful postures the strange company of ascetics seeking godliness through austerities and detachment from the world.

They were those who are "indifferent to pleasure and pain, insensible to heat and cold, incapable of satiety or want." Some of them held both arms upraised over their heads; withered arms, first strapped in that position until they atrophied, now sticking up gaunt and useless like pairs of antlers from their owners' shoulders. Some crouched in cages where they had grown into strange deformities from being able neither to stand nor sit, nor to stretch out at length. Some lay on beds of spikes. Others held out fists that could never be unclenched, with nails and finger tips growing out through the backs of their hands. A few hung head downwards by the ankles over slow-burning fires, naked save for a loin-cloth and a towel around the head. Yet their detachment from the world was not so complete as to exclude certain measures for attracting attention to their exhibitionism and the spreading of cloths upon the ground to receive pious contributions.

The fakir camps were located as far apart as possible so that the uncongenial sight of one another might not induce riot and bloodshed between the sects. On the three specially holy days of Magh—the new moon, the light half and the full—all the sects paraded in state down the roped lane to take their ceremonial baths, each at its prescribed hour. The harassed British marshalling officers were in an advanced stage of jitters lest their arrangements should miscarry and the different *akharas* meet and start tearing each other apart. On the day of the new moon of Magh, more than any other day, the nerves of the marshals were taut down under Allahabad's ancient fort. And this day I chose in guileless spirit to drive out upon the "Chiefest Place of Pilgrimage" in our car.

I was ploughing through the sand along the processional way when an infuriated police major galloped up on a big chestnut Waler and damned me well and properly to all eternity. He forced the car over against the wall of staring faces.

"*What* in God's name are you doing here in that ruddy chariot?" he roared. "D'you think we've nothing on our minds with all these blasted fakirs but that you must come bounding into the midst of it to brighten things up?" He was definitely not pleased. Of that I had no doubt at all when our ruddy chariot was shunted unceremoniously to the side and he made note of its Delhi Durbar registry. He swore he would have me interned in a fortress where the opportunities for shattering the peace of His Majesty's Indian realm would be less conspicuous. Then he galloped furiously away, it being time for the *akharas* to set forth on their parades.

The car was jammed against an edge of the solid wall of humanity with the side-rope of the processional lane carried round its protruding outline. The dispossessed front-row watchers settled upon it like a swarm of bees, blotting out its contours. We stood on the seats and from there looked across two million or so closely packed heads. Not far off, one of those seeking detachment from the world hung head down over a slow fire, swinging gently as an acolyte pulled now and again on the rope to keep him from actively cooking.

The comparative silence that held for a few moments after the police commandant had galloped away gave place to a wailing of native instruments, loud squawks from horns and conch-shells, and the beating of drums. The Nirbanis came trooping down the lane in irregular formations eight or ten abreast, about a hundred of them, naked but for necklaces of *rudraksha* berries. They were not pretty to look at. Their hair was long and matted, their bodies smeared with ashes, their bearded faces evil. Some carried bells. They were the "Supreme Geese," who were followers of Siva.

One amongst them walked in line by himself. He was short and thickset, and in no way detached from the world. He kept glancing proudly at the intense crowds on either side as he walked. He had the most colossal male organ a human being could very well carry, hanging to his knees, swinging from side to side like the trunk of an elephant. And as he went past, the barren women broke from under the side-ropes, swarmed out onto the lane to snatch and eat handfuls of the sand on which he had trodden.

"Some of these fakir lads establish quite a reputation for themselves with their charms against barrenness," remarked my irreverent officer friend from the Fort later that evening. "They pitch their wee shelter-tents out by the gates of the towns; the barren wives come to consult them in the privacy of evening. And oddly enough—or it may be naturally—their charms are often effective."

Hour after hour the different sects paraded past our outpost, which was like a promontory in a sea of intense faces. They were timed with extreme caution that they should not meet, yet followed in close succession because there were many. They did not meet. My driving up the processional lane caused no flurry of disturbance other than with the police commandant. It brought instead unmerited reward in an extraordinary view of the proceedings. The "Supreme Geese" returned in due course from their baths, and again the barren women broke under the ropes to snatch up the sand trodden by the master healer of their sorrowful state.

By late afternoon the way was clear. I beat an orderly retreat before the military police caught us up. We had planned to leave Allahabad the next morning at nine. We left instead at dawn, and I took the precaution to replace the DD registry plates with our pre-Durbar French plaques. Once the Allahabad district was cleared I put back the DD-1532's, and removed them no more until I reached New York twelve months later.

We continued to the end of the Grand Trunk Road at Calcutta; then struck southwards into the Madras Presidency. From southern India we shipped to the Island of Ceylon. I had an urge to sail across on a fishing smack with the engaging name *Virgin Mary of Tuticorin*, but was regretfully dissuaded.

We covered more than twelve hundred miles in Ceylon. With a thousand chanting pilgrims I climbed Adam's peak by torchlight to watch the sunrise cast and foreshorten its gigantic pyramidal shadow. We heard the singing fish of Batticaloa intone their plaintive cadences beneath the moon. With my father I sailed on the Indian Ocean in the out-rigged dug-out fishing canoes that reverse end for end but cannot tack nor keep moving for long without water flung to tauten their loose brown sails. I tried a hand at climbing coconut trees with a long belt and shark-skin creepers strapped to my calves. And I learned not to leave a motorcar in the jungle unattended.

This last lesson was acquired near Anuradhapura. For several hours we left DD-1532 alone in the forest, or so we thought. The car was not alone when we returned. It was in possession of a troop of long-tailed monkeys busily taking it apart. They had undone everything that would undo and were twisting and turning all the fittings that would twist. They had emptied the pockets and a canvas pouch, had seized on every loose article we had left in the car, and at our approach decamped into the trees laden with their spoil.

"Damn you, drop that, you imp of Satan! . . . that's my duster!" my father roared as he dashed in full sprint after a fleeing monkey. The agile looter easily outdistanced him, swarmed up a tree trailing the pongee dust-coat out behind, to shriek invective at the owner's head from the safety of a swaying branch.

My incensed parent returned panting from his futile chase and began to search the empty pockets of the car. His bellows would have shamed a sea-lion. "The fiends of hell! They've gone off with my tobacco! Dammit, *that's* too much!"

That was not the half of it. I took stock of the missing effects. The maps . . . the small tool-kit . . . my notebook . . . the list grew. They had taken everything removable. Many of the filched items were not replaceable in Ceylon. Woolly scarves, an Ingersoll watch, a handy oiler, a folding canvas bucket, a collection of wing-nuts off the car, the brass knobs of all the controls, the door-handles, the valve-caps from the tires, even the rubber bulb of the horn. The only loose equipment I managed to salvage was a rug its looter abandoned when it caught at the foot of his tree. They had unset all the external adjustments on the car, and to cap their injury hurled insults at us from above along with hard, inedible growths.

They went far beyond the efforts of the crows at the Galle Face Hotel that came in one's window to snatch any small bright object off the dressing table or a bit of toast from one's breakfast tray. The crows, at least, were not interested in our heavier clothing nor in sabotage of our mechanical gear.

"I only hope," growled my father, "that the tobacco and machine-oil make those monkeys damn sick!"

From Colombo my father headed back to business affairs in Europe while I took ship eastward with my mother for Rangoon. There, after a trip into Upper Burma, I picked up "Fig" Vorhees and bore him with us down the Malay Peninsula to Java. No road led through the jungly isthmus to Penang; so we coasted that stretch on a British ship. From Penang to Johore the roads of Malaya were the most perfect I had ever travelled.

Smooth ribbons they were, white and even, unrolling into a tropical density of vines and air-plants and tangled creepers draped on enormous tree trunks, barring all vision twenty feet to either side. Over them we rolled through virgin forest that thrummed to the drone of a myriad insects, the shrill *yeep-yeep-yeep* of tree toads and melancholy bird-calls of the jungle, from whose twilit depths unnumbered watchers followed our progress with wondering, mistrustful eyes. We passed also through clearings where the jungle had been turned into rubber plantations, miles and miles of *hevea* groves, from tiny shoots to scored trees in full yield.

"At this rate," grunted Fig, waving towards the *hevea* trees as we sweated at mounting new tires on the lugged rims that were the devil's own contraption, "rubber should become so cheap that tire manufacturers may put some of it in their products!" The torn string-and-fabric walls of two scarcely worn covers which burst less than an hour apart had a baleful effect in the steamy lowland heat amidst all that growing rubber.

We wound over passes across the dorsal range when the wooded slopes lay drenched in claret from the sunset and darkness cascaded down the mountainsides like an outflung cloak, heralded by throaty cries of nightjars flying just overhead. The tiny lanterns of mile-long bullock-cart trains picked out the road below in serpentine lines of yellow dots across the dark of the slopes. Now and again we would come on such a train creeping round a bend. Our headlights' glare caught the startled bullock faces two by two, reflecting off four blazing, opalescent eyes, and on the uptilted roofs of palm-leaf thatch from beneath which the drivers cried loudly into the blinding light and then melodiously, as we passed on, to calm their frightened beasts.

Sometimes the road, wet and glistening under tropic downpours, would be as covered with little frogs as though the rain had brought them. Sometimes it was carpeted in golden blossoms through the scented Gothic aisles of *angsena* trees, or edged by "Flame-of-the-Forest" trees standing in crimson pools of fallen bloom. And every rolling mile of it was perfectly kept as if the maintenance were done with a brush and manicure scissors.

"Where are the Malays?" Fig inquired the second day out. "I've seen Chinese and Indians, but where are the Malays?"

We saw Malays, but not often where labor was the thing in hand. We saw them on the verandahs of their little *nipa*-thatched houses, contentedly watching their coconuts and plantains and tiny paddy-fields ripen through nature's benevolence. We saw them in the dim interiors of huts built up on stilts away from the damp and the snakes; family groups of them squatted round the evening bowl of rice, fat babies happy on their backs upon the matting floor. We saw them waiting dreamily in canoes for fish to come and stick their silly heads into nets. But almost never did we see them at toil.

"Why *should* they work?" I queried. "Nature provides nearly everything they need for the asking. A month's spasmodic labor takes care of the paddy-fields. Why should they poison contentment with needless strife? Let the Chinese and the other funny aliens do that if they will, says the Malay. He just isn't interested in the things that call for sacrifice of peace of mind or would prevent his full enjoyment of a care-free existence. I've read about him. Now I'm beginning to appreciate his philosophy."

"We should have been Malays," murmured Fig, with half-closed eyes. The day was extremely warm and we had just had a flat tire.

"The Malay neither requires nor wants the material things that are purchased with worry and unrest," I went on. "He's indolent, if you like, with the indolence of a warm and generous climate—a beauty-loving, family-loving indolence. But he's not shiftless. He's a good craftsman when it comes to labor-saving devices. Look at his little bamboo wheels raising water to irrigate his fields. Clever, and work by themselves."

"I told you we should have been Malays," repeated Fig. "It's a matter of environment, of course. The Malay wouldn't last long with his present philosophy in, well, say New York, or even Florida."

"I grant that," I said. "But by virtue of his environment the Malay has decomplicated his existence. He's not nationalistic. He has a beautiful tolerance, and he isn't a bit jealous of the material gains of others, even of interlopers in his own country."

"Which is a good philosophy," Fig concluded, "if you can make it work."

The towns seethed with Chinese. Chinese pulled 'rikishas, with Chinese men and women of substance riding in them. All the shops were Chinese, half covered by huge signs vertically lettered in red and blue and gold. The more imposing residences were pointed out as "rich-Chinaman-bungalow." Chinese laborers in blue denim swarmed up the sides of open-cast tin mines on notched tree trunks, bearing baskets of wash-dirt on poles across their shoulders. Chinese capitalists had the courage and enterprise to open up Malaya, and their efficient, industrious countrymen, together with the Indian laborers on the rubber plantations, developed it. But the Malays remained little impressed or concerned with it all.

It is well established that the water-buffalo of Asia dislikes the smell of Western humans. Whether this is due to some innate quality in our odor offensive to buffalo noses, or merely to unfamiliarity, I do not know. Probably both. On occasions they translate their dislike into action.

We motored nearly the length of the enchanting isle of Java without misadventure, and from Soerabaja, where we bade farewell to Fig, who shipped from there to Saigon, we continued to the island's easternmost extremity. Forty miles or so from Banjoewangi, where the road looks across at Bali over the narrow strait, we met one such expression of dislike for Western odor translated into action. For a moment this threatened to end further progress under our own power.

The road was very narrow. It was built up like a causeway above the wet floor of the jungle. There had been no sign of human life over a long stretch save for a few small clearings in the forest—flooded paddy-fields without habitation. About mid-afternoon I figured that another two hours should bring us comfortably to Banjoewangi, well before sunset.

Suddenly out of a sunken paddy-field ahead of us there rose a mud-caked, amorphous mass, like some prehistoric amphibian monster erupted from the depths of a forgotten mere. It took shape slowly, a ton and a half or so of ungainly shape. It turned towards us, lowered its head, and snorted. It was one of the largest water-buffaloes I had ever seen.

I did not at all like its looks. Its pig-like little eyes were inflamed, behind nostrils twitching as they whiffed the horrid odor of white human blended with gasoline exhaust. It shuffled its front feet and made as though to charge. I reversed in hasty retreat.

"This is a fine load of mud!" I muttered. "That damned ugly brute won't get off the road and we can't." Its weight was about equal to ours. But its front was encased in a pair of heavy, swept-back horns that looked like thick dark hair parted in the middle, while ours had the vulnerability of radiator, headlamps and engine.

I smoked a pipe, hoping our amphibious obstruction would lose interest and lumber back to its wallow. It did nothing of the sort. For three hours we made passes at one another on the narrow causeway. I tried sneaking up on it in sinuous silence. The massive beast got set to charge. I tried rushing it in the guise of a dragon, emitting loud squawks from the horn and all the noise and flame I could produce from an open cut-out. That was not a good idea. Our tour just missed coming to an end then and there, forty miles from Banjoewangi. By some very fancy backing I escaped a furious lunge; the buffalo, by the grace of St. Christopher who protects foolish travellers, chose not to follow through.

Dusk began to fall. I lighted the headlamps, with no better effect than to show up two angry, incandescent spots of eyes.

"Looks like we're here for a nice, long stay," I said. "I can't very well back twenty miles on this road in the dark." There was no possible place to turn. Joseph, our native 'boy', had fallen under an illness at Pasoeroean, so my mother and I were alone.

We had abandoned hope for the night when out of the dusk there appeared a *deus ex machina* in the shape of a naked female child: one brown-skinned infant barely two and a half feet high, unadorned as the day it was born except for a heart-shaped silver ornament hung around its middle like a fig-leaf. It took a solemn look at the monstrous beast on the causeway. It twisted its fig-leaf thoughtfully. Then it said "Woof!" and kicked a ton and a half of buffalo in the stomach with its bare toes. The lowering animal snorted, wheeled about and shuffled off the road. Our naked god-from-the-machinery stared in silent wonderment at the car as we sneaked past.

There one had the disproportion between cause and effect.

After returning to Batavia I made a side trip with my mother into the East Coast and Batak Highlands of Sumatra. Motorcars were not entirely a novelty there among the vast tobacco estates, but I believe ours was the first brought to the island *en touriste*. On the way up into the Highlands large troops of monkeys accompanied us overhead, swinging through the magnificent jungle in a game that was highly diverting both for them and for us.

There were many kinds. Streams of small grey bodies flowed back and forth above the road between the treetops, racing ahead through the branches to cross back again before we caught them up. Other bands of brown impudence chased and tweaked one another to piercing shrieks in the excitement of the sport. There were little black fellows with very long tails, and shy black-and-white ones with thick and silky coats who peered suspiciously at us through the leaves. And now and again, though they were rare, we saw a great black ape swinging hand over hand through the forest, or bending down a heavy branch with a long sinewy arm while he explored it for possible tidbits with the other.

Three of them we watched close beside the car, scarcely forty feet away. They were orang-outang, the "Old Man of the Forest," found only in Sumatra and in Borneo. They appeared completely indifferent to us, regarding the car with comical solemnity like old and sulky black savages. Too powerful for fear, they entirely disregarded and were left severely alone by all the lesser monkey folk. Their every motion was deliberate. Yet when they passed arm over arm through the leafy branches they moved with surprising speed.

In my Sumatran diary one item kept recurring. "Paid Florins 2.50 to road-gang for digging car out of mud-hole near Siantar" . . . "Fl. 6 to jail-gang—38 Batak and Achinese prisoners—digging out of mud-hole at Kebon Djahé" . . . and so on. The clay roads of the highlands were peculiarly treacherous after seventeen days of rain. From the hole near Kebon Djahé, where the rescue was effected by a fanciful crew of jail-birds, we had just been able to crawl out on our stomachs under the canvas top.

Kebon Djahé was one of the most picturesque villages I ever came upon. Its flaring thatched roofs were surmounted by many-gabled cupolas with brightly colored figures atop and carved buffalo heads at the corners. Its earthen floor was enlivened by bare-breasted women with blue sarongs and huge coiled silver ear-rings, weaving cloth on primitive looms or pounding rice in hollowed logs beneath a skyline as fantastic in its way as that of Manhattan.

Above the splendid lake called the Toba Sea the car entombed itself once again in a clay trench cut by the rains down the middle of the road. The inland sea lay deep below, varicolored against the purple shadows of the circling mountains. Night was coming on. To dig the machine clear meant a job of some hours. I took one of the oil side-lamps and set off with our 'boy' Joseph to look over the lay of the land.

We came, after about two miles, upon eight or ten men. They were a road-gang, but had no tools with them. Would they dig us out? Yes, the leader said, in the morning. I learned from him that there was an empty rest-house some five miles back. With a little persuasion he agreed to assign two men as guides and to carry our bedding-rolls.

I did not much like the look of some of those men. It occurred to me that it might be well to have one of the more reliable of them camp in the car overnight to guard the luggage. But none could be induced to do this, though I offered perhaps a week's wages as reward.

"Why not?" I inquired through Joseph. "Tell them there is nothing dangerous about the car. It's dry and comfortable, and cannot move until I start it."

"Not car," replied Joseph. "Tigers. He say plenty tigers come down sure for eat him up!"

"But not in the car!" I protested.

"Oh no; he say tiger first take him out!"

My mother, who had remained alone in the car, was not wholly amused by the explanation.

Actually I only saw one tiger in Sumatra. This one I fell over in the dark. It lay outside a tiny isolated rest-house in the highlands. The tiger was dead, but the sprawl caused me a certain momentary emotion. I was not just then expecting to fall over a tiger, not even the still-pliant body of one freshly killed.

Orientations

I left my mother in Singapore while I went back into Pahang State in eastern Malaya to shoot seladang—the wild bison that can be among the most unamiable of jungle beasts. A friend who was to accompany me dropped out at the last moment because of illness. Wherefore I went alone, with a small party of Malay trackers.

On the way to the favored haunts of the seladang I motored to the end of the road—the only road—through the perpetual blue twilight of virgin jungle. There were rippling golden pools upon the road, the shimmer of gold in the air, as if shafts of brilliant sunshine had burst through the canopy of branches overhead. But the golden pools were not from the light of the sun. They were myriads upon myriads of yellow butterflies whose pulsing wings lit up the dim aisles.

Along either side the interlacing mat of the jungle hung on a framework of straight trunk-columns, nearly white, of giant *tualang*-trees, with magnificent ferns feathering the scarped ditches. From out of the tangle of vines and creepers long-tailed little monkeys peered inquisitively, throwing bits of stick and hard growths down at the car, or scampering along with it in great leaps through the branches overhead.

As the blue twilight faded into dusk the jungle burst forth in full-voiced evening chorus, alive with sounds half suppressed by day. Mournful cries of night-birds rose above the drum and buzz of a thousand different kinds of insects. Some winged thing followed along in our trail, shrilling like a peanut-stand just overhead. Small furred and feathered beasts made raucous noises out of sight, or scuttled furtively across the road.

Now and then there came a crash or a series of crashes in the thickets alongside, unexpected and startling; followed by a moment of intense silence. Some bigger animal on the move, one could not tell what. And once, just before reaching the outpost of civilization where I was to spend the night and pick up part of my outfit, we stopped for something indistinct that lay across the road close ahead. It might have been a large log. But it was not a log: for when my bearer got out to remove it, it scuttled off with a flash of malachite-green eyes.

"After seladang, eh?" asked the Public Works Department engineer who had been repairing the damage a recent washout had done to his road. We were having a whisky-and-water together in the rest-house.

"Hope you're not prophetic!" I responded. "I've been *after* big beasts before, sometimes so damn far after 'em that I've never seen anything but very stale spoor. This time I hope to be *on* them!"

"Good hunting!" he cried. "But don't let 'em reverse it and be on *you!* Never can tell about seladang." He paused. . . . "Might run into elephant out there too, you know," he added.

"I'm not after elephant," I said.

"No, but this could be amusing for you. There's a herd of wild elephant on a rampage. Been knocking native *kampongs*—villages, you know—all about, over by the river where you're going. Villagers along this side have the wind up thoroughly.

"Elephant are odd beasts," continued the engineer. "They can move through dense jungle with scarcely a sound, when they want to be quiet. Move fast, too. Tilt their heads, flatten their ears, throw their trunks up over their foreheads and scoot through the forest on enormous squdgy feet."

He passed me a Burma cheroot. "We grow used to these things," he apologized.

"Thanks, I quite like them," I said.

He went on. "Now and then wild elephants get an urge for excitement. It's a kind of mania with 'em. Want to raise hell, like a bunch of college boys out on a spree. Want to smash things. *Then* they move slowly through the forest, trumpeting, tearing down trees, making a monstrous racket. You can hear 'em booming away for miles. When they come to a native *kampong* they pass right through it, pushing the little thatched huts down with their foreheads, flinging the top-hamper over their shoulders and trampling the rest underfoot, roaring in savage glee."

"Jolly for the villagers!" I commented.

"The villagers get out, *quick*, when they hear the herd coming. This herd I mentioned has torn up three of the dozen scattered villages just a little west of where you're going. I *mean* torn up . . . or down, as you like. Malays say there's nothing left of 'em. Haven't been out there myself."

He poured out two nightcaps. I had been very entertained by his story.

"Thought you'd be interested," he said. "You might run into 'em, you know. If you do—well, I don't expect you'll want to stand on ceremony. Get away from wherever you may be, *quick*, and down-wind."

Next day, after the inevitable delays attendant on starting for anywhere in the East, I got together my outfit, my trackers and bearers, and set off at a latish hour. At that jumping-off place I had taken on a few last-minute provisions of which we seemed short. Because of the late start I did not try to rearrange the packs, but tied the extra supplies on top of them in the stiff brown wrapping-paper in which they were done up.

All day we tramped narrow jungly trails, the two trackers ahead, the bearers behind. My thoughts kept running to elephants more than to seladang. The Malays had confirmed the engineer's tale of the wild herd on the loose. The only difference in their stories was that the Malays said four *kampongs* had been destroyed.

That night we camped in an open glade deep in the forest. The bearers pitched my balloon-silk tent a little apart from the others. The cook prepared food over a small fire. During my solitary supper the moon rose above the jungle, turned the massive trunks of the virgin *tualang*-trees along the edge of the glade into immense, straight columns of white marble. In its ghostly radiance I sat and smoked, deeply contented, watching the leafy silhouettes streak with quicksilver in the moon-play and the shadow of the moon.

The shrilling chorus of eventide died down to a steady hum before I turned in, or it may have been that I was getting used to it. It seemed almost quiet in the glade, despite the insects and the night-birds that flitted through the whispering dark.

I slept well. And I dreamt, though not unpleasantly, of elephants. Elephants moving through the forest on enormous squdgy feet, booming in high glee as they flung sections of *kampong* over their shoulders.

Then suddenly I awoke, sitting erect with nerves taut. There was a deafening uproar outside—crashes of trees being uprooted, broken off short; branches flung about to an accompaniment of wild trumpetings and the thump of heavy feet on the jungle floor.

"God-a'mighty!" I cried half aloud, "it's the herd!"

I was thoroughly awake. With one great leap I plunged under the mosquito-netting and out of the tent, grabbing my express rifle as I went. Barefoot and in pyjamas I bolted across the glade, away from those formidable sounds. The moon was still overhead. There was no wind.

I streaked to the nearest and, as it happened, the largest of the *tualang*-trees, swung breathlessly behind its enormous trunk and crouched there to take my bearings. I did not see any of my Malays. They must have heard the coming of the elephants before I did and decamped without wasting an instant's thought. I felt a bit annoyed that the trackers should have left me unwarned and alone in my balloon-silk tent to be trampled or tossed to death by wild elephants on a spree.

The glade was a picture in etched sliver, every feature acid-sharp. And as I stared, tense-eyed, there came the gradual consciousness of a deep-pervading calm over it all.

For perhaps ten minutes I listened with nerves set like a tuning fork. Not a sound rose above the usual hum of the jungle and the pounding of my own heart. No crashes, no trumpeting. I could not understand it. The sudden arrival and disappearance of the herd seemed exceedingly odd.

I crept back across the glade with painful realization that I was barefoot and the jungle was full of poisonous snakes. The Malays were sleeping peacefully under their shelters of rubber ground-sheet. It had not occurred to me that I would have to warn *them* of the approaching elephants—the elephants that somehow had passed us by. As I came to my tent I heard a sharp crackling. It was not the echo of distant crashes. It was crisp, near, and low down. I walked around the tent.

On the other side, dazzling in the direct moonlight, lay a sheet of the wrapping-paper that had done up the last-minute supplies. My bearer evidently had left it there when he unpacked the camp gear. It lay flat on top of the rank grass close beside the tent, close to my ear as I had lain asleep.

On it was a field-mouse, a little jungly mouse with large ears and fluff-tipped tail. I do not know how the wee thing had happened to jump up onto the paper, but there he was, bouncing around at a great rate, not quite daring to jump again into the contrasting blackness beyond its edge.

At each bounce the stiff paper crackled—staccato crackles that in the quiet night (with an ear close to their source, while one dreamt of wild elephants) were the crashes of uprooted trees, of branches torn down and flung about; the pound of heavy feet approaching over the jungle floor, the trumpetings of enormous beasts in malicious glee. It was oddly realistic in effect.

My herd of wild elephants on the rampage was a lone, bewildered field-mouse.

It has often been like that. Fancied pachyderms have turned out to be field-mice, mouselike apparitions to be elephants. But sometimes, as though to support the law of averages, spectres seeming to possess the stature and innate malevolence of wild elephants have on closer view proven what they seemed. Nor were these pink elephants, either.

Taking off again from Singapore in DD-1532 with my mother and a Christmas Island "China-boy," whose name was written Chang Siu and pronounced Ching-Say, we touched wheels, so to speak, in Indo-China, at Hongkong, and in China proper. Such roads as there were did not connect with others nor offer in themselves any great facility for extensive motor touring. But in the Philippines I covered more than twenty-five hundred miles over routes that in the main were excellent —all the first- and second-class roads, the former as well kept as anything in Malaya; and a good deal of third-class track which was something else.

Warwick Greene, capable and entertaining Director of Public Works, was about to make an inspection trip of all the maintained roads in the islands. So I deposited my mother in Baguio, after first overcoming a slight opposition on her part, and joined forces with Warwick. We started with two cars, but his Hupmobile burned up the first day out and we continued together in DD-1532. He provided the facilities, including special depots of gasoline and a Coast Guard vessel to take us from island to island.

We were the first to arrive by automobile at Bangui on the northern-most tip of Luzon. The approach to this little fishing village tobogganned down the side of a cliff into a hip-deep river, in which Warwick descended to crank the engine that had stalled in a huge splash. This was highly entertaining for the villagers, who eventually provided *carabao* (the Philippine water-buffalo) to drag us back up the cliff.

There were a good many villagers and tribesmen who saw an auto-mobile for the first time during that tour. Some of the more intelligent ran to the side of the car and peered underneath to discover the hidden beast that pulled us. But many merely took one indifferent glance and turned away.

"It's just foreign magic to them," said Warwick. "So far beyond their comprehension that it doesn't make sense, so they won't even look at it. It's the same with some of the Igorots and modern weapons. I was up a few months ago among a head-hunting tribe which had never seen a firearm. I showed them a rifle—killed a goat with it out in front of them. Made a decent shot; the goat never even kicked. They were moderately awed by the noise and its result, but do you think they would look at the rifle? They would not. It didn't mean a thing to them other than an abstruse sort of magic—like a thunderbolt from Zeus or some other unfamiliar deity.

"Then I showed them a cross-bow we had taken from a museum of armor. They had never seen anything like it, but they understood its principle and could appreciate the power that drove the arrow right through a plank. They were fascinated by it. 'Now *that*,' they cried, 'is *some* weapon!' or words to such effect. 'Why haven't we seen anything like that before?' I had to let about thirty of them try it out."

We had a good many rivers to cross. Some, where the water was low, we ferried on bamboo rafts supported under the car's weight by swarms of native '*hombres*'; in deep water by various appliances from dug-out canoes to inflated skins. Some were shallow enough to ford under our own power, or for the car to be pulled by long lines of men and animals. In the latter event the procession made an entertaining picture: an elongated Thing like a sea-serpent winding sluggishly over the river, with the head of a *carabao*, its sinuous middle thirty to sixty-odd '*hombres*' in mushroom-shaped hats, its rear the upper part of DD-1532.

We climbed the Naguilian trail, then hardly a carriage road at best, with the rain falling at the rate of an inch an hour and the edges breaking off into thousand-foot abysses. On one crumbling brink we were held up for the night, and passed it amongst a crew of naked Igorots in a grass hut that stood an excellent chance of being washed suddenly off into space. The howls of half a hundred dogs tethered outside on their way to tribal fleshpots added the last touch of impending doom.

We visited nearly all the islands where there were any roadways available to wheeled traffic, once landing to cover six miles of newly made road; and stayed with provincial governors and other officials, merchants, cultivators and tribal headmen. The fine old Spanish churches with their heavy buttressing against earthquakes stood picturesquely in the towns and larger villages, but the friars had gone with the revolution.

"It's a pity not to have known them," said Warwick. "They were a carry-over of ecclesiastic feudalism, and extremely well informed. They were both the spiritual fathers of their villages and the physical progenitors of a large part of them."

The roads Warwick Greene was building on several separate islands, from money provided wholly by the Philippines themselves, shamed anything the United States could show at the time. Our half-submerged passages of rivers and slithery jaunts along mountain trails were on the third-class tracks as yet "improved" merely to the point of being passable by wheels, God willing and weather permitting. The first-class roads led without break across charming old Spanish bridges of moss-grey stone, or less picturesque but well designed American structures of reinforced concrete. Often where the old bridges had lost their archways, the new highways crossed through decorative ancient approaches refitted with American concrete spans. These were known as *mestizas*, or half-castes.

Cameron Forbes, the Governor-General, was absent in America; so I did not meet him until some years later. But Warwick Greene told me one story about him which bears repeating.

"In one of the northern provinces," Warwick recounted, "the local Filipino Governor was antagonistic, for political effect, to the American 'occupation.' When the Governor-General came there on an inspection trip, riding on horses with a small staff, the local Governor thought he saw his chance to belittle the G-G in public and so enhance his own importance before his friends.

"We were met at the border of the province by an escort which the Filipino Governor had sent out. They tried to surround our party and kick up dust and mud over us as we rode into the little provincial capital. But we were better horsemen and better mounted, so they got no great satisfaction out of that. Actually, with the G-G himself, we constituted the Governor-General's polo team, and recently had trounced the British in Hong Kong." Warwick grinned a bit at the recollection of that ride.

"After our arrival (the escort was no longer in sight) we bathed from kerosene tins and changed for the banquet being given in the G-G's honor. But as we proceeded into the room where the table had been arranged in a large U we found the seat of honor assigned to a Filipino *politico* of more than doubtful repute, and the G-G relegated well off to one side. It was a studied affront, of course. The invited guests were gaping to see what the Governor-General would do. We of his staff stood flabbergasted, with fire in our eyes.

"The G-G did not seem to notice it. He sat down at the place indicated without sign of surprise or displeasure. He appeared to be in excellent humor, asked questions about the welfare of the province, and talked with those around him throughout the long dinner.

"But he never unfolded his napkin. As each dish was passed him he declined it with a pleasant smile. He sat and chatted through it all without ever touching his host's bread and salt, his meats, water or wine. And that was the most perfect response he could have devised, before all those watching people. It effectively demolished the 'face' of his churlish host. What face that mingy little man had left," Warwick said, "when the G-G, as expressionless as an owl, thanked him in front of all the others for his hospitality, was a strained and sickly flea-color."

From the Philippines we went to Japan, after touching once more in China. There I ran fifteen hundred miles up nearly the length of the main island of Honshu. Much of this was quaint and original motoring. The little roads were for the most part smooth, but exceedingly narrow and very evidently not designed for motorcars. They meandered across mountain passes where the torrents were bridged by flimsy structures doubtfully up to our weight, clinging shelf-like to precipitous slopes. They tumbled into terraced valleys whose dumpy straw-thatched cottages sprouted masses of iris and red lilies from wide sod roof-ridges. They crossed broad lagoons and swift rivers by ferries which for our purpose had usually to be contrived from a pair of sampans roped together and decked by two narrow planks athwart.

Often they zigzagged over green basins checker-boarded in paddy-fields. There all other travellers had to take to the ankle-deep mud of the paddy as we approached, since the causeway was but very few inches wider than our track. Nearly all wayfarers were packing heavy burdens or dragging two-wheeled carts, yet never one showed any sign of ill humor. Instead they helped steer me round the right-angled zigzags on whose narrow reaches I had to back and fill with nice precision not to land the car in the flooded fields.

We broke through a whole array of small bridges, hauling the car out with the chain-falls that was part of our essential equipment, or with the aid of efficient and swift-working crews of men who seldom failed to rise from nearby fields and villages.

There were unpredictable difficulties in clearing some of the little towns. In almost every one a tiled overhang would have to be removed from above the entrance to a shop, or corners of projecting eaves, or the exposed stock of a stone-lantern store, before we could get by. And always we were pursued, surrounded, half-submerged by swarms of the very young and old; greeted and followed with shrieks of joy that rose above the clatter of wooden clogs on gravel or stone pavement.

In one little town a frightened horse suddenly veered through the wood-and-paper screenwork of a house-front, while women and children popped shrieking out from the sides. The horse passed on through the back of the house, wrecked a bamboo fence beyond, and then stopped in a paddy-field to snatch a furtive, unaccustomed meal. I made a modest offering towards repair of the damage wrought. It was accepted diffidently, with low bowings and indrawn breath. Everyone concerned, except the owner of the horse, thought the whole affair extremely funny.

Once an old woman followed me three miles on foot over a mountainous trail to a tea-house where I planned to pass the night on a walking trip around Fujiyama. The Oriental Secretary of our Embassy, Arnell, was with me at the time. He spoke Japanese remarkably well and with his reddish hair and long nose looked like the fox of Japanese legend, which made him the delight of all the village children. The old woman caught us naked in the bath. This did not perturb her in the least. She prattled a few words I failed to understand and offered me twenty *sen*.

"She's come," Arnell translated, "to return the amount she says you overpaid for the nested wooden bowls you bought in her little shop this afternoon." She had undertaken a six-mile walk, up and back, to return the equivalent of ten cents whose loss I had not even noticed. I could induce her to accept nothing more than the refreshment of a one-cent cup of tea. That was in the interior. Had she lived in a Treaty Port and so gained greater knowledge of the world she might not have chosen to walk six miles, at her age, to the same end.

I grew accustomed to having the *mousmés*, the little serving maids of the inns, gurgle with delight over my curious garb, my inarticulate ways and general clumsiness, as they undressed me and showed me how to lather myself over with soap and then rinse it all off with water from a bucket before getting into the hot bath. I was a little disconcerted the first time a very good-looking young Japanese lady tripped with smooth grace into the bathing quarters, bowed, went through the same process, and got in the sunken wooden tub with me.

The bath was very hot and I was being effectively parboiled. Though she slid into the water with no splash, the ripples from her slim displacement felt, when they played against me, as though they were blistering two layers of skin off my front. I had been ready to get out, but I thought it might be wiser to defer this move. So we lay there face to face quietly parboiling together, until she emerged a rosy olive, dried her lithe body with a steaming cotton towel, put on her kimono, bowed again and disappeared. Cooked to a turn, I then crawled out.

In due course I grew accustomed to this, too, and on occasion may even have timed my bathing hours accordingly.

At Gifu on the River Nagara I fished for *ayu* with ringed cormorants by night from sampans in the light of blazing fagots, and learned to disgorge the querulous birds of their catch with a motion like the reverse of milking a cow. From there we drove to Nagoya. Part way a wind sprang up, a capricious wind of oddly whirling currents. It grew swiftly stronger, rocking the car with angry thrusts that all but lifted us off the narrow road. When we reached the outskirts of the town the air and streets were filled with odd articles—empty wooden tubs rolling over the ground, long strips of blue and white cloth sailing through the space above, varicolored tin signs swooping down at vicious angles upon the cluttered road. On all sides the roofs were shedding their tiles and worried people strove to shore up their houses with poles lashed with straw rope.

"Plenty blow!" spluttered Chang Siu, our Chinese 'boy' from Singapore. "S'pose one typhoon come!"

One typhoon came: the worst in fifty years, the Nagoyans said. The rain swept cross-wise with incredible fury in dark horizontal sheets. Following the rain came a six-foot tidal wave to work a final touch of destruction along the coast.

We careened over heaps of debris and tangled wires to the courtyard of the hotel. This was a European-type structure and solidly built. The entire staff were struggling with long poles, bracing the walls, barricading doors and windows, propping up the second story with twenty-foot beams.

The wind tore the roof off a small shed and deposited this in one piece on the ground nearby. It was the only wooden roof anywhere about the compound. The others were tiled, and the tiles were coming off like autumn leaves after a frost.

Chang Siu and I fought with the wind for that little detached roof. With fearful struggles we managed to drag it over the car and rope it down. Housed then like a yacht for winter, DD-1532 rode out the storm.

Several times during the night I thought the hotel was coming down. There were no lights save for a few paper lanterns. By one of these I put myself to bed in a room that faced straight into the drive of the storm. The window was protected by a heavy iron shutter. Early in the night this bent in under the force of the wind and carried the window along with it. I clung to the drenched bed that the wind was bouncing savagely up and down. The crashes of falling poles and collapsing roofs outside rose above the staccato clatter of tiles like coal pouring into an empty steel bin. The building rocked as though in an earthquake. Yet it stayed upright, and remained in a manner covered.

The wind died down before dawn. In its broad swath of devastation there was no house that had not lost at least a portion of its roof; very many lay spread out in flattened little heaps of wreckage. Nagoya was noted for the number of its theatres. Not one remained standing. But the car rested unscathed beneath its well-lashed wooden roof.

"Have makee dly!" said Chang Siu with a delighted grin.

The car started on the first turn of the crank, but we were three days getting away from Nagoya. Even then the coastal road to Tokyo was not yet clear. It had been blocked, among other ways, by a succession of large junks deposited across it during the tidal wave. In places these were several miles from the coast. So we struck inland again, and fell through a lot more bridges.

We were in Tokyo for the funeral of the Emperor Meiji Tenno. It was an extraordinary ceremony. All along the processional route the houses were tightly shuttered: one did not then look down upon the Emperor, living or dead. The procession was held at night. Hundreds of thousands of people lined the torch-lit, sanded way; reverent people, waiting silently through the night.

After many hours of waiting the cortege came. It crept over the muffled avenue to a muted instrumental moaning. Long columns of torch-bearers in mediaeval garb preceded the body, with bearers of ancient symbols and regalia in the fantastic costumes of a legendary past, and musicians wailing on instruments of strange design and weirder tone. As the two-wheeled, lacquered catafalque approached, the waiting thousands lowered their heads like wheat beneath the wind.

The great gold-studded wheels turned with doleful creaks above the moaning of the dirges. Except for the distant boom of minute-guns those were the only sounds that broke the silence of the night. Sounds designed to represent the concentrated wail of a nation as the black-and-gold bier, drawn by an interminable file of white oxen, passed over the sanded streets of Tokyo between breathless rows of Japanese who never raised their heads.

Behind the catafalque the high dignitaries of state followed humbly afoot, in order of their rank. In the foremost line a space remained where General Nogi should have been. The aged hero of Port Arthur was not there. He had followed his Emperor more precisely—the traditional "following in death." At the first boom of the minute-guns sounding the Emperor's last salute General Nogi and his countess, kneeling together before a portrait of their departed lord, committed *hara-kiri*.

The old General left a message. His life had long been forfeit, he wrote, since he lost the colors of his regiment as a Sub-Lieutenant in the Satsuma rebellion, more than ever forfeit after he was forced to sacrifice so many of the lives of his soldiers in the taking of Port Arthur. Now he was released from continued existence by his lord's death to follow after him, and in following to protest against the politics he saw creeping into the army.

It was a gesture of supreme dignity from the Eastern viewpoint; unhappily, on the last score, in vain.

Our tour ended by crossing the United States in mid-winter. I believe it was the first trans-continental crossing made by automobile in that season. It was not one that commended itself to repetition.

We stuck for a week in the snow on the Continental Divide. There was a ranch of sorts, but its comforts were abridged by a squaw-man passing through an acute stage of D.T.'s. His stolid-faced squaw was inured to his mouthings. I was not, and in the confined quarters of a snow-girt cabin in the solitudes of the Rockies the howls of that reptile-tortured spirit had a shattering effect.

We stuck in many other places because the frost lifted in a mid-seasonal thaw. The main highways were very often impassable without the help of horses or oxen. In the middle of the pike that led to Washington, a few miles from the capital of the nation, the car sank to the level of its door-handles. "We are a young country," people said. "You have to expect such things."

The editor of the Automobile Club of America's *Club Journal* wrote: "With the coming of the motorcar has arisen an insistent demand for roads over which cars can make their way with some degree of safety." The demand for "some degree" of safety seems hardly excessive; yet it was apt. In all the countries of our eighteen-month tour the worst roads we encountered, with the exception of China, were in the United States.

I spent the remainder of that winter in desultory studies in New York. But by then the wanderlust had taken firm hold. My father's affairs, furthermore, were steadily shifting abroad. In the spring of 1913 I went again to Europe with my parents and returned no more for six years.

Northernmost Road

"There is no record," wrote the secretaries of the Royal Automobile Clubs of all the north European countries in reply to my queries, "of the Baltic Sea ever having been circled by automobile." And I was then at an age when it seemed exceedingly important to be the first to do this.

In the late summer of 1913 the project took shape. As it happened, one would have been hard put to repeat that trip for a good many years. The northerly routes—the few that existed—were practicable only during the three months or so of Arctic summer. The season was already nearly spent, and the following summer brought international complications to break the loop of Baltic roads indefinitely.

In a new six-cylinder Packard—not an exceptionally well-suited car for the venture—I set out with my mother from Aix-les-Bains in the Haute-Savoie, where she had been taking her annual "cure." Shovel, axe and pick, heavy tire-chains, containers for extra gasoline and oil, one-ton chain-falls, a coil of thick rope and other impedimenta lent an air of solid preparation a bit unusual for the well-kept roads of western Europe in summertime. My father joined us from England at Warnemunde, from where we ferried to Denmark, and thence across the Öresund that links the Kattegat with the Baltic proper to Sweden. From Stockholm we bore westward to Oslo—or Kristiania, as it was called then.

> *Yes, we love this country,*
> *As it arises*
> *Lined and weatherbeaten from the sea.*
> *—Norwegian National Anthem*

The scenery of southern Sweden was reminiscent of upper New England: lake-studded, rolling hills swathed in pine and spruce, the well-kept farms along the lake shores cheerful with bright red paint and white trimmings. As we approached the Norwegian frontier the rolling hills piled into mountains, into bold grey formations of lichen-covered rock and densely forested slopes of spruce or fir with wild ravines and narrow mountain lakes between. The red-and-white farms gave way to unpainted timber buildings more in keeping with the dour and solid character of the Norse farmer. Each farmhouse and its attendant barns were grouped close together on three sides of a hollow square for defense against the long, hard winter. The small farms tucked away in the solitude of upland valleys, laboriously cleared of their stones and timber, were expressive of the Norseman's rude struggle for existence against a Nature that is over-generous in precipitation and in very little else.

"*Ja,*" a Norwegian friend observed, "very few of our farms can support a family without some additional revenue from winter logging, or deep-sea fishing when they are near the coast. And this is one reason why so many of our farm folk have emigrated to *your* country!"

These upland Norse farms have a peculiar character of their own. Farming practices anciently imposed by a Nature so rugged and rainy make for curious over-all effects. In the fields the hay is draped like dark fish-nets on long lines, which the women keep turning over and over until it dries in spite of the rain. The mountain ash trees in late summer stand gaunt and naked. Their leaves and scarlet berries, stripped from the branches for cattle fodder, are festooned round the bare trunks in the manner of hula skirts. The corn hangs suspended in overlapping sheaves on tall poles. These, as twilight fades, give the fields the appearance of a fantastic concourse of figures clad in the straw rain-capes of Japanese farmers. In the gloaming the fields seem to be peopled with the ghosts of departed reapers met in formal state, bowing stiffly to one another in the first measures of a gigantic square-dance—a solemn dance under the prompting of ancient tree-crones, who wave bare and withered arms above their flounced hula skirts as they urge on the dancers over parallel tiers of draperies made of dark hay.

We usually put up at one of the larger farms along the main routes which were under contract with the local authorities as posting stations —*skyddstations* in Norway, *gästgiveri* in Sweden—where travellers could obtain horses, light carriages and limited overnight accommodations; or at Government telephone-and-telegraph stations. The rooming arrangements were simple but comfortable enough, and always clean. The food, as everywhere in Scandinavia, was excellent. Various types of cheese, hard black bread, potatoes, and coffee with cream served as the staples of every meal. Farther north one had reindeer meat and a variety of game—ptarmigan, black cock, huge grouse, trout, grilse and salmon.

Northwards from Kristiania the Telemarken and Hardanger Roads led into the *fjeld* which rivals, at least in certain places, the scenic grandeur of the Alps, though on a more intimate scale. Across heavily timbered mountains and bleak wildernesses above the tree-line we twisted and clambered far into the perpetual snows, zigzagging down again into deeply grooved green valleys. In the folds of Alpine upheaval lay many cold, blue little lakes fed from glacial cataracts or crystal-clear brooks.

One of these tranquil lakelets lingers in memory. It was the lake called Sandven, around whose rim the narrow road had been blasted out of sheer rock. It seemed then the most completely satisfying small body of water I had ever looked upon. Light blue and scintillating it lay, like a star-sapphire at the bottom of a vast, irregular bowl rough-hewn out of the rock. Down one edge of the bowl reached a long arm of the Folgefonne glacier, as though a gigantic polar bear were fishing for the jewel caught there in the mountain fastnesses. The beauty of it was breath-taking, with no blemish of Nature or the hand of man to mar its serenity.

The roads did not always run around the fjords, so sometimes we had to ship across by little fjord steamers. This, it turned out, was no matter of casual undertaking. Their tackle was not up to our weight; we smashed all their landing planks, broke through a dock, greatly diverting the population of at least two fjord towns.

After several hours of effort I managed to stow the car on a hatch aboard one of these small vessels of passage, at the ugly little town of Oddo that reeks of carbide factories but is superbly situated at the head of the Sörfjord. The car was surrounded by a lowing herd of fat cattle, bleating goats and sheep, horses, copper pots, churns and pans full of cheese and butter. Farmers and *sæter* maidens in gaily embroidered costumes, homeward bound from upland pastures to some of the small islands off the coast, stared at the procedure in amazement.

The *sæter*, or mountain dairy, was a unique though disappearing feature of Norwegian farm life. Each farm held rights in upland pasturage along a brook or mountain lake, often several days' march from the home fields. There, for the two midsummer months, the farmer turned out his cattle and flocks to graze, along with a couple of his daughters or young female relatives to tend them. The upward processions of cows and sheep and goats, horses laden with dairy paraphernalia and the brace of maidens balanced high atop, would set out soon after St. Hans' Day—the 24th of June.

Up in the isolated mountain pastures the farmer deposited his troop at two or three low log huts built as living quarters, dairy and storm shelter. He then returned with his horses to his hay making, and came again to fetch the *sæter* maidens and their charges eight or ten weeks later. One might think that what with milking the herd and flocks twice a day, straining the milk, making butter and preparing the sweet brown *mysost* cheese in great pans over a slow fire, watching for bears, bringing the cattle in to shelter during stormy weather, cooking and washing up and a hundred and one minor chores, the girls would have scant leisure to bewail their lonely state.

"*Ja,* but it's pretty dam' lonesome for t'em young girls up t'ere," explained one of our Norwegian friends. "T'ey get t'enking of t'engs and sorry for t'emselves; so now t'ey go off to America or get yobs in summer hotels. And soon we hav' no more *sæter.*" But the lonely maidens we saw tending their milch-cows and goats in the vast upland solitudes lent a distinctive touch to the scene, and their colorful little processions trooping back to the home farms were quaintly picturesque.

At Eide I saw an immense flock of ducks floating out in the fjord. "Eider ducks?" I inquired naïvely. They were, though the words have nothing in common—*Eide* being Norwegian for isthmus, while *Eider* derives from the Icelandic.

Several of the roads that we took, unaware of restrictions, were forbidden to motorcars. I would not challenge the wisdom of whoever forbade them. But though we had unpleasantnesses with the roads themselves we had none with the local authorities. Frightened horses were our major problem. On the thin ribbons of trails sometimes raised in causeways above the wet bottom lands, sometimes pitching up and down with gradients of thirty to forty per cent, the unfamiliarity of Norwegian horses with self-propelled vehicles was a menace to all concerned, but more particularly to the horses.

Sturdy bays from the Gudbransdal, strong cream-colored or roan *fjord* ponies, gave our strange contraption no more than one horrified glance before they plunged with snorts and squeals overside, whatever the nature of the terrain or the load they were hauling.

There was little traffic on the roads, yet my recollections of the Norwegian scene of those days—and in Finland it was worse—are interspersed with visions of horses misbehaving in odd and fearsome ways. Horses galloping off through spruce forests with fragments of cart dragging behind, horses lying flat and kicking at the poles of overturned hay-wagons, horses disappearing over cliffs with or without their attached vehicles, horses lying upside down in ditches wrapped in barbed-wire fence.

We tried every conceivable way of inducing the horses of Scandinavia to stay on the roads we made hideous for them, but with scant success. Whoever first sighted a vehicle would cry out the warning signal—"Horse!" I then stopped the car short, switched off the engine and ran forward with a coat to tie over the equine head. My father followed, and together we would try to unharness the animal. We would offer it sugar, carrots, or half an apple. With voices meant to be soothing we strove to distract its attention.

"Steady there! Good horse, good old Olaf! . . . *whoa!*" we would cry. And Olaf, had he not yet sensed the presence of the car, might perhaps submit to being led off into the woods, or sometimes even past the benzine-buggy itself. In specially delicate situations we tried camouflaging the car with branches of trees and wisps of hay.

But the horses one came upon unexpectedly stood not an instant on the order of their going. At once they swung around and made off, upsetting their wagon-loads of hay or grain, popping from two to perhaps half a dozen men into the ditch. The driving horses hitched to lighter vehicles would make a fair start at kicking these appendages swiftly to pieces. Then they would plunge away, strewing bits of broken shafts and singletrees behind, through the forest, through fences where there were any, into deep gullies, lakes, or down boulder-sown mountainsides.

We were a scourge and a devastation to the Norse farmers whose substance ran to ownership of horses and of vehicles. And yet—for we did our best to avoid accidents, and when they occurred, as they so often did, to atone in some measure for the damage wrought—there were few who turned ugly in their misadventures, nor any we met who attempted to exact more than might reasonably be due for actual loss. They did not esteem our self-propelled contraption highly—one could hardly expect enthusiasm under the circumstances. But they were comprehending and appreciative of honorable amends. Dour and often unresponsive they may be, yet I would be happy to think that the Norwegian *bønder* on whom we descended like a Satanic visitation retained for us a fraction of the high regard we held for them.

The *bønder*, the strong and independent farmer backbone of the nation, form a class hardly paralleled elsewhere in Europe, if anywhere in the world. Sturdy and self-respecting, they never have submitted either to feudal domination or the mortgaging hand of townsmen. It was they who shaped the policy of their country in recent years—an interesting blend of cooperative socialism with the conservative self-reliance of mountain peoples. In doing so they did not seek to bolster their own harsh economy by uneconomic subsidies at the expense of other classes and interests. And while they did not fully solve the social problems of a troubled age, they had advanced no little way towards a working formula until the Nazi hordes halted all further progress. It was a formula that brought their country through the alternate crises of inflation and depression in a manner few nations outside Scandinavia managed to achieve. That progress will be continued. The Norwegian *bönder* were among the chief causes of an accumulating sense of despondency in the hearts of the "Nordic" invaders.

The strong bay ponies of the Gudbransdal, the most well-favored valley of Norway, whose rocks have been removed by infinite toil of hand, regarded us with shuddering antipathy. But on the ancient road across the wild and desolate Dovrefjeld, that in winter is marked only by stakes set in the snow, we met not a single vehicle. The only building, as I remember it then, was the mountain refuge of Kostuen which has afforded travellers on the *fjeld* a warm security since its foundation by King Eystein eight hundred years ago.

From Trondhjem the Karl Johans Vei led eastwardly over the dorsal range back into Sweden. Along it is a little town with the ungenial name of Hell. I halted there long enough to despatch a few cards, duly postmarked with the name of the location, to friends who might have thought Hell my ultimate destination. "Just passing through," I wrote, "unscorched!" It was, in fact, quite cool in Hell.

The Swedish side of the Karl Johans Vei, I discovered too late to turn back, was forbidden to motorcars. It should have been. Its width was several inches less than the car's track. It was overgrown with grass and bordered with deep ditches, and so slippery from a heavy rain that an average of nine miles an hour was, from every aspect, a dashing achievement. From where it debouches at Östersund our way led through districts with sonorous names suitable to northerly marches— Jämtland, Angermanland, Västerbotten, Norrbotten and Lappland. There was much game along the road. Ptarmigan were everywhere. Hazel and black grouse and capercailzie flashed lustrous plumage in the autumnal sunlight. Wild duck and swan floated on the rivers. Deer and hare and red foxes strolled or scurried through the scrub birches. All the furred and feathered life of forest, lake and moorland so charmingly portrayed on canvas by Bruno Lillefors in Stockholm's National Gallery ran, jumped, flew or paddled within a stone's throw on either hand.

Lesser birds, very tame and disposed to regard our odd vehicle with noisy curiosity, frequented the fields around the scattered settlements. There were many varieties. The magpies as usual were the most gregarious. One morning we found a flock of magpies in a chattering group about the car watching a large greenish-bronze woodpecker vigorously drilling away at one of the front tires. The woodpecker's lack of success at his drilling threw him into a furious rage. With throaty imprecations he cursed the tire, then attacked it again and again while the magpies jeered from the sidelines. My father, arms akimbo, joined the magpies in their jeering.

"Do you know what those magpies are saying?" my father asked the infuriated driller. " 'A hell of a 'pecker *you* are,' they're saying, 'to let yourself be stymied by Monsieur Michelin!' " (Michelin made our tires.) The woodpecker rattled hoarsely and redoubled his effort. He kept at it until I had tied on the luggage and went to start the engine on the crank. Monsieur Michelin's tires stood up better under the attempted sabotage than they did on the Lappland road.

Between Norsjö and Vistträsk, just before crossing the Arctic Circle, the pungent smokes from four or five open tar kilns wisped languidly into the grey-blue skies. On these primitive stills the resin-fat pine logs smoulder for a fortnight at each burning, laid on saucer-shaped platforms, forty feet or more in diameter, that dish down to a hole in their center. The melted resin trickles into barrels from the logs cooking under a cover of turf and charcoal. Each cooking produces up to a hundred barrels of tar. The fragrance of pine tar hung heavy in the still air. On the road were only Lapplanders and a few lumbermen in larrigans, carting the barrels they had fashioned to hold the tar.

At Norsjö we found a little tannery that specialized in larrigans of reindeer hide. I was inspired to acquire a couple of pairs of these knee-high shoe packs, flaring upwards at the toes. They were light as feathers and softly pliable, yet waterproof and tough; ideal footgear for paddling about in cold water at each lake or river crossing where the ferry landings were not up to our weight. Unhappily they had one defect. They smelt to heaven with a fearsome odor of ripe and ancient goat. When not in use we tied them on the back of the car.

One early morning I woke with a start. The wind was blowing from the direction of the car, which stood about fifty feet beyond the partly opened window. My father, asleep beside me, woke at about the same moment. We looked at the open window and then at each other. "By

all that's great," my father said, "I thought we were being invaded by a
flock of wet rams!" I also could have sworn to it. But the fragrance was
not from a flock of wet rams. It was from our larrigans some sixty feet
away outdoors.

On September 25th we crossed the Arctic Circle, called *Norra Polcir-
keln* (North Pole Circle) by the Swedes. That night we slept in a farm
which was the *Rikstelefonstation* at Öfre Lansjark, one large room with
a great corner fireplace of stone; and we washed in the ice-water of the
lake.

The Lappland highway was a military road completed the previous
year to a point where the Muonio River defines the northern border of
Sweden against Finnish Lappmarken. Until the Petsamo road in Finland
was built some years later it was the northernmost connected highway
in the world. Beyond the raw little iron-mining camp of Gällivare,
where the road crossed the then most northerly of all railways, it passed
through country scarcely inhabited save for scattered Lapp winter encampments, in summer deserted. No traffic other than an occasional
Lappish cart laden with tar-barrels or freshly killed bull reindeer broke
the immense autumnal solitude.

> "A stone's throw out on either hand
> From that well-ordered road we tread,
> And all the world is wild and strange . . ."

The country was partly covered with stunted pines and birches, in part
with lichen-grown rocks and peat bogs carpeted in reindeer moss, with
many narrow lakes reflecting superbly the early Arctic sunsets over
distant blue hills. In the segment from northwest to northeast, save for
the road itself that led as far as the Muonio Elv, there lay scarcely a
man-made feature in the intervening wastes of two to three hundred
miles to the Arctic seas. The road was open about ten weeks of the
year. During nine months or so the whole countryside turns into a
limitless road of snow, but a road for reindeer rather than for motorcars.

Ferries were our chief source of trouble on the Lappland road. The
car was heavily laden. At Gällivare I had taken on a sufficient supply
of "benzine" to carry us through to the end of the road and back again
to the depots of the outskirts of civilization. As far as Gällivare we had
usually been able to pick up a few tins of motor fuel in the occasional
settlements, at apothecaries, or general stores. We carried five spare

tires which I had shipped ahead from London to Östersund, with a small vulcanizing outfit. All of these we used repeatedly.

There were many ferries, shallow, flat-bottomed barges of uncertain buoyancy, propelled by hand with a wooden clutch. The clutch slipped forward over the picked-up cable, gripping it taut for the haul while the ferryman walked it aft and drove the barge lumberingly ahead. Each ferry gave us anxious moments while we got the car on and off. One sank under our weight at the landing platform. We managed to pull the car out of the luckily shallow water with the chain-falls. One grounded hard for several hours in the mid-river shallows of the Torne Elv, and we might have been there for days had it not been for the timely arrival of some thirty Lapps in nine high-prowed canoes. They formed a highly picturesque rescue party as my father, the ferryman and I struggled hip-deep in icy water. The Lapps, inured to hardship and very self-reliant, are by repute not always very helpful in the emergencies of others. But the Lapps in those nine canoes all promptly jumped into the water with us. "*Hi yo ho!*" they shouted. Grinning and uttering guttural yells, they freed the ferry as though the affair were a prize contest which they had paddled many miles to enter.

From another ferry we watched a completely incredible sunset, a double sunset over a narrow lake running east and west, magenta-shot amidst the darkness of the pines. For, while we were crossing, there rose from one end of the lake a round, red moon just as the sun sank round and red at the other end. By some odd refraction the two globes appeared to hang in balance, identical in shape and color on either side, each just touching the water; two crimson spheres exactly alike glowing above the surface of the lake, their wine-red light-paths centering on our slowly moving barge as we passed across between them.

One hundred ninety-six miles north of the Arctic Circle by speedometer we came to the end of the road. The latitude was 68° 27′ north, where the Muonio Elv forms the frontier against Finland's northwestern corner. There were wild swan on the river, thin ice forming along its edge. I took a plunge with my father in the Arctic waters; we came out blue and breathless some ten seconds later. "Br-r-r!" my father cried through teeth chattering like a pneumatic riveter. "W-why d-don't *we* w-wear l-layers of f-f-fat and f-f-feathers like those i-insulated s-s-swan?"

At the road's end lay Karesuando village, the northernmost settlement in Sweden. Its permanent population of a few Lapp farmers, a Swedish postmaster-storekeeper and his wife, a Lutheran pastor and one or two other Swedes, would expand mightily with the coming of winter, due to arrive almost any day then, under the influx of some four thousand Lapps and ten to fifteen thousand head of reindeer. As soon as the early snowfalls should turn the country white again the scene around the tiny outpost would grow animated. The Lapps would throng to market, barter their surplus reindeer bulls, hides, cheese, fur boots, horn spoons and other handiwork of reindeer products, against coffee, sugar and salt, tobacco, steel knives, barley flour and like commodities.

There until the break of summer—the intermediate seasons of spring and autumn being scarcely discernible in the North—they would live in canvas or burlap tents stretched on birch poles and banked with moss. Some few families went in for the luxury of huts of stone and clay. The huts, like the tents, have openings at the top as exit for the smoke of wood fires constantly smouldering on the earthen floors within. Their semidarkness is none the less laden with a smarting acridity, to which the Lapps seem immune. They are nowise discomforted by ranges in temperature that would decimate people less inured. Garbed in wool and hides they face the biting cold of Arctic winter or the heat of birch-fed fires with equal unconcern.

Karesuando's Swedish pastor was an intelligent and sympathetic soul. He was fond of his four thousand "children," deeply attached to his work. The Lapps, he said, took a transitory delight in religious services.

"During the winter services my church is always full," he recounted. "There are a few Swedes, more Finns, but mostly Lapps. The Lapps flock to it, colorful in their gay costumes, knives dangling from their belts. They never remove any of their winter wools and furs, though the church gets quite hot from the fire of birch billets in the big iron stove. The men sit on one side of the center aisle, the women on the other. Their dogs always come along with them—great packs of dogs, filling the aisles, howling to the music of the organ, growling and fighting up and down the church throughout the whole service."

The pastor gave his sermons in both Lappish and Finnish or Swedish, depending on the proportions of the congregation. The Lapps would listen intently, but beyond all other parts of the service they delighted in the hymns played on the tiny organ.

"They sway to the cadences, chanting at the top of their voices in weird intonations and curious jargon—they understand practically nothing of the words of the hymns—while the dogs howl and yap through the general din. The worship of God in my church is not quite like the usual service," said the minister with a gentle twinkle in his eye, "but its informality suits my congregation and the Lapps love the simple ritual."

The next day I left the unpretentious log house that served as the parsonage and tramped away across country with a Lapp youth as my guide. After some hours we came upon a Karesuando Lapp family camped in the hills about twelve miles west. It was a large family, whose wealth, as with all nomad Lapps, was ambulatory, on the clacking hoofs of their reindeer herd. They met me with simple but unrestrained welcome. The Lapp youth stated briefly the innocent purpose of my visit as the parson had instructed him. He then took his departure, and I was led to the tent by the head of the family for the coffee and reindeer cheese that is the ceremonial of greeting.

Our conversation was limited, since we had but eight words in common. When these did not suffice I supplemented them with the universal language of signs and with rough sketches that greatly entertained my hosts. The head of the family and his wife were splendid types, short of stature but fine-featured, with keen eyes and kindly, intelligent faces. Their features were surprisingly aquiline, not at all Mongoloid like the majority of Lapps. Their hands and feet were small and shapely. Their age was indeterminate under a mask of seared and weathered skin. It might have been fifty, but could well have been ten years either way.

The picturesque Lappish costumes lent a cheerful touch of color to the camp. The men wore tight-fitting leathern breeches (seldom completely removed, I gathered, until they more or less wore off) tucked into gaily embroidered anklets over moccasin-like foot-gear of reindeer hide with turned-up pointed toes. Their dark blue coats were embroidered in intricate patterns along the edges and round the collars. Their visored red-and-blue wool caps sported big wool pompons atop. The women wore embroidered skirts with gay bodices. All the males carried sheath-knives and decorative leather tobacco pouches on thongs round their waists, and they smoked continuously.

Coffee taken, we went to the corral. The herd of 250 reindeer, headed by a magnificent pure white bull with a tremendous spread of furry antlers, had been collected for the biweekly milking shortly before my arrival. The cows were being lassoed by the men and milked by the women into small wooden bowls. They gave a very scant quantity and tried to hold back on that; whereat the women would punch them above the udder, milk vigorously as they relaxed, smack them again when they tautened up. The yield, though feeble, came out thick and rich as egg-nog.

During the milking the men perched on the corral rails. They smoked their long pipes and passed vulgar witticisms (I surmised) that kept the squatted line on the rails shaking in loud chortles of merriment. The women were less amused by their quips. One flared up in sudden wrath against her reindeer and her hecklers, kicked the recalcitrant beast in the stomach and with head thrown back poured forth a marvelous stream of invective while the men howled and slapped their thighs with delight.

"Hi-yi-yi!' they yelled. "That's big talk, but what of the milk? Kick her in the udder! Kick her in the udder!" or words to that effect. They were like a party of jeering schoolboys on a spree, showing off, with their womenfolk the butt of their humor.

When the milking was done the women bore away the proceeds in the little wooden bowls, an inch or two deep. The reindeer were then turned loose into the night behind their belled leader. The head of the family led me back to his tent. We sat cross-legged on the bedding, smoked for a while, and told stories. It is curious how far one can follow the simple tales of nomadic life with but a score of words. My vocabulary had increased slightly during the afternoon. But I became very involved in the tale of a herd of elephants, the like of which no Lapp had ever seen; and ended feebly on a note of confusion not quite cleared by crude sketches depicting comparative size. For the Lapps were interested in the milk and cheese value of such enormous beasts and I had never milked an elephant, nor was I well informed on the lactic production of the female of that species.

Then we ate jerked reindeer meat—a luxury brought out in my honor—with barley bread dipped in reindeer milk that had been diluted with water. There was also the staple reindeer cheese and, as always, coffee. The early dark had fallen. By the light of the fire we ate our fill, and soon afterwards lay down to sleep in a circle round the edge of the tent. We were, in that tent, four men, three women, six children and six dogs, sleeping all together beneath the conical shelter. The

Lapps have, in general, a reputation for hospitality, fondness of their children, and kindness to their animals. It was maintained in all respects in that tent.

The wood fire smouldering in the middle filled the tent with bitter smoke, from about a foot or so off the ground, though the peak was open like a tepee. I removed my boots and coat, which the others seemed to consider an effete and needless gesture. We overlapped a little, legs and heads, and the dogs turned occasionally. But they turned less than I, who might have spun a cocoon had I had the makings. For it was roasting hot on the fire side and bitterly cold on the outer, wherefore I kept turning my cooked parts to the cooling Arctic night, my chilled ones back again to the fire.

We rose in the morning dark, and had reindeer cheese and coffee for breakfast. There is a certain lack of variety to Lappish meals. The brushing of my teeth entertained the whole camp. They thought this enormously funny. *"Ho-ho-ho!"* they shouted, pointing. When I had done, they passed the little bristly brush round and round amidst gurgling laughter.

The men from the three tents performed a few functions about camp—the bulk being women's work—and then we set out together to round up the reindeer herd. A pack of some twenty mongrel dogs, in size from yelping terriers to bastard wolfhounds, with six of which I had slept, led us in the direction the deer had taken the night before. The Lapps glided over the rough ground in a curious swaying motion with no apparent lifting of their feet. About every two and a half hours we paused for coffee, heated in a little pot over a quick fire, and a snack of reindeer cheese.

Long before I heard it the Lapps spotted the tinkling of the belled deer. We caught up in due time with the browsing herd whose hoofs made an odd clacking sound, drove them slowly on a broad sweep back towards camp, then left the deer to fend for themselves through the night and be picked up again next day.

The whole life of the nomad Lapps is based on and with and by the reindeer. In summer they seek the highlands or the fjords of the northwest where mosquitoes are few, for mosquitoes are the reindeer's greatest torment. In winter they congregate in large camps where they can feed the deer economically, dispose of the excess bulls, and barter the products of the herd.

I stayed with them, following the daily routine, until I had gained a fair picture of the autumnal procedure of one Lappish tribe. As far as that experience gave me to judge, those people were happy. They were happy-go-lucky in any event, with a fine sense of humor—always ready to laugh at one another, at me, and at themselves. They were kindly and courteous. There was nothing mean about them. Their ideas of sanitation were on the primitive side; but I left with regret to return to Karesuando and the mechanism of the road.

Karesuando, according to all available information, was the northernmost point ever reached by automobile up to that time. We were not the first, unless it may have been for a few hundred yards. The Swedish Köpman, governor of the district, had arrived at Karesuando in a 12 h.p. "Maf" on August 5th the previous year when the road was first opened. But in no part of the world could one then have proceeded any farther north in a standard automobile on wheels.

From that end of all roads we headed back just before winter caught us. There was a reindeer market in full swing at Vittangi, the landing alongside its three or four scattered houses overlain with slaughtered bulls. From there we went down to Haparanda at the top of the Gulf of Bothnia, and continued through Finland to St. Petersburg—more than thirteen hundred miles south from the head of the northernmost road.

Baltic Loop

Four miles beyond Haparanda lay the Finnish border; yet to pass the granite monolith with the double-headed eagle of Imperial Russia carven on it took the whole of a day. None before us had ever applied for transit clearance of an automobile from Sweden into Finland. "But there is no precedent!" the Finnish customs officer kept pleading as one complication after another threatened indefinite delay.

Finland, then a Grand Duchy of Russia, enjoyed autonomy of customs. One could not cross its borders without a Russian visa to one's passport; but the customs triptych for Russia, issued and guaranteed by the Royal Automobile Club of Great Britain, was not valid in the Duchy.

Over the heaps of baggage and equipment spread out along the roadside for heavy-fisted inspection I argued the matter of transit privileges with four massive Finns, gravely polite and surpassingly slow. To answer all they wanted to know called for a knowledge of weights and measures, engineering and metallurgy, along with the fiscal and customs procedures of half a dozen other countries. The difficulty of tongue also entered into the matter. With three of the massive Finns we shared no word in common. The peculiar guttural flow of their remarks, borne upon a liquid stream of vowels, had a bewildering effect. This effect was achieved orthographically in the gargling name of one Finnish place whose fifteen or so consonants were liquefied by three pairs of umlauted a's.

The fourth Finn, chief of the post, spouted syllables meant to be French but so subdivided by a really phenomenal stutter as to make each utterance a sort of acrostic puzzle. Early in the proceedings he offered me a cigarette from a long metal case.

"*Fu-fu-fu-mez M-m-sieu fu-fu-fum-M-m . . .*" he urged, and continued in similar fashion while I accepted one, lighted it, and had half consumed the paper-tipped smoke before he could switch off that back-firing stutter.

After many hours of poring through irrelevant heaps of printed schedules and instructions ("But there is no precedent!") the chief raised his shoulders in a last, lingering shrug and asked if we could suggest a suitable amount as a deposit.

"Offer him 250 Finnmarks," muttered my father. I hardly expected that our stuttering friend would accept the equivalent of fifty dollars, the guaranty for some of the countries covered by our customs triptyches being about forty times that modest sum; but he seemed grateful for the suggestion. Over another cigarette—"*Fu-fu-fum-M-m!*"—the deal was closed. Pocketing the receipt we could not read, I informed my parent that he had kissed Finnmarks 250 goodbye.

"Those two rather inferior Russian cigarettes you bought me," I observed, "I think have cost you just twenty-five dollars apiece." My father, who never smoked cigarettes though he kept a pipe almost continually stoked, uttered muffled sounds of pain. I did not yet know Finnish character as we came later to appreciate it. The deposit was repaid in full when I drove across the eastern frontier of the Duchy some three weeks afterwards, without demur or delay, against the crumpled receipt.

Dark had long descended before the formalities were accomplished. We came then to Torneå, a dull town of low wooden houses facing on broad streets evilly paved in small round cobbles. The town, like most Finnish inland towns, was spiritless in its uniformity but for a fine little white church with a detached bell tower. From there we ran next day to Uleåborg, or Oulu, 101 miles in eleven and a half hours of highly fancy motoring.

There were three ferries. The first was adequate. The second stuck fast on a sandbar midway in the Simojoki. We removed the luggage and equipment by canoe before the combined efforts of the ferry crew of three, the canoeman, my father and myself, all struggling waist-deep in the icy water, could refloat the flat-bottomed scow. At the third we nearly lost the car in the Kiiminsjoki.

This last barge was low amidships, with high sloping ends. It had no reserve buoyancy. When I eased the car down upon it over two steeply pitched planks the weary hulk shipped a three-foot wave and all but sank to an accompaniment of loud yells from the four-man crew. One of the four was a little drunk. "Been to 'Merica, been to 'Merica! Sonvabitch, allright!" he kept chanting.

I had to take the debarkation with a rush, which drove the end of the barge completely out of sight. The car barely made the bank as the melancholy scow foundered in two fathoms' depth. "Hi-yo-ho!" yelled the crew. "Sonvabitch, allright!" added the jovial one with a grin of yellow fangs.

"You seem to have fixed it so no one is likely to follow us over the Kiiminsjoki in any conveyance for some time," my father observed. Yet when we gave the four hardies who had manned the ferry a small extra compensation for their troubles, they solemnly shook hands with us in turn. Then they set off to find grappling tackle with which to salvage their sunken barge. Our friend who had "been to 'Merica," probably as a sailor, waved to us as they disappeared. "Sonvabitch, allright!" he cried in cheery farewell. His mastery of that useful idiom gave him keen satisfaction. It placed him at once on a more intimate basis with us and set up his prestige before his less widely travelled fellows.

The road along the whole way to Uleåborg was cut by innumerable sunken culverts. These were miserable little traps, badly laid, all very rotten. At each approach I brought the car to a dead stop; yet we broke through nearly every one, racking the heavily loaded machine as the wheels shivered the mouldering wood.

There was an endless succession of rivers. We crossed three more big ones by railway bridges, many others over bridges of rotten plank. On two of the latter the car broke through the flooring, and at least one we left impassable by wheeled traffic after more than an hour of clearing away the wreckage with an axe and dragging the car out by the chain-falls. After that I drove alone across bridges.

The horses of northern Finland behaved in the most perverse fashion of any I ever met. They were ugly and hysterical. They brooked not the slightest interference with their mouths. A steadying hand on rein or bridle seemed merely to infuriate them the more, bringing out their inherent desire to smash things. Generally they wheeled around the instant they sighted us. In a shuddering, kicking frenzy they would gallop away from our monstrous apparition, the drivers standing like charioteers with feet outspread, leaning well back, tugging futilely on rope reins with leather-mittened hands. Charioteers in larrigans of oiled hide, short coats to the knees and fur-lined leathern hats turned up behind, pursuing one another at irregular intervals in an intermittent Arctic chariot race of seatless carts.

The drivers were nearly as frightened as their animals, but never as ugly. Sometimes they lost the reins, often their balance. In a conflict of wills the horses invariably won. Only in a padded van could one have got those maddened little beasts past or even close to the car. I always switched off the engine at first sight of a horse, but it was a gesture of utter futility.

One of them upset a long, flat wagon loaded with cans of milk. The covers popped from the cans; the milk gushed forth onto the ground as the pony rolled over and over amidst the debris, savagely kicking the 40-liter containers about. *"Gnu ualu uliaminki!"* yelled the driver, or sounds to that general effect, as he crouched on his hands and knees at the edge of the maelstrom. The pony continued to roll and kick, taking upon itself a rich coating of milk and a filler of reddish sand.

"I say your blasted gnu is an *uliaminki,* too!" my father shouted.

A quiet steed hitched to a shiny new sulky was tied to a tree in a farmyard some distance from the road. He never even noticed the car until after we had passed by, then proceeded methodically to demolish the sulky. Another plunged off through the forest dragging a small cart behind, fell over a cliff and lay dead as mutton, the wreckage of the cart strewn all about him.

None of the horses we met in Norway approached the standards of misconduct of the north Finnish ponies.

"It appears," observed my father glumly at the end of the first day, "as if motoring through Finland is going to be a damned expensive pastime!" To round out the day we blew two tires before reaching Uleåborg and ended long after dark in a driving snowstorm.

In a foot of snow we set out the next morning over a road as yet unbroken for the first 140 miles. It was tricky driving over the narrow, unfamiliar track that passed through thick forest with only rare clearings, but amazingly beautiful in the play of sunlight on the fresh snowfall. The snow lay nine or ten inches deep upon the thick branches of spruce and pines, along the tops of fences and on the roofs of the small, infrequent farm buildings. Clean snow, sparkling as with sprinkled diamond dust, shot with opalescent hues that softened the incredible atmospheric brilliance; set off by dark streaks that were the undersides of the evergreens. Mile after shimmering mile we drove in the silence of an enchanted forest with its scattered clearings etched in sharpness and purple shadow.

The snow lasted the better part of two days while we made the 140 miles at an average speed of eight miles an hour. During the night a dense ground-mist formed in the valley where we halted. It seeped into every crevice of the car. There it froze; and with my father I spent three hours the next morning—as also the morning after—first thawing out our vehicle with a gasoline blow-torch, then trying to get it started. Every connection, every joint and hinge, was frozen solid. The brake-bands were frozen to the drums, the doors frozen shut, the pressure line, pump, gasoline lines and a thousand-and-one moving or tubular parts were every one frozen into immobility or closure. The lock of the tool-box was frozen, the cover was frozen to the box, the tools were frozen fast in the depressions of their metallic tray as if they had been poured there molten. Once the car had been externally thawed we could still jump on the hand crank without budging it.

When we reached Nyslott the only gasoline I could pick up had been kept in a tar-barrel. This made starting in the cold no easier. The alleged motor fuel was a rich brownish-yellow, redolent of wood tar. It would not even pour through a linen handkerchief, let alone a chamois. But there was none other to be had for two days, by which time the exhaust-valves and spark-plugs had been gummed up as if set with cement.

Nyslott, or Savonlinna in the Finnish form of its name, is a charming old town built on several islands in a narrow lake. Its splendid thirteenth-century fortress-castle rises gaunt from the waters that mirror the massive stone towers, their grimness softened by a patina of grey-green lichen. In the open market on the street which fronted the hotel—very Russian in appearance—a dozen kinds of game-birds were being offered for sale.

In Nyslott I took my first Finnish bath. Following this ordeal I felt like the Alabama darky after his first airplane flight had scared him an ashen grey, who said to the pilot: "Mister, Ah thanks you for them two nice rides—mah fust, an'—mah—lahst!" For though some years later I returned for more punishment of the same but a slightly modified sort, I had never until then been washed with the terrifying completeness of that bath in Nyslott.

"*Soumi sauna?* You will take Finnish bath?" the hotel proprietor inquired.

"Why, yes, I would like to," I responded unsuspectingly.

"*Ah!*" It seemed as though there was something sinister in that *ah!* "I send leedle boy to show you." He assigned a tow-headed whelp who led the way to the public bath-house—a barn-like wooden structure, cold, deserted and smelling of wet steam. Here "leedle boy" induced me to remove all my clothing, after which he disappeared. Alone and shivering in my nakedness I looked around the empty hall with growing distaste. "A hell of a bathing establishment *this* is!" I yawped.

I was about to regarb myself when there entered an enormous woman who yanked the clothes from my hands and shoved me into one of the several box-stalls that gave onto the barn. It was an austere little oblong of a room with two wooden shelves one above the other along the side, a ladder leading up to them, and a half-length, triangular Russian stove in one corner. There was nothing else except for a layer of stones on the flat top of the stove, roasting over the fire within.

The female Colossus returned to the room carrying two buckets full of water, which she heaved onto the hot stones. She repeated this a dozen times until the little room became a steam-box in which I was being effectively parboiled. On the last trip she bore a bundle of birch twigs. These she dipped in the water and then laid them on the stones to steam. It struck me that all this augured ill.

With bearish grunts the horrendous Amazon drove me up the ladder, like a calf up the ramp to the slaughter-house, onto the top shelf where the steam hung densest. I made a futile effort to stop at the lower of the two shelves, but she would have none of it. On the upper shelf she stretched me out, and wielding the top part of a birch tree with an arm that would have shamed a Japanese wrestler, she beat me until the skin came off in layers.

One side after the other she flailed front and back, rolling my tormented body over and over as she might a large guinea-pig; thrashing me with a methodical, sadistic efficiency. I put up a feeble resistance, mewling weakly: "Woman, for the love of God, will you have a heart?" She had no heart. She was completely dispassionate. I suspected that she employed her spare time like Hackenschmidt, the "Russian Lion," whom some years before I had watched move cars round a New York garage by lifting their front or back ends with his two hands and swinging them about. She paid no attention whatever to my mewlings, and at last having borne my carcass down the ladder—clean as it had ever been since its initial bath after birth and about as weak—she dumped me limply naked onto the floor of the cheerless central hall and for a reviver doused me with six large buckets of ice-water in rapid succession. I tottered back to my hotel a cleaner and a chastened man.

"You like *Suomi sauna?*" inquired the hotel proprietor with a grin. "Here in Nyslott give very good bat'."

"I do not like *Suomi sauna* at all," I replied. "Bat' is right. I admit it is probably very effective, if one lives through it."

"Ah!" he said. "Even in small town all Finn take *Suomi sauna* every Saturday. W'en hav' no bat'-woman t'ey beat each odder, all in beeg room full wit' steam. Mens, womans, all toget'er, all wit'out clothes. Roun' and roun' in circle, each beat man, woman, in front, behin', until t'ey all clean. T'en in winter, t'ey run outside and yump in t'e snow."

Hardy folk, the Finns. The weaker ones, I presume, die young. To anyone looking for a really clean people I commend Finlanders—the ones who survive—as of any Saturday night, or even a Sunday morning.

Despite perverse horses, tarred gasoline and peculiar bathing practices, I had been in few lands more delightful than Finland, especially through the central lake district. No other part of the world, save perhaps the St. Lawrence basin, is so fantastically broken up by lakes. A large-scale map of the area looks as if someone had snapped a drawing-pen dipped in blue ink over and over against it. Amongst many rivers draining the area, the Vuoksi alone pours off through the Imatra Cascades the overflow of more than a thousand lakes. From such watery surroundings the Finns take their name: *Suomi*, the fen-dwellers.

The lakes are spattered with islands and ribbed by narrow ridges, each ridge wooded to its summit, each island to the water's edge. From the Punkaharju hogback of glacial moraine one can see a dozen alternate belts of blue water, pine-clad islets and strips of thickly wooded peninsula. The view from Puijo Hill near Kuopio recalled Matshushima on Japan's Inland Sea.

The pines, in the brief transition from summer to winter, were swathed in a fluffy counterpane of snow. Beneath them the carpet of thick green moss sparkled with a sugary coating over which ptarmigan —now white in their winter plumage—pattered like vague ghosts of the brown birds they had been but a few weeks before.

Apart from perhaps half a dozen ancient settlements like Nyslott, Borgå and Viborg, with their mediaeval charm, most Finnish towns are dully monotone. Helsinki has a character peculiarly its own. The capital of the Grand Duchy was even in 1913 one of the most modernly equipped and best kept-up cities in Europe. It had a garage fitted with both a ramp and electric elevators. It had comfortable hotels and excellent shops. Its University students strolled across the open squares in choral groups with strong, mellow voices. Its interesting modern architecture, not yet fully developed but pioneering well in advance of most of the world, breathed national consciousness through the medium of the massive granite boulders of a sturdy, rugged land.

"Yes, we are progressing," observed a Finnish gentleman of cultured and agreeable approach who had taken a keen interest in our trip. "Not only in our architecture. But too slowly! There is one thing that holds us back." He glanced over his shoulder, around the public room where we were having a glass of schnapps. "Russia! Russia has always held us back, tyrannically sought to suppress all our racial feeling, to destroy our very souls. We must break away from Russia!" This he whispered, and as if in confirmation, "I have myself been twice in exile."

"You will be there again, my friend," I thought, "unless you're careful!"

"The time is coming!" he continued. "Not yet, but I assure you it is coming sooner than some think. We are going to free ourselves from the corrupt, feudal hand of a hated overlord. We must bide our time, yet it is coming . . . you shall see it . . . it is coming!" To its coming we silently downed our schnapps.

He was not at all the type of revolutionary I had visualized. He was middle-aged, quiet, of distinguished appearance, obviously not the sort of person with nothing to lose. Nevertheless I, too, kept looking over my shoulder. Though I was much interested in his prophecy (which took four years in its realization) I had no wish to be haled before some grim inquisitorial court as a plotter against the Double-headed Eagle's imperial sway.

My father returned to England from Helsinki. On my way out of Finland with my mother there were two surprises. The first came at the Finnish customs house, and had to do with the refund in a matter of some twenty minutes of the 250 Finnmarks transit deposit we had paid on the customs entry of the car. In that day this would probably have taken at least six months in the more highly developed state of my country.

The second surprise was at the Imperial Russian customs station just across the Rajajoki River. Instead of my being dragged before an inquisitorial court, our passage was expedited with a courtesy and despatch as unexpected as it was agreeable. The only delay resulted from a remarkably thorough search of our baggage. Bombs and seditious literature rather than dutiable goods seemed to be the object of the search. We had no bombs. But the inspector found at least questionable literature in Sir Henry Norman's two fat volumes on *All the Russias* which the author had inscribed to my mother as a parting gift. From them the inspector tore fourteen pages, then returned the censored books with a bow.

"Not allowed in Russia," he explained in French. The offending pages bore principally upon Russia's drastic suppression of Finnish independent thought, wherefore the censorship seemed a trifle late. But the inspector was well pleased at his adroit discharge of duty.

We ran then to St. Petersburg over a wide, straight military highway congested with traffic for the last few miles. It was the first heavy traffic I had seen for a long time. People in St. Petersburg seemed reluctant to believe that we had come by automobile 1364 miles south to reach that northerly capital, on the same parallel of latitude as the top of Labrador.

Though I had been to Moscow and had traversed the length of the Siberian railway, I had not previously visited St. Petersburg. Externally the city was disappointing. Its vaunted Nevski Prospekt gave an impression of spaciousness and of little else. Its stuccoed pretenses of grandeur left the feeling of shoddy impermanence. Internally it was different. There was nothing shoddy about its stupendous art collections; and in catering to the sensuous pleasures of life no other city could surpass, perhaps none other equal, in that year before the war, the Capital of All the Russias.

There was a restaurant called the *Café de l'Ours*, of modest size though not such modest charges, rated high by the élite for its cuisine and its atmosphere of discreet gaiety. I frequented it both for these advantages and for its music. My mother was mildly ill for a few days; so I went alone, at first, and then with an amiable companion. The leader of the small stringed orchestra played delightfully. Among the many selections that I particularly liked was a little café-piece which had caught popular fancy along the Baltic. It was a simple little piece with an engaging lilt. I heard it in the Café de l'Ours for the first time. The orchestra leader took note of my pleasure over it, whereafter he played the lilting little tune each evening at my table. After leaving St. Petersburg I heard it once again in Danzig, and no more for seven years.

I was dining then at the Italian Roof Garden, London's newest restaurant with dancing as its *raison d'être*. My partner was the particular orb of youth and beauty in my firmament of the time. The lights were dimmed. We were sitting beneath twinkling stars in a blue heaven, which if artificial was realistic enough under the circumstances. The orchestra was muted as though to our conversation—dulcet and dreamy.

It is a curious thing how music can transport one back to where some melody was first heard and liked. There came a momentary pause in the muted tones of the orchestra; then suddenly, but without sense of transposition, I was no longer at that table, I was not in the Italian Roof Garden, I was not in London. I was in the Café de l'Ours at St. Petersburg, a place that had ceased to exist, in a city whose very name had changed along with the name of the country of which it no longer was the capital, in an era that had died and forever been interred under the avalanche of the war.

I had scarcely thought of the Café de l'Ours during the intervening years. But there I was, floating on a Baltic tune I had not heard for seven autumns. The orchestra was playing my favored little café-piece of 1913, very softly. It was a supper-piece rather than a dance tune.

My partner was not wholly pleased over my abstraction. Somewhere, as from a great distance, I seemed to hear her voice. "You have gone away," it said; "please come back!" Hardly recognizing the voice, I turned my head slowly in the general direction whence it came. The lilting refrain of the gay little Baltic tune was being played again. It sounded quite near at hand. As I turned my head, I looked straight into the face of the orchestra leader of the Café de l'Ours.

It was the same man, playing—after seven years of war and revolution and sudden death—the same piece towards my table to my lady-of-the-voice. He had not recognized me, I was sure, though when I spoke to him he pretended to remember. But it seemed an odd coincidence.

A few weeks later he played to us a new tune that I very much liked. And that one now takes me back to the Italian Roof Garden, another place that has ceased to exist.

From St. Petersburg our course led southwestward through Pskow, Dwinsk and Kowno over very wide, very straight military roads of reasonably well maintained macadam. The macadam gave way to round cobbles, roughly paved through the towns and sparse villages; miserable villages of a single row of half-story houses on either side set far back from the road. In many of the villages there was not one inhabitant who could read or write. Most of the villages were fearfully ravaged by syphilis. In all of them the whole adult population would be supine drunk on Sunday—the Lethean drunkenness that brought a moment's oblivion into the desolate round of their lives.

During the course of a single Sunday I dragged at least twoscore unconscious villagers from the middle of the road to safer repose alongside. At the outskirts of Ostrow, on one of the exceedingly frequent holidays, there was a great fair, wherefore all the occupants of all the carts were drunk as David's sow. As usual the horses were very frightened, their drivers too sodden to know what to do about it or care at all. An incredible number of carts upset into the deep ditches, popping out twelve or fourteen persons each time. The passengers fell in befuddled limpness, well padded in their winter clothing; so no single one was hurt.

Towering above the wretched, earthen-floored hovels of all but the meanest villages, in multiplicity over the dingy towns, the golden domes of great churches gleamed with the wealth of an impoverished community. Within them well-fed, bull-voiced priests moved about under columns of lapis-lazuli and porphyry and alexandrite, sold the tapers that the implorers of God's mercy offered in humility before silver and enameled ikons. These tapers, purchased with the kopek or two that stood between the buyers and utter penury, I myself saw—and more than once—snuffed out as soon as the suppliants' backs were turned, then readied for other implorers. Perhaps there was a shortage of tapers. I did not know; but the callous treatment of those earthy, unhappy peasants made a deep impress on my memory.

The contrast between the churches of Holy Russia and the abodes of most of those who attended them was as striking as anything I had seen up to that time. This, and the disparity between priest and parishioner, gave one to understand something of the reaction against the Church when the Tzarist regime broke down, and of the fearful reward visited upon a clergy which had ill acquitted its trust. There were, of course, exceptions on both sides.

At Kowno I had counted on finding a badly needed draft awaiting us. A fortnight in St. Petersburg had devastated the remnants of our letter of credit. With the equivalent of about eight dollars in hand I inquired of the manager of the hotel if he had any communication for me.

"*Niet!*" he snapped, and turned back. He was a peculiarly repulsive piece of work and his hotel, reputedly the best in Kowno, was execrable. The banks were about to close; the next day, of course, was another holiday. I expended half of our ready cash on a cable to London, then settled down unwillingly to wait.

Kowno in that day—it has improved moderately since—was a thoroughly horrid place. It was dirty, ill-kempt and foul-smelling; and so was its Hotel Metropole. That hostelry had all the earmarks of a large and disorderly brothel. It seethed with inebriated Russian officers and their blowzy mistresses, with unappetizing Jewish evening ladies and shifty-eyed men of evil mien. The food was odious. What with drunken yowling and crashing of glass on the ground floor, and the bedbugs and other unamiable crawlers that overran one's rooms, repose flew away on the wings of night to return no more whilst we remained in Kowno.

A reply to my cable was delivered the morning after the holiday. It advised that the draft had been mailed me care of the manager of the Hotel Metropole nine days before. First-class postal service from London to Kowno should not, then, have taken over four days at the most. Once again I accosted the manager.

"*Niet!*" he spat out. "I told you I had nothing for you!" Over his shoulder I noticed in a pigeon-hole of his littered desk an envelope bearing English stamps. I leaned across and snatched it out. It bore my name; it held my draft. It had been there nearly a week. The manager simply shrugged his shoulders. "You don't expect *me* to keep track of all the post that comes in here, do you?" he snarled. My hands itched to wring his scrawny neck.

In half an hour I returned from the bank with the proceeds of the draft. I had the luggage put on the car and tipped the servants who had tended us. I helped my mother aboard. Then I went to the manager's office for a last farewell, accompanied by our completely ineffectual courier-interpreter acquired through Thomas Cook in St. Petersburg. On the manager's desk I laid the exact amount of the bill, less the cost of the two cables to and from London and one full day, rooms and meals, for three people. I explained this to him in detail.

"If you had given me that letter when I first asked you if one had arrived in my name, I could have got to the bank before it closed for the holiday, I need not have wired London, and I would have been off next morning. The fact that you did not do so has caused me expense and inconvenience. Furthermore, I dislike your particular type of insolence, your whole demeanor, and your beastly hotel. Good day!" And I stalked out.

"*Niet!*" he shrieked, and a good deal more. There was a fearful row. I moved swiftly to the car—the engine had been left running—while the manager and an accumulating troop of servants clattered along behind. Some of them brandished brooms, all were frantically yelling "Stop thief! . . . Assassin!" or words of that nature. A boy pursued us on a bicycle. I rode him off, ducked out by a way I had plotted beforehand on which happily there were no police, and headed for Germany.

Then I began to have qualms. The manager probably would get the police to telegraph the frontier station. Our passports would be seized, I would be flung into jail on a whole file of exaggerated charges, would rot incommunicado for weeks and weeks, my mother would be interned, the automobile would be confiscated, and we would be inflicted with a gigantic fine in the end. They did things that way in Russia, I had been assured. The manager did not know just which way I was going, but there were only a few practicable ways out. The police, of course, would telegraph to all those points. Once more I approached the Russian frontier with misgivings. These were not allayed by the sight of four guards armed with rifles standing at the closed barrier. "Ah-ha!" I said to myself, "I don't like the look of *that!*"

Once again nothing happened. Our passports and triptych were stamped, the car and baggage cleared, without question or delay. It was none the less with a certain sense of relief that I left the black-and-white barriers of Wershbolowo behind. Kowno, a fortress of the first class with eighteen detached forts, the principal railway center and key to the borderline of Russia proper, was captured by the German forces of von Eichorn in August 1917. As to the town itself, I did not feel excessively distressed over this. Nor would it have been a fearful shock to have learned that the captors had hanged the manager of the Hotel Metropole.

We kept on through Königsberg, through Marienburg on the Vistula with its great red Balto-Gothic castle preserving something of the splendor of the Teutonic Knights—the first of the Junkers—whose glory was smashed at Tannenberg in 1410; through Danzig and Berlin. Here my mother, the last of my family-crew, abandoned me for the train. At Eisenach I crossed our outward route north, completing there the first recorded loop of the Baltic Sea by automobile—5718 miles as the speedometer read, including our incidental Scandinavian wanderings and the diversion of the Northernmost Road.

Left Bank, Right Bank

The winter of 1913–14 marked the culmination of an epoch whose charm, whatever may have been its defects, grows in retrospect out of the chaos of social and political upheaval that has followed upon its close.

Probably nowhere else could one have appreciated so well the zenith of that epoch, and the abruptness of its collapse, as in Paris amongst the students from a multitude of nations seeking knowledge within the gates of the University City—the "City of Enlightenment" which countless generations of their predecessors had made the most cosmopolitan city of the world.

Those last days before the collapse my student friends and I took in our stride. None could realize how swiftly the débâcle was shaping. With sophomoric intensity we revelled in the privileges of the *Ville-Lumière*. Our enlightenment was not confined to the arts. Paris was enchanting, joyously open to the student-stranger within her gates; sensations were fresh, life delicious. It is not among my regrets that I took her privileges as I did. With the majority of my associates I was destined soon enough for sensations of another sort. The "doomed generation" of Europe teetered happily on the greased skids to destruction, without thought of what was in store for them.

My family had an apartment on the Rue Benjamin Godard, in Passy, on the Right Bank (the conservative bank) of the Seine. But this I avoided as far as I appropriately could in favor of the less restricted and consequently more enticing Left Bank, where my student friends lived, took courses at the Ecole des Beaux Arts, daubed or worked at architecture in various *ateliers*, and misbehaved at night in the fashions of their choosing.

It was a mixed brigade in temperament as in nationality that forgathered each evening around the white marble-topped tables of the Café des Deux Magots, or the metal-topped ones of the Brasserie Lipp, on the Place St.-Germain-des-Prés. National groups tended to hang together, but in general pattern and in outlook we were of the University City and of the world at large. Our conduct was moulded to an unwritten code of behavior, long-established and essentially liberal, whose precepts applied with varying emphasis according to the quarter of the city in which one happened to be at the moment, and to particular circumstances. Within these generous bounds a student could live pretty much as he felt inclined; and usually he did, up to—or beyond—the limits of his purse and the shifting inclinations of youth. There was a complete absence of regimentation. One's private eccentricities were respected so long as they did not unduly interfere with those of others.

As a group we attained a tidy alcoholic consumption, but we drank for enjoyment rather than for effect. Each paid his own account. There was no pressure on moderate thirsts to keep pace with more enthusiastic tipplers.

The habitués of the Place St.-Germain-des-Prés led, on the whole, a bachelor existence in which amorous adventure was casual and incidental. The roving eye of youth had no great way to wander for inspiration beyond the curricula of daily activities. But among my Continental friends were some who made it no part of their evening routine to join the bachelor band at the two chosen cafés. They found solace from the loneliness of the night in the affections of regular mistresses. With their gentle solaces they lived in varying degrees of style and of comfort, according to the combined circumstances. Usually their amiable companions held jobs as salesgirls or *midinettes* at one of the big stores, where the weekly stipend was something on which not even a Frenchwoman could live alone.

The partnerships were variously formed. Two I knew to be the result of items inserted in the humorous weekly *Le Rire*, then a favored medium of lonely hearts. The items were of standard pattern, varied only to accord with particular specifications.

"Art-ptre, jn, gd, sn & sér, ch. amie 18–22, brune, pour chas. caf, jlie, bn fmee, jlies jbes, sne, sér, dès, affse: pour lia. sér; exp. photo; profs. rig. s'abst."

Which, as read by those whom it might concern, informed the unattached feminine world that an

"Artist, young, tall, healthy and sincere, seeks feminine friend 18–22 (as to age), brunette, to chase away *cafard* (the beetle of loneliness), pretty, well formed, pretty legs, healthy, sincere, pecuniarily disinterested, affectionate; for durable relations; send photograph; professionals keep away."

From photographic returns and the descriptions accompanying them the field of contenders would be reduced to several likely beetle-chasers. A few meetings brought further eliminations, in due course led to a satisfactory arrangement with the favored qualifier. On such basis of mutual albeit temporary loyalty, those informal alliances could well have served as models for unions more ceremoniously blessed.

For my part few social events were nearly so entertaining as the impromptu suppers served in ancient fifth- and sixth-floor attic rooms by these bohemian friends and their cheery solaces. They were intimate little parties, usually of four or at most eight, each couple supplying its quota to the simple feast. Most of the American students of my acquaintance were too well financed, too inhibited and unimaginative, to live in any such manner, where the rotting wallpaper hung in stained festoons and the eager helpmates contributed to the *ménage* from their miserable earnings. The unaffected gaiety of the young girls lent infinite charm to the dingy surroundings.

They cooked *poulet en casserole* over broken charcoal stoves in a manner to make one weep with joy, prepared pungent sauces in weird makeshift containers, "fatigued" the salad with a long wooden fork. We would usually sit on the floor, there being a paucity of chairs, with our bottles of wine (brought to correct temperature by immersion in warm water in a cracked *pot de chambre*), shouting with laughter at daring sallies and uncensored song, criticizing the efforts of others and making amorous passes with unabashed enthusiasm. The conversation would be frankly, but wittily, ribald; manners supremely informal. Yet there was a recognition of proprietary rights in partnerships which I rarely saw infringed.

"Thou shalt not seduce thy comrade's mistress," went the code, and this unwritten interdiction was honored by stricter observance than the Tenth Commandment in many a smug society whose matings had benefit of clergy. Very rarely would one of those sprightly Dianas of the *cafard*, implacable huntresses of the beetle of depression, be seducible, even during the protracted absence of her mate. They were faithful little mistresses after their fashion.

In that youthful world, enjoyment implied being interested or amused. So perhaps it does elsewhere, broadly interpreting the two qualifications. But on the Left Bank in '13–'14 the two words were synonymous. The current expression of approval, "*c'est amusant,*" covered anything from Gothic cathedrals, early Latin treatises on medico-astrology or lectures by eminent scientists, to a lovely lady's boudoir, her fashion of doing her hair, or duckling prepared *à la presse* as only Frédéric of the Tour d'Argent could do.

The summing up was not quite the reducing of descriptive effort to such adjectives as "nice," "swell," and "lousy." Rather it placed things in one of two basic categories: they amused or they did not amuse. And for those things that did not, we made no attempt to disguise a shuddering antipathy.

Now and then the trivial term covered deep emotion. Often it was supported by keen analysis of the finer and feebler points of the object so broadly classified. But outsiders of the Left Bank were sometimes a trifle confused at a student's casual comment on one of the world's great glories of religious architecture or painting: "It's not bad; it's amusing!"

Yet the phrase itself was catching. Criticism of artistic detail in Paris was not confined to students of the Left Bank. I saw, that winter, five *fiacres* lined up in the Place de Rivoli, on the Right Bank, facing Fremiet's equestrian statue of Jeanne d'Arc which had recently been regilded. The little leather-hooded carriages were blocking traffic down the Rue des Pyramides. Their drivers did not care in the least. They stood on their boxes, white top hats canted back off their foreheads, pointing with their whips at the offending statue while the scrawny remnants of their horses sagged between the shafts.

The statue *was* garish in its new coating of gilt, yet I could not quite visualize a like scene facing the gilded Sherman of New York's Plaza.

"*Horrible! Infecte!*" shouted the *cochers* at each other. "They've spoilt it!" After this broad appraisal of the Municipality's effort at beautifying the city, one of them summed up the general distaste of that group of ancient hackmen spiritedly gesticulating with their whips: "It is *not* amusing!" The rest concurred; a perfect testimonial to the penetration of Left Bank patter, whose stamp of disapproval was definite as the grave.

What did not amuse displeased, and was interred with assured, if verbal, finality. Happily, Paris afforded an infinite variety of things in the approved category.

They were good company, those students of the Left Bank who sought and found the "amusing" in life. Many of them were killed in action not long after. Others have disappeared in the aftermath of the war. Some doubtless are in jail or in asylums for the criminally insane—where they might have landed earlier in a less tolerant atmosphere. Some have lived to distinguish themselves in their several fields.

They worked hard when they worked, played with complete abandon when they played; those two approaches to a full life being fairly evenly divided. Certain ones from time to time disappeared for days, and even weeks, in intense if sporadic application to their chosen pursuits. Their reasons for withdrawal from circulation, and their hidden retreats, were respected.

Others would disappear for days and nights on ventures of a different type. About the third evening of such impromptu absence someone would organize a search party to track down the missing comrade, dig him out from obscure places where we felt he might be in need of rescue and should not in any event remain so long.

"We really ought to hunt up X——!" would be the rallying cry. "He was last seen at such-and-such a spot two nights ago—may be in the morgue by now!" And volunteers seldom lacked.

Now and then the stale scent of those hunts led to curious earth. Trailing one or two of our more notorious absentees, the huntsmen would sometimes take along an emergency costume. Experience had taught that in the sort of hole we might ultimately run to ground our prowling fox there would be a likelihood of his clothes having unaccountably been misplaced.

But mostly they studied and painted through the working hours of the day, sipped their beer or *apéritifs* each evening on the Place St.-Germain-des-Prés, supported and challenged with equal vehemence the various groups that were breaking with cherished traditions, and made love in an incidental manner as generations of their predecessors on the Left Bank had done before them. Together they contributed amply to the broadening of one's outlook on life.

Most of my friends were students of painting or architecture. The plunge into the modern had hardly begun in architecture, but there were undercurrents of revolt against the unimaginative adherence of the "Ecole" to nineteenth-century form. To appreciate the ornate stodginess of this style one had only to make a tour of the public buildings in the principal provincial cities, though it would have been unfair to blame all those mansard-roofed horrors on Beaux-Arts influence.

A group of us sometimes lunched at Thryion's little old restaurant on the Boulevard St.-Germain, where an excellent repast of hors d'œuvres, soup, horsemeat, greens and cheese, with a quarter-liter of passable wine, could be had for seventeen sous. Thackeray was among the illustrious who in their day frequented that simple second-floor eating place. There for the first time I heard the sacred high temple of architecture openly blasphemed. The torpedoing of venerated tradition always comes as a shock. I had taken the Ecole des Beaux-Arts for granted as the Supreme Arbiter of Things Architectural. "Which," one of our rebels observed, "is exactly how the superior staff of the Academy takes its collective, dull, and reactionary self!" Though not a student at the Beaux-Arts I felt slightly unhappy over such *lèse-majesté.*

Painting had definitely entered a period of transition. The cherished shibboleths having been thrown overboard by a few artists of original genius, a horde of imitators rushed wildly beyond them to exploit new techniques that might screen their inability to draw and the exceeding thinness of their talent.

The multiplicity of new "schools" and weird "isms" was infinitely confusing. They sprang forth overnight like aviation companies in America some fifteen years later, mostly to disappear about as swiftly. That certain ones received attention at all, beyond the point of inspiring ridicule, could be ascribed only to the spread of a sympathetic strike against "authority" and the academicians, and to the exploitation of a gullible public by the dealers; in no manner to any intrinsic quality of their art.

Though they had not yet reached the asininities of sur-realism, many of the canvases one was invited to look upon conveyed no intelligible impression whatever: neither of linear rhythm nor the meaningful use of color found in the guileless abstracts of savages. They were not intriguing; they were not even exasperating. Preposterous smears, these emotive excursions into the realms of synthesis failed to "amuse," in the accepted sense of the term. Yet while many of my friends shared my distaste for the completely obscure, to others this attitude caused surprise and pain.

"But you are atrophied emotionally!" cried a young French adherent to one of the more expressionistic phases of futurism, who undertook my enlightenment. He had perpetrated a horrific, incoherent canvas of which he was vastly proud. He called it *"La Brasserie Lipp."*

"That may indeed be," I admitted.

"Ah, but you will expand to it, *mon cher,* when I explain you the thing! It is the living spirit, the very breath of the café, that I depict! It is the atmosphere, it *is* the Brasserie Lipp of our senses. Listen to me! I enter, and what first? I look for a table. I see not one unoccupied. Ah, but yes! There, three men are paying off their saucers. Each has three counter-saucers in front of him; three drinks consumed. They have been long at that table." He pauses briefly to refill his glass of port.

"I move nearer to the table and wait close beside, scuffling with my foot the damp sawdust that lightly covers the floor. I think, for what one uses this sawdust? I tell myself: it is because some people spill beer, and some people spit. For such, it is good to clean with damp sawdust the tiled floor. It is soon swept up, and with it the spilt beer, the cigarette butts and spit."

"You bring all that into your painting?" I inquire mildly.

"Of course; it is there. One of the men at the table sees me waiting, and then all three sit a little longer. 'Kinds of a toad,' I say to myself. 'May they grow antlers, betrayed by their wives and mistresses!'

"I hear the two-toned taxi horns going '*eeh-aah, eeh-aah*' outside, like the braying of little donkeys. I whiff the sweetly pungent smell of benzole from the taxis; that smell which has become the so characteristic odor of our Paris streets. Finally they depart, those three. I sit down quickly and call: '*Garçon!*' Charles, he comes with his white apron enfolding his fat belly. 'Half a liter of dark,' I say, and Charles he cries across the room in ascending falsetto: '*Un demi br-un-e, un!*' I strike a match for my cigarette, holding it aloft while the sulphur tip burns off. God, how I detest that choking stench of sulphur!

"But the voice of Charles! Ubiquitous, he moves to and fro between the tables, deposits beers with their counter-saucers, crying the orders in tremulous tone: '*Quatre demi bl-on-des, qua-tre!*' and wipes his goat's-beard on his apron, each outward-curving side separately. I ask you, what would be the Lipp without that voice, that ridiculous beard, and, of course, the good beer? Nothing. It would not exist. So what use to portray the Lipp without those things, without their varied effects on our senses?"

"All that you have painted on the canvas?" I ask.

"But yes, my ancient, and more! How otherwise to express the thing? Behind me six, perhaps eight, Beaux-Arts students are as usual talking all at once, drawing *motifs* in the air with their thumbs. They think now of their *projets* and of the Prix de Rome they expect to win, forgetful of *affaires de cœur* of nights just passed. At small tables near the windows venerable bearded ones, two by two, play at dominoes and checkers. Intent, they plan many moves ahead in silence, then make little clicking noises as they advance their pieces. Too old, they are, to click at a living *jeu de dames*. But farther back in the room amorous couples throb lightly to love's preliminaries. Their thoughts are close and warm. I observe in the mirror furtive caressing of smooth thighs and firm breasts. I sense the whispered urging; and I paint them in the embrace of intimacy that soon must follow, for I am thinking ahead of them!"

"You have, then," I ask, "painted their thoughts as well, all these variously occupied people, and your own thinking, on the canvas?"

"*Mais, naturellement!* Is it, the Lipp, a musée of wax figures?"

I suggest that it might seem over-ambitious to attempt the portrayal on a flat medium, with brush and pigments, of a sequence of movement on both sides and behind, sounds and smells arising within the crowded café and from the street beyond; the mental processes of architectural tyros, of elderly checker players and absorbed lovers; and the overlying thoughts, shifting and sensual, of the artist himself.

"But *that* is what I have done! Bah! Wherefore these limitations of space and medium you would have hamper us? I annihilate them!" He does so with a bold stab of his thumb. "I sweep away the cobwebs of restraint. I paint what exists, the vitality, the reaction on all the senses: *l'esprit!* What gain the emotions from a dead photograph? *Mon Dieu!* You do not sense it, you cannot feel?" he cries, concerned over my lack of wit.

I look again at the dreadful canvas. There is not one line, not one daub, that conveys to me any suggestion; unless it were that an ape from the Jardin d'Acclimation had escaped to an artist's studio, had watched the process of daubing on canvas, and had duplicated this process under the stimulus of absinthe and acute pains in its head and stomach.

"My friend, I am sorry," I say, gently, for this enthusiasm is genuine though unrelieved by any touch of humor towards its objective. "There is too much for me. I wander, dazed, as in a forest which I cannot see for the trees, nor recognize the trees as such. Despite your explanation I grope in darkness, hearing nothing, smelling nothing, nor able even to think."

"Ah, you cobweb-bound! Emotionally stultified! Tied to line, understanding but the externals of form, color-blind and lacking imagination! So does a dog sense but one utility in a rosebush!"

Perhaps. But several young artists with both imagination and humor had a painting done under their supervision without direct human touch, and had it hung in the *Salon des Indépendents* of a few years before. They led a donkey to the Cabaret of the Agile Rabbit in Montmartre. There they taped a paint-brush to its tail and backed the small beast to a stretched canvas placed upon a chair in lieu of an easel. They fed the unwitting artist lumps of sugar soaked in rum, while they dipped the brush alternately in cans of vivid red, emerald green,

Prussian blue and yellow paints. The donkey switched its tail reflectively, passing the pigment-soaked brush across the surface of the canvas.

When sugar failed to produce the results desired they stuck brads into its behind. The outraged animal expressed itself by excreting before the improvised easel and snapping its tail back and forth like an amorous cat, leaving highly impressionistic streaks on the canvas.

The conspirators continued alternately to feed their colleague tasty *canards* and jab at its tender posterior until the canvas was completely painted over. They called the painting "And the Sun Put Itself to Sleep on the Adriatic," signing it with the mystic name J. R. Boronali—a slightly disguised form of the Rabelaisian ass Aliboron. They submitted it formally to the Salon, where it was accepted and hung in a choice location. People gazed at the monstrosity with awe; many professed to appreciate its obscure beauty. And the laudatory notices of some of the art critics described it as a work of genius.

In the spring some of the Left Bankers when momentarily in funds would now and then descend from the merry slopes of Montmartre to breakfast in early luxury on scrambled eggs with bacon, hot chocolate and brioches in the gardens of the Pré-Catelan. Then, it being rather late to make an appearance at home, I would occasionally repair to 23 Quai Voltaire.

Harry Cannon's apartment, on the top floor of one of an ancient row of houses overlooking the river, was my favorite refuge. It was a weary climb of six long flights after a night of wandering. During the hours of dark there was the added struggle of arousing the *concierge* by vigorous yankings on the bell-pull that rang in her bedroom, along with accompanying shouts of *"Cordon, Madame, s'il vous plaît"* coupled with the name of Monsieur Cannon. How heartily she detested the nocturnal habits of the students and their friends who clamored at all hours of the night for her to pull the wire alongside her bed and so release the bolt of the big door into the courtyard! But the haven was worth the effort.

Only once in Paris did I encounter anything in the way of serious physical altercation. This happened to be with a compatriot who joined one of our parties that extended well into the hours of daylight. I forget now who brought him along. He was a young mastodon of athletic prowess who carried neither his honors gracefully nor his drinks well.

The early and acrid distaste he formed for me started, I think, when I told him that the "Deux Magots" were grotesque little Chinese figures, not maggots.

Later in the evening he took exception to the arrangements of our best Montmartre cabaret toilets, so conveniently provided for the comfort of clients without distinction of sex. The necessity of relieving himself under the eye of an ancient beldame knitting socks beside the urinals, while female clients passed to and from the W.C.'s, aroused his ire. This turned to invective when the dilapidated hag shrilly reminded him of the tip customary for the privilege. The rest of us, quite used to the interior economy of Montmartre night-haunts and in no manner responsible for this, were coldly unsympathetic.

I do not recall what eventually caused our unamiable companion to lust for mayhem at my particular expense. We were breakfasting then in the Pré-Catelan gardens. Willie Iselin had brought as his guest Frank Moran, contender for the world's heavyweight boxing honors. Moran, whose conduct had been most circumspect throughout the evening, rather liked me; or in any case he disliked the mastodon cub. Just as our truculent guest was on the point of taking me apart Frank Moran cried out, "Hey!"—then tapped the mastodon once with a restricted version of the curious slow-motion swing he called his "Mary Ann." That restrained tap lifted some two hundred pounds of athletic fame clean over a Pré-Catelan hedge.

On the strength of this I bet most of a month's allowance on Frank Moran in his world's championship fight against Jack Johnson, on the eve of the assassination at Sarajevo—and lost. But there were many who felt Frank Moran should have had the decision.

One must have been unimpressionable indeed who failed to succumb to the appeal of Paris in that year of grace. The cleanliness of her, against the dirt and drab untidiness of most American cities! How she glistened after her early-morning bath, scrubbed, combed and brushed, not a hair displaced, highlights aplay in shifting patterns on the water drops that trickled off her lovely body! Very often, on our homeward way, we observed that matutinal bath of the unabashed First Lady of All Cities.

The lofty haven of 23 Quai Voltaire gave on a view so enchanting that I wept openly, one night in the late autumn of 1914 when the war was in full swing, at the thought that I might never see it again, or if I did it would perhaps be all devastated and smouldering. Even then the glory of the illumination had been dimmed, supplanted by the questing fingers of searchlights.

Until the war doused the lights, that view of an evening was one of the most exquisite the world could offer. From the ghostly contours of Notre Dame on the far right it swept with the bright ribbon of the Seine to the Mauresque outline of the Trocadéro on its Passy hillside at our extreme left. The one, a grey emblem of permanence and loving workmanship; the other, a sterile nineteenth-century imitation of an alien style, yet not unsympathetic in its evening silhouette. Between the lateral framing of those two edifices the whole of Paris of the Right Bank was unfurled.

We could count ten of the thirty-one bridges that span the river within the city's confines, their piers weaving fantastic patterns in the dark threads of the current. Reflections in green and red of navigation lights danced crazily in the swirling waters. Jolly little "fly-boats," beloved of Sunday trippers, scuttled with lowered funnels through the arches, corrugating the surface in gentle swells that swung the reflected arc lights of the banks in parabolas of quicksilver. On rainy nights the arc lamps glinted lineally on the wet pavements, centering like ribs on a spangled fan to our point of vantage.

Beyond the river in middle foreground an intricate open formation of lights spread through the Gardens of the Tuileries, flanked by straight rows along the Rue de Rivoli, to a blaze of illumination on the left quarter that was the Place de la Concorde (what travesty that name has been of late, O Concordia!). Thence they led in orderly double files up the splendid expanse of the Champs Elysées, unspoiled then by the garish shrimp and orange neon signs that later enticed other generations to cocktails, automobile salesrooms and purveyors of various fineries for expensive ladies.

The lights of Paris before the war were soft and mellow, the loveliest illumination of any city in the world.

At the top of the Champs Elysées rose the dark, rectangular mass of Napoleon's Arc de Triomphe, vaguely ponderous, commemorating the excesses of the Grande Armée; subsequently to shelter the first of the Unknowns who would represent the futile sacrifices of another war that had helped perpetuate war.

Down that glorious Avenue there used to come in the very early morn long processions of immense springless carts balanced on single pairs of seven-foot wheels, each pulled by four to six shaggy Percherons in line. Creaking ponderously under their loads of country produce, they rolled on their way to the markets of *Les Halles*. Their creaking through the empty hours somehow recalled the doleful sounds emitted in the silence of a Japanese night, when a two-wheeled lacquered catafalque drawn by an interminable file of white oxen bore what was mortal of the Emperor Meiji Tenno over the sanded streets of Tokyo between rows of Japanese who never raised their heads.

The streets of Tokyo are blasted now rather than sanded, and in Paris the carts of country produce no longer creak to *Les Halles* in such profusion.

Beyond the Louvre, facing us across the river, the great basilical pile of the Sacré Cœur gleamed white from atop Montmartre. With this Paris hill we were not entirely unfamiliar. Certain of us qualified as fairly assiduous explorers. Nor were our evenings at the Quai Voltaire spent always in quiet contemplation of the view, through the windows made notable by Bradley Delehanty's agile swarming across the entire front of the apartment, on the outside. Six long flights above the pavement he was, leaping from ledge to three-inch ledge where no self-respecting cat would have been tempted to risk one of its lives.

Quite a number of people within the apartment and on the street below experienced acute emotion during his passage, before his sweating comrades managed finally to haul him into the sixth and last window.

"For the love of God, man!" they cried. "You've given us heart failure!" The only reward for their pains was to be roundly cursed for having interrupted Bradley's return trip.

Few circus performers in sober state could have pulled that incredible stunt and lived to reflect on the processes of destiny.

"If I'd been sober, you silly damn fools, I wouldn't have tried it!" said Bradley.

There was a night when some of us went up on the "Mountain" and spent a good many hours in several favorite hangouts. Dawn was well launched when finally we decided to come down. The few waiting night-hawks of taxis refused to take us on the meter, demanding colossal sums to drive where we wished to go. We refused to be held up.

"But no, my ancients," we cried in unison, "Montmartre is a hill! Down it we will toddle in the bright and cheery dawn!"

We descended one of the steepish little side streets off the Boulevard de Clichy until it quartered into another, and came there full upon an astounding procession.

Three open victorias crept in snail-paced single file down the slope, fleshless relics of horses shuffling apathetically between their shafts. Three soiled white top-hats protruded at odd angles from the hunched-up bundles of blue cloth that were the dozing drivers on the boxes. Nothing was novel to a Paris *cocher*—least of all to a night-hawk of Montmartre; and so they slept. But this procession had elements of originality.

In the first *fiacre* a five-piece orchestra had somehow been wedged into the space provided normally for two and a half passengers. The musicians, leaning outwardly like the petals of an opening flower, were rendering a jaunty tune of the music halls, their arms and instruments all mixed up together in the general effect of a cubist portrait by Picasso.

The second carriage was stacked high with the early-morning production of a small bakery: succulent new-baked bread loaves three feet long. Between it and the third ran a diminutive messenger-boy dressed in the red uniform and pillbox hat of an English "Buttons." On each rearward trip the Buttons bore an armload of fresh loaves, as if feeding ammunition from an artillery limber to a field gun in action.

In the third vehicle a squat figure with the head of a ruddy Billiken stood on the seat, facing aft. He was propounding in rapid French a child's version of socialistic economics, the while he passed out bread loaves over the folded leathern hood to a multitude behind. For like the spuming tail of a rocket in slow motion there followed for nearly a block a horde of laughing, dancing people whose varied pursuits were apparent from the variety of their garb. In the manner of the Pied Piper of Hamelin the Billiken had drawn in his train most of the population of the Clichy quarter of Paris up and circulating at that hour of breaking day. A weird procession they made; a complete cross-section of the life of Montmartre streets at 5:30 A.M.

There were French workmen in blue smocks going to their daily tasks, lunch boxes of tin or paper in their hands. There were gilded playboys from South America and the capitals of Europe clad in "smoking," returning homeward because the *boites de nuit* had closed up or ceased to be amusing. There were weary musicians whose once-white little dickeys hung loosely disarranged around their necks; evening ladies from the night-haunts in slightly bedraggled dance-floor apparel, unsuccessful or early released from professional activities; and predatory prostitutes of the more dimly lighted avenues.

There were dismounted taxi drivers, *bistro* keepers who had just closed or were about to open their wee saloons, newsboys delivering early editions, singing out occasionally as though it were a reminder: *"Le Matin, Messieurs, Mesdames! Le Matin!"*

There were rodent-faced procurers and purveyors of various illicit commodities. There was a smattering of *clochards*—derelicts of Paris, without visible means of support but deeply attached to their accustomed nests beneath the bridges or in re-entrant angles of alleyways. There was a varied assortment of people returning from other people's bedchambers; of public service employees in dark blue uniform armed with spanners on long poles to turn off the street gas lights; of solid grocerymen and coffee-house keepers on their way to open their shops.

Arm-in-arm, broad grins across their faces, in evening clothes and workers' garb, night ladies and *pater-familias* out to earn the daily bread, they swayed and dance-timed down the echoing streets to the music of the orchestra: zigzagging behind the carriages, an ebb and flow of those going forth to fresh activities or returning after expended efforts, all at the same hour. And every one bore a long bread under the arm, or was skipping up to receive a loaf from the dispensing paws of the Billiken.

There was something familiar about the oratorical outpourings of the Billiken, so liberally providing his followers with the staff of life, as there was about his contours. I had not yet had a good glimpse of his face, wherefore I pushed closer. Then I yelled his name. He was a Princeton classmate of mine, very well known to me, whose extra-curricular activities while attending that ivy-clad seat of learning had brought him a considerable local notoriety. He was what the French call *"un original."* He looked at me without the slightest glimmer of recognition in his roseate eyes. He was very tight indeed.

"Le bon pain!" he cried. "It is all one needs, the good bread! That and music and love! Come then and get it! Take it thus from me, for I give. That is as it should be: when I have, I give; when I have not, thou wilt give me. And so shall we all live in tranquillity and dance to music and make love! *Ah, le bon pain!"* and he handed me a loaf a yard long while his cohorts cheered.

Other fresh arrivals came up for their quota. The God of Things as They Ought To Be rolled on in his chariot, his pipers playing stoutly, his queue of diverse character zigzagging gaily behind in dance-step, down the wakening streets of Paris towards the river.

Spring and the Four Arts

Never have Paris and her wooded environs been lovelier than in the spring of 1914. There is a quality to the seasonal beauty of the *Ville-Lumière,* a sensuality of light and atmosphere, such as no other great city possesses. It reached its perfect expression the year of the great débâcle; in the spring which held the swan-song of an epoch.

Though international storm-clouds were piling on eastern horizons, to imagine them as shortly to burst into a flood which would disintegrate Europe seemed preposterous in that sunlit, perfumed spring. Flowers were everywhere, great expanses of gardens, uncovered greenhouses riotous with color. The horse-chestnuts of the avenues and parks flowered in profusion, flaunting blossoms of pink and tinted whites. On both banks of the river the young men's fancies ran to seasonal form. While we flung no winter-garments of repentance to the vernal fires, we sought air. The urge for escape from stuffy ateliers into the blossom-scented open grew increasingly in the early afternoons. The ranks of Deux Magots habitués began to show gaps.

Some among us took to small picnic suppers in the Park of St. Cloud. There, when the escape was appropriately arranged, we would lie for hours beneath the flowering trees on the slopes overlooking the river. Suppers stood neglected while we played lightly at love, pretending to conceal affectionate gestures under thin coverlets of blossoms. To these bucolic pleasures our amiable partners responded with delight. Lazy hours passed deliciously while the international storm-clouds piled up on frontiers out of sight.

One beloved accomplice on the stolen afternoons at St. Cloud was a young Austrian sculptress whose charm, but for her innate good sense, might well have disrupted certain of those parties. She was usually the first to utter hunger-noises as the sun sank low, whereupon we would pull one another up, comb the petals from our hair, and nibble on the cold *poulet,* the sandwiches *aux foie gras,* with swigs from our bottles of wine.

She often led the discussion to contentious topics. She greatly admired the socialist leader Jean Jaurès and would get into fierce arguments over the probable effects on art and on life of his theories.

Her own views were expressed with clarity and conviction. She found me *sympatique* because I was tolerant of her—for that day—radical leanings and because I loved Austria; and possibly because she may have sensed a drift of my affections into less detached channels.

When the clouds of war burst over our heads I was in the Haute-Savoie. Jaurès had been assassinated the night before general mobilization was called. By the time I returned to Paris my enchanting friend had completely disappeared. Try as I did, I never could get the slightest trace of her beyond the portals of the Rue de Rennes flat where she took sorrowful farewell of her concierge on the day of France's declaration of war against Austria, and fled thence to the Gare de l'Est in a taxi with five pieces of luggage and three boxes of sculptures. She must have got across the frontier: I made sure she was not in any internment camp in France. But no address that I tried ever reached her, nor brought report of her whereabouts.

Sometimes, instead of picnicking, we would dine in one of the discreet thatched huts of the Restaurant Select near the Gate of Daybreak, or at the Hotel of the Sturgeon at Poissy whose cuisine was an unfailing delight. Sometimes we went out to Plessis-Robinson and dined on the uppermost of three platforms high in the branches of a huge chestnut tree. We ordered our dinner before mounting the steep steps that led to the top branches, and lowered a basket on a rope to haul up each course and the wines to go with it. One night, when the topmost deck had been reserved by a wedding party and we were ensconced on the platform below, the groom's attendants pulled the bride up in the basket. It was a long haul and the manager took a dim view of the proceeding, since the rope was dubiously up to her weight. But the revellers held him back while the bride sailed dizzily but intact into the treetop.

Now and again we would choose the terrace of the *Pavillon Henri-Quatre* in St. Germain-en-Laye, topping off splendid and costly repasts with huge portions of wild strawberries doused in thick cream. The combined outlay on a *partie carrée* ran from about eight francs (at five to the dollar) for the picnic foursomes on the slopes above St. Cloud, to perhaps a hundred on the terrace of the Pavillon, without strictly proportionate increases in enjoyment. But variety was our spice and there were those who abetted the cultivation of a highly expensive taste for *fraises des bois à la crème*, nowhere gratified so appropriately as on the terrace of the Henri-IV when the moon was at the full.

For the evening view from that sixteenth-century Pavillon was dangerously romantic. Over the silver-shot loop of the Seine, deep below, long spider threads of softly tinted arc-lamps centered on the heart of Paris. Moonlight etched in mystic outline Mont Valérien's somber fortress, turning the frosted basilical domes of the Sacré Cœur on distant Montmartre into a Himalayan peak, alive and throbbing above the blended lights of the city. Sipping Cordial Médoc after an excellent repast, with the moon-play on Paris and in our ladies' eyes, the world seemed a wholly entrancing place and we took due advantage of our setting.

With the advent of spring the Left Bank students turned their attention to preparations for the *Bal des Quat'z'Arts*. This ball of artists and would-be artists is not like other balls. Nor was its reputation, in those days at least, of "an orgiastic manifestation of rude and licentious studentry" wholly undeserved. Yet it was more than just that. "The Quat'z'Arts," I was told by a French friend, "has become a traditional feature in an artist's training at the Ecole. It is an essential part of his development in expression. It serves as his proving-ground in emotive analysis." By the same token it was not a seemly gathering for innocent maidens who might desire to remain so a little longer.

Well ahead of the event the ateliers started working on the decorations for their loges. With the artists and student-artists of the four primary categories—Painting, Sculpture, Architecture and Poetry—were "assimilated" those of the other Arts—Belles-lettres, Music and Drama. My assimilation came through one of the ateliers of the Académie Julien where a number of my friends were enrolled. It was scarcely possible in that year of grace to gain entrance to the Quat'z'Arts without some such background.

Through odd hours I daubed with irreverent groups of students on gigantic drops and side pieces for the loge. These were curious compositions, rendered with talent and a highly fertile imagination. The "period" chosen for that year's Bal was ancient Greek.

Explained our *massier*, student-treasurer and monitor of the atelier: "It is a period which lends itself well to our purpose. Its costumes are simple yet varied, decorative, and highly convenient." The latter quality became more particularly apparent during the middle stages of the Bal.

The general theme of the decorations was so carried out that from any reasonable distance the classic outlines were magnificent. Heroic structures of the Golden Age of Architecture and Sculpture were depicted against a background of dark and surly tempests or the pale blue of Athenian skies in spring. It was only on close inspection that certain peculiarities of detail revealed themselves; egg-and-dart mouldings ingeniously developed, decorative motifs worked out in the manner of Vaishnava Hindu temples—an intricate effect of satyrs and nymphs and animals, of reproductive organs stylized but not wholly abstract, saved from crass obscenity by cleverness of design.

"What, I ask you," inquired the massier as we applied color at close range to immodest detail sketched on the huge canvases, "is the significance of the egg-and-dart moulding adopted in every country where Classic or Renaissance ever touched?" He made his point clear with a few deft daubs.

"We are but aiding the uninstructed by making that significance more apparent," he continued. "The Indo-Aryans were less abstruse than the Greeks in their architectural design. Their *linga* and *yoni* are not so conventionalized, their decorative sculptures not at all. But both Hindu and Greek are bound to the same generic principles of life." That massier would undoubtedly have discovered in the Empire State Building the greatest phallic symbol of all time.

"Because we're not doing an Indo-Aryan period, is it a reason," he asked, "for us to be less honest in our presentation than the Hindus, so long as we adhere to correct form?"

Yet despite the honesty of our presentation the loge as a whole was a beautiful thing. The students took real pride in the drops and sets. Only when broken down into small elements without form or context did the canvases become noticeably pornographic: as at the close of the Bal when torn pieces were used in lieu of the costumes many of the revelers had misplaced, to whom egress was denied until they were in a manner clad.

With devoted effort we erected the sets in the big hall of the Marché des Gobelins, oddly enough located on the very spot where Jeanne d'Arc's ungrateful sovereign, Charles VII, just missed being burned to death in the course of a costume ball five centuries before. Until 1912, when the Moulin Rouge was turned from a *"Bal"* into a music hall, the Quat'z'Arts had always been staged in that enclosure of liberalism. And as always the puritanical had made strenuous but unavailing efforts to restrain the nude portrayal of the Four Arts.

For years old Senator Béranger led the protectors of public morals. His Quixotic attacks on immodesty caused one Quat'z'Arts committee to provide canvas fig-leaves for all its feminine guests. No more constructive result than this appears to have attended his efforts, aside from the placing of his naked effigy in a niche over the main portals of the Ecole. The latter was effected during a Quat'z'Arts night by an anonymous group of students resolutely opposed to his principles. It was discovered in the morning when the parade of scantily clad revellers reached the Ecole gates. Standing with possessive arms around their molls they hooted imprecations in high glee while the combined forces of police and fire brigade took several hours to get the replica down. The pure old gentleman died without having made any notable impression on the morals of the Left Bank.

On the afternoon before the Ball we met in various apartments to help one another into costume. The Deux Magots habitués then proceeded in small lots to the preprandial haunt, which filled rapidly with Greek demagogues, athletes, warriors and philosophers, accompanied by a smattering—amply supplemented later—of Grecian goddesses and courtesans, wood nymphs and Bacchantes. There was a dense crowd of onlookers in the Place St.-Germain-des-Prés who passed loud and inelegant comment on the costume of each new arrival and the groups departing to dine.

"But what's to keep your behind warm, soldier?" . . . "Oh, he'll find a way, though it may take two to do it; never fear!" . . . "Now *that* costume I call really convenient—for no matter what!" The bantering was thoroughly good-humored and we responded with dignity or in kind.

Apéritifs taken, a score or so of us drove together on three or four hacks to a Montparnasse restaurant—the Grande Chaumière—convenient to the hall. We did not sit *in* the hacks: that would have been *infra dig.* We put the drivers inside and ourselves on the boxes, on the roofs, or astride the horses, and drove a frenzied chariot-race up the Boulevard Raspail with four or more disunited Greeks to each pair of reins. By special dispensation of Him who watches over children, imbeciles and overenthusiastic students we reached our destination without having committed homicide, or even mayhem on any of our own teams. The *cochers* inside the hacks were not exactly pleased over the procedure and expressed themselves volubly but to no effect.

At the Grande Chaumière we dined upstairs in a private suite—
which was just as well—where wood nymphs and shepherdesses and
more courtesans awaited in an amiable frame of mind. It was an exceedingly merry dinner, if one would call it dining. *L'esprit de rapin*—
"the spirit of the student-dauber"—took full swing, with Bacchanalia on
couches in lieu of grassy slopes. As a dinner it was not quite like any
I had attended before.

We arrived at the Bal a wild lot of Greeks, along with a motley
following of Persian prisoners, African slaves and looted women from
the Mediterranean shores. There was an immense crowd outside the
hall, both of participants trying to get in and those gathered to watch
them enter. A cordon of police flanked the entrance and exits. As far as
I could judge their sole duties were to prevent the storming of the Bal
by the unauthorized, to discourage the rape of Grecian women in the
open streets, and, as the night wore on, to see that revellers did not
emerge, in exuberant forgetfulness, unclad.

The long queues of costumed arrivals converged onto a covered
passage that was lined with massiers and sous-massiers from all the
ateliers. At the start of the passage one's ticket was taken up and destroyed. Farther along, the passage split into Y-shape. He who was not
recognized and approved by some massier before reaching that decisive
fork found himself suddenly shunted out onto the sidewalk again,
bereft of ticket and of hope. Only the unrecognized males were so
shunted. For feminine youth and beauty the formalities of entry were
notably eased. Each atelier, in fact, had a special committee to herd its
ewe-lambs to the slaughter.

Secure in consciousness of work put in daubing canvases under my
massier's eye, I sailed through without incident. Ahead of me the
splendid thighs of Charles Lanier Lawrance extruded from an abbrevi-
ated warrior's costume. From behind came such anguished howls as I
had not heard since having assisted several years before at the unscientific slaughter of a pig. The accent was that of the once-jovial Billiken
I had come upon a few days past dispensing bread in the early morning
down a Montmartre street. There was now no trace of joviality in his
tone. He was invoking God, the Catholic hierarchy of saints, the
massier of the Académie Julien and the shades of Monsieur Julien
himself to restore to him the ticket that had been snatched from his
grasp, and pass him through the portals into the promised land. Eventually some friend in good standing rescued him. Had he not, a further

and unique touch to the fantastic composition of the Bal would have been lost.

Once inside, the tension eased—and how! The different groups gathered at the loges of their respective ateliers. The Bal was officially set under way by an amazing procession of floats and paraders, a phantasmagoria of the Four Arts at the height of their development in Ancient Greece. There was a swirling accompaniment of the life of city streets and sylvan dells—a singular type of life, were one to judge from its portrayal by the students of 1914; a life whose extreme lavishness in other respects was offset by a notable economy in clothes.

There followed still more amazing "shows" put on by the ateliers, each striving to outdo the other, each in its way succeeding. They were something to have spun old Senator Béranger in his grave.

I had been watching one of them with my eyes large, round and prominent when I was taken in hand by a dark-orbed shepherdess. She was an enchanting creature with an elfish little face and figure. Barring some four centuries of time she could have been the model for Correggio's Danaë—the more so after her scant costume had disintegrated under the impact of the Bal. She had the engaging vivacity of Latin youth, and at the ripe age of just over seventeen was among the more self-possessed young persons I have ever met. Yet with this she had a winsome gentleness and very firm ideas on the propriety of things.

"I don't like!" she announced of the febrile atelier show I had been watching in some astonishment, and led me firmly away. We turned our backs to it and were walking hand-in-hand about the floor when one of the decostuming waves hit us. The enthusiasts had begun a chant that now thundered across the spacious hall, growing in momentum like a drum-call to arms.

"A poil! A poil!" they yelled. "A poil!" (down to the hair!) and set into motion serpentine snap-the-whip dances expressly designed to shake the costumes off those snapped at the ends of the lines. This they accomplished quite effectively, along with the aid of many willing hands and a not excessive reluctance on the part of the snappees—affable young ladies who had given themselves up for lost before ever they entered the classicized portals. The Grecian costumes, more especially the female models, lent themselves admirably to this playful practice.

I made a futile effort to protect my charge, until she whirled past crying: "Inutile! . . . It's no use! . . . and anyway, it's in fun!" and came off the end of the disassembly line with nothing of importance in the way of garb above her little Grecian sandals. The whirl left her somewhat out of breath but perfectly composed in all other senses of the term. She might well have been Danaë herself and was as completely unabashed, though without thought of golden rain. She was by no means alone in her nudity, yet alone or against the others in similar state she had no basic cause for abashment that I could see. And what I could not see did not very much matter.

There was something particularly wholesome in her naturalness. It was all "in fun," as she cried out when she came whirling off the line, while the process of divesting most of the feminine guests and not a few of the males continued with hearty enthusiasm. The fun was exceedingly boisterous and some of it broad enough to have brought blushes to the face of a Minsky stage manager as the "spirit of the student-dauber" surged into full expression. Yet the wildness was essentially good-humored. Under any other approach such a party would have been utterly impossible, its participants carted off in ambulances and Black Marias.

One incipient brawl flared up for a few moments. In this a compatriot of mine was involved. In a mild display of disapprobation he had dragged a French student off a ladder by the beard. He did the French student no great damage other than to his feelings, but the Frenchman and his companions were outraged. Pulling off people's clothes was one thing. Other less innocent manifestations of the student-dauber spirit were carried through without unnecessary violence. But to pull a man off a ladder by the beard! That was something else.

"But no!" Danaë cried. "One does not do that! That is not in fun!" She was quite right, of course.

"Barbarian!" shrieked the Frenchman's coterie as a group of American comrades haled the tactless offender of all the proprieties out of sight.

We sat at supper on the ballroom floor in the midst of a cheerful crowd. One of them, a young gentleman of very correct demeanor, had been reduced to rather less than half a pair of running-pants, a pair of horn-rimmed spectacles and a single Attic sandal. Around him eight ladies sat in yet greater *déshabillé* save for their duality of footgear. Most of the other males of the group had retained the more essential items of their apparel. But the dignified and courtly manner in which

our denuded companion dispensed champagne and chicken wings to
that select supper circle caused one of the others to remark: "I say,
you know, I feel damned overdressed!" That feeling, to judge from
the appearance of some of them a bit later, did not outlast the night
with all.

The ravaging of costumes became pretty widespread towards the
end. In my buckled-on trappings of a warrior I managed to survive
without having to improvise from the canvas draperies in order to
depart. Others not so securely attired were less fortunate, but none
appeared to care. Our unfrocked companion of the supper floor was
upset only over the thought of losing his spectacles. Under the circumstances that loss could have been a great pity.

One would be surprised at how amusing could be the simplest
games of French childhood played in that festive environment with
amiable partners clad only in Grecian sandals. Some of the games were
not so simple, nor all of the dances. Before morning *l'esprit de rapin*
became somewhat confused with one of *rapine,* or more strictly *enléve-
ment.* Manners ran closer to type of the shaggy-legged satyrs, who
chased and caught not too elusive wood-nymphs on the slopes of
Parnassus behind the canvas scenery, than of the philosophers and
lyric poets. The shadows of the back-drops fell on scenes that might
have startled Bacchus himself and surely must have twirled the shade
of Senator Béranger. Across these my little Danaë's disapproval drew
a screen as opaque as any back-drop. That was fun carried too far, or
in any event not in its proper place.

Along about six-thirty in the morning the Bal transferred itself as
a unit to the grounds of the Ecole. The "*à poil*" process had then to be
reversed; the cordon of police outside would let none pass without
some sort of covering. There was a sudden scramble to locate misplaced items of dress. I managed to find a few remnants for my partner.
But there were not nearly enough pieces retrievable and moderately
intact to provide for all the clamorous nudes. In the turmoil rose a
voice I recognized as belonging to the degarbed Billiken I had last
seen making satyric sorties after evasive wood-nymphs. "Can't find
an'thing to wear!" it wailed. "How'm I goin' t' get out?"

A reply from somewhere on the floor advised him to get himself
up in a piece of Doric temple like other people were doing.

Many were doing just that. They raided the loges, ripping sections
from the canvas sets. Torn into strips, tied with string or pinned

together with nails, tne effect of the painted canvas stiffly encircling bare bodies was prodigious. Grotesque details of design stood out then unrelieved. In the way of comfort, empty barrels would have been as acceptable. But all undaunted they poured forth to form a procession such as perhaps could only have been held in Paris in the year 1914.

Between lines of solemn police the revellers serpentined on foot or rode on the tops of fiacres and taxis and busses down to the Rue Bonaparte. Songs not learned in Sunday-school floated high on the morning air through a clatter of garbage cans rolled from kicking foot to foot along the sidewalks. Sorry-looking warriors, retogged in the flowing draperies of courtesans or goddesses, brandished weird implements from insecure positions. Lady Godivas sat astride bored cab-horses, clutching immodest fragments of canvas back-drops that clearly had not been cut as riding apparel. Holding tight to Danaë on the top of a covered wagon, along with a dozen others in fantastic disarray, I swirled through the streets of Paris to the Academy of Fine Arts.

Dismounting, we passed through the open iron gates of the Ecole, above which Senator Béranger's naked effigy once had peered, between dense rows of faces gathered to watch the show. Within the enclosure the procedure became a little vague. Some bathed in a fountain, some effected exchanges of dress—feminine for masculine or vice-versa. Some just sloughed off their uncomfortable trappings and relaxed. By nine o'clock in the morning the majority had eased away to rest and recuperate. Leading my protégée out through the gates to hunt for a prowling fiacre I heard behind us a familiar voice crying aloud in the wilderness of the Ecole des Beaux Arts.

"Can't find an'thing to wear!" it wailed. "How'm I goin' t' get out?"

Arm in arm with Correggio's Danaë I slipped through the portals of the Ecole to a fiacre and back into the world of reality.

"Janitor, My Snakes Are Out!"

Herbert Haseltine, as befitted an artist of original stamp, lived in one of the most amusing habitations in Paris. On an *Impasse* near the edge of the Bois de Boulogne he occupied three little houses within a walled enclosure whose small garden gave romping space for a portion of his menagerie. One of the houses served as his personal abode, another sheltered his wife and children. The third contained the salon and dining room where they met for formal meals, along with the kitchen and quarters of some of the family retainers. The whole made up a sort of feudal village in miniature, not wholly convenient under a pouring rain but always quaintly entertaining. In and around the houses and the garden, overflowing into Herbert's studio on the Rue du Docteur Blanche, animals of varied types roamed or sat on perches, yapped and yowled and screeched in bewildering cacophony.

I never knew just how many dogs and cats inhabited the odd angles of that *enclos* on the Impasse Raffet. The dogs ranged in size from a gaunt greyhound to silky Italian *lupeti* of rare species which sat only on chairs or on laps. There were hutches of rabbits and guinea-pigs, ostensibly for the children. There were highly colored, raucous-voiced macaws with tails just missing the ground from five-foot perches, and littler birds trilling sweetly within small cages.

For a while a Syrian ram lent an odd Asiatic flavor to the compound until it butted itself out of the good graces of the family, in temper and appetite (not to mention odor) too formidable for even Haseltinian hospitality.

In the days before the war Major Jimmy Logan, cheery gourmet of enormous girth, was apt to arrive there at formal repasts bearing under his arm the *pièce de résistance* for another meal to come. "This," he would say, "is my *next* dinner here!" and extract a wide-eyed duckling or shrilling piglet from the folds of an overcoat that could have blanketed a hippopotamus. "My host and hostess will surely have to invite me again to help them eat it!"

His host and hostess were charmed, but invariably such living contributions to their larder joined the community of beasts prowling happily about the garden.

One of these offerings became the most privileged of all the furred and feathered denizens of the compound. Jimmy Logan-the-duck had a figure not dissimilar in section to a reduced scale of that of Jimmy Logan-the-officer who had sponsored the duck's entrée into the Haseltine menagerie. Oddly enough, Jimmy-the-duck's was the one voice among the weird medley of sounds that ever seemed to annoy Herbert. Its matutinal quacks under the master's window drew a shower of expletives, often of boots, aimed just behind Jimmy's bustling posterior. Herbert had perhaps twenty pairs of boots and shoes handy as ammunition. All of them affected the disturber of dreams no more than to add a minor note of alarm to its homely utterances and a momentary speed to its zigzag parade across the yard. The commands to silence that issued from the open window, along with loud supplications: "May the devil take that goddam duck!" rolled like water, or boots, off a duck's back.

It was in the lounge under Herbert's bedroom, which became my base camp in Paris in the early days of war, that his two young lions previously had slept. In time they grew a bit boisterous for the accommodations of 20 Impasse Raffet. A few months before I moved in they had been transferred to the Antwerp Zoo. If I may have been—as doubtless I was, at least in irregularity of hours—a somewhat trying guest, there seemed to be a certain latitude for one's behavior in the thought of a brace of lion cubs having been one's predecessor.

During the while their cheerful roars had added to the music from the other fauna in occupancy of 20 Impasse Raffet, the *enclos* became the object of a mass petition addressed to the Juge de Paix of the XVIth Arrondissement. It was claimed that repose within vocal range of Monsieur Haseltine's garden was being shattered by uncouth noises making day and night hideous. The petition contained unsympathetic references to a public nuisance.

Happily the Juge de Paix was a friend of Herbert's and lived beyond earshot of the Impasse Raffet. He seems to have been an appreciative soul. In any event his judgment did credit to his artistic sense.

"A sculptor of living things must have living things around him as inspiration and as models," asserted the Judge. "Furthermore, the effect of sounds on the human system is generally in inverse ratio to one's familiarity with them." People inured to the screech of streetcars rounding corners, for example, would soon grow to relish the mellow, picturesque roars of lions, he said. Particularly of such gentle young lions, mere kittens so to speak, as were in question.

"It is a matter of great pride," the Judge pronounced, "that the XVIth Arrondissement has been selected among all other quarters of Paris as the domicile of an artist such as Monsieur Haseltine. I myself, with many others, have been deeply stirred by the beauty of Monsieur Haseltine's works." With a fine French sense of realism the Judge, while congratulating the people of his Arrondissement on their singular good fortune in the presence of so eminent a genius in their midst, solemnly pigeon-holed the complaint. The lion cubs continued their cheerful roaring until shortly before I arrived to take their place.

In that entertaining little enclosure I camped with Herbert Haseltine whenever I stopped in Paris, from the time I returned from the
upland valleys of the Haute-Savoie, after the great war was under
way, until I left to join the British Expeditionary Force in October.
It was a camp of infinite charm, enlivened by a peculiarly Haseltinian
humor that was not quite like any other I had known. And my host's
temperament, with its liberal touch of artistic vagueness, seemed to
take without dismay my partly unavoidable but wholly atrocious
irregularity.

Sometimes, when Herbert was off on his special occasions, I would
turn up alone at the Impasse Raffet for dinner. Then, the focal point
of a solemn trio at table, I passed morsels of food alternately into
expectant mouths—my own, the rakish greyhound's on the right, Jimmy-
the-duck's on my left. As table-mates these companions behaved in
exemplary fashion. So patiently they would wait, with not a sound (at
that hour of day), though now and then a gentle nudge of nose or
beak when I read or nibbled too long. It did not matter at all what I
gave them: meat, rice, grapes, dessert; each swallowed his offering
with an appreciative regard and shortly nudged for more.

Those two were great friends. They shared a joint contempt for the
other vertebrates harbored in their garden. Each morning the greyhound would gambol across the yard in twelve-foot bounds to place a
softly spread paw of greeting on Jimmy's back; the duck would squat,
waggle its absurd tail and quack a welcome.

In Herbert's atelier on the Rue du Docteur Blanche, backed up
against the Bois de Boulogne, various other animals were housed. The
first time I entered there I was assaulted by a large and wholly
unamiable monkey intent on mayhem. Through no fault of the assaulter
the hurt was chiefly to my feelings.

"Good thing you had on your coat," Herbert remarked reflectively.
"That damned irritable brute bit my concierge clear through the
shoulder. Oh, the concierge can still do his job when he feels inclined,
but I've had to pension him for the rest of his life. Sometimes I think
I may have to get rid of that monkey."

There was also in a corner of the atelier a box of snakes that came
in handily, somewhat later, in the matter of a lease.

Plaster casts of earlier Haseltine sculptures filled the studio's corners, with sketches in clay of new conceptions awaiting completion,

spread on modelling stands around the floor. Splendid things they were, done with such exquisite technical mastery that one expected the muscles to twitch when a fly alighted on the smooth skin of the sculptured animals in repose. His best-known groups in action were there, "Polo" and "Riding Off," one or the other of which embellished most cavalry and hunt clubs on either side of the Atlantic; "The Bullfight" vibrant with the swift pathos of a Spanish ring; and in more tranquil tempo "The Meadowbrook Team" filing slowly onto the field.

Herbert was himself an accomplished horseman. There was a story of a youthful exploit when on a bet he rode back through the streets of Rome after a hunt on the *campagna*, followed by enthusiastic young bloods of his age, to the portals of the palace his mother occupied on one of the Seven Hills. While his hunting friends cheered lustily from their saddles in the street below he rode up a circular stone staircase to the second story above the ground, from where he saluted them over the neck of his hunter through an opened Renaissance window.

I never learned the exact details of that story. One would suspect it was the horse that deserved the greatest credit. In any case, so the tale ran, it took many hours and the sweating labor of several astounded retainers, with a goodly number of his mother's best blankets, to get the versatile animal safely down the stone stairway after the bet had been won.

For some while Herbert had been planning to connect his group of little houses into one. He embarked on this project several months after my departure, the war by then having settled into a stalemate of apparently indefinite duration. His aunt in Rome had consented that he and his family should occupy her Paris apartment for the few weeks during which the work would be in progress.

Herbert was, I believe, his own architect. One after another of his contractors threw up the job in despair each time he returned from delvings in southern France, or Spain, or Italy. On each return he brought with him a large iron grille, a Romanesque staircase, a whole fronting of Gothic windows or other massive items which would not fit into the portions of walls already built, yet which he insisted on incorporating therein. This, of course, meant that much of the completed work had to be torn down and started afresh. All non-military construction was at best subject to indefinite delay. After a year or so his aunt intimated to Herbert that she might like to revisit Paris before her demise. Could he, she inquired, make it convenient to find other quarters for the balance of the time needed to finish the alterations to his property?

Herbert could, though without notable enthusiasm. He found somewhere in the neighborhood an apartment that seemed to meet his requirements. Depressed as to prospects of any early end to the doing over of his manor, he signed a long lease. One special privilege he exacted from the lessors: he was to be permitted to introduce into the apartment such small animals as he might wish for companionship or as "inspiration" for his work. (His work, in actual fact, was done in his studio, and to no great extent in the modelling of small animals.) The war had so restricted the demand for large apartments in Paris that concessions on long leases were granted almost cheerfully, which was very far from the case either before or after. But while Herbert perhaps put no specific mental reservation behind that particular clause, the manager little suspected what he was letting himself in for.

As soon as Herbert and his family had moved into the new apartment his artist's temperament suffered a devastating blight. There was, for no obvious or correctable reason, something about the atmosphere of the place he simply could not abide. It was more than merely uncongenial; it crushed him. This he made known to the manager, with a proposal that the lease be cancelled. Herbert could express himself effectively in four or maybe five languages. The *gérant* on his part was not manager of several Paris apartment houses for nothing, nor did he lack a certain resistance to the odd whims of his clients.

"But Monsieur Haseltine, it seems you forget," he said with that tolerant superiority of one who discusses logic with a child, "these are war times and difficult for owners of property. You may, of course, vacate the apartment if you are unhappy here. You might perhaps sublease, subject to our approval. But as to cancellation . . . !" French gérants have a manner of shrugging their shoulders which is at once infuriating and singularly expressive of the *impasse* into which the conversation has led. Even Haseltinian ingenuity could not insinuate itself through that impasse—not directly. He retired from the field with colors furled, pondering flank attacks.

The next day and for some days thereafter many sizable boxes with ventilating holes in their tops or sides arrived and were borne up the stairs to his uncongenial quarters. Boxes of parrots, boxes of monkeys, boxes of snakes. Up by way of the elevator came crated items enclosing dogs, cats, rabbits, and lesser fauna.

Early risers, a few mornings later, stumbled over several large snakes lying in the courtyard. These, it so happened, were dead. Herbert allowed as how they had been dead for quite a while before he threw them out the window. He had kept them, he said, with the thought that some time or other they might come in handy. The other occupants of the apartment house experienced a certain emotion when they found four-foot reptiles, unusual in a Paris courtyard, spread across the way to their morning activities. They were not especially pleased about this and were rude to the concierge, the custodian and janitor of the building, who seemed to have no good explanation as to why the egress should be cluttered with dead serpents.

"Silly excitement!" said Herbert when the concierge arrived at his apartment door in a fine frenzy. "Those snakes were dead and I didn't want them any more. They were too big for the scrap-basket. I always throw my dead animals out the window." From there on he took pains to cultivate the concierge's growing suspicion that a completely insane artist was being harbored in the higher levels of that respectable building.

Pleased at the success of the preliminary skirmish with spent snakes, Herbert proceeded to throw his forces into action in more subtle manner. The provision in his lease for bringing small animals into his apartment, together with a hearty desire to be ejected therefrom, placed him in a peculiarly unassailable position.

Several days passed in comparative tranquillity before the night he sprung his strategic coup. On that evening the concierge had watched Herbert conduct his lady to a waiting taxi outside. Behind the shaded glass partition of the loge on the ground floor, where the concierge lived with his dour wife, two pairs of eyes followed his movements. "It's he!" whispered the man to his peering mate. "The artist! I tell you he's completely cracked!"

A moment later Herbert returned to the loge. He stood at the door as though in deep thought. Then he called the concierge. The reluctant janitor half opened the door. In the dimly lit interior his wife crossed herself. Herbert drew a handkerchief from his coat pocket, replaced it, stared blankly at the man until the silence grew tense.

"There was something I wanted to tell you," Herbert muttered. "Now what the devil could it have been? Believe I've forgotten. Oh, now I remember!" He brightened up and placed a genial gloved hand on the concierge's shoulder. The man shrank back a little under the gesture.

"I'm going out." This appeared fairly obvious. "It may be late before I get back. Oh, *quite* late.

"Just now as I was dressing I went to look at my box of snakes, and do you know, I found it nearly empty? Can't imagine who could have loosened the cover." He glared suspiciously at the concierge for a moment. "I searched the apartment . . . couldn't find a single snake. Must have gone out by the service door: there's a gap where it meets the floor—*you* know, I've complained to you about that. There's no telling how many got out; I've not counted my snakes in a long time. Perhaps forty." The concierge's eyes were beginning to grow large, round and prominent.

"They're *very* valuable, my snakes. I wouldn't lose one for anything. So please go and look well over the building at once and, of course, notify all the other lodgers that Monsieur Haseltine's snakes are out. The other tenants might be surprised, you know, if they weren't warned. Probably there are other doors with gaps where they meet the floor, or that have been left ajar; and some of these poor lost animals will have taken refuge where it is warm and dark—you know, in closets and in and under beds—that's what they like. They're quite harmless except for a few, and those can be easily told by their diamond-shaped heads. With *them*, of course, one ought to be a bit careful. And generally they all will come out to a little warm milk."

The concierge emitted gurgling, suffocated cries. He was now pawing the air, never very fresh in a concierge's loge.

"Wait!" continued Herbert. "I've not finished. Now you and your wife will go get together some cardboard boxes and cotton, and warm a little milk. And when the other tenants find any of my snakes in their rooms they will let you know, and you will collect the snakes. Don't forget to tell people to be a bit careful of any with diamond-shaped heads. Take *them* in the back of the neck; you know, behind where their ears should be. Of course, you won't be able to see their ears; they haven't any. It doesn't matter . . .

"*Do* be gentle with them; they're quite pleasant to deal with if you know how. You doubtless will find some in the corridors and on the stairways. But don't delay in notifying everyone, as I've told you, for the tenants might be upset on finding snakes in their rooms, unless they were forewarned. Just tell them it's *quite* all right, these are Monsieur Haseltine's snakes and very valuable. They will understand. Tomorrow I'll collect the lot from you and you shall have a tip for your pains."

The concierge was by now "pushing cries," but Herbert waved him aside with large and sweeping gesture. "No, I cannot wait longer; this has already delayed me. I told you that I shall be very late, but I know that everything will be quite all right in your hands. Good night!" And he rushed off.

There was truth in the warning of a late return. As to the rest of it, the picture was drawn from a highly fertile imagination, though I believe Herbert had supported it by a strategic planting of a few lively though harmless snakes which he felt prepared to sacrifice to the attainment of his objective. And while Paris concierges by and large are not an essentially sympathetic class, one can rather feel for the unhappy custodian left with a situation on his hands that was singularly devoid of comfort.

He seized the telephone and in growing desperation fought through the usual run of wrong numbers to arouse the gérant—the non-resident manager. It is entertaining (I confess to a certain lack of esteem for Paris gérants) to picture that worthy, settled in slippers for a quiet evening at home, when he received the good news—an unknown quantity of live serpents crawling all over his best apartment house. He ordered the concierge to start at once a round-up of the errant snakes while he rushed to the scene. Upon this task the concierge proceeded with marked distaste, supported by a coal shovel and a wife advancing gingerly with lifted skirts, a broom thrust out before her. Perhaps they may have hoped it was all an impossibly bad dream, the inconsequential wanderings of a diseased mind. But soon they came upon snakes alive and slithering along the corridors and down the stairways.

The story is saddened (if one cares for snakes) by the fact that Herbert's advice as to warm milk and cotton-lined cartons was disregarded in the round-up. The noise of the chase, of unscientific attempts at scotching innocent serpents, brought tenants to their doors wondering what on earth all the clamor could be about. What they saw in no wise served to lessen their wonderment. The gérant arrived to find the building in uproar from top to bottom.

I am uncertain as to just what happened when Herbert eventually returned. He had, I believe, taken the precaution to arrange that his

children and servants should be away for the night. The concierge had
no keys to the auxiliary locks on the Haseltine apartment. One of the
more masterly features of Herbert's coup was his vagueness as to what
number of snakes might be loose. Herbert could be singularly vague
when he chose.

Disheveled, humorless people in various stages of undress were
still milling about the six-story building in search of more snakes.
Herbert, on returning, expressed grief and outrage over a small heap
of mangled serpents. He ignored the fury of the gérant and a searing
personal unpopularity among all the other inhabitants of the building.
He disclaimed any idea as to whether the lost snakes had all been
tracked down. He countered the threats of damage suits to follow with
one of his own for the slaughter of his valued specimens. Then he went
to bed, to pass a more restful night—or what was left of it—than most
of the other tenants, the gérant or the concierge.

In the morning his lease was cancelled. Herbert shrugged himself
and family from the apartment. He moved his menagerie back to the
studio, with his depleted box of snakes that had not been quite full
before. On his way out he paused to fire a final Parthian arrow.

"I think," he said coldly, "there must be a *few* more snakes you
have not yet located. Be so good as to advise me when you find them."
This closed the incident as far as he was concerned. So, at least, the
story went as told to me.

Herbert's whimsical humor could be an effective instrument of
deflation. The more objectively he used it, the more detached and
impersonal was the manner in which he wielded his foil. Once it caught
me completely off guard.

He gave a small luncheon at the Grand Vatel on my first appearance in Paris in British uniform. I wore this new distinction with
becoming modesty, or so I thought, though it may have been that a
touch of self-consciousness did not wholly escape my host. I happened
to be the only one in uniform at the luncheon.

Herbert had selected the Grand Vatel for the excellent reason that
it was among the few places in Paris where one could still count on
being served a repast such as made gourmets weep for the disappearing art of the *cordon bleu*. And lest our weeping should unduly sadden
the occasion, the wine-waiter was directed to apply himself to the
uncorking of numerous tall, narrow bottles of a magnificent Schloss

vintage from the slopes above the Rhine. The shape of those bottles proclaimed their Germanic origin to all who chose to look. It happened, that day at the Grand Vatel, there were rather many who chose to look.

The phobia of war passions discountenanced the drinking of German wines, even as the playing of German music was stopped throughout the embittered years. This appealed to Herbert as the height of absurdity; the more so since the wine we drank was French-owned, for many years immured in the well-stocked cellars of the Grand Vatel. And nowhere else in Paris could that particular golden glory be found.

On the strength of this Herbert chose to carry a liberal attitude somewhat further. He expressed himself on and off in German, as being appropriate to past associations with the pleasant district of the Rhineland, revived through the mellow product of its grape. I felt waves of warm color suffuse my cheeks as people at neighboring tables stared at us in amazement.

He had brought along his two Italian *lupeti*, rare silky-haired toy dogs with long, fluffy tails. Halfway through luncheon, while the rest of us were leaning forward to catch one of his stories, he whistled the two little dogs up to his lap and from there onto our backs. They sprang gaily, one after the other, then circled round and round the table, leaping from shoulder to hunched shoulder like flying squirrels. To them he spoke in Italian, and variously in German, French or English to our lowered heads. My head was lowered rather more than the others to hide a searing embarrassment, for the other people lunching around us in the restaurant were beginning to show an increasing interest in this performance. Snatches of their remarks drifted across to my flaming ears.

"But what can they be?" I heard. "Animal tamers, a performing troupe? But, *mon Dieu,* they speak German and drink German wine! And one of them speaks Italian to those trained little dogs! They would perhaps be Swiss? But what does such a circus troupe do in Paris at this time? And that one in English uniform, what is he? Spies, surely enough, that's what they all are! They must be drunk or they wouldn't give themselves away talking German! The one in English uniform looks very nervous . . ."

The one in English uniform was by this time decidedly nervous. The voicing of suspicion had become general. In tense whispers the manager and the head waiter were urged to call at once the Secret

Police, the Préfecture, the General Staff. One would not wholly blame them, but the well-intentioned saviors of the Allied cause did not stop to figure that if we had been spies we might perhaps not have chosen quite so public a setting to talk volubly in German, unless we had been very drunk indeed.

Herbert and his other friends, happily, were well-known clients of the Grand Vatel and highly esteemed by the management. The scene was in some manner explained as the eccentricity of the artistic temperament. Wherefore nothing came of it beyond scathing comments on propriety (not entirely unjustified) which disturbed our host not in the least; and the crimson waves of embarrassment that swept across my face. It was fairly drastic treatment for self-consciousness, or seemed so at the time; but I went out well inoculated against recurrence of the symptoms.

I tried to get back at Herbert, something over three years later when he had become a Captain in the Camouflage Service of the American Expeditionary Force. I never fully succeeded. The nearest approach was when I saw him off one day in an automobile with a particularly crusty and humorless General. Herbert had one of those little Italian dogs with him. The General glared at it. "Put that damn lap-dog outside!" roared the General. And Herbert had reluctantly to obey.

2 – In a World Aflame

When the Storm Clouds Broke

Item from my diary, dated August 1, 1914, at Aix-les-Bains in Haute-Savoie: "Dog Show opened today. Sparsely attended. Some ladies with little pets on exhibit complained that fear of international conflict is spoiling show . . . Town in state of tension, with little news. Drove mother to bath at Source, later to Casino. Tea with Underwoods at Villa des Fleurs. Head waiter, passing cakes, whispered in my ear: 'The Order for General Mobilization has just been posted!' This about 4.30 P.M. Hurried out to see *affiches* being put up all over town, crowds gathering before them, talking endlessly but undemonstrative . . . tense with suppressed excitement . . ."

That searing, fateful announcement with the crossed tricolor atop: "ARMEE DE TERRE! ARMEE DE MER! ORDRE DE MOBILIZATION GENERALE!" It stopped one's heart-beats for a moment as blue-smocked brushmen pasted the clamorous sheets swiftly, methodically, on blank walls, on the fronts of public buildings, on the sides of churches. Walls bearing the stencilled motto of the Republic—subsequently abolished by Pétain and now again restored: *Liberté—Egalité—Fraternité!* Walls with the blunt injunction: *Défense d'uriner.* Some with both. Walls with sculptured figures of the Virgin and Holy Child . . .

"Every Frenchman subject to military obligation is to obey forthwith the prescriptions of his Mobilization Book . . . This Order applies to ALL MEN not at present with the colors . . . The first day of the Mobilization is *Sunday the 2nd of August 1914.*" The date was stamped in. The proclamation itself had been printed and distributed throughout France and the Colonies long before—awaiting the moment.

Knots of old and young, of men and women and wide-eyed children clustered before each posted sheet of destiny, lips forming slowly, syllable by syllable, the momentous words. There was no hysteria; no outburst of enthusiasm, nor any of anti-war demonstration. Scarce a voice was raised above the low burr of conversation, save as someone read the Order in precise monotone for others who could not read, for some who could not see. The conversation was dispassionate. There were queries, half muttered, with furtive, sidelong glances: "*Ça y est.* So it has come! It is then really to be war? And the harvest, what of that? . . ."

Or simple statements, without show of the hidden pain: "My husband leaves tomorrow . . . my elder son goes Monday; the younger is now with the colors . . . Maurice and Jean depart tonight, we must make our adieux . . ."

Even the fringe of importunate gamins was for once abashed.

But in that charged atmosphere one bent and toothless crone detonated suddenly. Withered claws outstretched to the east, bloodshot eyes rolling in their sockets, "*Ah, les salauds! Les assassins!*" she shrieked. "They come again to burn, to pillage; they come anew to kill! Is it that I know them not, *les sauvages?* They who slaughtered my first-born, who left my man a cripple, my daughter a widow? Is there to be no end then, is there to be no halting of this scourge?"

In blistering invective she called upon the gods in heaven to extirpate those who had forced mobilization on a peaceful people.

The taut nerves of the crowd vibrated but did not snap. A few of the younger men stiffened, clenched their jaws; youthful mothers with drawn and anxious faces tried to hush babes-in-arms whose startled wails rose with the shrieks of the ancient beldame. People led her away, shuffling slow splay feet in enormous, misshapen shoes.

"*Calmez-vous, Mère Poulard,*" they said. "It is not yet war"; while she kept screeching imprecations in cracked falsetto against the enemy of forty-four years past.

"She comes from the north. She went through it all in '70," they muttered as though some explanation were necessary. Some tapped their heads. "Half crazy, but . . . she remembers things . . ."

Throughout the evening the crowds milled around the proclamations. New arrivals replaced the ones who withdrew to their homes for hasty farewells, to collect a few items of personal kit before departure, or speed parting reservists whose standing orders called for them to report on the first day. They moved as in a daze, in a spirit, it seemed, of numb resignation. There was as yet no war. It might still be avoided; mobilization was merely protective. Yet while I saw that evening and throughout the next few days in Haute-Savoie not the least spark of spontaneous enthusiasm, I also saw no Frenchman who had not accepted as inevitable the destiny writ between the lines of the Mobilization Order.

And on that most momentous day of all recent history, the day on which *finis* was written upon an era, I attended a dog show where a group of ladies not immediately involved in the impending disaster, whose silly little canines had been placed on exhibit, murmured in dismay: "This dreadful situation! It is spoiling our Dog Show!" And later, when they began to realize the implications of the Order, cried plaintively: "But this may interfere with our cures! It is said that all the younger male bath attendants, even many of the doctors, are being called to the colors! It is too distressing!"

In the evening I ran down by car to Chambéry. The little town, though it was an entraining center, showed scarcely more outward excitement than Aix-les-Bains. Crowds of civilians were grouped about the streets, filling the cafés. There was an almost complete absence of uniforms. On the outskirts I passed one small body of youthful reservists in civilian garb marching behind a large tricolor flag carried high on a staff. They were scheduled to report on the first day of mobilization and were on their way. They had flowers in their caps, in their buttonholes, in their hands. Their faces were flushed with wine and they sang the "Marseillaise." It was as near an approach to enthusiasm as I saw in Haute-Savoie.

The next day I went for a long swim in the Lac du Bourget. Over the scarcely ruffled surface of the lake I looked, objectively and with a slowly formulating realization, upon an unimportant and incongruous little figure, a slightly plaintive marionette bearing a trivial load of minor personal problems like fagots on its back. While I looked the figure receded as though drawn by invisible strings, growing steadily smaller, until it became but a tiny manikin in a vast, empty theatre whose stage was a lake. The modestly proportioned Mountain of the Cat, with the Pass of the Cat incised over its shoulder, etched a somber backdrop through which all the other players in the pantomime had been called to the colors. I suddenly recognized that manikin as myself. Then I saw it dump its fagots and depart to join the other players.

That afternoon I slipped again down to Chambéry and volunteered my services with the French Army for the mobilization or for war. The harassed officers threw up their hands.

"But *mon Dieu, Monsieur*, we have more Frenchmen than we're able to handle expeditiously! How would you wish that we utilize the services of a foreigner? . . . Though it's very *chic* of you to offer yours. But we're extremely occupied, and now, if you please . . ."

"*Messieurs*, I have a very good automobile of which perhaps you might like to avail yourselves."

"Ah, *that!* . . . yes, that we could use!" they chirped.

"But only with myself as its conductor!" I added hastily.

"And if we should requisition it?"

"Surely you will hesitate to requisition, at this time, the property of friendly foreigners whose nations you may hope to incline to your cause?" But of this I was not too sure.

There happened to be in Chambéry an acute shortage of transportation for the mobilization staff. After prolonged consultation between the officers, and an investigation of my credentials, my offer was accepted for mobilization service. I was given a special *laissez-passer* valid anywhere in Savoie and Haute-Savoie, by day or by night. The car, of course, was what they really wanted. I came into the picture as a not over-welcome adjunct. The car, incidentally, was my father's, not mine. But he was in London; I felt I had forestalled possible requisition, and it seemed a good wedge for certain more ambitious and vaguely forming plans.

The service to which I was assigned was not particularly spectacular. I hardly expected that it would be. Yet in that kaleidoscope of moving scenes it produced two pictures whose impression has remained on the retina of memory.

The special pass exempted me from the restrictions of the nine-o'clock curfew. During the daytime, running about on courier duties, transporting staff officers and civil authorities, I met a constant influx of groups of reservists coming in to report to their units; coming on foot from the valleys and mountain villages, coming in carts and by busses and local trains. All were in rough peasants' or workmen's clothes, with small bundles tied up in a kerchief or in gunnysack or paper. At the outskirts of Chambéry these groups were broken into lesser bodies. One rarely saw more than half a dozen men together, tramping unostentatiously through the streets towards the barracks. The steady inflow of small parties, in no order, attracted less notice than the passage of larger groups in some sort of formation. Their numbers nevertheless were considerable. And apparently they disappeared, swallowed up in the maw of the *caserne;* for one saw no outflow and astonishingly few uniformed men about the streets.

Young civilians in small batches, being poured into a vast and bottomless receptacle from which nothing came out.

Nothing, that is, by daytime. For in the dead of the night when the curfew kept honest people—and those who were not, or at least it was so intended—within the confines of their habitations, there exuded from the barracks and marched down to the entraining depot platoon after platoon of uniformed men, four abreast. Men in red pantaloons, blue-coated, accoutred, armed. With serious faces and packs on their backs, hobnailed boots crunching the paved streets that otherwise were in dead silence, they proceeded without lights, without music or singing, without colors displayed. To orders hoarsely whispered they moved as to a surprise atttack. Platoon after platoon, forming companies, forming battalions in the trains they filled in the dark; trains that pulled out one after the other in ghostly silence, headed—though of this probably none was aware—for disaster in Alsace.

Several times I was called on to transport a Staff Lieutenant whose duty it was to check the progress of mobilization from the more remote districts. We penetrated several of the upland valleys to points where they dead-ended in the nearly passless Alps that separate Savoie from Italy. And up there in the wee hamlets whose primitive habitations sprawled in tiers, their roofs held down by large flat stones against the ferocity of the winter winds, I saw queer Things. Things that the fables of Hans Christian Andersen have made familiar to children of many countries: gnomes and dwarfs and little creatures, misshapen, with big heads and squat, short-legged bodies. From almost every cottage there peered out of the dark recesses of open doorways one, sometimes more, of these creepy little creatures, following the car's progress with round, unblinking eyes.

The harvest had not yet been garnered in the upland valleys; the young men had been called to the colors, and all the able bodies left behind—women of all ages, old men and children—were in the fields. So none remained at home to look after the helpless, those unhappy results of long inbreeding in the isolated hamlets whose sole egress was down the valley. Down the valley—a journey rarely taken by the more venturesome, save when the young men went on their military service; and never by most of the inhabitants, even so far as the small town at the valley's mouth. And now the oddly shaped little Things squatted unattended in the openings of the hovels perched on the edge of gigantic formations of Alpine upheaval. Squatted and stared with immense, inquisitive eyes, like the eyes of night-birds in the daylight, at the unaccustomed object that moved slowly on wheels across their foreground.

I was appalled by their number, discomfited by their relentless, unfathomable gaze. I could feel those uncanny eyes penetrating my back as we retraced our way down the valley. What could they be thinking? For their stare, though unresponsive, was by no means completely vacant. But the Lieutenant was an unimaginative soul.

"*Ah oui, les Innocents,*" he said. "There are many up in these valleys. They are quite harmless. They do not think." He shrugged his shoulders. "Usually their relations keep them out of sight; but in such times as these, when none can remain in the houses to look after them in the daytime, they emerge."

My first impressions of war were of small parties of agrarian and village youth ceaselessly converging on a grim, grey barracks where they disappeared, where some occult metamorphosis occurred, and in the secrecy of the night, without benefit even of the artificial stimuli of music or of cheering, were poured forth remoulded in standardized mass formation . . . all individuality of appearance and of thought extracted. In the silent dark, shunted off by battalions to an unknown destination . . .

And of driving an anachronism through valleys in the *massifs* of the Alps peopled by gnomes out of illustrations for Hans Christian Andersen fairy tales. Creatures that should have squatted on great toadstools in a mediæval forest; queerly shaped heads turning slowly on hunched shoulders as they followed one's every movement with intense but uncomprehending stares from the dark doorways of Alpine farmhouses.

After fourteen days of mobilization duty in the Haute Savoie I was relieved at my own request and proceeded with the car to Paris. For eight weeks, while the German hordes surged almost to the gates of the *Ville Lumière* and were thrown back in the brilliant counter-attack on the Marne, I served as a temporary Attaché to the American Embassy. During this period I made numerous trips to the French coast in connection with the evacuation of American citizens, and two memorable ones conducting our two official military observers (Henry T. Allen and Frank Parker) to the shifting "front" during the crucial struggles that saved Paris and changed—for a time—the course of European history.

One evening in early October I went with Herbert Haseltine to the Travellers' Club in Paris for a drink. We were joined at cocktails by a personable British Staff Captain named Frank Rattigan, resplendent in his red tabs, an unusual linguist and (this I learned later) of great appeal to women, who was then doing liaison duty between the British

Expeditionary Force and French Sixth Army. Before the night was long advanced he had started the mechanism to have me appointed a volunteer "automobilist" (complete with car) in the British Army. There was a group of twenty-four young British sportsmen, mostly with Rolls-Royces or Lanchesters, who had been appointed by the War Office to drive Corps and Division Commanders and certain special staff officers in the B.E.F. A few days following the evening with Rattigan I was appointed the twenty-fifth of this group.

I sailed into the British Army, so to speak, over the bar of the Travellers' Club.

Shortly after having had O.H.M.S. (On His Majesty's Service) painted on the windshield of the Packard, I was ordered to report with Rattigan to the Belgian front.

Albert, King of the Belgians

During the Battle of the Yser, in October and November 1914, King Albert's headquarters as Commander-in-Chief of the Belgian Army were in the Reception Room of the sixteenth-century *Hôtel de Ville* at Furnes, where the Inquisition used to meet some three centuries before. It was a beautiful Flemish Renaissance room, all of oak, with magnificent carved doorways and embossed Cordova leather covering the walls. Above a splendid mantel hung portraits of Ferdinand and Isabella of Spain, painted on wood in 1602 and of great merit.

My first meeting with the King was supremely informal. I crashed into him in the dimly lighted corridor outside that room on the day I reported for duty with the British Military Mission to the Belgian Army. I all but knocked him off his feet as I rushed around a corner when he was approaching from the other direction.

"*Sire!*" I cried. "I am so awfully sorry!" I was indeed very confused. His calm and courteous manner, while I stood stiffly at salute stammering apologies, at once put me at my ease. It was characteristic of his whole bearing.

King Albert was one of the few completely admirable figures the great war found in high capacity; one of the fewer whose reputation time has enhanced. Unostentatious, simple and direct, serious-minded, he kept his head through terrific stress, his temper under severe provocation, while others around him were losing theirs. Pretentions and grandiloquent phrases left him cold. He seemed completely without vanities. And he was no mere titular figurehead as Commander-in-Chief of the Belgian Army.

He actually commanded his forces, determined their disposition and strategy, was their inspiration to amazing fortitude when they were battered and exhausted beyond the point of normal physical endurance. His soldiers never lost their confidence in him. They revered their leader with a devotion and loyalty that subordinated all conflicting emotions. Conflicting emotions did exist. Those weary, dispirited troops felt badly let down by the Allies, whose promised relief had week after week been deferred. They believed their country had been sacrificed to a plan of campaign of advantage only to France. The Belgian Field Army had fought a series of gallant but losing battles against greatly superior forces. Its morale was shattered by constant retreat; its strength reduced by heavy losses. It had no reserves. Desperately it needed a chance to recuperate and reform.

The opportunity was not granted. The Germans swept on along the coast. King Albert, against the counsel of the French High Command, determined that his army should fight on its own territory as long as any territory remained on which to fight. Probably no one else could have aroused those exhausted, ill-equipped troops to the feats of resistance that blocked the way to the Channel ports and kept it blocked until reinforcements finally arrived.

"I shall hold the line of the Yser at all costs," he announced in his slow, quiet tones; and he did.

The King's General Order of 16 October 1914 threw a harsh and revealing light on the situation of his command on that date, as on some of the measures he felt necessary to employ in coping with that situation. Among other things, he ordered "the officers of the General Staff to be distributed amongst the troops in the front line. They will remain there during the fighting, encouraging others instead of grumbling themselves . . ."

The King was not entirely happy with his General Staff, nor with all of his commanders. Some individuals of the staff and many of the combatant officers showed the utmost tenacity. The losses among the officers who could least be spared were heavy and difficult to replace. More than twelve thousand of all ranks—over twenty-five percent of the total effectives—fell during the first few days on the Yser. The troops had been told to hold their positions for forty-eight hours until the French came up to relieve them. In most parts of the line they had held for ten days, with no relief in sight. The survivors slithered in mud above their knees, frayed out, their units dislocated, most of their leaders casualties.

The King appreciated better than Foch the grave need of reinforcements if the Yser line was to be held. He did not at all concur with General d'Urbal's low estimate of the fighting value of the enemy. He was right, and d'Urbal's attempted offensive was a complete failure. Had it not been for King Albert the Germans would have swept through to Dunkerque, and in all probability to Boulogne.

The 26 October was one of our very worst days. The Belgian 1st and 2nd Divisions broke and streamed back into Furnes, swamping that small town until the picturesque old Grand' Place on which faced the windows of the King's and the Mission's headquarters was a seething mass of mud-covered, ragged and ill-fed men, dazed and in the last stages of exhaustion. Battered field-guns and empty limbers rolling towards the rear pushed through them and beyond. There was nothing between General Headquarters and the German bayonets southeast of Nieuport—just four miles away—save for this disorganized, shattered rabble.

Why the Germans did not follow through was perhaps the will of Fate. They also were weary, and evidently did not realize how complete was the break. In the unhoped-for pause the routed elements were rallied. King Albert, clinging to the small fragment of national territory still in his hands, called for reconsolidation of the line on the Nieuport-Dixmude railway embankment. During those tense moments I had many intimate glimpses of the King, a superb figure in a situation which must to him have been immeasurably distressing. In this he weighed swiftly and calmly the chances of sacrificing his whole remaining force by prolonged resistance, based his decision on a correct conception of German tactics and the nerve-strength of his own people, and ordered the broken troops back into the line to fight out the battle on the Yser to the end. It was primarily their love for and belief in their monarch Commander-in-Chief that took them back.

The collapse of a considerable part of the forces plunged the Belgian Staff into utter consternation. By 11:00 in the morning they had drawn up orders for the general retirement of the Belgian Army across the

French frontier. The King flatly refused to consider such a move. He rejected every proposal for further retreat. Colonel Tom Bridges, chief of the British Military Mission, was with him on and off throughout the day. Those two were much the calmest persons in Furnes. But Colonel Bridges could get the King no reinforcements. That evening, after the situation had been temporarily reestablished, they went together in Tom Bridges' car to St. Omer where Field Marshal Sir John French had his headquarters. Sir John, though sympathetic, could not spare a single battalion to send to the Yser.

I was in and out of our office during most of the day, several times in the King's private office with messages when Tom Bridges was in conference with the Royal C-in-C. There was no great standing on ceremony during those crucial moments. Uniformed people—some of them high staff officers—were running in circles all over the place. Yet the King's room was pervaded by a notable calm. It seemed to spread from that remarkable personality. It made a deep impression on me. The demeanor of King Albert under intense stress, his deliberate movements, his calm, slow voice, had the most tranquilizing effect of any human contact I have ever experienced.

That impression has persisted throughout the turmoil of the ensuing years. For in some manner that was not quite obvious, aside from the Gendarmes rounding up disintegrated units, the shattered ranks were rallied. Weary and dispirited men trudged back to the knee-deep mud of their trenches in the fenlands, made infinitely more loathly by the gigantic bursts of heavy shells. The line was reconstituted. It all sprang from the unwavering determination, the calm assurance and slow, tempered voice of one splendid spirit.

He was not spectacular. He did not go out and declaim to the tired mob, attempt to revive them with oratory and the waving of a brilliant sword. That was not his manner. His influence went deeper than that. He showed himself only for a few moments, standing at his window while a batch of about a hundred German prisoners was marched through the disorderly Grand' Place under a heavy guard of Gendarmes. They were all that remained of a German battalion which had filtered through the lines near Dixmude in a heavy fog the night before. They came in for a loud hooting from the soldiers and the fear-stricken remnants of the civilian population, then decamping with an unkempt horde of refugees from towns and villages beyond the lines. The King watched the prisoners' passage. His presence was well-timed and had an effect. I wondered if he had staged that *coup-de-théatre*. Probably not; his temperament was not that of a showman.

During one of the most critical moments of that confused day, when field telephone messages of a gravely discouraging nature were arriving from the edge of the sector that had crumbled, the King noticed me standing by for an order from Colonel Bridges, staring at the lovely sixteenth-century mantel that framed the great fireplace.

"It is a beautiful thing, that old mantelpiece, is it not?" he remarked in his slow, steady voice.

"*Sire,*" I gasped, "it is indeed beautiful!" But I think what I saw at that moment was not a carven mantel. There was an aura rising above it. It was the spirit of Albert, King of the Belgians.

Four days later, when I returned from where the Belgian 4th Division was holding stoutly near Dixmude against furious attacks, portions of the 2nd Division, long past the limit of their physical resistance, had broken at Ramscappelle, were rallied and sent back into the line, broke once again. The Germans occupied Ramscappelle village in strength.

They were then west of the railway line and 3¾ miles from the edge of Furnes as the crow flies. There was nothing much in between, though counterattacks were making some progress. The Belgian General Staff again prepared hastily to withdraw.

King Albert took Tom Bridges and Prince Alexander, second-in-command of the Misssion, to lunch at his small villa at La Panne where each night he returned to the consoling and courageous spirit of Queen Elizabeth, active with her Red Cross work in that unpretentious little seaside resort. The King quietly affirmed his confidence that the Belgian and French counterattacks, then going strongly, would succeed in holding the Germans and, he hoped, restore control of the railway embankment.

"In any event," he said in his even tone, "I have no intention of withdrawing from Furnes until the Germans are entering the outskirts of the town." He meant that. The three returned to Furnes immediately after lunch. They passed into their respective offices. The Belgian General Staff remained where it was.

The same afternoon I drove Prince Alexander to St. Omer to see Sir John French. On the way we talked of the phenomenal composure of the King. The only sign of strain he had shown during lunch, the Prince said, was a restrained irritation over the attitude of the French. "The King feels it damned unjust," Prince Alexander continued, "for the French to impugn the stamina of men he has been forced to keep on in the lines under repeated protests of their unfitness, long after they have reached a pitiful degree of exhaustion, have lost their officers, most of their equipment, and nearly all semblance of unit organization." King Albert held that French reinforcements could and should have been brought up earlier, though of this he did not speak at the lunch, Prince Alexander said, now that some reinforcements actually were arriving.

I had been in our office that morning when a Major of the Belgian Staff reported glumly: "Our artillery has less than seventy rounds of ammunition left per gun. This will not last through the day, and we cannot get any more."

All their arsenals and factories had been captured one by one during three months of constant fighting. The liners of their cannon were worn out from rapid fire and the use of French ammunition not entirely suitable for the Belgian guns. Now even this ammunition was no longer available, at least for the moment.

On 1 November the German artillery began the bombardment of Furnes with 150 mm. shells. One shell fell in the town every four minutes between 1:00 and 4:45 P.M. There were few duds. The King was lunching at La Panne. In the Grand Quartier Général the bombardment caused confusion and turmoil. Once again the Belgian Staff prepared to quit Furnes.

King Albert returned from La Panne shortly after lunch. He passed through the emptied Grand' Place on which the firing was directed— ranged on the tower of the Palais de Justice alongside his headquarters —and proceeded quietly to his office. After this we heard no more about any withdrawal of Belgian General Headquarters.

Most of the shells fell a trifle short. One dropped about thirty yards from the King's office, in a direct line with his window. Another unfortunately hit the fine old Hôtel de la Noble Rose across the Place, one of the most charming sixteenth-century Flemish buildings in town. Its explosion demolished the upper part of the building. Four soldiers of the French Mission were killed, and an officer wounded, upstairs. Members of the Belgian General Staff lunching in the oak-panelled banqueting hall below scuttled out like ants from under burning grass. One could hardly blame them.

The King remained throughout the bombardment. An artillery officer plotted a chart from the first dozen or so bursts showing that the median line led directly to the King's office. King Albert was entirely unmoved. He calmed the highly nervous staff. His courage was of the quiet kind that shows up best in emergencies. I could not imagine him losing his poise, or giving the least outward indication of physical fear.

The principal figures on my immediate horizon of that time were a remarkably interesting trio for a youthful volunteer to be thrown with at such a moment. King Albert, Colonel Tom Bridges, Prince Alexander of Teck were big men, immense of stature—all, I think, over six-feet-two. They were big as well in their qualities. All three were courageous, undaunted by calamity, broad-minded, far-seeing. Only in their manner of expression did they differ.

The King was reserved, quiet almost to the point of shyness, but in no wise a nervous shyness. He was one of the slowest spoken of men. "I .. make .. my .. own .. repairs .. to .. my car," he said to me when we were discussing the relative merits of his Minerva, Tom Bridges' Rolls-Royce and my (actually my father's) Packard, now assigned to Alexander of Teck. He frequently sought relaxation in the pit in overalls, greasing and working on the mechanism of his car.

He wore a modest uniform of dark blue (the Belgian Army had not yet gone into khaki) without decorations save when he honored some visiting Allied commander or statesman. He was often unaccompanied even by an aide-de-camp. And he kept pretty much out of view save when he had occasion to encourage or command his troops.

He visited the trenches, always without fuss. He never sought the limelight. But he understood better than his Staff, more clearly than any of his advisers, the temper of his soldiers and the dispositions to take in the light of the general situation and of the troops' capacity.

The Grand' Place at Furnes made an effective setting for the strange array of characters and of property that passed across the scene in those days. Its sixteenth- and seventeenth-century buildings had looked down on many medleys of armed men in centuries past: on Burgundians and on Spanish, Dutch and grey-eyed English, ruddy Knights of Flanders and thin-lipped Inquisitors of the Church; on warriors with pikes, with halberds, in heavy armor and visored helmets; on warriors with crossbows or wide-mouthed arquebuses.

The Renaissance windows and decorated gable-ends now looked

down upon gatherings more motley than any of past centuries: on men of a dozen races and tongues in a wide variety of martial costume, with weapons of destruction far deadlier than their predecessors'.

Belgian troops, wearing "uniforms" of weirdly diverse type and color supplemented with odd items of civilian garb, shuffled wearily back and forth, ragged and encrusted with clay. Infantry of the line, *chasseurs à pied,* grenadiers, sappers, cyclists, dismounted cavalry, foot-slogged past on their way to the trenches. Gendarmes on bicycles, on foot, on horses, marshalled hordes of empty-eyed refugees to points far from the homes they had fled—drear caravans of the expropriated, swelled by the bulk of Furnes' six thousand inhabitants.

More Gendarmes marched field-grey files of German prisoners across the Place to interrogation in the Palais de Justice. Batteries of French 75's, 105's, 120's filed past on their way to the line. Empty French and Belgian caissons clattered back to Bray for ammunition. There were traffic jams where tired artillery horses had fallen on the slippery paving blocks, where armored cars with bad visibility had hooked into ambulances full of groaning wounded, cleared to an ac-companiment of archaic oaths in Flemish and French and English.

Autobuses from the boulevards of Paris transported swarthy Chasseurs d'Afrique in red riding boots and white burnouses to oozy trenches in the fenlands where spectacular horsemanship would avail them not at all. Old friends, those familiar, round-nosed *de Dion* buses still bore the placards of their urban runs—*Opéra, Passy-Bourse, Champ de Mars:* a singular appropriateness to the last.

Belgian machine-gun companies equipped with small limbers and caissons mounted on pneumatic-tired wheels rolled silently towards the lines, drawn by sturdy dogs of Flanders whose early training had been on milk-routes.

There were blue-clad French Marines sporting red pompons on their berets, brown-skinned Moors and Algerians, huge Senegalese with white eyeballs agleam in shiny moon-shaped faces of black lacquer. French infantry tramped past in blue coats and red pantaloons. Grey wagons of supply columns rattled interminably over the *pavé.* Khaki-colored British ambulances of Dr. Hector Munro's Field Hospital slipped through wherever an opening afforded. And sometimes General Grosetti, the gigantic Corsican known as the "Bull of the Yser," who bewildered his colleagues with proposals for general attacks on all occasions, would ride by with his escort of French Hussars.

In one corner three cars stood often side by side at alert along with those of the Grand Quartier Général: the King's Minerva, Colonel Bridges' Rolls-Royce, and my Packard with O.H.M.S. (On His Majesty's Service) painted on the windshield. Here British motorcycle despatch-riders waited for urgent messages from the British Mission to carry in the rain over the slithery paving of the cambered roads. For it rained four days out of five, and when it did not rain there was usually a white ground-mist through which the steeples of churches, the dislocated arms of old windmills showed as vague phantom shapes pointing grotesquely in the fog.

In the nearby Church of St. Nicolas woebegone refugees knelt in prayer down the center of the nave between the side aisles where soldiers in torn, mud-caked clothes and bloody rags lay upon straw, cleaned their rifles, joked, wrote letters or slept like dead men, their arms and accoutrements stacked along the walls beneath the dusty figures of Saints draped with clotted bandages.

Usually the Place was a kaleidoscope of movement. Sometimes it seethed with disintegrated elements falling back, having lost their trenches and their units, halted there and hastily reformed, marched back to the lines with mounted Gendarmes to see that they did not again lose their way. And sometimes it emptied as though stricken by God, when the German artillery ranged on the three towers that marked the town in the nearly featureless lowlands.

Once in the early morning during a fortuitous lapse in activity the Place was cleared; a staff car with one wheel gone being the last object dragged away. Detachments of mounted Belgian Gendarmes and French Hussars lined up in double ranks on the four sides. At 8:50 a German plane dropped one bomb which exploded with a great crash some seventy-five yards away. Had the bomber timed his shot ten minutes later with a bit better aim he might have had an interesting bag. For at nine o'clock King Albert and President Poincaré, Generals Joffre and Dupage, Belgian Minister of War de Broqueville and French Minister of War Millerand, arrived in two cars and inspected the guard.

The King and the President of France drove slowly around the Place. The others walked. The inspection was not unduly prolonged. The President and the War Ministers had no desire to gain first-hand knowledge of the bombardment of Furnes, even though the Battle of Flanders had by then, to all practical effects, been won.

The dignitaries visited the King's office for a few minutes and departed, while I stood with the rest of the Mission at salute on the steps of the Hôtel de Ville. The King seemed fully a third again the stature of Poincaré. Alongside the King's tall dignity the President appeared an utterly insignificant little figure, squat, bearded and shapeless in a grey sack suit and felt hat.

Just before the celebrities first came on the scene a Belgian military photographer set up a motion-picture camera in the center of the Place. It happened that the apparatus was of German make. He left it for an instant to fetch his reels. Out came two little dogs, who sniffed at the tripod and then turned up in unison against two of its legs. Pleased at that effort they trotted away, wagging their tails. The rows of bared sabers around the hollow square shook as the solemn honor guard broke into rumbling guffaws.

"They were dogs of Flanders," the King commented afterwards with a quiet twinkle in his eye when the story was told him. "And the enemy has not crossed the Yser." The enemy, because of King Albert and his men of Flanders and Walloons, never did cross the Yser.

Prince Alexander

On 27 October 1914 Major His Serene Highness Prince Alexander of Teck,* brother of Queen Mary of England, arrived in West Flanders to be second-in-command of the British Military Mission.

Tall and distinguished in appearance, handsomer in his visored military cap than without because of encroaching baldness, he had a happy bearing that lacked any trace of pompous formality. He was kindly in his human contacts, internationally minded, a fluent and entertaining conversationalist. He regarded the war with deep personal regret—the war that was the very salt of life to Colonel Tom Bridges, a God-given opportunity for his talents and his training; that was stark tragedy to King Albert of the Belgians.

Prince Alexander had a less unemotional temperament than those other two, who seemed to have no nerves at all. He was courageous rather than fearless. While I served with him for but a brief time, he

---

* When King George V, in 1917, discarded the former Germanic style of the British Royal House—Saxe-Coburg and Gotha—in favor of Windsor, Prince Alexander relinquished his princely title, also of Germanic origin, and became Earl of Athlone. He recently served as Governor-General of Canada.

was as likable a senior officer as a young alien "automobilist" could
very well have had.

The road was grey and greasy in the morning mist when I drove
my new chief out from Dunkerque to his new post. All the roads of that
sector—the few passable ones—were grey and greasy, built up like
causeways above the soggy polder with its network of canals and
ditches. Those near the battlefront were lined with the carcasses of
cars that had crashed against trees or run into one another in the night,
had been smashed by shell-fire, or overturned into the deep feeder
channels along the sides. Ghoulish drivers with a weather eye out for
spare parts and accessories had stripped the melancholy wrecks of
everything removable. Some had burnt. Segments of a goodly number
showed through the surface of the water, upside down six feet below
the road. Others sprawled half in, half out, clinging to the edge of the
causeways like uncouth amphibian monsters. Driving over those narrow
strips of shell-torn *pavé* at night without lights, in the usual rain or
fog, was in no sense a joy-ride.

The Battle of the Yser—the battle for the Channel ports—was then
drawing to its climax. The remnants of the Belgian Army were entrenched in a spongy morass in the last stages of exhaustion, thinly
extended in shallow, watery trenches dug in land lower than the sea
behind the barrier of the coastal dunes. For the past ten days men on
land had fought against water, ships at sea against infantry and horse
artillery. Cavalry, field batteries, siege-guns, armored trains and cars,
foot soldiers and marines, gun-boats zigzagging over the Banks of
Zeeland, aircraft and every auxiliary service then devised, moiled about
in the narrow sector with manpower that was Belgian, French, German,
British, Arab, Moor and Senegalese, at moments all mixed up together.

Prince Alexander felt his first need was to familiarize himself with
the local situation which the day before, when the wornout Belgian 1st
and 2nd Divisions broke and streamed back into Furnes, had been
about as bad as it very well could be. It was a bit better now, as the
German failure to follow through had given King Albert the time he
desperately needed to reconsolidate the line.

Along this line, whose length ran from the dunes to Dixmude, I
took Prince Alexander on his first tour of the Belgian positions. Aside
from the modest defensive value of the canalized Yser they were not
impressive positions. The country lay flat and without feature. The line

was thinly held, the wire scanty, the trenches sketchy in the extreme. In the soggy lands adjacent to the Yser, though their flooding added to the defensive strength, no trenches could be dug save in a few "high spots" and along the narrow Nieuport-Dixmude railway embankment; nor very deeply there. One could drive in a car almost to the front line at several different points (though the practice was not encouraged) over roads that led to the several Yser bridgeheads variously held by Belgians, the enemy, and Admiral Ronarc'h's Brigade of Breton Marines.

We had not proceeded far when we were nearly blown off the Nieuport road by two French 120 mm. cannon, placed hub to hub down below the shoulder of the highway under a heavy camouflage of branches. The guns fired together at the precise instant our heads passed some seven feet in front of their muzzles and perhaps a fathom below the trajectory of the shells. The cannon had been well concealed. It was the unexpectedness of the thing that made it disconcerting. Prince Alexander merely gulped and blinked, but I saw him pass a hand furtively along the far side of his head and snap his fingers several times close to his ear.

"Sorry, Sir!" I shouted. "Those damn guns weren't there yesterday! Hope the concussion didn't break your eardrum!"

"Don't believe so!" he shouted back. "But it left a swarm of bees in my head!" It had in mine, too.

Later the same day we were driving fairly fast along the narrow built-up road to Pervyse when a German high-explosive burst on the cobbled center strip directly in front of us. The air suddenly filled with paving blocks, and a piece of shell screeched through one front mud-guard. I could not stop in time—we had no four-wheel brakes in those days—to miss crashing into the jagged crater at considerable speed. The car bounded thirty feet clear, not quite turning over. There was a clatter of inauspicious sounds before it finally came to rest.

"Close!" said Prince Alexander. "Can't say I want 'em closer than that!" We clambered out to look over the damage. One tire was torn to ribbons and every leaf of the left front spring had been sheared through the middle. "Neat job you did holding her on the road. Pity about the spring," he said.

I effected a very rough repair to the spring with rope and a billet of wood, while more shells kept bursting alongside, ahead of us and behind, just off the road. Prince Alexander smoked cigarettes and talked steadily, handing me the tools.

"Well done!" he cried when the makeshift job was completed. "Thought for a moment we were cooked. How did you happen to have that billet of wood—carry it purposely to mend broken springs?" he asked as we drove on, the unsprung front wheel chattering over the torn road.

"No, Sir," I replied. "I carry it as a base for the jack when I have to change tires. We get a lot of punctures out here." He had reason to know that before long; we averaged better than three a day.

At Nieuport there stood in an obtuse angle of the Belgian line a venerable stone tower known as the Tour des Templiers. It was the sole but splendid relic of a twelfth-century Templar monastery and establishment that had been burnt by the English in 1383. From its top one could look upon General von Beseler's 33rd German Reserve Corps striking furiously at the Nieuport bridge hard below, and correct the fire of Admiral Hood's Monitors on the German batteries that we were able to spot by their flashes in the flat and featureless landscape. The Monitors were shallow-draft river gunboats built for Brazil's Amazon patrol. There were three of them, each mounting two 6-inch guns forward. They scuttled back and forth over the Zeeland shoals like fat wild ducks with clipped wings, firing merrily. They were extremely effective against von Beseler's ground forces. Sometimes I took a hand in spotting their fire with Dennis Schoppee, a British naval Lieutenant loaned us by Admiral Hood.

On the night of the heaviest of the attacks Prince Alexander and I lay stretched out atop the eight-hundred-year-old Templar tower. The canalized Yser forming the main Belgian line of defense curved outwardly from beneath our point of vantage, a tarnished silver ribbon under the starlight and intermittent flashes of the shells. Behind the rim of the dunes the sodden fields glinted like oily lead, magentasplashed where scattered farms burned fiercely. Above their pyres heavy palls of red smoke hung in angry, incandescent shapes. The flames threw into relief the bloated corpses of milk cattle, the smaller dots that were the human discards in the game, half floating in odd postures on the reddened, watery field. Over it all, around and below, the ceaseless flashes of the guns and bursting shells gave an effect as though the whole astral system were disintegrating.

On the tower five French Lieutenants lay stretched flat on their stomachs directing the fire of their field-gun sections just behind. They cried their corrections to a telephonist who chanted these aloud into the night.

"*Deuxième pièce, 3800 mètres!*"

"*Deuxième pièce, 3800 mètres!*" sang the echo.

The whistle of shells past our ears from the batteries behind had the sound of air rushing continuously through a great ventilator. Now and again the flow would be broken by the short, high-pitched scream of German shrapnel ending in a sharp *CRACK!* as it burst overhead, while we lay like frozen slugs in the meagre protection of the parapet.

"Some ruddy German gunner is getting too damned close for comfort!" grunted Prince Alexander.

"*Première pièce, 200 mètres à gauche!*"

"*Première pièce, 200 mètres à gauche!*" chanted the echo.

A long fluttering whine marked the passage high above of each 6-inch shell from the Monitors zigzagging over the Zeeland shoals. I had learned to pick out that sound from all the deafening jumble of noises. It was not always easy to spot the burst amidst the multitude of others, against the rippling light from the mouths of cannon like the play of phosphorescence on a tropic sea.

Guns of all shapes and sizes contributed their special tones to the racket, tearing the night apart with their flashes. It was as if one looked down upon a clattering inferno whose floor was partly covered with a turbid liquid that glowed blood-red where angry volcanoes erupted through. From them rose crimson smoke-columns like the Yggdrasil trees of Scandinavian mythology, binding together earth and heaven and hell with their branches and their roots; while in between all the devils in Hades were trying their hands at various Satanic mechanisms for shattering the unfortunates trapped in their toils.

The German attacks were disrupted that night before they ever reached our lines. Gradually the seething play of flashes faded into darkness. Neither side then possessed the immense supplies of ammunition that later were hurled back and forth for days and nights on end. Silence of a sort, after that convulsion of sound, descended like a great blanket, acting as an opiate on taut nerves. For a little while longer the Prince and I lay flat on our bellies atop the massive Templar tower, staring out on an arena where the dying flames of a dozen scattered farms and villages glowed under the placid stars.

On some nights when not otherwise assigned I went out alone, during the attacks between Ramscappelle and Dixmude, to try my hand at a new activity. This led to curious results. Wandering beyond the Belgian outposts after dark I got half awash in the inundations amidst hundreds of German corpses.

From these bodies I took identifications. Their shoulder-straps bearing regimental insignia—later abolished; their wrist-tags or necklet identification disks; their pay-books worn in a slit pocket in the back skirt of their tunics; the little diaries so many then kept in greatest detail—forbidden soon after—carried in their breast pockets.

My trophies, dried out, cleaned of blood and other matter, proved to be useful when tabulated. They helped identify at least two German divisions whose presence had up to then been unknown.

For a number of nights in succession, until the Battle of the Yser finally ended in stalemate across the inundations, I went out on these lone, macabre expeditions. Twice I was surprised by attacks that kept me submerged up to the neck for several hours surrounded by wallowing enemy troops. But *they* sought the drier strips of rising ground; I kept to the hollows where the water was breast-deep, while the attacks lasted. By then I had learned to feign death, lying bent over as if blasted by a shell or drowned. There were so many bodies; one that managed to breathe under its armpit was not likely to be noted in that mass of cadavers sunk in mud and water.

I developed something of a special technique. In the dark, doing a compromise between wading and swimming, I could tell at once by touch as I bumped into an object whether it was a fresh and therefore interesting corpse, an old one, or just a gas-blown cow. There were quantities of bloated cattle, fine dairy cows that at one time had supplied England with much of its milk. From these I sheered off at the first contact. Except once, when beneath a disconcerting glare from star-shells and shrapnel I lurked under the inflated entrails of a decomposing Holstein.

But on touching a recently killed body I sensed in a grim way the satisfaction of a gold-miner on striking pay dirt. Hurriedly I would feel through its pockets, cut off its shoulder-straps with a sheath knife, run my hand over its wrists and around its neck for an identity tag, and shove the garnered trophies into a haversack. I would come back wet through and slimey, covered from head to foot with mud, gore and human insides.

One could not always be right, of course. Some of the floating islands, those that had been too long dead, were not pleasant contacts. Many of the cows were about set to explode like gas-mines if one hit them too hard. It was not very savory duty. But the acquired faculty to distinguish in the dark a fresh corpse from a spoilt one, by superficial touch and without unnecessary loss of time—for my progress averaged probably less than a fifth of a mile an hour—developed in its ghoulish way to be of some value to the Allied cause.

On certain nights I stood telephone duty in the Mission office at Furnes. There was a night I was alone in the office, when an irritable voice at the other end of a very poor connection kept asking for Colonel Bridges or Prince Alexander. I replied that they were both out, but that I was on duty to take any messages.

"And who might you be?" asked the voice.

I explained this as best I could, three times over. Each time the same petulant voice came back: "But who are you?"

The third time I gave way to rising irritation, uttered a tired noise and bleated, "And who the hell might *you* be?" Somehow, as soon as I let it out, I felt that was a mistake.

There was a very slight pause, followed by a different voice. The connection also had cleared. Calm and acid-sharp the new voice came back: "This is Kitchener speaking, who did you say you are?"

I do not recall just what I stammered then. The connection by some mischance had been put through to what was perhaps the most guarded telephone in London. It was now Field Marshal the Earl Kitchener of Khartoum, His Britannic Majesty's Secretary of State for War, speaking from his innermost sanctum in the War Office. He had been the one who had asked, through his Aide or Orderly Officer, to speak to Colonel Bridges or Prince Alexander. He evidently had heard my last, impetuous bleat. As a Warrant Officer-Automobilist without a Warrant, attached to a member of a Mission then headed by a Lieutenant Colonel, I found little background for eloquence. I suspected that few others, of recent years, had asked "K of K" directly: "And who the hell might *you* be?"

Furnes, four miles behind the front line and under intermittent bombardment, was far from an ideal place for General Headquarters of the King Commander-in-Chief. Of this the Belgian Staff was only too keenly aware. But the King refused flatly to move back off Belgian soil.

The King, living at La Panne, a few miles away on the coast, usually had lunch brought to him at his headquarters in the Hôtel de Ville of Furnes. The members of the British Mission ate wherever they could find food. There were casual messes, very bad, in the Hôtel Royal and the fine old Hôtel de la Noble Rose. These were both disrupted by the shelling. Shortly after Prince Alexander arrived, and the tension had eased very slightly for the moment, it was decided to form a British Mission mess. Colonel Bridges instructed Captain Rattigan, who had not yet left us, to find a cook. Rattigan passed this on to me. I, having learned something of buck-passing in military service, passed it on to Poupart.

Henri Poupart was a Frenchman whom Rattigan had managed to "wangle" as an orderly while on liaison duty with the French in front of Paris. How Rattigan had succeeded in keeping him after having been transferred to the Belgian front I never knew, but there he was, red-pantalooned and blue-coated, spending much of his time unpacking and repacking our kits from or onto my car while the Germans wavered just beyond the outskirts of the town.

"Get us a cook," I told Poupart. "A good cook!" I had not up to then talked to Poupart about his past life. Poupart advanced the suggestion that if he were provided with a stove he thought he could cook palatable enough food for a mess.

"Yes, yes," I cried, "I know; all Frenchmen cook well! But this, my old Poupart, is to be a very special mess and the brother of England's Queen will eat at it. So we must find a very special cook. Please go at once and see if you can locate such a one. Perhaps among the Belgian troops you will find a suitable *cordon bleu*."

"Yes, sir. But if you permit me to mention it, I have many times served *Son Altesse Sérénissime*. I think his Serene Highness well esteems my cooking. And His Majesty, His Serene Highness's brother-in-law, would say a good word for my ability in that line, I feel convinced."

"His Majesty?" I was beginning to blink a little at these titular bombs. "And what, pray tell, may His Britannic Majesty know about your cooking?"

"Why, sir, I have for the past eight years been chef to His Majesty King George V. It was only my mobilization which caused me unhappily to take leave from that position."

I reported in triumph back to Tom Bridges. "I've found you a cook, sir," I said.

"Already? Any good?"

"I haven't yet tried him but I rather expect he is." Prince Alexander came in. "Sir, would your brother-in-law's late chef at Buckingham Palace do for your mess?" I asked. He stared at me. I explained the matter. Then he grinned.

"Why, yes, I fancy he'll do," said Prince Alexander. So Rattigan lost his orderly and the British Military Mission acquired the chef of their sovereign.

(Henri Poupart served as chef to the Mission, which Prince Alexander headed after the departure of Tom Bridges to command a Division, until the end of the war. He then returned to Buckingham Palace, and for nearly eighteen years continued as chef to King George V. In 1936 he was released by Edward VIII—at the instigation, it was said, of the then Mrs. Wallis Warfield Simpson. On the accession of King George VI he was reinstated, and retired permanently at his own request in 1938 after thirty years' service. When I last heard from him just before the second phase of the war he was living quietly near Vichy.)

Late on 30 October, after the overstrained Belgian 2nd Division had broken at Ramscappelle, I drove Prince Alexander to St. Omer to see Sir John French. The British Commander-in-Chief still was in too tight a position at Ypres to spare so much as a company to reinforce the Yser. Not to return entirely empty-handed, Prince Alexander provided himself from the officer's canteen with two boxes of very good cigars for King Albert.

"The cigars the King is now smoking," said the Prince, "are really quite the nastiest in the world!"

They were poor enough in all truth, but I had sampled nastier. A day or two earlier I had distributed a couple of boxes of the cheapest French monopoly cigars, left over from an expedition on the Aisne, to the troops in the Belgian front-line trench along the Nieuport-Dixmude railway embankment. Colonel Bridges had thought this a good idea for the moral effect it might produce of Allied support—tangible if not very substantial. The odor of those cigars was wholly appropriate to the pervading stench of lyddite and decomposition. But they were well appreciated where better tobacco might have tasted flat and insipid.

I returned with Prince Alexander from St. Omer after dark, in a cold, slanting rain. The sentries at the barrier-posts along the way had not been chosen for their I.Q. I carried a leather map-case whose celluloid pockets enclosed on one side our bright red Belgian Staff permits and grey British Expeditionary Force card passes; on the other side the *Carte Taride* of northern France. At each barrier two or three dripping Territorials, sometimes more, would pore laboriously over our credentials. Not one comprehended in the least what was written on the passes. But after the same tiresome delay at each halt, we were allowed to proceed.

On the French side of the frontier the post was occupied by a solitary guard with the earmarks of an ancient hop-farmer. He took my map-case to a shielded light and stared intently at it, wrong side up, while the rain trickled off his beard in a steady stream. After several minutes he returned the case with a motion to proceed. *"C'est bon, passez!"* he announced. What he passed us on was the road map of northern France, upside down.

"Some day, just by the law of averages, we should meet a literate man at one of these posts!" remarked Prince Alexander in weary resignation. As far as I know, we never did. But at the next barrier, on the Belgian side of the frontier, we met one who at least was alert.

We had the Belgian password, good only within the Belgian lines. The word that night was *"rose."* From St. Omer we had brought back with us a young French staff officer whose attributes included a clear baritone voice. As I drew up to the Belgian barrier our French companion led a bob-tailed chorus of three, one of them the brother of England's Queen, as with rain-drenched faces thrust into the night we burst into the first bars of a currently popular French song. *"Oh, Mademoiselle Rose!"* was its title. The sentry passed us at once, with a grin.

Furnes was still in Belgian hands when we returned—we had not been quite sure that it would be. Later that night in the Mission headquarters the Prince and I were discussing the afternoon's events with Major Thompson, when a Belgian Staff Major came in to report. The Major was in high elation.

"Our troops recaptured Ramscappelle a few minutes ago!" he announced. "And they have now been ordered to charge the railway embankment."

The Belgian Staff Major begged Prince Alexander to telegraph at once to King George the news of Ramscappelle's recapture. This the Prince agreed to do, providing the Belgians should hold Ramscappelle throughout the night and advance as far as the railway embankment

just beyond; which they did. When we were alone a little later Prince
Alexander grinned broadly at the picture of King George receiving an
urgent private message—"Belgians have retaken Ramscappelle . . .
Alexander."

"I can see my brother-in-law in his library at Windsor Castle poring
over the map of northwestern Europe," he chortled, "sputtering to himself: 'Now where the hell is Ramscappelle?'" But Prince Alexander
kept his promise to send the message.

Ramscappelle, before it was completely demolished, was a tiny dot
on a large-scale map, a wee village of a few score Flemish families. Yet
the recapture of that momentarily critical position was a stout feat of
arms on the part of the wornout Belgian troops.

Several times I went with Prince Alexander to the Dixmude bridgehead, and once with the King. Dixmude had been held for twenty-five
days against an enemy six times their strength by Admiral Ronarc'h's
Breton Marines, Meyser's Belgian Infantry Brigade and, during the last
fortnight, two battalions of Senegalese. The Bretons and the Belgians
had been called upon to hold out for ninety-six hours. They had yielded
no part of that all-but-impossible position until after three and a half
weeks it was battered to pieces, enfiladed and rendered utterly unten-
able. On 10 November the Württembergers finally occupied the drear
remnants of the town. But we had opened the Nieuport locks and by
then it was too late for the Germans to advance farther in the spongy
area of the flooded lowlands across which it was impossible to move
artillery, or to outflank the main force of the Belgians. The loss of the
bridgehead was no longer vital.

I was there the afternoon before it fell, and again during the morning the defenders were forced to relinquish it. Around the bridgehead,
in moderately well protected trenches—somewhat better than the Belgian though not so good as the German—were the Breton Marines and
Senegalese, all mixed up together. They had burrowed into the sodden
ground as if holing in for the winter. The trenches were connected with
covered passages, constantly broken down by the shelling, from which
they emerged no more than was absolutely necessary. Then they scuttled like crabs from one point of cover to another: enormous land-crabs
with the shiniest, blackest faces I have ever seen. Those were the
Senegalese. The Marines were like little blue-black bears clambering
out of a clay wallow. Straggly pompons that had once been red drooped

from their berets. Tough they were, squat and fuzzily bearded, for most of them were very young; the mud of weeks caked hard all over them.

The stand of those youthful sailors at Dixmude under their Breton Admiral was one of the grandest feats of resistance of the whole war. Meyser's Belgian Brigade also put up a splendid resistance. Together they stiffened the Senegalese. Those huge black men, fierce enough fighters in a charge, would never have stood the pounding alone by themselves. One of the Marine officers told me the Senegalese did not understand taking prisoners.

"They simply cut off their heads," he explained. I do not think this was usually true, under their French officers, though it undoubtedly happened sometimes. "Most of 'em keep souvenirs of German ears," he said. "Some have long strings of them." But those tropical Africans lost their verve in the Flanders winter.

The day we lost the bridgehead I went into Dixmude with Louis Neilson. It was a grim sight but for one absurd touch of comic relief. The little town sheltering formerly four thousand souls had been pounded to fragments by its attackers, thoroughly pillaged by its defenders. Its fifteenth-century Church of St. Jean that gloried in the finest Gothic rood-screen of all West Flanders stood a gutted shell of shattered walls, the tower bent at an extraordinary angle. Württembergers held the site of a chateau on the northeastern edge, several times taken and retaken in fierce bayonet fighting. From this their machine guns commanded many of the streets and areas laid open by the shelling. Their snipers waited around the edge to pick off anyone who might expose himself. Through the scrambled ruins crept an occasional French patrol, spattered by German shrapnel and high-explosive.

In the midst of the shapeless wreckage one little house remained insecurely perched between two large shell-craters. Its windows and doors were empty openings; its roof and sides gaped with jagged holes. The interior was littered with rubble, with splintered window-frames, broken glass and roof tiles. And inside it, on straight-backed wooden chairs just within what had been the entrance, sat two ancient Flemish crones admiring how the world was being unmade. Keenly curious, they gazed out upon the fantastic scene of devastation over which shells screamed continually and burst with tremendous crashes close around.

They were not in the least frightened. They grinned and tried to chat with us, but our Flemish was weak and their hearing nearly extinct. It was, I suppose, because they were too deaf to hear the infernal racket, too old to understand the danger, that they took it all as such an entertaining show. For they seemed quite happy and very, very interested in what was going on around them.

"How do you suppose they subsist?" asked Louis. I could not say. Behind sunken lips one of them showed two teeth in her lower jaw; the other boasted three in the upper. That was all the dental equipment they made up between them. But their eyes were clear, peering all about like inquisitive squirrels.

Those two amazing relics had remained there throughout the whole bombardment that had demolished every other house around them, through the attacks and counterattacks and the hand-to-hand fighting up and down the streets. They could not be induced to leave. It had been decided not to attempt to remove them forcibly because of their great age. They were perfectly sane. Patrols and ration parties sometimes left them a little food from which to make a gruel, we were later told.

They were the only human beings, civil or military, still existing in the distorted mass of debris that was Dixmude town. And there, undoubtedly, they were when the Württembergers forced their way into the town that afternoon, perched on their two little wooden chairs, peering keenly through gaunt holes in the walls of their house at the interesting newcomers.

To round out his first-hand view of the Belgian positions I led Prince Alexander well out beyond our front lines along one of the roads that ran westwards into enemy territory, to a Belgian outpost of three or four men crouched behind a little barrier of paving stones and earth. The barrier edged a shallow trench some ten or twelve feet long cut in the surface of the road, without overhead protection. To the sides were neither landmarks nor horizon, only leaden water and dull, beating rain. The post and road out to it lay under spasmodic rifle fire, bracketed from time to time by bursts of shrapnel: leisurely white puffs, two by two, that spewed a nasty metallic spatter.

We skirted the line of little trees flanking the road. Woefully thin little trees, widely spaced, their spacing accentuated by the effects of high explosives. They afforded scant protection. The Germans had a disagreeable habit of picking off men on their return from the outposts. Those men whose bodies lay unburied along the roadside had mostly been killed ducking back after being relieved. It was much easier to get up to the posts than to return to the lines intact.

Probably nowhere else on the entrenched front could one have walked out a mile or more beyond one's lines with a fair prospect of getting back. But this war in an amphibious area that lay lower than the sea was unlike anything else in the West. Usable trenches could be dug only in the embankments or high spots that afforded something in the way of dryish land and a field of fire over the flat meadows. In the central part of the sector between Nieuport and Dixmude, once the inundations spread, the lines were separated by three thousand yards or more. Between them, perhaps two hundred yards apart on the raised causeways across the marshy polder, were the outposts: the German posts better built and more strongly held than the Belgian. On thick nights the Germans would sometimes creep up and rush the Belgian posts in the fog, shooting or bayoneting the pickets before the latter were aware of what was upon them. Life in one of those outposts was peculiarly devoid of charm.

In the churchyard of Pervyse the monuments and tombstones of at least twenty generations of the revered dead, interred with all the solemn ritual of the Church, lay upheaved, broken and disorderly, the bones and skulls of the remains strewn over half the village. Duly sanctified remains, blasted from the hallowed ground beside the ancient edifice to God—the church which had protected them through the centuries, that was now a fantastic, gutted outline around an altar-table still supporting a few scorched ornaments amidst the wreckage of the collapsed choir.

When we came back from the outpost the Germans were unpleasant. They shelled and shot at us with deliberation while we hugged the unimpressive line of trees. Prince Alexander, though his nerve was as cool as if we were on a treasure hunt, found the protection of those trees inadequate. I have the recollection of a tall figure whose sister was Britain's Queen, dodging every now and then behind a little tree some nine or ten inches in diameter while bullets and shell splinters sang brief but wicked songs.

"I wish," sputtered Prince Alexander with a certain emphasis, "they grew bigger trees here and spaced 'em more frequently!"

The Other Side of the Wire

One night in Furnes I was taken by Captain Goldsmith of G.H.Q. to look at a civilian he had secreted somewhere behind our Mission headquarters. Goldsmith wanted Colonel Bridges to see the civilian, but I was alone in the office. So he led me in the dark to a back room in the Hôtel de Ville where a sombre little man sat on the edge of a wooden bench.

"Mark him well and remember his features," said Goldsmith. "For he is being 'sent out' and when he comes back—*if* he comes back—it may be necessary that someone here should recognize and identify him."

He was a sad-looking little man, narrow-eyed with dark cropped hair and a straggly yellow mustache. It was interesting to hear the final instructions given him in the dimly lighted room where witnesses for the Inquisition once waited their call. He was going to Bruges, behind the German lines.

He did not come back. But it happened that I was to see him again. Not in Furnes, nor anywhere I expected soon to be. I met him, some five weeks later, in the shadows of Bruges Cathedral.

The Battle of the Yser settled into stalemate and I went to Calais for a few days' rest. The flat country, usually depressing, was extraordinarily beautiful under a two-inch blanket of white, all the trees and bushes covered with fresh snow, frozen and glistening in the unaccustomed sunlight. Flocks of grey-backed crows, the big hooded crows of the northlands, walked boldly about on the crusted surface of the snow. General Foch whirled past in his bright red Rolls-Royce, trailing an ethereal cloud that sparkled as though of powdered diamonds. In a superb wintry sunset with a pink sliver of a new moon hanging low, the grimness of war seemed oddly remote.

While strolling across the Place d'Armes in Calais a voice in English behind me caught my attention. "I suspect that you are being closely observed," it said. "This town is reeking with 'their' agents."

I looked sharply around, to find that I was being tracked by Lieutenant Alec Waley of the Carrier Pigeon Service at G.H.Q. The last time I had seen him he was crawling, large, bald and monocled, through dung-filled Belgian lofts after elusive birds. "You don't know how damn temperamental these blasted pigeons can be," Waley had then observed.

This was about the time his French sergeant had advised against his choice of a certain pigeon for a specially delicate mission. "*Mais non, mon Lieutenant,*" the sergeant had protested; "*ce Henri n'est pas un pigeon sérieux!*" (this Henry is not a serious-minded pigeon!) Swift and keen of eye but unreliable, a philanderer among message-carriers of serious purpose.

Now I looked at Waley in a vaguely startled way. "You're stalking me as though I were a strayed pigeon," I remarked lightly. "I'm not a blinking pigeon. What about a drink?"

"I have a message for you from Colonel Kirke," said Waley. "It is very private." We repaired to the inner office of the Commissaire of Police and for an hour talked on the subject of Colonel Kirke's message. Waley kept glancing over his shoulder every minute or two, which soon had me doing the same thing. The message was very private indeed. It came as a complete surprise. That evening I tramped nearly ten miles alone, milling the matter over in my mind. Before I returned I had reached a decision.

By the fifth of December I was in Brussels. A little more than a month later, after returning to England at Christmastime to report, I descended at the Hotel Adlon in Berlin.

It was an intensely interesting experience to wander among the armed forces of the opposite side whose components I had seen only as prisoners being herded into barbed-wire camps, as dead and wounded on the fields, as shadowy forms moving in distant trenches or advancing deployed across the flat meadows by the Yser. I watched, at first in a sort of daze, their formations marching past in full-throated song, uncovered as their colors swept by (lest someone ram a bayonet into my behind), dined and drank with German officers and listened to the damnation of England. It was an experience that with somewhat greater maturity I perhaps would not have chosen to repeat under identical circumstances. Yet it afforded so intimate a view of the other side of the picture, such an insight into the mental attitude of those people who were tramping rough-shod over the fair face of Europe, as I would not have wished to forgo.

Practically without exception they held that the war had been forced upon them by the machinations of their continental neighbors.

The war was none of their making, except in so far as the steady cultural and commercial progress of the German people had inspired jealousies on the part of others who were not keeping pace. They maintained, and mostly seemed to believe, that the French had been the first to invade Belgium. They did not hate the French—a misguided people who appeared to need another lesson as in 1870–71, a lesson which this time they would not so quickly forget. The Napoleonic days when French forces swept through and repartitioned a disunited Germany were over, they asserted.

They were mildly annoyed by the Belgians, a silly little nation that had deliberately chosen the wrong side. But the English had betrayed the Anglo-Saxon race. The English they hated. Yet even that hate was more in evidence among the officer classes than the ranks.

And though their attitude seemed somewhat naïve under the circumstances, it was nevertheless an attitude of firm conviction. Those who had told them what to think had done an effective task. It is perhaps only with Germans that quite so thorough a job of predigested thinking can be done for an entire nation.

I went on a number of gay officers' parties in Berlin where the wrath of God upon England was called for in lusty toasts. These were usually followed by what my companions held to be typical examples of English culture as expressed in the English language.

"*Gott strafe England!*" they shouted, clinking their glasses: "WATER-CLOSET! GODDAM!" Throughout the evening every so often they would get together, arms around one another's shoulders like college lads giving a cheer, and yell in unison, "*Ein, zwei, drei:* WA-A-TER—CLO-SET!" This never failed to bring loud guffaws. Doubtless that elegant expression was recalled by the generally international use of "W.C." on the doors of public toilets.

The familiar inscription was then being effaced throughout the Fatherland in favor of a more native appellation. When Britain declared war on Germany after the violation of Belgian neutrality, the officers and men of the regiment named in honor of Queen Victoria tore the emblematic VR's (Victoria Regina) from their shoulder-straps and threw them down the drains. The rest of the country followed suit by removing "W.C." from public toilets.

Berlin at that time was occupied by a horde of German-American Jews, hopeful of making handsome profits from the emergency, and more anti-Allied than the most Prussian of officers. There were also a remarkable number—and the German capital has never lacked their allurements—of predatory evening-ladies who offered their commodity in every place and circumstance. The Adlon from lunch-time on was filled with them, of the more expensive variety. They ogled one from the bar, from the tea-room, from the writing-room, in the elevators, in the corridors, in one's bedroom when they could bribe a servant to momentary forgetfulness with a pass-key. Some were extremely good-looking and very smartly dressed, those of the latter category usually Austrian or Hungarian. At times they were strongly tempting, but the fear of an undefinable position kept me on a narrow if not very straight path.

And in the Friedrichstrasse, where the convalescing wounded paraded throughout the day, they were so thick from about five o'clock on that one young Bavarian officer punned the situation in the quaint English of which he was inordinately proud: "Our Friedrichstrasse in der daytime mit der wounded is filled, und by night mit der fallen!"

But there was nothing casual about the way in which the nation or its capital were taking the war. The spirit of self-sacrifice, the national leaning towards regimentation which the leaders so effectively exploit, were everywhere apparent. I met none who doubted the outcome of German victory, though many felt that the struggle might end with the German arms still holding much the same lines as they held then, in January 1915.

The Russians they considered stupid and inefficient barbarians, good cannon-fodder without proper equipment, sacrificed in huge masses to graft and inept leadership—which was not, at that time, so very far from the fact.

In Berlin, from a source that was high (just one step down in descent from the "all-highest"), well-informed and temporarily indiscreet over numerous bottles of wine, I gained some very interesting information about German aviation expansion and the program for the bombing of London from Zeppelins. I visited the depot bases of many of the German corps, formed a fairly close idea of replacement plans and of the then scarcely credited potential manpower that could be trained, organized, equipped and sent out not only to replenish but to swell the combatant forces. I passed through munitions centers on the Rhine and elsewhere, including a portion of the vast Krupp works at Essen, and industrial plants in many parts of western Germany. The most effective mobilization of industry the world had ever known up till then was infinitely impressive, frightening in its scope, its determination.

I was followed on and off, and watched, I knew; but only once arrested. Two days before I planned to leave Germany I became the guest for six extremely uncomfortable hours of the *Kommandantur* at Weimar. Normally I made no notes by day. But that day, from over-confidence and having picked up more data than an unretentive memory for figures could keep clear, I pencilled some rough jottings on a card carried in the pocket of my overcoat. They were unintelligible to anyone but myself, yet it would have been difficult to explain them as innocuous travel or shopping memoranda.

I realized, when invited to accompany a plain-clothes Inspector to the Kommandantur, that I had somehow to get rid of that card. And this I did, managing to slip it under a desk blotter and later to retrieve it. I never quite knew how this came about, in the presence of four highly suspicious officials, without its being remarked. I have no apti-tude for sleight-of-hand. It seemed to happen automatically, almost without thought. Yet my mind was seething with thoughts that brought moments of acute discomfort.

The searching of my person was Germanically thorough. It re-vealed nothing incriminatory. To four hours of exhaustive questioning I replied with specious naïveté.

I had no very good excuse for being in Weimar, but maintained that if the authorities did not want travellers it was up to them to stop one when he presented a ticket, not for the traveller to decide whether or not he might be welcome. They had reports of my presence at perhaps half the places to which I actually had been, including four or five of no military interest visited advisedly. My chief line of defense lay in several letters to and from certain prominent German industrialists. These provided a useful background.

The letters concerned the ostensible purpose of my trip, which was to interest the German industrialists and through them the Govern-ment in a process for producing motor fuel from coal. I knew very little about the process, but had learned a fairly plausible patter. Probably it would not work. Its beauty from my point of view lay in the fact that it would need months of expensive experimentation to prove or dis-prove it.

In connection with this matter, some acquaintances sent a telegram just before I left England to their associates in Edinburgh. I did not see the message until after they had despatched it. The wording was unfortunate for wartime, though its purpose was to be helpful to War Office Intelligence. *"Friend of ours leaving for Frankfurt have you anything for Kaiser,"* it read. It created something of a stir in the various counter-espionage departments of the British Isles. Kaiser was the name of my acquaintance's former correspondent in Frankfurt. The counter-espionage bird-dogs thought the reference was to *the* Kaiser.

After six hours of interrogation and study of the documents with which I was provided, the Major-Kommandant of Weimar was persuaded of the innocent purpose of my trip. The plain-clothes Inspector was not, but his voice was overruled. Happily there was no Gestapo in those days.

I knew, of course, that my hotel room and baggage would be gone though with a fine-tooth comb while I was being detained. This thought did not worry me unduly, but when at length I was released the first thing I did was to saunter back to the hotel and brush my teeth. I had inscribed from time to time certain notations in an improvised code on a strip of oiled paper about half an inch wide, at night under the bedcovers, with a hard pencil and a small electric torch for light. Except during the actual process of notation the strip of paper reposed tightly rolled in the center of a large tube of evil-tasting German toothpaste. It was tiresome and messy having to remove half the toothpaste in bed each time I wrote up my notes, then insert the roll of paper and replace the paste through the bottom of the tube. But it made a neat container which if squeezed merely expelled toothpaste from one end or the other.

I breathed more freely on finding that the searchers of my baggage had not tampered with that tube. Yet through this temporary satisfaction there paraded certain thoughts in no way making for repose, thoughts of too many weak points in my armor for any tranquillity until I could see an international frontier disappearing behind. I more than half expected to find a posse waiting to hale me back from the little border station just short of the Netherlands boundary. But there was no posse, and neither before nor since have I crossed any frontier with such a feeling of relief.

The tour I had made in occupied Belgium before proceeding to Germany had been really very entertaining. I went up the valley of the Meuse in German troop trains, heard the young enemy soldiers rejoicing in the beauty of the slopes around Namur. *"Schön, schön!"* they kept crying. *"Ach, sehr schön!"*

We passed the burnt and gaping ruins of the church in Dinant, of various buildings in other places over which had rolled the tide of invasion. And of these they said, "It is a pity; yes, it is sad, but military necessity, you know . . ." What did *they* know? They did not know in the least what it was all about, those ill-informed, enthusiastic youths. And they differed from their Nazi-inculcated successors of twenty-five years later.

"We will fix that up after the war, when we return the country to the Belgians. For we don't want territory," they said. "We would live at peace with our neighbors. But they, our neighbors, would not let us." Just as the sound of the cannon was in no wise different on that side of the line, so the field-grey rank and file regarded themselves as defending the cause of an aggrieved nation.

One evening in Bruges I ran into my rodent-faced acquaintance of the inner room of the Hotel de Ville at Furnes. He did not expect me and was considerably perturbed on first sight. Later we met in the shadows of the Cathedral. He poured a lot of miscellaneous information into my ear, most of it on troop movements of too local and temporary a character for my purpose. I had no means of getting information out except as I went out myself. British General Staff Intelligence had organized an efficient grapevine into Holland for the rapid relaying of such identifications. Most of its elements were unknown to each other. They were entirely unknown to me.

The rest of what he told me concerned the peril of his own situation. This I could readily appreciate but could do very little about. I heard that he was apprehended not long after.

And in Antwerp, one dark night when I was walking from a restaurant back to my hotel down an unlighted street, there came a whisper in French over my shoulder from some black door-alcove.

"Be very, very careful! This is a friend. You are being closely watched!" And was gone. I never saw its face. It gave one an eerie feeling, that disembodied voice of warning in the pitch dark. My room had evidently been visited in my absence. Yet I slept well and nothing came to interfere with my orderly departure through the electrified flood-lighted wire along the Dutch frontier.

But when I came out of Germany I breathed a very deep sigh of relief. No more of that, I whispered to myself. That episode is over! The friendly air of England had scarcely been inhaled before I was arrested as an enemy agent.

The War Office bailed me out in fairly short order. I spent a week writing my second report. It was received with a good deal of interest. I was told that parts of it were shown to Lord Kitchener, the Secretary of State for War—"K of K," whom once I had asked on the telephone, "And who the hell might *you* be?"

The most important parts—the estimates of German manpower, of the enemy's replacement program to meet the "war of attrition" counted on to crush German aggression, of munitions production; the aerial warfare plans and some phases of the mobilization of all industrial effort, were at the time somewhat discounted by the powers that were. Yet those prognostications turned out to be pretty accurate.

Sixteen days after submitting my second report I returned to France a Second Lieutenant in His Britannic Majesty's forces. On 14 April, my birthday, I was assigned to duty in the Ypres salient, and remained in that graceless area for more than two and a half years.

The Mistake of Corporal Beaulieu

Ypres, during the first weeks following the battle that began on 22 April 1915, was one of the least hospitable spots on this globe. It was burning fiercely in a dozen different places. Because of the incessant bombardment, it was "out-of-bounds" to all troops except for detachments of sappers trying to clear a passage through the debris, an occasional burying detail, or small ration parties when a momentary lull offered them a chance of getting through. The upturned streets were mostly impassable, though the sapper detachments strove heroically (we had no bulldozers in those days) to fill the shell-holes with the wreckage of human habitations, loose paving blocks and fragments of Gothic sculpture.

The air reeked of lyddite, of wet, burned debris and decomposition. Savage, half-starved dogs prowled the streets, feeding off the bodies of horses and other animals that the harassed burial details had not covered with chloride of lime. For a while I was there alone, living the existence of a hounded woodchuck, scuttling from the shelter of one cellar to another. Every so often one of the infrequent ration parties would report being fired at by snipers as they scurried across the Grand' Place and down the rubble-cluttered street to the Menin Gate. The men reporting these stories were too experienced to have mistaken shell-splinters or shrapnel for bullets.

"The buggers is snipin' at us in Wipers, all right!" they insisted.

From one such party I took a soldier by name of Private Morgan to point out exactly where he and his companions had been potted at within the walls of Ypres. We crawled, crabwise, along the south side of the Grand' Place towards the Menin Gate. Our progress was spasmodic under the heavy shelling which kept us flinging ourselves on our faces in the debris. The Grand' Place was a scene of utter desolation. Its middle was spread with the remnants of a 4.5 howitzer ammunition limber that had connected a few days before with a direct hit. The whole of the contents had exploded in one vicious burst. Pieces of horseflesh lay about in shapes not readily distinguishable as having belonged to six separate animals. A burial party had removed the remains of the crew in a blanket.

We were making moderately good progress between shells when there came a thinnish, unmistakable sing. "Br-zz—*ping-g-g!*" it went. I looked around but saw no place from where it might have come. It was rifle fire, sure enough. And then there came two more. The second passed close behind my head to strike the corner of a smashed wooden shutter projecting from a heap of rubble. I took a hasty glance at the hole through the woodwork, got a fair line on whence the bullet had come, and scuttled on. The third shot missed Private Morgan by a couple of inches. Neither of us was enjoying this especially.

We edged around the Place but could find no possible shelter for snipers on the opposite side. There was nothing but brick and mortar lying in jagged chunks, scarcely twelve feet high in the largest piles, over all of which we crawled.

I tried to remember what had formerly been in that sector of the Grand' Place. There came to my mind a second-rate hostelry with a good wine-cellar, in whose taproom junior officers used to forgather before 22 April to drink a few bottles of a tender Pomerol. The hostelry was styled the Hôtel de l'Epée Royale. Nothing now remained to indicate where even the foundations had been. But one evening I had gone down into its cellar to help the proprietor bring up another half-dozen bottles. The wine lay on shelves in deep niches; the stairway was at the back. And I remembered that there was some four inches of window space looking out over the sidewalk, for I had seen legs moving jerkily past the narrow opening, casting distorted shadows from the rays of a shaded light that glimmered in the entry above.

There was no trace of all that now. But after a careful survey, crawling on our bellies, we found a tiny opening which the debris had not quite covered. It was just a dark spot, the size of a hand placed sideways; and there was a narrow stretch of sidewalk clear of rubble before it.

"Ha!" I muttered. "In there is where the snipers are holding out!" It was the only possible location. But how to get into it?

While we wormed over the heaped wreckage in the back—it seemed for an endless day but may perhaps have been an hour—a score or more shells burst on the ruins, unpleasantly close. We retired a short distance until the range shifted. They were medium-sized shells, 105 mm. howitzers. I decided to plug up the front opening and leave it at that for a while until we could get more hands to dig, and a supply of grenades. But when we came back from the ungracious shelter of adjoining debris one of the shells had flung aside several wagon-loads of brick and mortar, exposing a hole the size of a derby hat just about where I had guessed the cellar stairs should be. I reached down and at full arm's length fingered the edge of a stone step.

We dug out the hole by hand until it was perhaps three feet in diameter, wide enough for a body to pass through slantingly, with the edges of four steps partly uncovered. Down it I shouted in uncouth German: "Come out here, you silly dopes, before we heave a hand-grenade to share amongst you!" But we had no hand-grenades, and there came no response.

Several times I repeated this, with variations, in German, French, English and a guttural mouthing that was an approach to Flemish. Not a sound came out, save the garbled echo flung back against the pounding of my own heart. Yet as I listened with an ear set for anything above those reverberations it seemed as though there was a crunch, as of a step on broken glass, and again repeated. One . . . two . . . like a heron stepping after fish in shallow water.

Into that dark hole I stared with acute distaste, then looked at Private Morgan squatting on his knees awaiting my next move. Now why the hell would *you* have to be here, I thought. You rabbit-faced, unimaginative little blighter. If only I were alone . . . the sensible thing would be to go away, fetch some grenades and additional help, do the thing up properly. I began to wish more shells would fall on us. But no more came. They were touching up a different quarter. And the trustful, expectant face of that soldier forced me to some sort of gesture.

Without enthusiasm I announced: "I'm going down. I'll call you if I need help. Don't shoot at anything unless you're sure what it is. It might be I." Further contemplation was merely making the prospect more repugnant.

"Yes, sir," said Private Morgan. And from the uninviting depths there seemed to come the faint sound of another crunch on broken glass.

Feet first, arms tight to the sides, I went down into the slanting hole. There was no other way to it. My right hand gripped a cocked automatic, my left a feeble electric torch. My body completely filled the hole. On about the fifth step the loose rubble slipped out from under foot. I coasted down the next eight or ten steps on my back. There was a sharp flash of light with a loud report, and a glimpse, instantly blotted out, of a rifle barrel pointed quarteringly past my right side. Then I managed to spring, firing at the same time into the dark without aim. I struck an erect body which fell over backwards, myself on top of it; and I remember bashing its head against the hard ground. Holding tight to that inert figure with the muzzle of my pistol jammed into its neck, I yelled for Private Morgan. The little man came bumping down the steps. But nothing more happened.

It was very dark in the cellar. I had dropped my flashlight. With exquisite caution we looked over the situation as far as the light of matches would carry, which was not far. First off it revealed that the body to which I was clinging was dressed as a Canadian corporal. There was no trace of any bullet wound from my shot in the dark. He seemed to be dead, the back of his head smashed and damp with blood, but we trussed him with our belts to be on the safe side.

We did not yet know what else might be in that cellar. There was utter silence. I retrieved my torch—a solid piece of equipment: even the bulb had not broken. Then we combed the cellar in detail. There appeared to be no one else in it. The floor was covered an inch or more deep with broken bottles and red wine. Under the small, unblocked opening of the little window giving onto the Grand' Place were about two dozen empty cartridge cases, and another Canadian rifle.

The bricked-up wine niches had been torn open and emptied. Our search ended without finding any other signs of life. In the right-hand corner by the foot of the stairs was a heap of coal, beside it a pair of boots. I kicked the boots; they merely waggled. They were attached to feet. We pulled at the feet. Morgan dug away the coal, and together we dragged out the body of a Canadian private. One side of his head was blown off. The body was soft and warm; that man had not been long dead.

"Blimey!" said Private Morgan.

I began then to picture the affair. It was towards the pile of coal the corporal—if he *was* a corporal—had fired when I slid down the stairs, blocking any light from the hole. The two had been in the cellar since possibly the second or third day of the battle, which would make ten or eleven days. Very likely they *were* Canadians, authentic battle-stragglers who had lost their unit in the mêlée of the attack, had taken refuge in the cellar from the shelling and had lived on red wine after the building had come down above them, sealing them in.

They had sniped through the small gap of window at passing parties in the belief that these were the enemy. Too drunk to recognize uniforms, thinking to hold out to the end, they had sought to sell their lives as dearly as they might.

And then had come some quarrel. The one had killed the other, buried his body under the heap of coal. This could not have been many hours before I slid down the steps. At the noise I made, the corporal in his drunken stupor probably thought the man he had put away was coming back to attack him; wherefore he shot quarteringly past me in the general direction of the coal heap. That mistake may have had a certain bearing on my subsequent activities. For, drunk as he doubtless was, he could not very well have missed had he aimed at me with a rifle from four feet away.

This conjecture as to what had taken place proved correct, in so far as it was ever possible to establish the sequence of detail. While we were still examining the dead body, the trussed one started to groan. We got him out with considerable difficulty, and none too gently. He was a tough specimen. To my surprise he lived; to be duly court-martialed on the charge of murder and sentenced to death.

His record in action had been excellent. On the strength of this the reviewing board suspended the sentence. He returned to the lines as a private and, I later heard, was killed in circumstances that did him credit. Corporal Beaulieu was one of a number of cases of battle-stragglers separated from their units while fighting, taking to cellars for shelter, and—with wine and beer their only sustenance for days—firing on their own forces in the belief that they were surrounded by the enemy. I located several more in *estaminet* cellars in Ypres, all pretty drunk but full of fight. After that we had no further reports of sniping in the town.

At the field general court martial the prisoner was invited to name any witnesses he might wish to have called to testify in his behalf. He thought for a long while. Then, very slowly: "Why, yes," he said, "there was . . . a private . . . with me in . . . that cellar. . . . I think . . . I would like . . . to have *him* called." It came out that, so far as he could remember, only one other person had been with him in the cellar at any time. This was the soldier of whose murder he was now accused. Corporal Beaulieu recalled nothing whatever of the incident in which the one witness he cared to summon in his defense had been effaced by his own hand.

Sergeant Koch's Tactical Error

Sergeant Koch of King Edward's Horse was an Afrikander whose father had fought the British in the Boer War. He himself had served as a noncommissioned officer in the German Colonial forces of East Africa, and had received a German medal for gallantry in tribal action. He spoke both German and *Uitlander* Dutch, which was useful in Flanders. He had a liking for patrol duty between the lines, and had come to my special force on his own application with the praises and appreciation of his officers. His regiment was at that time dismounted, doing odd details in British First Army.

We were out together one night with an eight-man patrol to look for an underground passage reputedly connecting one of the eastern casements of the Ypres ramparts with a subterranean storehouse, built by Vauban as part of the Ypres defenses. The vault was believed to be located somewhere between the lines due east of Ypres, which would have placed it roughly 3400 yards from the Menin Gate. We went out by "Hellfire Corner," thence by communication trenches along the Roulers railway embankment, and finally crawled through our wire to look over a couple of craters, one of which might have some connection with the fabulous passage. (It was not entirely fabulous: I found later that such an underground way did exist, though long disused and choked with earth and refuse; but the vaulted chamber lay well inside our lines.)

One of the craters made a convenient breathing spot for patrols. The breathing was not very good because of the remains liquefying in the crater's lower part; but the rim at least afforded a tiny refuge from snipers in the naked expanse of no-man's land lit with ambient star-shells. Its bottom was filled with a greenish seepage, gurgling and noisome.

German patrols also visited that crater at times, and then ours, if aware of this, avoided it: honor among thieves of entrenched privacy. Often two opposing patrols would pass close by one another, moving turtle-wise in the night, and neither would disturb the other on its lawful occasions. For an aggressive attitude, presupposing fairly equal numbers, would merely bring retaliation and render patrol duty still less attractive thereafter. It was only patrollers who felt such compunctions, of course.

But on this night it was desired that our patrol should bring back a prisoner for identification. And though we failed to get a live one, we managed to upset the patrolling protocol of the sector. After resting for a while within the shelter of that unlovely pit, we crept up its inner slope, each gripping an automatic pistol. As we neared the rim my outreaching right arm shoved the muzzle of my pistol almost into a face that suddenly appeared over the edge from the other side: a face under a heavy German helmet, wide-eyed and aghast for a split-second.

There was no conscious effort as my trigger finger contracted. And doubtless because of the tensity of one's nerves, there seemed to come no sound above the general crackle and popping all around us. But there was a curious effect of the face slowly coming apart, the upper portion with the helmet and a monstrous pair of eyes spurting upwards, leaving a jaw without superstructure protruding over the crater's rim. My own face must have reflected something of the surprise of that other, fantastically disintegrating some twelve inches beyond my outstretched right hand. It seemed most odd that the other should split itself in two like that, in silence.

"*God verdomme!*" I heard Sergeant Koch mutter behind my left shoulder. "You have spoilt him!" Koch had been particularly keen to get a prisoner. And we knew we were in for something after that. The spoilt patroller would hardly be alone.

We scrambled to the rim, and from this vantage point blew the rest of the German patrol down the gently sloping side before they knew what it was all about. They left three more dead. We did not lose a man, then. But the devil's own tattoo broke loose before we got back under the searching star-shells to our own lines. And two of our eight were hit—one drilled clean through by a machine-gun burst, the other punctured by shrapnel and raising a fearful din about it. Two of the patrol managed to bring the latter in alive. They did this at no small additional risk to themselves. One of them was Koch. His team-mate kept pleading tensely with the wounded man: "For Christ's sake will you shut up yer bleedin' mouth, you silly bastard? You'll be 'avin' the lot of us stretched out yet!"

The wounded man died soon after they got him to the trench. And then the men who had risked their lives to get him in, with others of his own company manning the fire-step, shrugged their shoulders; and someone grunted: "Well, there's another bloody lump o' meat to put under before it starts to stink us out!" It was often like that as one became callous to death. Men took the most desperate risks over and over again to carry back to trenches and field dressing stations those who still had a chance to live. But when the last breath was drawn, what remained became merely carrion; something to be disposed of hurriedly before its presence should add to the other miseries one had to bear in those grisly trenches. Such callousness was the offset to the mental collapse termed 'shell-shock.'

Patrolling was always a highly speculative venture, with a strong likelihood at the end of being shot at by undiscerning sentries nervously manning one's own fire-steps. We contributed little that night to make it less speculative in the sector east of Ypres.

I had grown quite fond of Sergeant Koch during months of close association in action of such sorts. And so I was sincerely distressed when trouble came to him in the shape of an Assistant Provost Marshal from First Army area. The charge was forgery and misappropriation of funds; specifically of the proceeds of a large personal draft—for £200, I believe it was—in favor of a wealthy Canadian mate of the sergeants' mess of his old unit.

Koch, it appeared, had learned of the expected arrival of the draft through the indiscretion of his messmate in promises of gay parties to come. He then had himself detailed as mail clerk for the unit, opened all the Canadian's incoming letters until the right one arrived, meanwhile acquiring proficiency in imitating his colleague's signature. With the latter's pay-book 'borrowed' for the time being as identification, he cashed the draft at the Credit Lyonnais in Béthune.

This initial success he followed up with a tactical error. He took two girls employed by the bank out on a festive party, during which the consumption of champagne was notable even for wartime. After this he applied for and obtained transfer to serve with my special establishment in Second Army.

It was months before he was tracked down. I insisted on fair identification, and paraded seven sergeants in a large, dimly lighted council chamber of the Mairie at Poperinghe. It was not easy to find in a hurry six other sergeants approaching the stature of my big blond Boer. The two girls whom the A.P.M. had brought up recognized Koch at once.

"It's he!" they cried, pointing to Koch. "*C'est bien lui,* the big, handsome one!"

He called me as a character witness. I gave him an excellent character for the period he had served under me—gallant, energetic and dependable. But the court found him guilty. He was sentenced to three years' imprisonment and reduced to the ranks. The loss of his sergeant's stripes hurt him most of all. I never saw him again. The imprisonment was suspended, and I believe he, too, was later killed as an infantryman in the lines. After the sentence he thanked me for my testimony.

"*Women, God verdomme!*" he blurted out with infinite disgust. "You turn your pockets inside out for 'em and *that's* what they do for you! Be *damned* to all women!" said *Private* Koch.

Champagne with the Corporal of the Guard

In the late spring of 1915 when it looked as if the Ypres salient—which was nothing more than a deadly shell-trap—would have to be abandoned, I was ordered to run a secret telephone line underwater or underground from the Etang de Dickebusch through Ypres and out beyond. The Etang was a pond dug in the year 1320 to supply the town of Ypres with drinking water. From it the line had to follow the course of the Dickebuschbeek, a little brook that flowed into the Ypres moat, and thence to be led around the southern section of the moat and along the vaulted Yperlee beneath the city. Because of secrecy the work of laying the line could be done only by night. It took three nights and a bit over, with the aid of Lieutenant Lindley of Second Army Signals during the first two. Since other things filled my days, I had no chance to sleep for seventy-four hours.

I wonder whether I could have carried on that long without feeling excessive fatigue had I eaten any regular meals. I kept gnawing now and then on slabs of cake chocolate and hard biscuits, washed down with gulps from a water-bottle filled with the splendid ration rum of those days, long aged in wooden casks and mellow as honey. Once the job was done, a full meal in an advanced artillery dugout put me out completely for ten hours.

On the first night Lindley and I laid the line down the Dickebusch-beek to the moat. On the second we took it along the southern expanse of the moat to the spillway under the ramparts by the Lille Gate. To this end I had procured a boat, an ancient, square-ended rowboat with many shell-splinter holes through its flat bottom and straight sides. We plugged up the holes as best we could; it still leaked like cheesecloth. The constant efforts of one man bailing barely kept it afloat. Lindley did the bailing to an accompaniment of smothered blasphemy.

"If you know of a better boat, go get it!" I remarked. There were no better boats, nor any other, in the moat of Ypres. On its sides was painted *Ecole de Natation*—"Swimming School." I had found the tired hulk in the foul, reeking backwater at the northeast extremity of the moat where once there had been a swimming school.

"As a lifeboat, it's not a bad swimming school in itself," commented Lindley without enthusiasm. We called it the "Lucy," since our cruise in it took place a few days after the sinking of the *Lusitania* with nearly all hands on board. We were not superstitious.

The *Lucy* was equipped with one oar resembling a frayed slab of palmetto, and a life-preserver that sank like an anchor when we tested it out. Across the fetid waters of the moat we sculled the wretched craft at about a mile an hour through a night whose darkness had the density of black marble, illumined by a ghostly silver semicircle of star-shells on three sides and red pillars of smoke from burning quarters of the town that glowed fiercely under the ebon sky.

Part way around the bend a gaunt section of wall was thrown into sharp relief by the fire behind. Through it a shell had pierced a jagged hole fashioned rather like a shield—a crimsoned shield across which passed silhouettes of mounted men two by two, six-horse teams straining on their traces, the barrels of cannon and tops of artillery limbers. The silhouettes appeared out of the darkness, were outlined for a moment as they moved slowly past the shield-shaped opening against a scarlet background, disappeared again into the darkness beyond. It was like an impressionistic stage setting, utterly unreal, weirdly picturesque.

From a nearby dugout in the ramparts came the incongruous strains of a piano, not badly played. An unknown British soldier was running practised hands over the keys while Ypres burned, a nostalgic British soldier, striking chords on a piano toilsomely removed from some shell-torn house in town; with bursts of high-explosives and the doleful howls of an abandoned dog as his accompaniment. The music lent an odd, Neronean touch to that strange scene of unreality.

We had a rough passage under the two stone causeways across the moat at the Menin and Lille Gates. Both were being heavily shelled with 6-inch shrapnel mixed with high-explosives. In running these gantlets the remarkable sluggishness of the *Lucy* was a fair test of one's fatalism.

"Liking it?" I called to Lindley.

"Why . . . not awfully! Are you?"

"Well . . . not particularly!" I responded.

Three times during the night we beached our craft just before the leaky hulk filled up with water and was about to sink.

The third night, when I took the line over the spillway from the moat through a passage under the ramparts and down the vaulted Yperlee, rain was falling in steady Flanders fashion. The smell of wet burnt debris hung heavy on the air. Laying that section called for two operations, since the passage was blocked by a heavy iron grille embedded in the ancient stonework. At the upper end, by the outlet from the moat, a very old and rusty chain attached to the sluice-gate let one down monkey-fashion into about four feet of water. From there the wire could be passed through the grille and later be spliced on the other side. Some forty yards from the passage there was fortuitous access into the Yperlee through a jagged shell-hole in the vaulting.

The Yperlee is a brook that runs under Ypres from south to north, completely covered over by the structure of the city. It debouches into the Yser Canal on the northern edge of town. A short way from the Lille Gate the stream divides in two branches which join again not far beyond. On the little island thus formed was located, early in the tenth century, the whole town of Ypres, a group of mean houses clustered for protection around the Castle of the Three Towers of Baudouin-the-Bald, 2nd Count of Flanders. From those small beginnings the town had grown to 200,000 souls in the thirteenth century by virtue of its flourishing cloth trade. The political and religious struggles of the next three centuries ruined this trade, and the population dropped to a remnant of 5000 impoverished hangers-on. It had revived to about 19,000 at the outbreak of the war.

With the growth of the city the course of the Yperlee disappeared beneath the houses and paved streets built over it, nearly forgotten save as an overflow channel and a convenient sewer for the habitations located near to its flow. For though Flanders towns were not usually equipped with sewage systems, holding to their ancient cesspits of early days, the Yperlee served such purpose for those who happened to live above it.

I started off with a pair of waders and in less than a hundred feet fell into a deep hole, filled up the waders, and got thoroughly wetted to the skin. It was next to impossible to operate in that weight of saturated clothing; so I doffed everything but boots and socks, left the soaked clothes somewhere under cover, and re-entered the Yperlee naked save for a haversack and a canteen of rum. The latter item helped combat the nauseous vapors of the vault.

The Yperlee was a grim passage, rank with the accumulated filth of a thousand years, lined and festooned with queer growths, its bottom overlaid with discarded pieces of metal from battle-axes to bits of bicycle. The slowly flowing water, thick and poisonous, was covered with an evil brown scum over which crawled black Things with many outstretching legs.

When I came to the point, marked by a small shell-hole above, where a branch of the wire had to pass through the side of the vault and the foundations into the cellar of a house at 13 Rue Basse, I had come close to the end of my own rope. The foul atmosphere, made no sweeter by the stirring up of ten centuries of deposits, got me feeling very sick. Unlovely echoes threw back from my splashings: gruesome chortles, sinister and horrid. I sensed an acute need to get into open air. Quite definitely I did not want to pass out and drown in that noisome channel.

Lurching back to the shell-hole exit, I managed with fast-failing strength to clamber out over its rough edge of shattered brick and cement. The struggle removed most of what little skin still adhered to my frame. The outside air was reviving, though it reeked of gas and lyddite like rotten pears, against a basic odor of damp, burnt wreckage. Very soon I awoke to the fact that the quarter around the hole in the Yperlee vaulting was being viciously shelled. Taking a deep breath I made a dash for the casemate in the ramparts by the Lille Gate.

Just before I reached this point of comparative safety a 6-inch shell made an all-but-direct hit where at the moment I happened to be stretched out flat on a not overfilled stomach. No fragment touched me, I think, though a good many fast-moving pieces of stone and brick did. Crawling from the debris, I made the casemate on the next plunge. There was a sentry stationed within. Two companies in support were then located under the ramparts. The sentry looked a trifle surprised at the storming of his redoubt by a blood-flecked, naked man. I had warned the corporal of the guard early in the evening, some eight hours before, that I was doing special work in the vicinity and did not under any circumstances wish to be disturbed. Now, as I entered, the sentry yelled for the corporal of the guard. I had forgotten that I had nothing on but my boots.

The corporal of the guard recognized me. He asked if I had been hit. "Don't think so," I said. "Not very badly in any case, but I'm feeling a bit weak." He washed me off with an old carriage sponge, using up some six ampoules of iodine on my surface, and threw his greatcoat around me. Then, without expression, he produced a bottle of champagne. It had been looted, of course.

"I'm thinking maybe you'll be needing this, sir," he remarked. I could not think of anything I needed more. I asked if he would share part of it with me.

"I've had mine for tonight, thank you the same, sir," said the corporal of the guard. Squatting on the ground beside a charcoal brazier, naked under the corporal's greatcoat save for my boots, I drank the whole of that champagne in a few great gulps and felt decidedly better.

We did not give up Ypres. My line was not used for the purpose for which it was intended. But from that night I had a more sympathetic feeling toward the military looters in the broad ribbon of devastation euphemistically called "the lines" who had the sound sense and discernment to uncover buried *caches* of champagne. The few extant *caches* would soon have been lost in any case in that continually pounded Empty Space. The corporal apparently had made a fairly good haul.

"Any night you might be passing this way, and feeling a bit done in, I'd be pleased to give you some, sir," said the corporal of the guard.

Bill Mitchell

Where the River Marne is but a tiny stream, purling through lush meadows below the hill-crest town of Chaumont, there nestles alongside one bank a Renaissance shooting lodge known as the Château de Chamarandes. Built for the mistress of a king, its shady arbors have abetted many a court flirtation, its walls have echoed to intimate royal parties gathered to hunt the boar and stag and other game that roam the wooded uplands.

In this picturesque setting Colonel William Mitchell established his headquarters while laying his plans to command the Air Service of the American Expeditionary Force then in formation. Here I joined him on transferring from the British Army. It was a romantic spot, though romance was somewhat tempered by the comparative celibacy of the mess and the frigid temperatures of January 1918, when a glass of water would freeze solid at the breakfast table within six feet of the open fire. The mess was excellent—one could trust Bill Mitchell for that —and brought a succession of guests, at a time, unhappily prolonged, when few A.E.F. messes inspired any great desire to repeat the experience of a meal. It was well stocked with choice liquors and vintage wines. On special guest nights we went in for wild boar and a château Burgundy with notable effect.

Among our more frequent visitors was the rotund Jimmy Logan, then sharing bachelor quarters with Frank McCoy up on Chaumont hill. Whenever Jimmy Logan arrived to partake of our fare Bill Mitchell would insist on segregating the dogs—we had a good number, including my black Belgian griffon "Dickebusch"—lest their morals be corrupted by Jimmy's stories.

"Hold on a minute!" Bill would cry. "Can't have our dogs' characters ruined by lewd and bawdy tales!" The dogs would be shoved out, protesting, to the servants' quarters. "There! Now, Jimmy, shoot your latest!"

Bill Mitchell was the exact opposite of a hide-bound conformist. I had an opportunity to observe this side of his character soon after I joined him. The occasion had a bearing on uniform regulations.

The regulation uniform of the U.S. Army of 1917–18 had not been devised for trench warfare in northern Europe. It was neither practical nor smart. The breeches took a strangle-hold on various parts of one's anatomy, whatever the posture one assumed. The so-called blouse was thin and tight-fitting, with no split behind and so short that the slightest bend on the part of the wearer exposed and accentuated the line of his rear façade. Its pockets were designed to carry nothing of a thickness much greater than a sheet of paper. In the air the stiff, standing collar that choked one's neck at every turn of the head was the invention of the devil.

The Paris-made uniforms in which I turned out were not very strictly regulation. I was prepared, if without marked enthusiasm, to conform to any uniform regulations generally observed. But in this respect Bill Mitchell was not the preceptor to swing one into line. For while I was sometimes criticized for wearing breeches of a lighter shade than my tunics, or "blouses," Bill Mitchell rejoiced in breeches several shades lighter than any of mine. And his tunics were splendid, but far from regulation.

Shortly after I reported to him we made a flight together in a two-seater Spad powered by a Lorraine engine. Few of those contraptions ever came off the assembly line, which perhaps was just as well. The engine was misbehaving as usual, so we made an emergency landing on an airfield that happened at the moment to be in the throes of a visitation by an Inspector General. The Inspector General was an elderly Colonel of the line, very old-school and thoroughly versed in his Regulations. He caught me just after I crawled out of the cockpit, wearing field-boots without spurs.

"Colonel," I attempted to explain, "spurs are useful equipment on a horse, but they're apt to be a dangerous encumbrance among the loose control wires of a Spad." That did not matter to him in the least. I was a field officer. Regulations laid down that field officers wearing field-boots should be equipped with spurs.

"You are improperly dressed and I shall report you accordingly!" snapped the Colonel.

Up then breezed Bill Mitchell, nattily turned out in a chocolate-colored tunic of rough texture with bellows pockets and a deep split in the back of its long skirt. His well-cut breeches were of pale fawn-color; his field-boots, built by Bunting at around $90.00 the pair, were unadorned with any vestige of a spur. The mournful eye of the Inspector General passed up and down this horrid sight. It left the old gentleman aghast and speechless. Not so Bill Mitchell.

"Colonel," Bill cried out cheerfully, "I hope you'll give me warning before you descend on my headquarters for an inspection. For otherwise you might find me with my bow incorrectly strung and my arrows not suitably stacked in their quivers!"

I heard no more about any lack of spurs. Bill Mitchell dragged me away. As we passed the Squadron workshop he called for the sergeant-mechanic.

"Bring piano-wire," he commanded, "and small tools!" Thereupon he devised two pairs of appendages to our field-boots, shaped in the fashion of spurs, with a little twist behind in lieu of a rowel.

"Now," he said, "no one can challenge us with being improperly dressed on *that* score, for there's nothing so far as I know in Regulations that specifies the *size* of spurs we have to wear in airplanes!" And, to my regret, no one ever did again.

Bill Mitchell's expectation of commanding all the combatant elements of the American Air Service (as it was then called) in France had been momentarily clouded by the arrival from the United States of Major Benny Foulois with the temporary rank of Brigadier General. The advent of this officer accompanied by a considerable staff, few of whom had any practical experience in air operations, was a highly explosive topic with my C.O. There was no noticeable love lost between the two camps. Some of the Foulois entourage were capable enough officers in their way, but Bill Mitchell referred to them generically as the "Carpet-baggers" or "that bunch of Nurses' Aides."

In due course General Benny Foulois moved up to Toul with the title of Chief of Air Service, First Army. At the time First Army was not operational, nor was there very much in the way of an Air Service. Bill Mitchell withdrew in a dudgeon to a manor house in the midst of a large wood. From there he conducted two simultaneous wars, international and internal, while exercising command of an anomalous organization called First Brigade, Air Service. He was successful on both fronts. General Benny Foulois was relegated to the Service of Supply, and Colonel William Mitchell took command of all air operations in the Zone of Advance.

Shortly before this occurred I was relieved by General Foulois, without word of warning or explanation, of my command of 1st Observation Group to which Bill Mitchell had appointed me. I reported back somewhat dejectedly to my chief at his *manoir* in the woods.

"Don't you worry," he said. "That bunch of Carpet-baggers are after me, not you. But, goddammit! our Air Service isn't going to be run forever by people with the tactical conception of a pack of Nurses' Aides! Now, I need some Night Reconnaissance. Go organize it."

"May I pick part of the personnel from the Squadrons I know?" I asked.

"Sure, any who'd like to be transferred. You're the Group Commander. But don't denude the Zone of Advance of day-flying pilots!"

"What about flying equipment?" I continued.

"Go get it! Ought to be able to get some in Paris. Try Breguet."

"By Colonel Mitchell's verbal authority?" I asked.

"Certainly! I'll confirm it later in writing if necessary."

"And touching on the matter of transportation," I continued. "I've nothing but 1st Group's Cadillac and I promised to send that back to McNarney from here."

"Now don't start bleating to me about transportation! I haven't enough to keep myself moving, and, as you should know, I have to be on the go all the time!" No one would have accused Bill Mitchell of being static. We happened to be standing then by one of the windows that looked out upon a long, open-fronted shed in which, from left to right, I could count the noses of one 90-h.p. Mercedes runabout, a 70-h.p. Renault landaulet, two Cadillacs, a Fiat light van and a couple of little open Fiats. I let my glance run slowly and perhaps rather obviously along that line of cars, then turned back towards Colonel Mitchell.

"*Hell!*" he cried, "most of those damn things won't run when I need 'em worst. How much longer are you going to hang around here pestering me? Take a car from the end of the line if you must have it, and get started before you think of something else to ask for!"

"From the left end?" I inquired innocently, looking at the Mercedes.

"Good God no! From the *right* end—as you face it from here!" I saluted and he grinned a little. One had to know how to take Bill Mitchell when his usual good humor had been tried. He could be gruff as any Kodiak bear.

"Now don't bother me any more than you have to," he went on. "I want that Night Reconnaissance in a hurry, but I'm having troubles of my own just now, as you know." I did know. "Get on with it; and if I catch you so much as putting a hand on anything but a Fiat down in that shed . . .!" I scuttled off, with what seemed fairly broad verbal powers, my personal kit and one 15-h.p. Fiat touring-car to organize a Night Reconnaissance Group.

The Fiat was a pitiful little wagon after a nicely broken-in Cadillac. It had no power and was rough as a sledge on bad roads. The Air Service had bought some thirteen hundred of them. Warwick Greene, my friend of five years before in the Philippines, was now a Major in charge of transportation allotments to Air Service units. He told me some of his difficulties. No one wanted anything but Cadillacs. One staff sergeant in charge of mechanical transport at an Air Service headquarters which had just received fifteen of the little Fiats looked over these new acquisitions with infinite scorn. He drove one of them about three miles and back, then carefully removed and threw away the fifteen crank-case drain-plugs and called out all his drivers.

"Now you take them goddam Wop cars out and drive 'em till they quits, see?" he instructed. "Won't be very long. And don't you put no more oil in 'em, neither!" After which he reported the Fiats unserviceable and without difficulty persuaded the Transportation Officer to requisition for Cadillac replacements.

Warwick Greene tried to work out in detail General Mitchell's transportation requirements for his headquarters staff. This was after Bill Mitchell had become Chief of Air Service of First Army, *vice* Benny Foulois. He was then a Brigadier General. Warwick proposed a few Cadillacs, some Fiats and a sizable number of Model T Fords. The Fords, he explained, were very handy on rough roads. (Fords were not in those days so well or favorably known as now.) Captain Kelleher, Bill Mitchell's Adjutant, stared at Warwick Greene in amazement.

"*Fords*—good God!" he exploded. "Why, General Mitchell wouldn't have his *baggage* moved in Fords!"

While I was still at Francheville in command of 1st Observation Group, Bill Mitchell arrived unheralded to make an inspection of that command. It was the 14th of July—not at all the day for an inspection, I thought. I had obtained his verbal permission by telephone several days before to absent myself from my station on the afternoon and evening of the French national holiday, but this had slipped his mind.

I had been working at high pressure to round out the keen but unseasoned squadrons of 1st Group into a coherent unit. We had reason to believe that the Germans were going to attack somewhere in our neighborhood on the 15th; but, having made dispositions for such event, I felt that a few hours relaxation would do Paul Meyers, my Operations Officer, and me a world of good. Orders, prepared by Paul, were in our pockets. They read:

Headquarters, Observation Group, 1st Army Corps,
July 14, 1918.
Major Melvin Hall A.S.S.C. and 2nd Lieut. Paul D. Meyers C.A.C. will proceed from this station to Paris, France, for temporary duty in connection with aviation. Upon completion of this duty they will return to their proper station. Motor transportation will be furnished.

By Command of Major Melvin Hall.
OFFICIAL—Emil Schwab, 1st Lieut., Adjutant.

These orders, duly stamped with 1st Group's official seal, appeared to cover the situation. I had just returned from dropping a message on French VIth Army Aéronautique headquarters. My second-in-command was standing by to act in my absence. Sandwiches were ready in two little packages. The Cadillac was fueled and washed. Paul Meyers and I were about to step aboard when there blew in from the east in a cloud of dust a familiar fawn-colored 90-h.p. Mercedes runabout with Colonel William Mitchell at the wheel, accompanied by his French aide-de-camp. The Mercedes was followed by the robin's-egg blue Renault bearing another officer, a sergeant-mechanic and a driver. My Colonel announced that he had come to inspect 1st Group.

We went through the inspection carefully but without wasting a single minute. It was gratifying to be told, as we finished the tour of the field, that he was well pleased, though he did not fail to remark sharply on two or three as yet uncorrected deficiencies which I had been turning into headaches for our supply people. It being then about midday, I invited the Colonel and his party to lunch with us.

"Won't be able to stop," he said. "I've four more inspections to make today!"

"You must eat somewhere," I protested, "and my officers will be very disappointed if you don't stay."

"Sorry, can't today; haven't any time for lunch."

"Then let me give you some sandwiches," I said. "We always have a few ready." We usually had, especially when we were about to take off on a mission of somewhat uncertain possibilities.

"No thanks, won't stop to eat. Must get along now. Good-bye!" He drove away in the 90-h.p. Mercedes followed by the bright blue Renault, heading, as he had come, in an easterly direction. I waited with Paul Meyers while the dust settled, and for a few minutes more in case he should return for something he might have forgotten. Then we hopped aboard the Cadillac and burned up the road to Paris, some 100 kilometers to the southwest. We averaged perhaps 80 kilometers an hour. The road was remarkably free of traffic. We were not once held up at control posts until we came to the gates of the city, and there were stopped for no more than a minute. The "City of Enlightment" opened up to us. I turned to Paul Meyers.

"What about the Crillon as a point of take-off?" I asked.

"Fine!" Paul responded. Leaving the car a short way up the Avenue Gabriel we proceeded to the Hotel de Crillon bar. It was downstairs in those days. Not many people were in it at that hour. I saw only three, resting their elbows on the bar. There was something distinctly familiar in the contour of the central of those three backs, as in the smart cut of uniform and boots. I approached with Paul trailing close behind, then clicked my heels loudly in salute. The three backs turned. The central one was that of Bill Mitchell.

"Colonel," I said, "you got through those other four inspections pretty quickly!" He glared at me for an instant, then burst into a roar of laughter.

"*Hell,*" he cried, "*you* didn't waste much time getting here your-selves! If you'd only told me you were going to Paris we might have come in together! Those other inspections—I didn't say they were purely military, did I?—are right in this town! What'll you drink?" We indicated our pleasure.

"Never did want my responsible officers to act like a bunch of cabbages when they don't have to!" he added. "Not when they deserve a moment's change. I know you can do with one, and I certainly can." We made the other inspections together that afternoon and evening. He was quite right, they were not purely military. We found hordes of friends in the capital. Some of my former haunts had reopened; Bill Mitchell and a rapidly gathering coterie knew a lot of new ones. By midnight we were a large and very cheerful party, celebrating Bastile

Day in appropriate style. But a little before dawn the three of us were
back at our posts of command, considerably refreshed and ready for
any emergency—as Bill Mitchell always was.

That morning at four o'clock the Germans attacked across the Marne
between Chateau Thierry and Dormans in the last great enemy offensive of the war. The first phase of it was just off my immediate front,
but the next days produced plenty of action for us all. Bill Mitchell's
talents were thereafter to have wider scope.

Some people never did understand Bill Mitchell. He was wild as a
night-hawk at times. Few could keep up with him in his restless energy,
his intense concentration on the development of an air arm fit to
contribute in real measure to the winning of the greatest war the world
had yet seen; interspersed with equally intense, whole-hearted play. He
had a rare ability to mix the two, yet not to do this on inappropriate
occasions. And he was one of the most picturesque characters the war
produced.

Those who served under him loyally and well for any length of time
were devoted to him, held infinite respect for his breadth of vision, for
the clear tactical and strategical conception of the man, his imagination, his boundless enthusiasm and immediate grasp of new and threatening situations. He frequently demanded the next-to-impossible and
usually obtained it. He was wholly unperturbed by calamitous reversals.
I went back somewhat dishevelled to his headquarters in the Argonne,
when I was commanding 1st Observation Wing, very late one night
after nearly every mission I had out—including one tranquilly taking
pictures of our heavy artillery emplacements several miles behind our
lines—had been shot or driven down by peculiarly vicious groups of
Fokkers with bright red tails. The von Richthofen "Circus," or a substantial part of it, had come up unannounced to cause us acute discomfort over the stretch of front we then were facing. Their smallest formation seen that afternoon comprised thirteen planes, with many of
twenty-six or more, which was extraordinary for those days and boded
no good.

Bill Mitchell did not blink an eye. But during the night he rearranged the whole tactical order of our operations. We went out next
day with squadron formations as protection, eighteen planes covering
each individual mission. This he followed up with the greatest concentration of aircraft the world had seen up to then, or would see for a

good many years. He borrowed nearly the whole of the British Independent Air Force and the French *Air Groupements* of the East and threw them, with everything we had that would fly, on one gigantic raid. More than 350 aircraft went out in echeloned formation (with 1000-plane strikes a commonplace towards the end of World War II this may seem small, but at that time it was a stupendous effort): every aircraft that was capable of carrying an effective bomb-load heavily laden with high explosives. For several hours First Army skies were mottled with the aircraft of three nations (I saw no Germans playing around that formidable groupage). Their droning synchronized into a steady rumble as of drums beating a titanic tattoo. It was the most spectacular aerial gesture of the whole war, and it made a distinct impression on a front where the enemy had for one ill-chosen moment ventured to threaten General William Mitchell with a destructive superiority in the air.

"By God, we'll show 'em something!" he said joyfully. And we did.

Bill Mitchell possessed the capacity of a great commander for active warfare. This he demonstrated on many occasions. He had a clearer view of the potentialities of the air arm than anyone of his countrymen. He contributed more than any other to the bringing of an undeveloped and ill-organized branch of our military service to the high state of effectiveness it could claim in the last three months of the war. As an aerial strategist his mind was of the first order. And for all his ambitious projects, his sometimes overwhelming demands, he was unwaveringly loyal to those who were efficient and kept faith with him.

He was at his best when in full control of large-scale operations. Temperament and a supreme self-confidence fitted him better to command than to take orders from others. Many were jealous of him. Some called him insubordinate. So perhaps he was, when lack of confidence in the understanding or the judgment of others brought him into conflict over matters of aeronautical policy and tactical employment. So was Sir Douglas Haig when he lost confidence in Sir John French, his superior officer and Commander-in-Chief of the British Expeditionary Forces in France, caused the latter's recall and succeeded to his command. So have been many outstanding leaders in warfare, though I do not suggest insubordination as an essential quality for leadership.

In Bill Mitchell's relations with the abler commanders of our ground forces there was only the most whole-hearted loyalty and cooperation.

It was in its way a prime misfortune for Bill Mitchell that the war did not continue a few months longer. Had it done so, he would in all likelihood have been given command of an Independent Air Force made up of bombardment elements, deep reconnaissance and special combat units from all the Allied forces in France. Undoubtedly he would have done well with such a command. The bigger the job, the better he fulfilled its opportunities.

In the years from 1919 to 1926 he contributed immensely to the building up of American aviation from its post-war slump. It was in many respects a disheartening task for a man of his temperament. He was opposed, usually with more vehemence than intellect, by the stolid traditionalists of the older services and their supporters. Later, as the conflict broadened, he began to weaken his case by overstatement, to antagonize too many persons by sweeping generalities and immoderate criticism. This was unfortunate in all ways. For when, because of this, his voice came no longer to be heeded by those shaping the destinies of our nation and its defenses, the most far-seeing counsellor on military preparedness that America had produced in his day was disregarded. In the end this helped to kill him. At his untimely death in 1935 I lost a revered commander and beloved friend. The country he so deeply loved and to whose growth he devoted himself unswervingly had soon after to swallow grievous humiliation, spend incalculable treasure and count the expenditure of a vast number of lives in catching up with the precepts Bill Mitchell expounded to closed ears a decade and a half before the unhappy events he foresaw.

We Broke the Armistice

The Armistice of 11 November 1918 caught me at my advanced headquarters near the small village of Rampont in the Argonne, not entirely unprepared, nor insensible to what it implied; yet after forty-nine months of combatant action the booming of the guns at eleven o'clock on that November morning had a curiously hollow sound.

The let-down was tremendous. It could hardly have been otherwise. The whole structure of one's psychology had been refashioned in the war mould, pressed into terms of combat, into manners of handling men and machines whose primary purpose was to destroy and to resist being destroyed. Even one's tastes had become attuned to the fragmentary pleasures of moments behind the lines—elemental pleasures of eating and drinking and making merry, in the face of an excellent chance that on the morrow one might have no further interest in such matters.

Over the space of more than four years the processes of destiny had shaped one's outlook to a scheme of things which abruptly ceased to exist on the stroke of eleven of a November morning, one's own objectives not as yet fully attained.

Bill Mitchell sensed something of that let-down. About two weeks after the Armistice had gone into effect he called me to his headquarters. "I'm going to take command of the Air Service of the Army of Occupation," he said. "For a while . . . won't dare stay away too long. Have to get back to stir 'em up at home before they all die of flatulence and the only relics of our Air Service are set up in the Smithsonian!

"So," he explained, with typically large and generous gesture, "I'm planning to turn the Rhine over to you when I've finished with it. But some of the bright boys at home have had you ordered back to be Chief of Air Reconnaissance Training or something equally idiotic. Maybe you can duck out from that order—I'll try to fix it with General Pershing. But you'd better be out of touch for the moment so it can't catch up with you. Anyway, I want to know something about the German airdromes we're going to use.

"Now you take a car and mooch along with the forward line of our troops as they advance into the territory we are to occupy. As soon as any German airdromes between Luxemburg and Coblenz are uncovered, you look 'em over. Report to me anything of special interest; but I won't expect to be able to communicate with you while you're jumping about for the next two or three weeks. Take along some of your officers who may need a change, if you feel like it."

Within a few hours I was on my way. Three days later, by an odd chain of events, my companions and I found ourselves "mooching" along, not with our forward line but well out in front of it, in the midst of the retiring German Army. Whatever the cause, this impromptu adventure in breaking the terms of the Armistice turned out to be highly entertaining.

Armed with General Bill Mitchell's blessing in the place of written orders, supported by four jovial flying officers and my small black mascot dog "Dickebusch," I set out in the general direction of the Rhineland. The first night we spent at Luxembourg, where on a later occasion there took place another party that lingers in nostalgic memory, with the ever-irrepressible Bill Mitchell the leading spirit and the youngest of the Grand Duchesses our amiable hostess. Late the following afternoon we entered Trier shortly after its occupation by the advanced elements of Third Army.

I had last been in that oldest of German towns in January, 1915; strolling then amongst the *feld-grau* troops of the enemy with a nonchalance I did not feel, doubling on my tracks, glancing over my shoulder to see if I were being followed, in constant dread lest my presence should arouse the suspicion it merited in fact.

Gone, now, was the field-grey. The only uniforms were the olive-drab of my own army; and where before I had sneaked as with a price on my head, this time I swaggered in blatant ease amidst glum civilian faces. Such change of status, ordained as it were by Fate in the very center of the German wine industry, demanded appropriate recognition; which it received. By persistence and the suborning of a dour *Herr Ober* I managed to entice from hidden sanctuary a number of bottles of a gorgeous Mosel vintage—Berncasteler Doktor 1905. We dined on venison steak, the best in all my memory. With the repast I sequestered two venerable cup-bearers, their instructions precise and to the point: "Keep on bringing Berncasteler Doktor until we tell you to stop!" As the evening progressed we entered enthusiastically into the spirit of the thing. We toasted the German Secret Service with lusty "Pfuis!"—this in connection with my previous visit of nearly four years before. We drank the health of the about-to-be disbanded German Flying Corps, and of ourselves who had played some part in causing its disbandment. The dour *Herr Ober* regarded us with cold and acrid distaste.

We had hard heads in those days. In due time we called a halt on our ancient cup-bearers. With the fine sense of well-being that comes from having all the Berncasteler Doktor 1905 one could desire, we betook ourselves to bed—"In Germany, by gad!" It was for me the culmination of four years of combatant strife.

Bright and early in the morning I went out to refresh my memories of Trier's majestic Roman ruins, to rejoice again in the splendor of her churches. We then inspected a couple of freshly "uncovered" flying-fields nearby, and set off anew for the point reached by Third Army's advance guard along the road to Coblenz. I did not know exactly where this might be. It could not be very far, and I thought it a simple enough matter to run down the road until we came to it. But in this I reckoned without the Fate that so often plays tricks in one's most guileless designs. We never did come upon that point. All unaware, we filtered right past it. The hand of Fate held a joker in my memory of a road.

Close upon the small village of Eller the main Mosel valley high-road disappears straight into a mountain. It comes out by Cochem on the farther side through the Kaiser Wilhelm Tunnel that is 2⅝ miles long. The River Mosel loops around the mountain known as the Ellerer Berg. Along its bank a little secondary road meanders past Ediger and Ellen to rejoin the main route at Cochem, some 12½ miles as the river runs.

I had motored over both routes in days before the war and remembered well the beauty of the little river road. Wherefore we decided to take that longer way, branching off from the highroad before reaching the tunnel.

It happened that the entrance to the tunnel marked the farthest point of Third Army's occupation up to that time. No main body of troops had yet come so far, nor had we passed any for a good few miles back; but there was an advance-guard at Eller with sentries posted at the tunnel's mouth (this I learned later). The sentries had orders to permit no passage beyond that point until the advancing columns should arrive and be pushed on through the tunnel into the next zone. For reasons known best to the officer in charge of the advance-guard, not a sign of which we ever saw, there were no sentries posted where the river road branched off.

And so we came to Cochem around the scarp of the Ellerer Berg, to find that small, immensely picturesque town dead and deserted below its old imperial castle on the hill. There was not a soul in its streets. Its mediaeval half-timbered houses, its many inns, were tightly closed. This seemed very odd. One of the inns showed signs of recent occupancy, whereupon we pounded on its doors. Behind an entry that led into what might have been the proprietor's quarters I thought I detected sounds of labored breathing.

"Open the door!" we shouted. "One intends no harm—but if you do not open we will break it down!" There came muffled whispers from within; after repeated calls a bolt was drawn. The door opened very slowly for a few inches. From the crack peered the face of a middle-aged woman, a face grey with terror.

"Why are you hiding thus?" I asked.

"We are afraid!" Her every look confirmed it. "We fear the soldiers!"

"What soldiers?"

"Why . . . why, the German soldiers! We have seen no others."

"There are no German soldiers here," I said. She stared past me in surprise. "*Nein?* They were here this morning. You are not German soldiers?"

"We are American officers. You need not fear the American soldiers. Did the German troops harm you? Where are all the other people of the town?"

"Hiding, as ourselves, in back rooms and in their cellars—those who have not gone away. No . . . the troops have not really harmed us. But some of them—you know, there are many now who talk of strange things and do not listen to their officers—*they* frightened us very much. They took all our food and wine and some of our things, and we were afraid for our young girls."

"How many are you?" She opened the door a little wider—there were eight or ten adults in the small room, women of various ages—one might have been eighty—and two old men; with as many children. They had no food left, they said, except for a few dried grapes. We gave them a loaf of bread and some tinned supplies from the car. They were pathetically grateful.

"The American soldiers, they will all be like you?" the woman asked me.

"Oh yes, have no fear. It is quite safe, now, for you to come out. But we must go on. *Auf wiedersehen!*"

"*Auf wiedersehen!*" they cried, and we pushed on.

"Now where the devil can our advance-guard have got to?" I mused aloud. "Seems damn queer we haven't come to them, if German troops were here this morning!"

"I think there's a weasel in this somewhere," said Curtis Wheeler. We wound along the lovely valley whose slopes were covered in vineyards, the slate peaks crowned with a succession of towers and crenelated walls of feudal castles, and suddenly around the bend came full upon the retiring German Army.

"Hooray!" yelped Curtis Wheeler. "I knew there was a weasel in it!"

I thought quickly. "We've done it now," I said. "If we go back we'll probably run bang on to some humorless General and have a lot of rude questions asked us—haven't any written orders, you know. If we go on we'll be breaking the terms of the Armistice." (Annex No. I, Section II: "The Armies of Occupation of the Allies and the United States shall enter these different zones on the expiration of the period allowed to the German troops for the evacuation of each zone. . . . Evacuation of the territories situated between Line 5 [two-thirds the way from Trier to Coblenz] and Line 6 [the Rhine] to be completed within 27 days after the signature of the Armistice.") We were just eight days ahead of schedule. "It might well be an amusing experience; and it might get us in the devil's own jam. I don't want to drag you lads into anything without your eyes open."

Curtis Wheeler looked at me with feigned astonishment. "Would you let an *Armistice* deter you?" he asked. The rest chimed in joyfully. "That makes it a hundred percent! Let's step on it!"

"So be it, then," I said, "and on our individual heads. To Coblenz it is!"

"*Nach Koblenz!*" they shouted. And Curtis Wheeler burst into his latest theme-song:

> "*First* you ring the bell, *then* you ask for *Anna*;
> *Then* you put a nickel in the old *pi*-anner!"

I stepped on it: the Cadillac shot past the marching columns of infantry, guns, transport; mile after mile of steel-helmeted faces staring amazed over their left shoulders as we passed. Yet no one tried to stop us. They were in pretty straggly march formation, but a strong Klaxon horn on the Cadillac together with a broken exhaust-manifold that made an infernal racket when I tapped on the accelerator cleared the way before us. Probably they thought it a German staff car until we got past each unit. Through all the din rose the clear tones of Curtis Wheeler's voice in snatches of ribald song, echoing from Mosel hillsides over the helmeted heads:

> "*Anna* comes down, *smell*ing of *cologn*-a,
> *All* dressed up in a *Jap*anese *Kimon*-a . . ."

It grew dark and I turned on the headlights. They swept the field-grey backs, glinted on gun-barrels and steel tires, casting distorted shadows on the walls of the cliffs; playing on row after irregular row of 'Boots—boots—boots—boots, movin' up an' down again'—the feet of the German Army returning whence they had come.

As we swung in an abrupt curve around the jutting spur of a mountain the headlamps threw full into a deep, rocky cavern. For an instant only, but it made a flashlight picture that was vivid and portentous. The cavern was crammed with men. They were sitting on the ground, leaning against the walls, their rifles and equipment stacked alongside. In the center a soldier stood on an ammunition box. His tunic was unbuttoned, his right arm upraised with fist clenched, his mouth open. The whites of his eyes and teeth shone in the glare of the lights. He stood there tense, impassioned, and ugly. It could be only revolution that a man would declaim with such a look on his face.

It was an eerie picture, instantly blotted out in the dark yet forever fixed in memory: the sowing of the seed of social revolt, the dynamics of disorder getting under way, by night in the tenebrous depths of a cave.

We had this picture in mind as we drove into Coblenz. The streets were jammed with soldiers and civilians in large groups. They went separately or mixed together; and in every group men were expounding theses we could not hear. I had no wish to stop—unexpected and unexplained—in their midst. Luckily I remembered the way. With flashing headlights, Klaxon squawking and the roars of an exhaust whose naked flames lent a touch of the spectacular to our progress, I forced a path down the Rheinstrasse to the river bank and with a broad sweep to the left drove into the grounds of the Riesen-Fürstenhof. There I drew up alongside a row of Benz and Mercedes staff cars.

"This *used* to be a hotel," I said. "I've stayed at it. Don't know what it may be now." I observed an Army standard at the entry. "Curtis, you and Paul Mathis go make arrangements for our reception. Tell 'em the American Major and his staff have arrived, that I want suitable accommodations for five officers, and we will be pleased to dine in half an hour." About ten minutes later they came back. With them was a German in civilian dress. He looked a bit bewildered.

"There's some confusion here," said Curtis Wheeler. "They say they didn't expect us, and the hotel is an Army Headquarters or something. But I've told 'em it doesn't matter—they must fix us up at once."

"Can't understand why they should not have been advised of our coming!" I snapped out.

The German addressed me: "Sir, I assure you we knew nothing of it. We had not expected any Americans here for another week"—"Most extraordinary!" I interposed . . ."But I will do the best I can for your comfort," he continued. "Rooms are now being prepared; they will be ready shortly when the effects of the officers who are occupying them have been moved out."

"Very good, we will wait another few minutes," I replied. "And who might you be?" He was, I think he said, the son or the nephew of the Riesen-Fürstenhof's proprietor. He had been furloughed from military service a day or two before, had just got out of uniform. Now he was managing that property which up to the present time was utilized as Staff Headquarters and officers' billets. Perhaps it would be so employed by the American forces? he inquired.

"Oh, quite likely," I responded. "We'll look it over."

A soldier came out to announce that the rooms were ready. In formal order we filed in to the vast caravanserai. The night was cold, wherefore I wore two coats. The basic one was a "British Warm" with an opossum collar. Over that I wore a long leather wind-breaker whose collar was of coonskin, and I carried like a Field Marshal's baton a leather-covered knob-stick loaded with lead. These trappings, my staff assured me, lent an impressive dignity of appearance as I led the advance-forces—very advanced forces—of the United States Army into occupation of the Rhineland. Without flags or fanfare, in dead silence but for our measured tread that echoed through the halls where N.C.O.'s with Iron Crosses stared stonily, we took over the German Headquarters at Coblenz, or at least a section of them.

"Couldn't have gone off more smoothly!" remarked Curtis Wheeler; "the ceremonial entrance into the capitulated Headquarters of the enemy. Simple but really beautiful and inspiring in its solemnity, you know: your passing through the Arch of Triumph of the Riesen-Fürstenhof's portals in your coats of many collars leading your staff two by two; with the conquered foe's official deputy one pace behind on your left pointing the way and turning over to you the keys, and three ex-enemy warriors in single file behind bearing your kit and little black dog. Now I think we should have a spot of brandy."

The three ex-enemy warriors were impressed into polishing our boots and belts—Curtis Wheeler glowering over them, egging them on to greater effort with alternate promises and threats in his fluent German. "God-in-Heaven, that won't do for us! Must make 'em *shine!* Want to see our faces in 'em!" While we were removing the stains of travel, our furloughed-soldier manager-host asked to speak with me. I could feel there was something on his mind. "In the matter of your dinner . . ." he began gravely.

"Yes, we'll be ready in fifteen minutes," I interrupted. "I know it's a bit late but that cannot be helped." We had eaten nothing but chocolate and hard bread since a very light early breakfast, and I did not intend to be put off by whatever excuse he might advance.

"Oh, it's not that!" he said. "There is food. But you see there is only the one dining-room, which is the Staff mess. The other rooms are being used as Army Staff offices. And it so happens that the Commanding General with his whole staff are this night giving a farewell banquet to the Burgomaster and the other civil authorities of Coblenz, with their ladies, in that room. It is very awkward. There is no other place where you could dine . . . except in your rooms. And it would be most regrettable were there to be an unpleasant incident."

"Oh that's *quite* all right," I said easily. "The General's banquet will not disturb us at all. A pleasure, indeed. There is some place in the dining room for another table, for five, is there not?" There was, he admitted, though somehow the thought seemed to bring him no great consolation.

"Fine. Have it set right away. We'll be down at once. Present my compliments to the General and say I regret to intrude on his farewell banquet, but we are very hungry and we *never* dine in our bedrooms. And there will be no incident so far as we are concerned."

The prospects pointed to a diverting evening. Highly pleased with ourselves we descended the stairs in formation, Dickebusch bringing up the rear. Our host met us at the entrance to the dining room. "His Excellency is seated at the far end of the table," he announced in a dispassionate tone, and swung open the double doors. Down the length of a table that seemed to stretch interminably, over a multitude of wine-glasses, flower vases and other accessories of formal banquet, I looked straight into the eyes of His Excellency Colonel General von Einem, expressionless as a sphinx.

For perhaps three long seconds we stared thus at each other in the charged silence of that room. Then I clicked my spurred heels and bowed stiffly from the waist. Under the circumstances I was not prepared to salute him in other fashion, but military courtesy required an appropriate gesture. The General rose to his feet. The click of his spurs came back like the echo of a pistol shot as he returned my bow in similar fashion—the rigid fashion of German etiquette. All the other officers and civil dignitaries then rose, turned quarteringly to face towards me and bowed together, their features blank as death-masks.

The rattle of spurs and heels had the suggestion of distant musketry. As I moved on towards my table in the farther corner of the room they reseated themselves, momentarily.

Four times more the whole ceremony was repeated as my officers filed in behind me one by one, bowed in their turn and passed on to our corner. This, Paul Mathis remarked, was doing it up in style. "Lucky for them we didn't come in squadron formation, eighteen in a row!"

Somehow the banquet never seemed to get in swing after that interruption. Conversation dragged; the toasts and farewell speeches were listless, lacking in either fire or pathos. This we could not well fail to remark from our vantage-point some twenty feet distant. "Damned queer," we mused over our replenished glasses of Piesporter. "You wouldn't suppose *our* presence here would have a dampening effect, would you, when we're so ready with joy and good cheer to join into the spirit of the occasion!"

In point of fact our audible comments as well as our behavior were really quite circumspect. They were so, at all events, until the banquet had broken up and, after a final round of spur-clicking, formal bows that it was now our turn to acknowledge in rising, had left an empty dinner hall to us. By this time we were no more than half through our own banqueting—quite evidently on the same sumptuous menu offered the Commanding General's party. As we reached the dessert course our helpful manager-host came in to inquire if all were well. Very well indeed, I affirmed; whereupon we drank to his health and the hospitality of the Riesen-Fürstenhof headquarters. There again seemed to be something on his mind. After a slight hesitation it came out.

"You will permit that I offer a suggestion or two in your interest?"

"Certainly," I said, "though I do not promise to follow them."

"Of course you will follow your own best judgment." He proceeded to his point. "The officers from the General's party have joined a number of others in the Rathskeller. This is the last night they are to be together. Today"—I glanced at my watch, it was already past midnight —"some of them start on the withdrawal across the Rhine. There will be drinking—a good deal of drinking; and as you may appreciate, they are not in a very happy frame of mind." I could imagine it.

"They have been . . . well, frankly, a little perturbed over your unexpected arrival here tonight. I am fearful that a seriously unfortunate incident might befall should you and your party visit the Rathskeller this night . . . if I may suggest it."

"You may," I said. "We have no desire to intrude our bright and merry faces into the drowning of their sorrows." Our host seemed to breathe rather more easily.

"One other matter," he continued, "as to Coblenz itself. Disturbances have broken out in several sections. Riotous elements among the populace, bodies of demobilized or furloughed soldiers—with some others, perhaps, as well—are circulating around the town in an ugly mood. There is talk of communistic revolt, as in Russia." The picture within the cave on a Mosel mountainside, not far back, flashed again in my mind. "Even the steadiest of the troops, feeling that they were undefeated in a military sense yet are now to suffer from defeat, are in a reckless, almost a desperate humor. Should you wish to take the air I would recommend that you stay on the Quay, and not go very far. In the center of the town this night I fear you would be in grave danger."

"We are accustomed to danger," I said. This sounded a little smug, but I did not care to let a possible implication pass. He inclined his head. "And we came through the center of the town to get here. However, we have had a long and somewhat strenuous day. I hardly think we need seek further distraction tonight, either among those who wish to drown their sorrows without our help or amidst the riotous and reckless. In any case I thank you for your kindly advice!"

In the morning I had further occasion to call upon his good offices, once again to slightly irregular ends. "I wish to fill my tank with benzine (gasoline)," I announced. He looked vaguely distressed.

"There has been no benzine obtainable in Coblenz for a very long while," he replied. I waved my hand in the direction of the grey Mercedes and Benz cars lined up outside.

"And those? What do *they* run on, hot air? Or would it be Rhine-wine?"

"They are the Army Staff cars." I was aware of this. "They draw their benzine from the Army Motor Transport dump," he explained.

"Quite so. That's what I meant in the first place; you didn't suppose I wanted to *buy* the stuff, did you? Just how do I get it?"

"You would have to have a requisition signed by the Kommandantur. The dump is on the other side of the Rhine, across the pontoon bridge. There will, as you must know, be troops retiring across that bridge all the day through."

"I may have to hold up their retirement for a bit, in that case," I remarked. He looked at me for a moment; then, "I'd better get an

Unteroffizier to go along with you," he said quietly. He appeared to be growing used to my ways.

Accompanied by a German sergeant and Curtis Wheeler, I drove to the Kommandantur in the middle of the city. I advised the sergeant that if the requisition were not in my hands within ten minutes there would be hell popping loose upon his own and all the Kommandantur heads. In exactly nine minutes I was invited into the office of the Major Kommandant of Coblenz. He stood up.

"You are the American Major?" he asked.

"I am," I said. We exchanged salutes.

"You wish benzine?" I confirmed this. "How much benzine?"

"Oh, my tank full and about twenty liters extra. Say one hundred liters."

"And the purpose?"

"For the advance-reconnaissance of the forward zone of occupation!"

"*Ach so!*" He seemed a little puzzled. I looked at him coldly. "You will be good enough to expedite the requisition," I said in a firm tone. "I am in a hurry." He sat down, and as I leaned ominously over his shoulder he filled in, signed and stamped a yellow requisition form. I signed the stub with a flourish; we again exchanged salutes and I walked out with the yellow paper in my hand.

"When you *do* bluff, my dear Curtis, there's no use being half-hearted about it!" I remarked as we drove to the pontoon bridge.

"And that's the truth," he agreed. "So far it has worked like a charm!"

It worked like a charm the rest of the way. I had the sergeant break the solid columns of traffic double-filing across the bridge. We took our place in their midst and, with the retiring German Army in front and behind, rolled slowly across to the right bank of the Rhine. Below the fortress of Ehrenbreitstein from whose ramparts floated a large and defiant German flag—unready yet to cede its place to the Stars and Stripes—we drew our benzine from the Army dump.

"Now make this snappy!" I ordered the N.C.O. in charge. "We have no time to waste in argument!" He made it snappy, and I took along a can of motor-oil for good measure. There was a certain gratification in the whole procedure.

The return trip was more complicated. One of the double columns had to be held up for the full length of the bridge while we beat back against the traffic. Our sergeant proved an effective aide-de-camp. Assigning another N.C.O. as our guard, he returned on foot to the left bank and halted the retirement. He must have told a fairly impressive story of our importance. But the amazed expressions of the German officers, as we rumbled over the pontoons, were lacking in cordiality.

"God, but wouldn't they love to turn us over, car and all, into the Rhine!" whispered Curtis Wheeler, a trifle obsessed by those glowering, hostile faces.

"Don't suggest it," I countered, "or maybe they will."

They did not. Uncheered but triumphant we returned to our headquarters in the Riesen-Fürstenhof. I felt quite pleased with that little expedition and said so. "Chalk up another *coup* for 1st Observation Wing! First to cross the Rhine! We've blazed the trail, the Army of Occupation can followed along any time now. And we're all set for further advance-reconnaissance; tanks filled up and everything—all with the compliments of the German Army Command!"

We spent five days on the Rhine. Because of a long and happy connection with British Second Army it seemed to me that the obvious thing to do was to include in our "reconnaissance" the Rhenish zone which that Army was about to take over. Somehow it did *not* seem quite expedient for us to greet the American forces on their arrival in Coblenz, nor to go back the way we had come. I had a distinct feeling that our trail-blazing efforts might not be properly appreciated by our own High Command.

Just before we left Coblenz two passenger boats came steaming down the Rhine. They passed in line astern close to the quay where we were then standing. They seemed to be packed with people. I wondered who these might be, until suddenly a tremendous cheer burst from the leading boat as she listed heavily to port with her passengers crowding the near rail.

They were British prisoners of war going home. Some of those poor devils had been shut up within dismal barracks and barbed-wire enclosures for years; since August 1914, it might have been. There were a good many of them who were not quite whole, though the more gravely shattered wrecks were probably not among those deck-loads. As they spotted us standing by the river's edge in our British Warms they took us for British officers—the first they had seen, save as fellow prisoners, since their capture. Their cheers roared across the Rhine, re-echoed from the cliffs of Ehrenbreitstein . . . broke then into snatches of "Tipperary." From this they swung to "*Are . . . we . . . downhearted?*" and the massed decks rocked under the thundering "*NO-O-O!*"

They waved caps and mufflers, empty sleeves, crutches. Through the general uproar one caught light-hearted quips: "*Where's the blooming Kaiser? . . . We want LITTLE Willie! . . . Could do with some girls —mademoiselles—fräuleins! . . . Give our love to von Hindenburg! . . . WE WANT BEER!*" Unquenchable, the British Tommy.

We stood alternately at salute or waving back at them as they passed on down the Rhine: two boatloads of cheerful derelicts heading homewards after a long absence, and I for myself was unabashed at the tears wetting my cheeks. Down the river towards freedom they passed in the two aged, listing boats, from whose freighted decks there drifted back like an echo on the still air: "*And . . . are . . . we . . . downhearted? . . . NO-O-O! . . . Bloody well NO-O-O!*"

At Cologne we happened to see the other side of the picture. We were there a day or so before the first unit of the British advance guard came in. The British troops had not been expected quite so soon; but because of the growing insecurity and fear of the Workmen's and Soldiers' Council, the civil authorities had themselves urged General Plumer to push forward his occupation of the city. The first unit of occupation, a Lieutenant with a troop of cavalry, was not sorry to find us there. They had no food or forage, and the Lieutenant was a bit anxious about their situation.

I was standing on a corner of the Dom Platz when another unit of the advance guard swung slowly out of the Burgmauer into the Cathedral square. It was an armored car, dappled, grim, the head and shoulders of the gunner protruding from its open turret. Ready for action it came; and the look on the gunner's face under a canted steel helmet, his arms resting lightly across his gun controls, was the perfect expression of his Army's humor on occupying the enemy's land after four years of ghastly struggle. Resolute, completely self-assured, cheerful and without vindictiveness—but: "Anyone around here like to start something?" it said.

The car stopped alongside where I was standing. "Which way, sir, to the Hohenzollern Bridge?" the gunner asked, and hopefully, "Any trouble here, sir? Riots?" None in this section, I told him, pointing the way. With that indication, British Second Army, my former Army, took over its main bridgehead.

We moved out through Second Army, then advancing towards its last objective. Several times we were halted by angry Brigadiers demanding to know whence we came and why. I explained myself out of these situations without serious qualms. Were we actually to be arrested I felt I could count on my friend Colonel Percy Laurie, Provost Marshal of Second Army, for a speedy release and most likely a good dinner thrown in.

We returned in due course to our own area, via Aachen and Liége. When a few days later I recounted the story of the trip to Bill Mitchell, over a long-necked bottle which was part of the Rhenish trophy I had brought back, his comment was typical.

"So you upset the terms of the Armistice and took over the Rhine just eight days ahead of the Allied Command, did you?" he asked. "H'm, not a bad effort. But, *hell!* if *I* had slipped across the Rhine the way you did I'd have kept right on to Berlin!" He probably would have at that, and have smacked his lips over his Piesporter or Berncasteler Doktor in the shades of Unter den Linden.

3 – On the Golden Road of Central Asia

The Golden Road to Samarkand

WATCHMAN (*at the Gate of the Moon, Baghdad*) "What would ye, ladies?
It was ever thus.
Men are unwise and curiously planned."

A WOMAN "They have their dreams and do not think of us."

VOICES OF THE CARAVAN (*in the distance singing*) "We take the Golden Road to Samarkand!"
— HASSAN

Unwise and curiously planned I doubtless am. And when I set out on the Golden Road to Samarkand I took my lady with me.

After three years as Air Attaché at the American Embassy in London I had resigned from the army, married, and accepted a five-year contract with the Persian Government to assist in reorganizing the financial administration of Iran. The latter undertaking, as it turned out, involved a number of things not normally classified as finance. But these added immeasurably to the interest of that experience.

We went out by ship to Bombay and then up the Persian Gulf, a voyage of extraordinarily colorful evenings down the golden moon-paths in blue seas flaming with phosphorescent jellyfish, under enormous stars.

At Karachi the *Varsova* of the British India Line filled up with a wild crowd of deck passengers—slant-eyed Sarts from Bokhara way, Baluchis with oiled locks to their shoulders and dirty white trousers hanging in shapeless bags, tribesmen of a dozen different stocks from little-known upland valleys, turbaned or hatted in brimless conical felts stained with sweat, and with incredibly long scarves wound round and round their middles. Men, women and children, of all ages, drawn by their faith to make the pilgrimage to Kerbela and Najaf.

Some spoke dialects no one else on board could understand. Few had ever before seen the sea or any ship that might ply on it. They

181

slept in rows on small rugs and wadded quilts, or fanned the fires of tiny charcoal braziers over which they cooked odorous foods in the grease of the fat-tailed sheep. With them were lambs and goats, miserable and bleating, tied to every hatchway and stanchion; ducks and chickens hitched by the legs to the odd items of baggage cluttering the deck. Five times a day they went through the genuflections of their prayers, invoking God in endless monotone. They were all very sick when the sea was rough under the cold *shamal* that blew like a ripening typhoon.

When it was smooth they squatted on their hams for hours on end and stared uncomprehendingly through the rails. The unbroken stretches of water were beyond their ken, as also the barren red islets set in the greenish sea—the "Great Sea of Sunrising" that we call the Persian Gulf, where man made his first feeble attempts at navigation before the Mediterranean ever floated a keel. Yet it was all God's work and they were going through it to the shrines of the martyred grandsons of His Prophet, wherefore they faced the terrors of the unknown with fatalistic confidence but not inquisitively.

From Baghdad we went by the newly built railroad to Khaniqin near the Persian border. The roadbed was very "green" (Green was the name of the engineer who had just laid the line and deplored the pun). The passenger equipment comprised one mid-Victorian "First Class Carriage" condemned and discarded years before off one of the Indian railways. This box-like affair was perhaps thirty feet long and was divided into two compartments with no passage between. Into the after compartment, at the end of the long train of little "goods wagons," we heaved our luggage and ourselves just before the engine took off with a tremendous jerk. The end compartment seemed a good idea, for the view and other purposes (we were to be on it for thirteen hours). It was not a good idea. As soon as we started it took on a synchronized motion with the waves of the roadbed that flipped our hapless bodies like popping corn up and down between the hard cushions and the ceiling. I extracted our solar topees from their winter packing and we wore them to keep our skulls from being shattered against the roof. But the battering became unbearable.

So we changed from the after compartment to the one ahead, running alongside on the desert while the train was in full motion. We could outsprint the Baghdad-Khaniqin express even when loaded with our hand baggage. The express was scheduled to do the 98 miles in a little over thirteen hours. This would be an average of approximately seven and a half miles an hour, but we did not make it. Shortly before eight in the evening, when the train should have been drawing near to Khaniqin but was still some seven miles away, we ran off the track. The tracks spread enough to let all the wheels of all the cars run off at once. I did not know just where we were; there was no one to ask, there was no light, no heat, and the desert was dark, cold and uninviting. Two hours passed. Then above the howls of the prowling jackal packs came a deep and booming voice calling my name. I shouted acknowledgment of our presence into the dark.

"I'm Osborne!" the voice boomed back. Osborne was the manager of the Anglo-Persian Oil Company's operations at Khaniqin. A moment later a tall, rangy Englishman swung himself into the compartment.

"Leave your gear," he advised. "You come along with me. My men will take this stuff. I've brought a trolley. We've seven miles to go. Green wired me that you were coming."

We moved up to the head of the train and crawled aboard the "trolley," a battered handcar. Josephine, whom I had married in Paris on the way out and whose preconceived ideas of a honeymoon were henceforth to be rudely revised, perched on an elevated plank seat with Osborne. I had to lie flat and curving outwardly like an agitated caterpillar to avoid having my head bashed in by the pumping wooden handles. After about an hour of this we came to Khaniqin.

"My bungalow is a bit rough," Osborne apologized. "Ample room, though, and it's reasonably well stocked." It was very well stocked indeed, more particularly with liquid commodities.

"Any friend of T. C. Mitchell can have anything I own," said Osborne. I did not then know just what he meant. T. C. Mitchell was one of my colleagues on the American Financial Mission. He had passed through Khaniqin a few weeks earlier. At one time in his wanderings he had been Director of Customs in Liberia.

There, in the capital city of Monrovia, the Minister of Finance had kicked his dog. The Minister of Finance was very black and T. C. Mitchell hailed from Georgia. Mitchell was not used to having black men kick his dog, so he kicked the Minister of Finance down the stone steps of the Ministry. There were certain repercussions to this. Mitchell was placed under open arrest, fined ten thousand dollars—he thought the amount, which perhaps still remains on the books as collectible, flattering both to himself and to the Minister of Finance, though in different ways—and left Liberia rather hurriedly in the dead of night with the connivance of a steamship captain whom he had befriended.

Before all this happened he had made a tour to investigate the alleged encroachments of France on Liberia's northern borders, I believe it was. He took with him two palanquins, carried through the dense jungle by relays of ebon-hued men. In one he rode, when he was not scouting. The other bore his special supplies, including several cases of snake-bite medicine, produce of Scotland aged for ten years in the wood. Mitchell felt that being alone with a barefoot force, and likely to be shot at now and then by unfriendly natives firing poisoned arrows through blow-pipes, he might need quite a lot of snake-bite cure. He was a provident soul in his way.

It happened that one evening while Mitchell was dining in lonely state in the jungle the headman of his retainers appeared before his tent and announced that a strange Thing had crawled into camp. Mitchell went to see what sort of Thing it might be, and found an inarticulate object that crawled on its hands and knees like a human child, but was much longer and thinner and more matted than a human child could possibly be. An emaciated Thing which made plaintive, voiceless gestures with its mouth.

The Thing was Osborne. Mitchell brought him back to life, grubstaked him and sent him, when he had recovered, back to England. Osborne was the roving son of an Anglican clergyman, who had been deserted by his porters in the wilds of West Africa while trying to capture a live white baby rhinoceros (an unusual beast even in the jungle) for a British zoo. Alone he had walked and crawled an incredible distance through the jungle to fall upon T. C. Mitchell just a little before he would have died of exhaustion.

After hearing this I understood Osborne's remark: "Any friend of T. C. Mitchell's can have anything I own!"

In the morning, amidst circles of kneeling camels and the heaps of our baggage borne in by squads of porters during the night, we found a brace of unbelievably derelict Model T Fords awaiting, venerable relics of the British Expeditionary Forces held together with baling wire and goat's-hair rope. They were not vehicles one would deliberately have chosen for crossing the Zagros ranges in the depths of winter. A pair of verminous-looking bandits lunged forth to announce themselves as the cars' owner-drivers and immediately to haggle for higher pay than stipulated by their contracts. After much profitless palaver I loaded the twin Lizzies to their tattered canvas hoods. Then, as the shadows lengthened, we pursued our way as far as the little frontier town of Kasr-i-Shirin. The Persian Vice Consul at Khaniqin insisted on accompanying us, though I had wished for no part of him. He tried his best to dissuade me from starting until next day. It would be dark before we could arrive, he protested, and the way held an evil reputation from the frequent raids of Kurdish brigands. But I was already overdue, the Governor at Kasr-i-Shirin expected us for the night, and the sudden descents of robbers were by no means confined to the hours of darkness. I determined to get on while the weather held fair. The Vice Consul came along, unwanted and in an acute stage of jitters.

Thirty miles is no great distance in a modern vehicle along a concrete highway. In a pair of overloaded tin Lizzies, on a stony track subject to the raids of brigands, it can be quite a stretch. The Vice Consul, as soon came out, wanted my support in securing transfer to some other post than Khaniqin. Before we had gone five miles I would gladly have sponsored his immediate transfer to hell. As an undesired escort he was tiresome; with the gathering dusk he became a dangerous nuisance, brandishing a cocked automatic from the front seat in gestures of juvenile dramatics. The clacking of false teeth no better anchored than his nerves rose above the rattle of our bounding Lizzie. And his narrow, greyish hand, covering vaguely with a pistol the whole landscape of western Iran, tended to take our minds off the beauties of the scene.

For it was quite beautiful, as a stage setting for one's entry into unfamiliar territory. The winter sun sank blood-red and enormous through the desert floor behind, dyeing the snow-covered peaks deep coral on the barrier ranges we had soon to cross. A little mud fort upon a bare hill, pinkish in the setting sun, marked the Persian frontier. The fort was occupied, and this our shivering escort took to be a very bad sign. Yet we swayed unmolested to the edge of Kasr-i-Shirin as the stars came out huge and brilliant in the blue nightshade of the sky.

Men met us bearing candle lamps with flaring glass shields, flanked by others carrying rifles and shotguns. We were led, it seemed for miles, through narrow, ill-paved lanes, muddy and exceedingly bad walking. The Governor's house lay hidden behind a courtyard, where the Governor awaited in formal state. All the "notables" of the dilapidated town had been invited to dine. They all came, wearing their best collar-studs of gold or turquoise in collarless and tieless neckbands.

We had first to receive their visits of politeness, in our bedroom, whose emptiness for purposes of repose was accentuated by a four-square row of little tea-tables and stiff-backed chairs. There was no possible privacy. There never is in Persian guest-rooms. Only in the *anderun*—the women's quarters, where I might not penetrate.

From each new entrant came the same stereotyped inquiries concerning our health. Through rounds of tea in small glasses we sat vainly hopeful that the reception would soon end. Conversation was limited to banalities within the grasp of one small functionary who spoke a little French. Time passed slowly, and not a soul moved.

I did not know just how to dismiss such a gathering gracefully. In this as in most other things our feeble interpreter offered no help. The customary procedure was to wait in the room of reception, which was usually one's bedroom, the announcement of dinner—an indefinite hour depending on the progress of the cook. Through the cigarette smoke I began to catch signals of distress from Josephine.

"Might we," I explored hopefully, with appropriate gesture, "wash off the stains of travel?" This brought servants bearing ewers, shallow copper basins and bath towels. I lacked in Persian, as did our interpreter in French, certain expressions of delicate usage. Eventually the idea in mind was somehow conveyed to our host, whereat he called aloud and retainers sprang to the summons. Regally Josephine was ushered through the solemn ranks by four servants holding candle-lamps, down the stairs, to a doorless convenience in one corner of the courtyard. There was no concealing the purpose of that descent, accomplished in a dead silence broken only by the tread of her heavy-soled shoes on the stone steps. The servants' sandals made no sound.

Clump, clump, clump down the steps and across the courtyard. Then there was a pause. Four ingenuous servants, ever helpful, held flickering candle-lamps around a conventionally shaped aperture in the tiled floor off a corner of the courtyard. I heard a weary voice utter one of the eight or ten Persian words then at its command. *"Burroo!"* it cried. "Begone!" Not a very polite word, but it had the desired effect. The four candle-bearers scuttled off to far corners of the courtyard and examined the structure of the walls.

A few moments later *clump, clump, clump* up the stairs; a flushed little face arrived surrounded by a retinue of candle-bearers. In the

polite silence that hung over the room the only unveiled lady outside
the *anderuns* of Khaniqin resumed her seat at my side.

We were nine long days on the road from Kasr-i-Shirin to Teheran,
a matter of 470 miles, easily feasible now in a day and a half. The
ancient caravan track had in places been realigned by the Russians,
metalled by the British Dunsterforce. It crossed the Zagros *massif* over
a series of passes running up to 7600 feet altitude. These were formidable obstacles in the snows of January for Model-T Lizzies. Up them
the antique relics of flivvers bucked and stalled and boiled with radi-
ators spouting like garden sprinklers. Where the snow lay deep or
drifted we had to be pushed for miles on end by gangs of a dozen to
forty men, who all the way kept up a rhythmic chant and synchronized
their heaving to its beat. Eight or ten men pushed each car, the rest
pushing them.

"A-*lee!* ah-hah, A-*lee,* A-*lee!*" Slowly, from forty throats in unison,
over and over again repeated, echoing musically through the snow-
covered ranges: "A-*lee!* ah-hah, A-*lee!* A-*lee!*"

I asked of Elishah the chauffeur what the cry signified. It bore a
crude resemblance to the French *allez!* Elishah was an ex-Turkish
Christian refugee, a Chaldean, who upon a time had passed some while
in the stockyards of Chicago. From this venture he retained a smattering of colloquial English that was altogether weird and often wonderful. He held a hearty contempt for most things Persian.

"Oh *that!*" he snorted. "They holler up to Ali for to give some help.
You know, they think he all same Jeez Christ. But he not an' can't do
nothin'; for he just or'n'ry sonvabitch like you'n me!"

But it may have been the inspiration from Ali that got us up the
passes.

The descents were something else. Down the slopes we plunged in
maniacal disregard for any other thing on the road, as also for life and
limb of the cars' occupants. The way behind was left strewn with
sprawling donkeys, camels and drovers. Our chauffeurs on meeting a
caravan merely leaned forward on their steering wheels and yelled at
full voice: "*Khabadar! Khabadar!*" A futile warning, "Take care!" as
one hurtled in murderous frenzy straight at some tangled mass of
animals. It never once occurred to that pair to slacken speed. The
donkeys would be spread all over the road, horses and mules in somewhat tighter formation, camels in long lines hitched nose-to-tail by

goat's-hair rope. Whether they were tangled or not, we soon tangled them.

The terrified animals veered off in one direction or another, galloped away shedding their loads as they went. Some were knocked down when others barged into them, or fell under the weight of their own loads. The camels would throw their heads in the air, snapping their ropes, sprawl awkwardly and make off in ridiculous, stiff-legged gallops, slithering over the snowy surface. When they fell they had a long way to drop and came down hard. It was an unpleasant thought they they might split themselves in two on the slippery going. Camels do that sometimes.

There was no manner of telling the rule of the road from the rugged individualism of our chauffeurs. It was only in Teheran I learned that one was supposed to keep to the right. Elishah and Reuben were Chaldeans. I do not know if they were typical, but they were a very odd pair indeed. Reuben spoke only a dialect none but Elishah could understand. Elishah's Persian was as little polished as his English. They were continually tinkering with the cars to keep them running at all, forever pottering about on things they should have done long before, just when we wanted to be off. Not once did we get started within two hours of the time I set.

Each morning, to an accompaniment of choice stockyardese oaths on the subject of everything Persian and the singular ancestry of his car, Elishah would predict, until we passed beyond the country of the Kurds over the barrier ranges: "Today plenty snow, plenty robbers!" We met with plenty snow, but no greater brigands than Elishah and Reuben.

There was no way to make those two lunatic chauffeurs drive with any sense or consideration. Descending the Assadabad Pass, Elishah ran clean over a bedazed greybeard—fortunately padded in heavy winter garb and so not gravely damaged—knocked two donkeys off the road, hit a camel, skidded down a ditch, and was finally crashed into from behind by Reuben with the baggage car. Over that sequence I blew up. There was a brief argument with Elishah, closed with a drawn revolver. I had by then reached the point of *wanting* to kill our driver, and he knew it. Until that moment I had merely been afraid that I might have to. From there on I drove across the passes.

The passes were magnificent. They followed one after another through the folded formations of the Zagros, with bleak wind-swept plateaus between. Nights we spent variously in caravanserais; in little mud-built telegraph section offices and rest stations; with the Financial Agent at Kirmanshah, where for five hours we went through the preliminaries and the substance of one dinner; on the earthen floor of the small house of the sub-governor at Assadabad; and with the Manager of the Ottoman Bank at Hamadan. I expected that the Financial Agent of Hamadan would come out to greet us and offer hospitality as had his colleague of Kermanshah. There came instead a frock-coated secretary.

"The *Pishkar* is very sorry not to welcome you himself," announced his deputy, "and to entertain you as he had so joyously been expecting. But unhappily at this auspicious moment of your arrival he finds himself in jail!" It seemed that there was a lack of cordial understanding between the Financial Agent and the Commander of the Western Division.

Through ten inches of snow on the level, with much more in drifts, we did six miles up the Aveh Pass in something over four hours. Close to the top, as the early dark closed in like a thick blue fog, we stuck fast. By Ali's grace this was no great way from the only building within miles. The building was not impressive in itself, but at that stage one was glad enough to find shelter of any sort. Its mud walls, stiffened with the bones of dead pack animals, enclosed a space of some eighteen by twenty feet. Its flat roof protruded perhaps five feet above the snow line. The purpose was a refuge for *chavadars*—for camelmen and muleteers and drovers of donkeys; a *chai-khaneh* where they could drink their bitter tea and warm themselves at a fire.

The fire glowed red on the mud floor, filling the room with an acrid wood-smoke that burned one's eyes and lungs as from the fumes of strong acid. It was impossible to see through the frowst more than five feet, until I lighted my gasoline lantern; and then perhaps ten. Shadowy figures crouched about the floor, one could not tell how many. What with drovers and part of a gang of snow shovellers, the tea-house tender, our chauffeurs and ourselves, we might have been thirty. There was a door, one tiny window sealed with opaque glass, and a pit in the center which held a well surrounded by heaps of offal. The place had the ripe odor of a goat's nest with a strong manurish flavor.

I set up our camp beds along one wall. Loud squawks of chickens and the surprised bleats of a sheep mingled with my curses as I fell over things in the dark. I strung a rubber ground-sheet on poles to make a screen of feeble privacy for Josephine. It was not a cleanly task to erect this through the festooning network of thick black soot built up by years of naked flame from chimneyless oil lamps.

The squatting *chavadars* watched us through the smoke. They gurgled like their own camels, spat lustily, emitting formidable belches. Some slept, and their snores shook the ground on which they lay as though an earthquake were rending the Zagros *massif* apart. It struck me that this could account for the high proportion of casualties when earthquakes shatter Mid-Eastern towns. People who sleep on ground habitually rocked by such stupendous snores would not notice the preliminary shocks of an earthquake until their mud-built houses collapsed upon them.

By a special dispensation of Ali no more snow fell during the night. In the morning, propelled by all our companions of the *chai-khaneh,* we managed to break through the top of the pass to where a gang of shovellers had worked up the other side. Yet it was far from plain sailing. At two the next morning, three-quarters frozen, we reached Kazvin. The last forty-mile stretch lay through a subzero gale interspersed with patches of icy fog. Even Elishah's blasphemy failed towards the end under the insatiable demands of the radiator. In the pitch dark of that wind-swept empty space, water in liquid state was as easy to find as flowering aloes. We had looked forward to Kazvin's Grand Hotel, the first semblance of any hotel since Baghdad. Reality brought disillusion in a forlorn set of barracks, little warmer than the night outside, a foretaste of the immense gloom that was the Grand Hotel at Teheran. Those two were our first and last stops at hotels in Persia.

We came to Teheran numb, in a state of utter exhaustion, at midnight. The baggage car had been lost. Reuben—I learned next day—ran it off the road somewhere in the frozen fog. At the Grand Hotel there was no open fire, not the least warmth of any kind either external or internal, nor even light. In the way of welcome there crept to the door a blear-eyed night porter with the mental acumen of an armadillo, who held an oil lantern in one hand and showed no wish to let us in.

With him I held a three-cornered argument through the intermediary of Elishah, whose linguistic deficiencies were filled in by oddly inappropriate oaths. All of this led at length to our being shunted through echoing, barn-like corridors to an evil little room in the back, that was drear and cold and smelt of the manure-pile one could not see until morning, just outside. It smelt, too, of the mattress on the narrow, three-quarters bed: an article of curious shape like the back of a camel, stuffed with straw, whose odor suggested some earlier use of its stuffing as horse-bedding. The armadillo shuffled off and disappeared. A few hours later callers began knocking on the door while we still lay on the camel-humps of that reeking mattress in postures of acute discomfort.

The capital city of Teheran in those days was a diversified but not very satisfying mixture of moderately ancient Eastern architecture with an indifferent attempt at Westernization along the lines of a Balkan capital. It comprised a few shapely mosques and associated structures of the Mohammadan period, an immense covered bazar partly glassed in, and a heterogeneous jumble of other buildings mostly of little merit. For all its vast expanse it lacked special character, apart from its high earthen walls pierced by twelve minareted gates with gaily tiled faces (since demolished under Reza Shah's passion for modernity), and a setting of immense natural beauty against the slopes of the Tokjal Range.

Down the main avenue ran a horse-drawn tramline between narrow, disconnected sections of sidewalk that broke off without warning into gaping mudholes. Long strings of camels filed through the sloshy winter mud to caravanserais near the bazars. Horses, mules and donkeys tacked back and forth under a variety of burdens such as the skinned carcasses of fat-tailed sheep. Human beasts of burden shuffled at obtuse angles balancing heavy loads on wedge-shaped hassocks upon their backs. Those persons who could afford a conveyance moved about in Russian droshkies drawn by scarecrow horses, with evil-looking cut-throats on the boxes.

There were only a few scattered electric lights in the city. The Grand Hotel was so lighted—feeble stabs at light that flickered continually and went out about eleven-thirty each evening. The hotel also boasted a European-type bath, a galvanized-iron tub attached to an oversized samovar that burned wood. This contraption took an hour to heat the water and the charge was a dollar.

There was a so-called telephone system, with connections to most of the principal government offices and Legations. It was usually quicker and far more certain to send a messenger on foot. There was coal available for the hearths or stoves of the well-to-do, shaley stuff brought down on donkey-back from high in the Tokjal range at a price of around thirty-six dollars a ton.

There were shops that sold strange European and American articles, brands of which one had never heard, at enormous prices. There were shops exposing dried fish from the Caspian with plaintive, staring eye-sockets; and shops that specialized in the more intimate inner parts of various animals.

There were some lovely things for sale in the bazars, if one knew how to look. Many *objets d'art*, silver, embroideries and even Persian miniatures, had been smuggled out of Russia by Tzarist refugees: loot from the débâcle of the Bolshevik revolution, often obtainable at extremely low prices—selling, not asking, prices.

There were oddities to be found on the streets wherever one chanced to look or to step. A few days after my arrival I clambered from a droshky, garbed in my morning coat but without top hat, to make a formal call on one of the cabinet ministers, and barely missed a disastrous collision with a blind man carrying a large, uncovered basket full of eggs on his head. This in its way was suggestive of how some of the cabinet ministers were carrying the burdens of their responsibility.

My top hat had not yet arrived. It came along eventually. In Iran most things come to him who waits. The waiting is not what matters; it is the variety and the unexpectedness of the things that come. My top hat arrived in due course—long-overdue course—on the post *fourgon* from Khaniqin.

The *fourgon* had been several weeks on its way. By mischance my sole-leather hatbox was stowed in an after corner of the springless wagon. There the heavy iron tire of the rear wheel had rubbed continually against it, eroding a hole in its side and through that a mouth-shaped gap in the hat. This was distressing, as there was no good way of replacing the topper without many months of delay and an expense that would probably amount to the cost of four such hats in London or New York.

Ingenuity is a part of one's essential equipment for life in Central Asia. By then I had begun to acquire the nucleus of a battalion of retainers. To Abu Talib I gave order: "Get me the hide of one very black cat!" This he duly produced. Cats are available almost anywhere in Persia. I cut a suitable furry piece of skin and glued it inside the gaping void in my hat. With nail scissors the hair was clipped to appropriate length, the edges inked in with India ink: and there was my topper, proud as could be—if one did not look at it too closely. This none did. Few men of the European colony would look very closely at another's topper, lest a return look should find a hat bought off some departing Secretary of Legation whose head was a couple of sizes different, one way or another, from that of the hat's present possessor.

The patch turned somewhat green in time, an unhealthy and betraying shade, but India ink always freshened it up for state occasions. I wore the hat only half a dozen times in Iran, being dressed in formal Persian style for the more important ceremonies. And I did not try to sell it, as was customary, on leaving—my conscience would not have been quite clear. Eventually it grew a crop of toadstools when I left it for a time in the dank godown of Raffles Hotel in Singapore. No catskin treatment could then correct its moth-eaten and harrowed appearance, after the fungi had been plucked.

In some respects Teheran occasionally reminded me of that hat.

King of Kings

The titles of His Majesty the Shah of Persia are legion. They extend to such sonorous honorifics as Pole of the Universe, Vice Regent (or alternatively the Shadow) of God on Earth, King of Kings. Yet the embodiment of all these when I arrived upon the Persian scene was not a force that counted greatly in the rehabilitation of Iran. Ahmed Shah Kajar, last descendant of a dynasty established through treachery and assassination some hundred forty years before, preferred the fleshpots of Europe to the Augean task of restoring his disintegrated country. In his official greeting he assured the American Mission of his satisfaction at our coming, promised support in our undertaking. But his own support was failing fast, pale and flabby as himself, and he had little to offer others.

On the voyage out from Bombay, Captain Fitzherbert of the *Varsova* had regaled us with tales of his previous trip with Ahmed Shah as passenger. The Master of the *Varsova* had been particularly struck by the Shah's insistence on having pillows in his bath.

Ahmed Shah, returning to his country from Paris (his last return, as it happened), debarked at Bushire. The Persian Navy had been ordered out to meet him. The Persian Navy consisted of one rotting gunboat called the *Persepolis* and a lesser craft. Both had lain long in Bushire roadstead with skeleton crews, for years unpaid, living off the salvage of the ships' fittings. The denuded hulks could not be budged. The Officer Commanding the Port borrowed a launch from the British trading company Mespers. Flying a gigantic Persian flag, he put-putted out the ten miles to the anchorage to greet the Shah. The Commander felt that a royal salute should be fired in His Iranian Majesty's honor, but he had no cannon. So he drew his revolver with a fine flourish and started shooting in the air just as the Shah got halfway down the ladder. Ahmed Shah thought it was an attempted assassination and scampered like a frightened squirrel back to the security of the *Varsova*.

"It took a bit of persuasion to get him off the ship after that," Captain Fitzherbert told us.

I came to Teheran in time to attend a "Grand Review of the Troops." The Shah had arrived in the capital some six or eight weeks before. This was the first public display of the new Persian military might developed by Reza Khan, Minister of War in title and dictator in fact, wherefore it was a show of more than ordinary interest for those who watched it. It was a show of peculiar interest, sinister in implication, for an uneasy Kajar head under a brimless *kola*—the Persian official headgear of that day—fashioned from unborn lambskin. The head of Ahmed Shah Kajar rested intranquilly on his fat shoulders. His emotions as he viewed the march-past of his forces sprang from other things than pride in their martial display.

The khaki-clad columns swung by in the long march step adopted from the Russians. They sang after the fashion of Russian troops, in Oriental cadences that blended oddly with the strains of Wagner to which they marched—a Wagnerian rendering unlike any I had heard before, or ever since. Their rifles, carbines and cannon were remarkable in divergence of types and origins. One suspected that supplies of ammunition for those weapons might prove illusory in the field. Yet as a whole the parade was not unimpressive. What it lacked in armament was made up in an extraordinary display by detachments of wild-riding irregulars from the four corners of Iran, wearing enormous turbans or woolly shakos and waving ancient scimitars, whose fanciful acrobatics in the saddle would have rejoiced the hearts of any rodeo audience.

Of greater interest than the review itself were the two principal reviewers. Ahmed Shah—legitimate dynastic incumbent of the throne, King of Kings, Pole of the Universe, Shadow of God on Earth: a short, fat and timorous young man who obviously was deriving no comfort from his immediate surroundings. And Reza Khan—illiterate opportunist, sometime trooper of the disbanded Persian Cossack Brigade, towering, dour: a ruthless personality in a weak and shifting court, soon to induct himself onto the seat he was to declare vacated by his sovereign.

The Shah, garbed in a black frock coat, rode to the reviewing stand astride a large white charger with a purple tail. Purple tails are the imperial prerogative, dating back to early Roman times and to the dye from certain shellfish of Tyre reserved by emperors for their greater glory. The dye for the last scion of the Kajars was probably German aniline, yet still stood as the outward representation of power.

Ahmed Shah was ill at ease. With the aid of many servitors he dismounted and walked slowly to the reviewing stand. Hesitantly he acknowledged the hollow plaudits, the low bows of his courtiers. A pale and flaccid youth, he looked the part of one who would call for pillows in his bath. He was nervous and frightened by the whole affair, afraid of his towering Minister of War, afraid of assassination; frightened of what the review might develop toward his personal discomfiture.

Nothing developed along that particular line save for one small *coup de théâtre* which I observed with interest from the next box. It passed unnoticed by most of the assemblage, but not, I think, by Reza Khan.

The columns of troops in close formation swung past the reviewing stand where Ahmed Shah sat flabbily on an armchair, Reza standing stiff and enormous behind his right shoulder. The Shah from time to time gave some mild sign of approbation toward the devoted efforts of his War Minister, feeling in his heart only fear and hatred for that unpolished usurper of power. Reza, harboring little but contempt for his royal master, paid outward deference, though with none of the requisite servility, to the Majesty he had already determined should be the last of the Kajar line.

The late-afternoon sun dipped toward the horizon, casting long shadows. One such shadow fell across him who was called the Shadow of God on Earth. His Imperial Kajar Majesty disappeared, blotted out, as it were, beneath a shadow far deeper than himself—the shadow, long and ominous, of Reza Khan.

It was a prophetic touch, in its way.

Ahmed Shah Kajar not long thereafter betook himself to Paris for his "health." And there, for his health, he remained until deposed by the one-time trooper he had been forced to accept as his Minister of War. A few years later he died obscurely in the American Hospital of Paris, his only notable success in life having been a fling at speculation on the Paris Bourse. Ahmed Shah, last of the Kajar Dynasty, counted not at all in his country's program.

The only one who did count was Reza Khan. The dour personality of this man completely dominated the Government. His strength of purpose, or more of will, stood out as a Messiah's in the confused and feeble conglomerate of a tottering regime. It was by no means a wholly altruistic purpose. Yet in his fashion Reza Khan had something of the fibre of a patriot.

His major objectives—beyond the mere acquisition of power—were fundamental to Persia's sovereignty. He planned to weld the disrupted fragments of the nation into coherence, first consolidating its forces under his personal leadership. He would wrest the country from alien interference in its autonomy, alike from the "protection" of Britain and Russia. He undertook to subdue and disarm the turbulent elements within its borders—the nomad and seminomadic tribes which comprise a third of the total population and become unmanageable whenever the central government is weak.

And, with the help of a Mission from a disinterested power like the United States, he aimed to reform the financial administration, restore the solvency of the country, develop its natural resources and modernize its archaic system of communications.

An admirable program in itself, and not easily to be attained in a State that was penniless, shot with internal corruption and impotent in external relations. Reza was probably the only man in the country who could have approached it. Within a very few years he had made considerable progress toward these ends. The cost of this progress was high in many ways, in personal liberties, in security of tenure and of life itself. In these costs he bore no share; yet, except for the unhappy peasantry, perhaps those who suffered the brunt were not too greatly deserving of sympathy. And while the methods he followed were utterly unscrupulous it may well have been that the ends justified the means, that in the peculiar structure of Persian society no other means would have succeeded—even to the treatment he accorded most of his own supporters in the end.

The rest of the Cabinet were men of little character, the usual miscellany of ineffectual, aging hangers-on, of experienced and selfish politicians, and young and grasping opportunists whose integrity it would in many cases have been a euphemism to call doubtful. Energy and disinterest do not often go hand-in-hand amongst the Persian governing classes.

The Prime Minister, Ghavam-es-Saltaneh, held the distinction of having moved directly from a Teheran jail to the chair which supported —at least in theory—the head of the government. He was a well-educated member of a prominent family, an astute but politically unreliable gentleman with a reputation somewhat tarnished from too personal an interest in the Anglo-Persian Agreement of 1921. That interest, it was alleged, had netted him the tidy sum of £30,000—a *douceur* for which a good many politicians, not only in Persia, would support a fair degree of tarnish. As Governor-General of Khorasan, Ghavam-es-Saltaneh had fallen into disfavor through an unsuccessful conspiracy against the government in Teheran.

Reza Khan, while consolidating his own power with the army, was content to see in the Prime Minister's chair someone able to deal with the written word more effectively than himself. When a periodic cabinet crisis early in 1922 left the government without a head, he decided that Ghavam-es-Saltaneh's capabilities could for the moment be employed to better advantage as Prime Minister than in penal servitude.

All this was typical of the situation when I reached the capital city of Teheran, sometimes called the "Foot of the Throne" since all life supposedly stems from the person of the Shah. It was emblematic also of the curious inconstancy of Persian fortune which elevates and deposes, though not in any general levelling, with such fine disregard for previous circumstances as to shape society on a remarkably democratic basis. Here was a hereditary monarch fearful and unhappy on his ancient throne, soon to depart his country and his throne forever (though not, indeed, of his own volition), to make a killing on the Paris stock market and die unwept in the American Hospital at Neuilly. Here was a Commander-in-Chief of the Army and Minister of War who a few years before had been a lowly and illiterate trooper, who three years hence would crown himself King of Kings of Iran. Here sat a Prime Minister who by invitation of that one-time trooper had left the inhospitable earthen floor of the local jail for the Prime Ministerial desk, and by the same authority in the following year would be chased clear out of the country to return no more until the forced abdication (by the Allies of World War II) of the self-elevated King of Kings eighteen years later.

Such constant flux in social relationship has written the history of Iran throughout the ages.

The rise of Reza Khan from the ranks of the Persian "Cossack" Brigade to be Dictator of the Iranian scene came like the unfolding of destiny. Reza was in no wise loath to accept it as such. Fate had set the stage; Reza, knowing well his countrymen's disabilities and weaknesses, alert to every opportunity and ready to shape each to his ends, played his part as though foreordained.

Persia was ripe for dictatorship. Reza was temperamentally fitted for the task. Few such strong characters have emerged above the irresolute mass of his countrymen since Nadir Shah rose, likewise from lowly origin, to be King of Kings two centuries before. Reza's qualities were not at all amiable ones. They inspired fear rather than love. He was arrogant, ruthless, lacking the least trace of gratitude. He stopped at nothing to achieve the objectives of an illimitable ambition. He was in no way ascetic in the amassing of an immense personal fortune within a short space of time. Yet withal, and despite a very limited educational equipment, he was a man of outstanding capacity.

Some weeks after my first official call on him as Minister of War I was invited to his office to discuss a matter of special concern. He sat on a high-backed armchair, erect and massive, in khaki uniform. He was a big man, physically powerful, large-featured, with cold brown eyes set in a greyish face. There was little of humor in that face, no trace of human kindliness. It was an immobile face that very rarely smiled but could express the savage temper he often loosed.

He asked briefly if I would help him organize an Air Force. "And I have the money for it!" he snapped.

It would have been an interesting but ungrateful task. There was not, as far as I know, a single Persian at that time with pilot's training or flying experience. There were few with enough mechanical knowledge or aptitude to make a satisfactory overhaul of a Ford jitney, let alone an airplane engine. There was nothing in the way of flying material in the country, and little enough of ground equipment.

My contract with the Iranian government called for different activities. It was not on the program that I should remain longer in Teheran. I offered a few suggestions for the formation of an Air Force and then set out for East Persia. As it developed I was well clear of a vexatious matter.

The Persian Air Force started off with three Flights, each from a different source. The pilots, while Persians were being trained in France, were of three nationalities. They spoke three different languages—none of them Persian. There were few Persians able to comprehend any of the instruction books in French, German and Russian; fewer, if any, who could understand them all.

The French Flight had two-seater Spads. It would have taken a stroke of genius to find an airplane of that time less suited to Persian conditions. This Flight crashed in detail over the whole of South Persia during its period of formation and was heard from no more. The German Flight had Junkers. The Russian Flight had aircraft said to be Russian but with a striking resemblance to Junkers, though apparently lacking the stamina of their prototypes. The German Flight was the only one that served any useful purpose. It did good work of a sort, chiefly in transporting Reza's commanders on "inspections" and missions to intimidate the tribes; its aircraft standing out in all weathers, its pilots quiet and efficient—and making good use of their opportunities to study the aerial geography of Iran. But with such a background of international jealousies, hotchpotch of equipment and lack of all basic facilities the attempt to produce a prefabricated Air Force (of a strength of eighteen aircraft) from alien air was foredoomed, and whoever took a hand in it could hardly have enhanced his reputation.

I returned a year and a half later on a trip to Teheran from East Persia by automobile—the third car ever to pass over that fearful track. The capital was then in a state of bewildered suspense over Reza Khan's trial balloon of a Republic. This, like many of his steps, followed somewhat after the model of Mustafa Kemal in Turkey. Telegrams despatched by Reza's order, representing the "unanimous voice of the people" in favor of the deposition of the Kajar Dynasty and establishment of a Republic under Reza, poured in from the provinces. For several nights running this "expression of popular demand" was celebrated with fireworks and long-winded speeches. Then it all ceased as suddenly as it had started. The trial balloon collapsed under the violent opposition of the still powerful Moslem clergy. Reza issued a general order forbidding any mention of such an ungodly thing as a Republic. But while the fireworks were still brightening Teheran and the provincial capitals, several Deputies with an estimable desire for knowledge came to me for private enlightenment.

"We are, it seems, to have a Republic," they said. "God willing, that is a very fine idea. Now you who come from a Republic doubtless will be able to tell us something we would like to know. Just *what* is a Republic?"

By the time of my next return to the capital, another year later, Reza had consolidated his position. His thoughts no longer ran to any such uncertain mechanism as a Republic to give him absolute sway over his country. Shortly after I had taken up the post of Acting Treasurer-General (with an office located in the former Russian Bank building whose entrance was flanked by a sentry-box where Trooper Reza had at one time mounted guard) he summoned a Constituent Assembly to meet in Teheran. The hand-picked membership voted without dissent to depose Ahmed Shah Kajar and all his line. In his place the Assembly selected Prime Minister, Minister of War, Commander-in-Chief Reza Khan to be Regent of the State. Of this the ultimate issue was not in great doubt, nor long delayed.

The Treasurer-General, among other responsibilities such as the Mint and the Royal Palaces and Buildings, had theoretical control over the Crown Jewels of Persia. These had been evaluated a few years previously by an appraiser, from Cartier I believe it was, at more than forty million dollars. They ranged from the Peacock and Nadiri Thrones to chests of uncut emeralds, from the great *Darya-i-Nur* diamond to gewgaws of large intrinsic worth but incredible ugliness. The historic value of many of the set pieces, the crowns and sceptres, the inlaid and jewelled swords and staffs, bows, quivers, shields and hatchets, would be quite impossible to determine. All together they made a staggering collection.

Some were kept on exhibition in a very badly arranged royal museum in the Gulistan Palace. Much of immense value was stored in dank and gloomy little treasure-chambers in the Palace depths. The brass or wrought-iron chains and locks to the chambers and the chests inside them were at that time sealed with the seals of the Treasury-General, the Ministry of Court, the Ministry of War and the Major-domo of the Palace. Every time any of the doors were opened the seals had to be broken by the head or a responsible representative of each of these offices, the locks afterwards resealed with their official seals. The process became a trifle tedious through repetition.

During my tenure of office the Regency gave Caesarian birth to a new dynasty, the Dynasty of His Imperial Majesty Reza Shah Pahlavi and his issue in perpetuity. The family and dynastic style he chose—Pahlavi—was the word for the ancient Persian language of Mazan-deran, the area from which Reza haled. (As a result of his choice the Imperial Bank of Persia had hastily to change its telegraphic code-name.) Pahlavi was the language of the northern Persians in the days of Darius the Great, from whom His Imperial Majesty had succeeded in the relatively short space of three months in tracing his lineal descent.

In the Royal Treasure were many crowns, some of them very famous. But Reza in the usual Eastern fashion ordered a new Pahlavi crown to be built for him, together with a new palace. The former task he entrusted to a Czarist Russian refugee jeweller whose life, were the work not finished before the coronation set for a few months later, was threatened with certain extinction.

There came constant calls for jewels lying in obscure corners within the treasure-chambers, now destined to adorn the Pahlavi crown. I never learned just why those calls nearly always came at night. A message would arrive by hand or telephone, often at a singularly incon-venient hour. Usually it would come from the Amir Lashkar to whom Reza had delegated his own quasi-personal Ministry of War.

"His Imperial Majesty requires, before morning, the central of the three large diamonds on the left epaulette of Nadir Shah's Dress of State," the message would go. Or it might be some other less precisely located jewel, or a dozen or more. "Will you of your kindness meet me at the Gulistan Palace at four hours after sunset, and bring with you your seal? I have advised the others concerned." And though the hour often interfered with one's prior arrangements, those nocturnal forays in the treasure-chambers of the King of Kings were never dull.

Accompanied by retainers bearing tulip-shaped candle-lamps we would enter through high-arched passages into dark and musty little rooms. At the outset the breaking of the seals was something of a ceremonial.

"I break the seal of the Treasury-General!" I would announce, and do so.

"I break the seal of the Ministry of War!" the Amir Lashkar would cry, following suit. And so on with the others. The ancient Major-domo would then fumble at the rusty locks with palsied hands. Servants held their candle-torches aloft as we peered within, our shadows cast in weird forms like Javanese dolls across the dust-streaked walls and cobweb festoons.

The Major-domo's lists were usually at fault, as was his memory. Happily so for me, for in looking into a multiplicity of chests and cabinets where the object of our search was rarely found at once, we came upon surprising things. Chests full of uncut emeralds, for instance; huge emeralds that never had been set, filling more than half the cubic space of a fair-sized Saratoga trunk. There came to mind Sinbadian tales, read in my youth, of persons plunging their naked arms to the shoulders in raw jewels. So I took off my coat, rolled up my sleeves and did likewise for the trivial fancy of being able to say that I, too, had done this.

"You had better watch me well," I advised the Amir Lashkar, "lest some of these bits of stone should stick!" I made similar gestures in a chest of unpierced pearls, large pearls from the Gulf, whose lustre doubtless had suffered through disuse and needed the touch of warm human skin.

The Amir Lashkar was an irreverent young man with a sense of humor and of pageantry, and the treasure-chambers were beyond any fancy-dress costumer's wildest dream. We rigged ourselves up in astonishing regalia: with jewelled swords and bucklers, in coats of gold-mail and coats encrusted with pearls, in ancient inlaid helmets and diadems and other weirdly shaped headgear heavy with the jewels adorning them, and royal uniforms whose epaulettes were set with gigantic diamonds and other precious stones. Under the dim light of candle-lamps borne by solemn servants we peered at our images reflected on crinkly, spotted mirrors to get an idea of the effect.

On the shelves of one cabinet I came upon some forty-odd *kolas,* all identical: round, brimless hats of unborn lambskin, a minor item in the wardrobe of the deposed Ahmed Shah. The Amir Lashkar produced a *kola* with a gold and pearl egret and an enormous diamond on its front. Casually we tried it on, but the Amir Lashkar was not satisfied. Shortly he turned up wearing an elaborate jewelled armband set with one of the more astonishing gems of this world. The central piece was a diamond of perfect color the size of a match-box.

"Recognize it?" asked the Amir Lashkar nonchalantly.

"*Mashallah!*" I exclaimed. It was the *Darya-i-Nur*—the "Sea of Light," blood-brother to the *Koh-i-Nur*, the "Mountain of Light" of the British Crown, and more than half again as large; a flawless bauble weighing 186 carats. I tried that on too, setting the *kola* at different angles on my head, crossing my braceleted arms under my chin and regarding myself with approval in a painted mirror held by one of the servants.

"Now, does this not go well with my Western style of feature?" I asked.

"Not bad," admitted the Amir Lashkar, "but I think it suits me rather better than your European physiognomy." I would not agree to this, though the argument was possibly academic. The occasions when I was apt to wear the *Darya-i-Nur* were likely to be limited.

The next time I saw the "Sea of Light," together with other ornaments and regalia I had sported by candlelight in the dim recesses of the Gulistan treasure-chambers, was during Reza Shah's Coronation. I came up from Shiraz for the ceremony, and attended it in the court dress of high Persian officialdom. This consisted of a *kola* (of felt rather than unborn lambskin, and unbedecked by any diamond) and a gown of Kashmiri shawling. The gown had long, tight sleeves, a skirt almost to the ground, and no pockets. It was a very warm gown. It was also extremely expensive, but I had been fortunate in being able to borrow one from a high state official who happened to be in jail and not needing his at the moment.

The Coronation was staged with Oriental splendor in the Hall of Mirrors, whose museum pieces had been rearranged under the direction of Vita (Mrs. Harold) Nicolson. Previously its priceless royal treasures shared space with such relics as sharks' teeth and a stuffed monkey; its magnificent Gobelin tapestries and Sèvres china service, gifts of Napoleon, were interspersed with faded photographs of Mozaffer-ed-Din Shah's tour of Europe; its prehistoric Luristan bronzes set off by such mementos of that tour as a toothbrush, a homœopathic medicine case with little bottles of pills in a row at each side, and a fluted seashell with the gilt inscription "Souvenir of Brighton."

At the far end of the Hall reposed the world-famed Peacock Throne—a disappointing enamelled-and-jewelled dais whose glory, valued once at £6,000,000, had been dissipated by faithless custodians since Nadir Shah looted it from the Moghul Empire. In front of it was placed the smaller but resplendent Nadiri Throne.

Shortly before the Shah's entry came his small son, the Crown Prince (now in turn Shah), very serious and military in khaki uniform; followed by a double line of dignitaries bearing on red plush cushions various items, of which some had once, if but for a brief moment, adorned my figure. In gowns and uniforms they advanced at solemn pace: the Prime Minister holding the Kiani Crown, the Minister of War with the Jahavgasha Nadiri Sword, other Ministers carrying the Pearl Crown, the *Darya-i-Nur*, the Inlaid Staff; the Minister of the Interior with the "Royal Golchagh." A file of Amir Lashkars carried the Sceptre, the Royal Shield, the Inlaid Sword, Ismail Shah's coat-of-mail, the Inlaid Quiver, the Safavi Sword, the Shah Abbas Sword, the Royal Hatchet, the Bow of Nadir, and lastly a large framed photograph of Reza Shah, inheritor of all this.

In front, on the right, came Taimurtash, the Minister of Court, whose "heart stopped beating"—as hearts so often will under a taut bowstring held round the neck—a few years later at the behest of his Imperial master. He carried the new high-domed Pahlavi Crown which Reza, seated then on the Nadiri Throne, lifted from its red plush cushion with his own strong, coarse hands and set upon his own head, buckling on immediately thereafter the Jahavgasha Nadiri Sword.

The guns boomed the royal salute. Through the low-salaaming assemblage His Imperial Majesty, a little less grim-faced and dour than usual, stalked slowly out of the Hall to the State Coach that bore him through the beflagged streets of the capital, past the striped sentry-boxes where afoot he used to stand lonely guard. In the golden Coach behind six white horses, with his new crown on his head and wearing the "Royal Garment"—a cape as stiff as armor with brocaded pearls—ex-trooper Reza was escorted with all the lavish pageantry of the East to his new palace.

After the ceremony Tom Pearson and I stood in the now almost empty Hall admiring its new arrangement of ancient glories. We remarked the Prime Minister standing by the side of the Nadiri Throne, fumbling with the 200-carat uncut emeralds that dangled in festoons from its jewel-overlaid surface. The Prime Minister, Foroughi, was a kindly ex-professor of philosophic bent and impeccable honesty. Tom Pearson and I joined him where he stood peering through his spectacles at that King's ransom of precious stones set in gold, trying to fit something into their overflowing pattern.

"Your Highness," said Tom, "may we be of assistance?" Foroughi looked at us in a vague and detached way.

"Why, I don't know," he answered. He held up a fair-sized cabochon emerald between his finger-tips. "I stepped on this out on the floor. I thought it might have fallen off the Throne, but there seems to be no place for it nor is there any other one here like it." We peered together at the Throne. Just then Josephine returned up the enormous length of the Hall and called to me. I went over to her.

"Vita Nicolson is in a state of near collapse," she said. "She has lost her most treasured heirloom of the Sackville-West family—a cabochon emerald. I'm afraid there's not much likelihood of her finding it again after that crowd milling about on the floor, but I thought it just possible you might be able to do something about it."

"Why, yes," I said, "I can. Please present my compliments to Vita Nicolson and tell her that you arrived just in time to stop the Prime Minister from fitting her heirloom onto the Nadiri Throne!"

Under the control, again in principle, of the Treasurer-General were also the Royal Stables. The deposed King of Kings had no great love for riding nor much for other outdoor exercise, but tradition required that there be maintained for the Shah a large stable of horses. Those that had been reserved, at least nominally, for Ahmed Shah's personal use were all white stallions with their tails dyed the imperial purple. There were many of these, eating their heads off in the Royal Mews.

Reza's huge frame required large mounts. He had come into possession of no few of his own and had little interest in those left by his predecessor. He gave or sent away a number of the latter. The rest he ordered turned over to the Central Division of the army which was then trying to develop a polo team.

The ancient game of polo had long disappeared from Iran until it was revived by a British officer, Major W. A. K. Fraser, during the last war. While I was in Teheran we played two or three times a week on a field that made up for its uneven surface in a setting which was perhaps the most picturesque of any polo field in the world. The field was located on the lower slope of the snow-clad Tokjal range whose 11,000-foot peaks glowed in springtime in spectral shades under the afternoon sun, with Demavend's superb 19,000-foot cone behind; a mountain as perfect in form as Fujiyama and a third again as high.

Down-slope from the field lay the walls, minaretted gates and domes of Teheran and in the middle distance a robin's-egg blue shrine, with mauve-flowering Judas trees close at hand. And on this field we played polo against teams of the Persian Central Division mounted on pure white Arab stallions with purple tails.

I played with the British Legation team against them in games and in practice tilts that ran to an indefinite number of chukkers and various combinations of players. Some of the Persians were excellent players individually, but I never met a Persian four with any conception of team-work. They zigzagged all over the field, barging into opponents and their own team-mates with equal zest, shouting the one English word of polo that they knew—"*Cross! Cross!*"—as they vigorously crossed anyone who happened to be on the ball.

The "ponies" were a weird and wonderful collection. They ranged from 14.2 to well over 17 hands. Few were even half trained, many not at all. The Persians rode the standard Persian saddle—a close-coupled wooden tree open in the center, fairly high in pommel and cantle, with stuffed leather pads ending short of the knee and providing no effective grip. Their stirrups were flaring iron contraptions, square-bottomed with sharp corners and ornamental triangular side-pieces, such as one finds in museums of ancient armor. Their bits were V-shaped, with long side-irons, the point bearing hard on the roof of the horse's mouth at any pull on the rein. Wherefore the horses, though their mouths were as if case-hardened, had learned to hold their heads almost straight in the air.

All were stallions save only the geldings of the British Legation escort, ridden by some of the British team. Polo on half-trained stallions has a peculiar zest of its own. They would squeal, bite and kick at man or beast approaching alongside. Armored breeches and boots would have been useful equipment. Now and then they would dash clear off the field, their riders tugging futilely at horse heads upraised like angry swans. The unceasing quarrels in the lines where the spare ponies were tethered rent the air with shrill and raucous sounds.

Major "Wak" Fraser, a high-handicap player of the Indian Army and the one primarily responsible for the revival of polo in Persia, played back on the British Legation team. Because of him and some semblance of team-play we generally came out ahead. One soon found that in the unavoidable collisions with Persian players crossing all over the field it was the Persian in most cases, riding hard and with a fine sense of balance but no grip, who came off, shot out of the saddle as if catapulted. The field was often spattered with unhorsed Persians.

There was one day when the Central Division's acquisitions from the Royal Stables were being tried out along with a number of newly arrived officers. The imperial dye had not yet worn off the tails of the white stallions. Some twenty-odd of varying hue were tethered in line beyond the tents pitched down one edge of the field. There was a bar tent, a tea tent, dressing and equipment tents, which some of the more wealthy devotees of the game had set up. We had just finished a chukker and were riding off the field when an ungodly commotion broke loose in the pony lines.

It happened that a villager had gone that day to town to sell a fat-tailed sheep. He had sold the sheep for a good price. Now he was returning home, singing in high-pitched quavers that reflected his contentment with his journey. His blue turban was tilted to one side, a pink rose tucked over an ear. One hand he held as a sounding-board alongside his opened mouth, the other behind the ear that was unadorned, the better to enjoy his cadences breaking on the quiet air of late afternoon. With face turned skywards he sang away to himself in the fullness of his heart. Singing thus, he passed by the farther end of the field, up-wind, riding at a slow amble a mare in heat.

The stallions tethered in line below the tents swung suddenly around as there was borne to them on the gentle breeze an alluring aroma. With one accord they snapped their tether ropes; neighing loud and fearfully they galloped off in the direction of the wind. The direction of the wind lay straight up the line of the tents.

Through the tent-ropes they dashed, squealing, kicking, biting at one another. The tents went down like a row of card houses. There was a crash of glass and crockery as the tea tent collapsed. We could see Legation ladies diving out from under its fly like frogs escaping a net. The next crash signalled a major disaster.

"Oh my *God!*" one of my team-mates cried, riding off the field beside me. "There goes our bar!" Above loud yells, male and female, curses of grooms and of polo players, rose the lusty squeals from a score or so of stallions whose thoughts were not on polo.

I took one quick look to make sure that there were no serious casualties in the wreckage of the tents apart from the unhappy break-up of the bar, then galloped after the clattering tornado of horses. They were well away. All one could see was a dazed villager flat on his back staring into the sky, blue turban and one pink rose on the ground beside him; and in the distance a cluster of white rumps with purple tails disappearing over the curve of the slope beyond the Judas trees.

In the summer following the Coronation the German Minister, Count von der Schulenburg (later German Ambassador to Russia and liquidated by Hitler in 1944), came to visit us in Shiraz, accompanied by his dragoman Ghassim Khan. Ghassim, a Persian, had been attached for years to the German Legation and had an amazing memory of all those who had ever stopped or dined there. He recalled days not long past when he used to hand out leftovers from the Legation kitchen to a tall soldier standing sentry duty in a green-and-white-striped box before the Legation gates. The tall soldier liked the Legation food. He would shove it into his mouth with his thumb, wash it down with a long swig from a bottle of arack. The name of the tall soldier was Reza. That was all there was of it, just a first name, like Ralph. Trooper Reza. The name had grown since then. It was now His Imperial Majesty Reza Shah Pahlavi (May Whose Reign Be Everlasting), King of Kings of Iran.

That was in 1926. For fifteen years Reza Shah consolidated and enlarged his power by savage repression of all potential opposition to his will, and by continuing to play off—a well-established Persian formula—the strong, interested Powers against one another. In his attempt to recast the whole social and economic life of Iran, mould it into a form of Western civilization, he was an overt and not too successful copyist of Mustafa Kemal Atatürk, but lacked his genius. He built an extremely costly and uneconomic railway between the Persian Gulf and the Caspian Sea (which served the Allies of the World War's second phase very well in their efforts to supply Russia). He renovated Teheran with wide avenues and some quite good public buildings. And he started a number of modern industrial ventures under German tutelage in a country where the camel caravan had been the basic concept of movement and the processing of the opium plant that of government-controlled industry.

He decreed and enforced on the reluctant subjects of an ancient and primitive state a form of European dress fitted neither to their habits nor their pockets. He organized a military force sufficient to assure internal security, and for a time there was security in many parts of Iran where none had been before. He built several very good hotels on the Caspian Sea for tourists who could not get there in any numbers unless subsidized by the governments that found tourist traffic a profitable form of infiltration.

But the great mass of the people became more and more impoverished under these modernizing efforts, though Reza and his closest collaborators built up immense fortunes—the latter's accumulations usually accruing to Reza in the end. He gradually lost contact with the people. He was loved by none, cordially hated by many, feared by all. And his savagery was prodigious.

His handling of external relations was based on well-founded traditions of evasion and duplicity. But when the impact of the war swung towards the Middle East he was caught between the German political and technical influence he had encouraged and the imperative need of Britain and Russia to eliminate that threat; and this became his undoing. He misjudged the desperate seriousness of the two Great Powers he had so often played off against one another, acting now in concert for the first time in twenty-four years. The self-installed King of Kings was swept from the Nadiri and Peacock Thrones with little of the ceremony in which he had inducted himself upon them fifteen years before. He was escorted on a one-way trip to Mauritius. This might have been interesting for him, as he had never been farther afield than Istanbul and Najaf, but under the circumstances was probably not. He did not care for Mauritius, so he was escorted on to South Africa. Ex-trooper Reza, ex-King of Kings and Pole of the Universe, died not greatly lamented in Johannesburg in 1944.

The Ex-Chief Eunuch's Descendants

The American Mission offices in Teheran were besieged from early morning till night by swarms of petitioners. Armies of unemployed functionaries camped in the halls, each to spin a long tale of intrigue as the cause of his being without assignment, though righteous and capable beyond all his fellows. There were pensioners who had received no remittances for months running into years, and government employees bewailing strange irregularities in the manner of their salary payments. "Influentials" came to offer specious argument in lieu of tax settlements. Personages of varied importance sought to intercede on behalf of relations and acquaintances; veiled women pleaded for husbands and brothers and sons whose excessive defalcations had landed them in disfavor.

But of the masses of petitions that poured in upon us, the oddest was one which came to Tom Pearson as Director of Personnel. It had to do with the restoration of a pension on which payment had been long in arrears, though in this of itself there was nothing unusual. The unusual feature lay in the nature of the grant. It was a pension in favor of the ex-Chief Eunuch of a former Shah's *anderun*—the Imperial harem—and his numerous descendants.

"I am confused," announced Tom Pearson. "I do not understand this matter!" Whereat officials of the Pension Service tried to enlighten him. The ex-Chief Eunuch was a most worthy man, they said, who for more than a quarter of a century had borne in admirable manner the responsibilities of his charge. Nor were these light responsibilities in any way of speaking. His Majesty's *anderun* then comprised a good many hundred women: what with wives, concubines, daughters and female relations, retainers, servants, slaves, and so on. It was a post of delicate nature and of trust, that called for diplomacy of a special kind and carried with it high rank.

Now, having been honorably released from such responsibilities these many years, he was greatly in need of the pension that had been granted him on his retirement; the deserved reward for long and faithful services, which lately had been in abeyance because of the Government's lack of funds. For though he owned certain properties in the north, their revenue was insufficient for the needs of a retired official of so dignified a background, along with a sizable family. He had, said Tom's informants, assigned a portion of his pension to his offspring as custom provided.

None of this brought Tom Pearson to much clearer understanding of the case. "It appears hardly so much a question of custom," he commented, "as of—issue, shall we say? For it would seem that a Government grant in support of the children of the former Chief Eunuch might be open to certain technical objections!"

"True!" affirmed his advisers. "It is indeed an unusual case. For God in His wisdom willed that he who formerly was a eunuch should be one no longer!" Even this failed to dispel the confusion in Tom's mind.

"Perhaps," they suggested, "you may wish to discuss the matter with the petitioner in person? He is living now with his family in Azerbaijan and could be brought here to Your Excellency's presence." Tom did so desire, and in due course there appeared before his presence the quondam Chief Eunuch of the Persian Court, a diminutive but dignified old gentleman with white and thinning hair, whose numerous offspring had remained behind in Azerbaijan.

Simply, though in the manner of a practiced courtier, he reviewed the strange train of events that was his history.

"Your Excellency's kindness is great," he began. "To Your Excellency all matters will be made clear. By Allah the Merciful, the Loving-kind, they be a true tale!" True, and a singular story, the tale of the ex-Chief Eunuch of the King of Kings.

In restrained and courtly voice the petitioner proceeded: "Your Excellency's servant was still of tender age in the household of his parents when the King of Kings, Nasr-ed-Din Shah, visited Azerbaijan on a tour of state. And on this occasion it was decided that your servant's father should offer your servant in gift to the King of Kings, as one suitable for service in His Majesty's female quarters. For, as it happened, no operation upon your petitioner was needful to such end, nor indeed possible, since God in His wisdom had forestalled the necessity and had provided in your servant a person to be trusted in all circumstances."

(Medical evidence confirms the occasional appearance of "natural" eunuchs, though the complete phenomenon is rare. Eunuchoids, they are called: "born eunuchs in their mother's womb," in the words of the Bible. Such a one the petitioner had been at that starting point of his career.)

"And so it came to pass, when the King of Kings arrived with his retinue, that your servant's father had converse with a Great One, who was even such a one as was your servant; but an operated-one, not a natural-one. This Great One rejoiced in access to the ear of the King of Kings. To which, by the grace of Allah, he brought the father of your servant, who led your servant by the hand. There was kneeling as in prayer, and some talk of the works of Allah by the Great One who was an operated-one.

" 'May His Majesty the Vice-Regent of God on Earth live for a thousand years!' cried your servant's father, and spoke somewhat of his sorrowful situation; but the Great One spoke more. There was further talk of the works of Allah. And then your servant was exposed: whereupon much wonder was shown at the evidence of God's wisdom. After which it was heard that His Imperial Majesty, the Vice-Regent of God on Earth and Pole of the Universe, would deign accept the gift of his devoted subject, whose unhappy situation would be graciously improved. Your servant's father retired, low-bowing and moving backwards, but your servant remained. Until that moment your servant had not realized that he was the gift in question."

There was thus opened to him an interesting new prospect as novitiate of the Shah's *anderun,* though at the beginning he was frightened at the separation from his relations. Because of the special favor of God, the petitioner explained, he was shown consideration beyond his stature and grew to a position of trust. So that in course of time he rose, after the death of the Great One who was an operated-one, to take charge of the well-stocked female quarters of His Iranian Majesty.

"Your servant brought great credit to his office through serving honorably and well"—the ex-Chief Eunuch saw no object in prolonged self-effacement—"until there came a day in the *anderun* when he felt strange sensations. So painful were these feelings that your servitor lay writhing on a cushion, with a large group of the *anderun's* population staring at him in amazement. But after a while the pain ceased, and he found himself possessed of certain bodily appendages which until then, by God's will, had been absent. And from that time your servant was no longer a suitable one to be in charge of His Majesty's *anderun.*"

The transformation apparently had been complete. Whereupon, realizing only too well that not merely his position of trust but his life was in grave danger, the chief of the *anderun* pondered on how best to extricate himself from an awkward and unprecedented situation. An ex-eunuch, neither an operated-one nor any longer a natural-one, in charge of the harem of the King of Kings.

"In his distress your servant called on His Majesty's principal Hakkim—the Shah's doctor, who was a friend," Tom's petitioner continued. " 'I have a prayer to make to His Majesty,' said your servant; 'will you be my intermediary?' And the Hakkim answered, 'What nonsense is this? You know well that in your position you may make your prayers direct to the Sovereign even when others close to his ear are unable to reach it. What foolish talk is this between friends?'

" 'May I be your sacrifice!' said your servant. 'But this touches on a matter that cannot well be explained without your professional wisdom and support, or otherwise my head is in the balance. You know that I be designed as it were by Allah for just such service as now I hold?'

" 'How should I not know?' responded the Hakkim. 'Am I not His Majesty's own doctor?'

" 'That is as it is,' said your servant; 'but know now that Allah in His surpassing wisdom has changed the design. And where I used to pass about my duties with only the thoughts appropriate to my guardianship, I am now bitten by unseemly sensations. Oh, Hakkim! It is not well that I remain longer in this capacity, for—by Allah! there will be a trouble such as I have spent many years guarding against, and already I feel my head insecure on my shoulders!'

"He listened with a detached air, and it was clear he thought your servant had eaten too much of an evil weed. 'Thy stomach is upset, my brother,' he said. 'I will give you a pill; in the morning you will feel better.'

" 'A *pill* you think to give?' cried your servant. 'And will you not have a look at me?'

"He had a look. 'By Allah!' he exclaimed. 'It is indeed a miracle!' And he agreed to go at once to the Shah and intercede for your servant's life, which had become a tenuous matter."

The explanation of the sudden change in the state of health of His Majesty's Chief Eunuch must have been exceedingly complex, even for one so skillful in his diagnoses as the Shah's principal Hakkim. It was a change that called for the immediate, but honorable, release of this tried and faithful servitor, with a pension on which he might live in comfort to extol the works of Allah and the graciousness of the Shah.

The Shah's humor as he listened passed through the phases of cold and uncomprehending disbelief, whereat the Hakkim trembled for himself as much as for his friend; of violent insistence that the matter be corrected with a sharp instrument in the customary way ("Yet for that," advised the Hakkim professionally, "it must be feared he is too old"); of paroxysmal rage in which the sword of the executioner was loudly invoked; and of coarse mirth which left an uncomfortable feeling as to the outcome.

In the end the Hakkim prevailed. Convinced at length that there had been no defiling of the Imperial harem, yet that continuity of the same services he had relied on these many years was no longer desirable, the Shah was content to recognize how inscrutable are the works of Allah. And he granted, if perhaps not with very good grace, the honorable release and pension eloquently pleaded by the Hakkim.

"So," concluded the petitioner, "your servant retired to Azerbaijan, with a pension barely sufficient to support himself, after those many years at the 'Foot of the Throne.' And there he took a wife and by the grace of Allah begat offspring." Quite a brood of offspring, it appeared. The ex-Chief Eunuch had done well in the brief space given him, even though Allah's grace may have seemed to fall oddly in the matter of parentage.

"And Your Excellency's servant assigned his pension in part to the maintenance of his children and his children's children. Wherefore Your Excellency will recognize the injustice of withholding the small sum so deserved for long and faithful service, and so greatly needed for the support of your servant's descendants!"

The Golden Road—Second Stage

> *"Sweet to ride forth at evening from the wells,*
> *When shadows pass gigantic on the sand,*
> *And softly through the silence beat the bells*
> *Along the Golden Road to Samarkand."*
> —HASSAN

From Teheran the Golden Road wanders eastward to Khorasan along the eroded slopes and barren spurs of the Elburz Range. In that day it straggled somewhat vaguely, as a road would that had been laid out and worn for untold centuries by the tread of naked feet and the hoofs of laden animals. It was passable after a fashion by wheels, but the wheels of post-carriages and springless *fourgons*, not motorized wheels. No motor vehicle had ever been over it up to that time.

After several weeks in Teheran I combed the *chapah-khaneh*—the postal service—for a carriage with springs reasonably intact and some pretentions to comfort for a drive of 585 miles by day and night, drawn by relays of four horses, across two-thirds of Iran. The product was a Russian-built *kaleska*, a kind of landau which pitched and rolled over rough ground like a seagoing yawl. It had a folding leather hood and two deep seats facing fore and aft. When the well between the seats was filled with our small luggage, overlaid by rugs and kapok mattresses and with pillows at the back, one could stretch out at about three-quarter length. After one got used to it the posture was not bad for sleeping. It would have been a good deal better had Josephine not contributed one item which hardly simplified the arrangements. She came to our point of departure towing a great leonine beast on a chain, a tawny, long-tailed sheepdog with enormous yellow eyes.

"Good God!" I croaked. "What do you propose to do with *that?*"

"Isn't he sweet?" she said. "Bob Hadow gave him to me. His name is Marco. He can run part of the way, and he'll keep our feet warm in the carriage at night."

He did neither. He was not that kind of dog. Whenever we turned him out of the kaleska, unless we turned ourselves out as well, he would run alongside for a few hundred yards howling like a banshee, then stop short with one great paw uplifted in sign that he had broken down. The hills echoed with his awful laments. And nothing would do but that we halt and take him in again.

Within the kaleska he arranged things comfortably, for himself, at our feet. He did not keep our feet warm. He squirmed and shoved until our legs were projected upwards and outwards at cold, ungainly angles. I would as soon have shared the kaleska with a full-grown giant panda as with Marco.

After we arrived at Meshed I got back at him partly, in an indirect manner. We were riding one evening over the valley, with Marco galumphing alongside, and passed a flock of very young fat-tailed lambs that had just been separated from their dams. There were fifty or more of the little woolly things turned loose to fend for themselves in a harsh and milkless world. With joyous bleats they espied and surrounded Marco, butting and squirming their way on both sides in frantic search of a warm supper. Marco fled under the horses for protection. The lambs followed after, baaing loudly, their little fat tails slapping up and down as they ran. They thought him their collective mother. I never saw so shamefaced a dog.

The Golden Road was rough and stony. It crept through deeply seamed reddish hills, wandered over desert plateaus where giant dust-devils whirled across the surface, threatening to immolate carriage and occupants. It crossed countless snow-fed torrents whose silt- and gravel-laden floods foamed about the doors of the high-swung kaleska on their way to lose themselves in the saline desert to the south. Often it followed the beds of watercourses, dry most of the year but now in frantic spate.

In the glimmer of the first dawn we entered the "Gorge of the Head of the Valley," the Caspian Gates through which Alexander the Great chased Darius Codomannus, last of the Achemenians. The narrow defile of seven miles' length led steeply downwards between furrowed sides of pebbled clay that exuded salt in great white streaks. The kaleska had no brakes, the harnesses no breeching. In Persian fashion of tooling loaded carriages down sharp descents, the driver walked backwards in front of his team, beating vigorously on their noses with a broken whip and uttering peculiar bubbling sounds. Several gazelles strolled across the track. From the top of a hill the morning star flared like a gigantic ball of magnesium light. Road-guards stood at attention by little mud forts against the skyline, saluting our passage. They knew we must be personages of importance, with our fine kaleska and mounted escort.

Some of those escorts had odd histories. Three who awaited at the border of Khorasan and escorted us for two days were ex-brigands of the gang of one Ramazan Barsuri of Fars. He and his men had been condemned to death but permitted to expiate their crimes by becoming road-guards instead of being hanged. They were typical caravan robbers with the faces of cutthroats, but made good road-guards as long as they were properly controlled. Set a thief to catch a thief . . .

The Caspian Gates opened onto a salt-encrusted plain which caught the sunrise in a myriad luminous points, dazzling as Arctic snow. The plain was framed on the north by hills of weird coloration, a chocolate-brown base deeply furrowed in parallel straight lines, narrow and close together, against which enormous S's of yellow and red gave an impression of fat double dollar-signs on an accordion-plaited skirt.

In the middle of Damghan's bazars our superior kaleska broke down. This was not greatly to be wondered at, since the cumbrous vehicle had obviously never enjoyed much in the way of maintenance and was now carrying, besides ourselves and the driver, some 450 pounds of baggage, Marco, our head-servant Nasrullah, and a post-boy perched on the luggage-net swung between the rear wheels.

"Here it can be repaired," announced Nasrullah, "and the pistachios are famous throughout the land." There was a blacksmith's primitive forge close by. As to the pistachios, I have never tasted anything of their kind so delicate. Nor were the melons of Lasgird, perfectly kept through the winter in cellars filled with chopped straw, soon to be forgotten.

The post-stations, ruined caravanserais and dirty little teahouses where we halted to change relays, or for Nasrullah to prepare food over a charcoal brazier, were pretty uninviting. Their mud walls were strengthened by the bones of animals, their interiors dark and fetid, the approaches to them leading between skeletons or half-picked carcasses of horses, camels, donkeys and goats. At some stops Nasrullah even showed a certain squeamishness.

"In there it is not good," he would whisper. "In there are stranger-biters!"

The *gerrib-gaz*—the "stranger-biter"—is a tick whose bite brings a dangerous, sometimes deadly, relapsing fever. It affects only strangers, the local inhabitants having become inoculated through long and intimate relations. It proceeds on its nefarious quests by dark, wherefore travellers forced to sleep in the villages and ancient caravanserais infested by the bug generally surround themselves with lighted lanterns or candles, like corpses lying in state.

Appropriately, the name of the most notorious village of the bug's habitat was Mehmandoost, "Guest-liking."

Along the road wound caravan after caravan of camels, horses and donkeys. The donkeys staggered and zigzagged under sacks of grain, great loads of firewood and camel-thorn, long logs trailing in the shape of inverted V's, and panniers filled with all manner of things from dung-cakes or turquoises out of the mines above Nishapur to opium-sap and new-born kids. Each little beast wore a blue necklace or a blue bead on its ear or tail to ward off the Evil Eye. Each had its nose slit, or an additional pair of nostrils cut above its regular ones, to afford added breathing power on the dusty roads—a sort of auxiliary air-intake as it were. All had a look of complete disillusion—the cumulative effect of short rations and scant care, overloading, continual prodding on sore posteriors with a sharpened stick or whacking with a length of chain, and jabs in the neck with a pruning knife to keep on the course set.

The horses were little larger and scarcely less blighted than the donkeys. All were stallions or mares; they do not geld horses in Persia. Underfed and overworked, galled, spavined and mangy, those of the postal service, at least, still had the spirit to show their spleen at the harshness of their lot. Squealing and fighting with one another, biting and kicking at whoever approached from either end, they vented their ill-humor at all opportunities. In Persia a horse is an *asp,* and the *asps* of the *chapah* were as malevolent as any serpent.

We changed relays some sixty times; at each *chapah khaneh* three to four *farsakhs* apart, and on the road wherever we met another post vehicle going in the opposite direction. (A *farsakh,* the *parasang* of the *Anabasis,* is the distance a laden donkey can walk in an hour, or about 3.8 miles theoretically.) There was no change without a fight, nor did the new relay ever fail to start off with a tremendous plunge before our driver could get himself back upon the box.

"These *asps* are not good!" growled Nasrullah in fine understatement after having been knocked to the ground, bitten, kicked and variously trampled upon. Yet one could hardly expect amiable behavior considering the treatment they received.

To all things there are exceptions. A tiny box of a carriage about four feet square rolled out of the haze below the snowy peaks and stopped for rest at a mud hovel where we had halted a few minutes earlier. Through the slats of the window shutters I could glimpse its interior packed with an incredible number of men and women and children in what must have been an agony of acute discomfort. A splay-footed moron of fortuitous breeding brought glasses of dark brown tea out from the hovel to the human sardines.

While they sipped the bitter brew an ancient hostler in the shape and size of a gnome disentangled himself from the luggage-net behind and shuffled forward to inspect his weary charges. Multicolored wool pompoms embellishing their noses, foreheads, saddles and loins contrasted oddly with their decrepitude; their shrunken necks were hung with bunches of nickeled bells. The little old gnome examined their eyes, first wiping the mud from his own. Whistling like a teapot, he passed his hand over their steaming flanks and mud-plastered bellies. Then, standing on tiptoe, he kissed on both sides of its face the offmost of the four—a shrivelled, broken-kneed *asp* with a turquoise-blue bead in its tail.

"Beautiful!" he murmured and clambered impassively back onto his perch atop the luggage as the sardine-box creaked off across the plain.

Khor, in old Persian, is the Sun; Khorasan, the Region of the Sun, or of the East. In that once mighty principality, probably more persons have died a violent death than in any other territory of equal size in Asia. A battle-ground throughout the ages of the Central Asian races, its towns have been devastated by repeated invasion, its inhabitants the prey of prowling bands who supported themselves by rapine. These characteristics have not changed markedly in the course of time. The Turcoman bands still maintain the tradition of their predecessors. From behind the Jaghatai range (named for a son of Ghengiz Khan) they sweep down continually, when the central government is weak, on swift, snaky-necked horses to plunder caravans and pilgrims, bringing sudden death to the hapless villages in their path.

Along the way from Shahrud to Nishapur the isolated buildings were grouped around fortified *robats*—mud-walled fastnesses erected against the robber bands, and in some of the fields, as at Maiomai, there were little individual "funk-towers" with tops of thorn to which cultivators surprised at their work might flee for refuge.

At Maiomai we were held up several hours until dawn because of an expected Turcoman raid. The raid took place a few miles farther east. Quite apart from it the enforced halt at Maiomai's Shah Abbas caravanserai was a not ungrateful interlude, whose end came in a melodious awakening. After the false dawn had faded and the true dawn streaked the eastern sky with faint rose there broke upon the silence of the night the voice of a muezzin calling to prayer from a nearby but yet unseen minaret. The call was in a clear tenor of lovely tonal quality.

"God is great!" the muezzin sang. "I bear witness there is no god but God! Come ye to prayer! Prayer is better than sleep!" That simple village muezzin, I later learned, was famous throughout Iran. With him we too bore witness that prayer was better than sleep—such sleep as one might get in a rocking kaleska with its broken springs bound up in goat's-hair rope. Certainly it was far better to awake and listen to the splendid prayer-call echoing in mellow cadences through the star-lit dark.

Other voices took up the call, filling the early morn with tremulous notes. Gradually these faded into a new tone growing out of the east, a rhythmic booming of camel-bells signalling a caravan's approach to where we waited under the great plane-trees of Maiomai's central common. In the half-light the swaying head and misshapen body of the lead camel seemed part of an improbable, prehistoric beast, like a monstrous lizard peering suspiciously from side to side with little reptilian eyes as it picked its way on cautious padded feet. On top of its load slept the head *chavadar,* the guardian of the convoy. His doubled-up figure was grotesquely swathed in a shapeless felt coat, with rudimentary sleeves, closed at their ends, sticking out with an absurd effect of auk's wings. From shell-encrusted, embroidered collars around the camel's shaggy neck swung a great bell which beat a resonant bass to the varied tones of the bells that came after.

Camels followed in seemingly endless single file. Each supercilious nose attached by a length of goat's-hair rope to the tail of the camel ahead was held high in the air, as if its owner suffered in martyred silence from the offensive odor of his mates. On every swaying neck there hung a bell, or dozens of bells, ranging in size from clusters of shrill little sleigh-bells sewn in tinkling necklaces to huge, deep-voiced iron drums beaten out of Russian oil containers. The most favored and effective in tone were of heavy brass, three or four bells of graduated size one within the other; the outermost adorned with conventionalized figures of camels and dragons in high relief, the lesser ones serving as tongues for those next in size. Their melody, unhappily, is no more heard.

Camel transport has been superseded in Iran by the motor truck of modernity, the fetish of Reza Shah. In more ways than one this was a great pity. Under the stress of the recent war motor transportation broke down and there were by then insufficient camels to supplement it. On the aesthetic side the loss was irreparable. The long, swaying lines of camels tied nose to tail were immensely picturesque; and I know no music to stir one's roving blood like the bells of a Persian caravan passing through the dawn.

We just missed the Turcomans at Miandasht—"Middle of the Plain." Several of their towering sheepskin hats remained stuck on poles in the ground outside the lonely brick fortress-caravanserai as evidence of the raid that had by-passed Maiomai.

"And where are their heads?" I asked the commander of the small garrison of road-guards.

"Ah, we killed some of their horses, but the sons of dogs got away." The commander waxed boastful. "Thick as grains of sand they were. We drove them off in a great fight; the sons of burnt fathers were lucky to escape with their heads!" Actually the Turcoman marauders had held the garrison invested for a night and a day in a vaulted chamber without food or drink while they plundered the *chapah khaneh* and several caravans at their leisure.

The plain was a flaming yellow ocean of flowering assafoetida plants four feet high, with only the red brick caravanserai in the middle to break its sweep, like a coral islet in a golden tropic sea. Beyond it, for fifteen miles of undulating plateau, the ground lay hidden under a riotous carpet of color—pale lavender of wild irises, yellow and white of marguerites, armeria bushes like soft pink cushions, green sage, yellow tulips, rock roses, yellow salvia with dark centers, pink and red thorn bushes called *tangez,* astragalus, amaryllis and many others, all blended against a background of yellow sulphurous hills streaked with green and blue salts of copper.

Outside the few larger towns like Sabzevar and Nishapur we were met in formal state in the pleasant Persian ceremonial of greeting that is known as *istikbal.* The Governor's carriage waited two *farsakhs* or so beyond the gates to bring us in. Two gaily caparisoned led-horses of honor, with an escort of very irregular cavalry, formed the spearhead of the official entry; local chiefs of administrations and other "notables" in a dozen droshkies, mounted attendants, retainers and a miscellany of other welcomers on horses, mules and donkeys, made the retinue.

Greetings having been exchanged, the cavalcade galloped into town in a choking cloud of dust between police guards posted along the route of viceregal progress. Peasants ran in from the fields and lined the road, bowing low. Great crowds waited at the town gates. The covered bazars through which the cortège passed were packed with Persian New Year buyers.

Our mounted attendants galloped ahead. "*Khabadar!*" they shouted, "*Khabadar!*"—Beware! The vaulted arcades echoed to their throaty cries. It never occurred to riders or drivers to slacken their furious pace lest they crush the humanity swarming in those narrow passages.

All work halted as we approached. The noisy hammers of the coppersmiths ceased their *tap-tap-tapping.* The felters and carders of wool stopped strumming their harp-like instruments. Cobblers and potters and fashioners of donkey-saddles rose from their knees; and the dyers of cotton cloth stood by their vats naked to the waist, colored deep indigo from their own brews.

The whole life routine of the town took a respite as we clattered to the inevitable reception in our bedroom, with the long-drawn-out banquet to follow in the Governor's earthen mansion.

Between Zaafarani—"Of Saffron"—and Shurab—"Brackish Water"—a band of seven local brigands used to operate with considerable success on travellers passing along the way. Among the many they pillaged was a new Chief of Police *en route* to Meshed. They sent him on his way stark naked.

But they were captured in the end. Now they stood by the roadside in a row of seven rectangular pillars of mud-brick and clay. Walled up alive where they were caught, sealed in with a coating of plaster, they stood as a concrete reminder of the insecurity of their trade.

A couple of stages beyond them the road crossed a stretch of the saline soil known as *kavir* which absorbs water like a sponge and gives its name to the vast salt desert called the Dasht-i-Kavir that spreads over much of northern central Persia. In the rains and freshets of early spring this soil becomes a treacherous and often impassable morass. In summer and autumn it is baked hard as stone by the sun, with a bubbly salt-encrusted surface that glimmers like moonlit foam on a windy shore. It was now in the former state.

Under certain atmospheric conditions all objects on its flat crust are strangely distorted by the refraction of light. Flocks of goats in the middle distance appear to be camels of incredible size. Camel trains float over the ground with the effect of a row of gigantic trees. Diminutive mud *robats* loom out of the haze as though they were enormous mediaeval castles. One of these hung suspended before us in the thick air above the plain like a mysterious and illusive city of the *Arabian Nights,* a town of vast proportions surrounded by dark, unfriendly walls hundreds of feet high, as we toiled across the dismal waste where no feature broke the emptiness save that distorted image. Both mystery and grandeur vanished with our approach. The image returned to earth; the shrunken city resolved itself into a mean mud ruin harboring two relays of broken-down horses and their opium-sodden attendants.

For seven miles our driver whistled, clucked and shouted at his straining *asps.* Several times the kaleska seemed stuck for good, water seeping above its floor-boards. One of our escort lost his mount. The animal gave a sudden plunge, divesting itself of both rider and saddle—no very difficult performance in view of the state of its equipment. The horse made off towards Nishapur shedding bits of saddle which fell all to pieces once its rotten girth had broken with the lengths of frayed rope that held the whole together.

The man picked himself out of the tacky mud and floundered off on a four-mile walk to the next post-station. In no uncertain terms he invoked the Moslem hierarchy to bear witness to the awful parentage and character of his steed.

"That *asp* is the son of a dog whose father was the son of a whore!" he yelled. "Its mother was a serpent's egg and its mother's mother . . .!" By then the ill-begotten *asp* had left most of a quarter-mile sprinkled with items of saddle and equipment to be retrieved in detail from the sea of mud by their outraged owner.

A trick of the mirage added a final touch of the ridiculous. The fleeing *asp* began to expand mightily in stature. It assumed mastodonic proportions. Passing quite out of the class of terrestrial horses it sailed calmly off the earth, a dark, fat and somewhat shapeless Pegasus soaring heavenwards above the surface of the plain.

In this manner we came to Nishapur. The present town's five centuries of existence cover but a fragment of the history of its oft-devastated site. Less than an hour's walk from its gates lie the mounds of former citadels, now shapeless and disappearing, where greater precursors flourished and were destroyed. Of these the most brilliant in its day was the city called Shadiakh where Omar Khayyam lived and died eight hundred years ago.

The Nishapuris of our time are a degenerate, opium-sodden lot whose town retains scant suggestion of the glories of its traditions. They are also wholly indifferent to the fact that its principal title to fame throughout the Western world lies in a garden three miles away. Many pilgrims visit that garden. Shoeless, humbly and in prayer, they pass in their hundreds through the carved wooden portals of a saintly mausoleum to kiss the tomb of the martyr known as the Imamzadeh Mohammed Mahruk who was murdered and burnt in the middle of the eighth century.

Not one in ten thousand is aware that the plain white sarcophagus in the east wing, beyond the blue-tiled dome, holds the bones of Omar Khayyam. If he were, he would feel only pious distress that the remains of a Sunni and an avowed free-thinker should be sheltered in the same sepulchre as the burnt grandson of a Shiah saint.

Even among the literate classes few Persians hold Omar in high esteem as a poet. As a mathematician of note, yes; an astronomer and scientist, a philosopher whose unorthodox leanings are condemned by the religious; but not a first-rate poet. Fitzgerald's free rendering of Omar's quatrains are undoubtedly more musical to ears attuned to English than are the original verses to those accustomed to the Persian idiom. But their philosophy is that of Omar the Tentmaker.

Invading tribes of Ghuzz destroyed the city of Omar Khayyam a few decades after his death. I found its principal mound had been rented by the Administration of Public Domains to an illiterate donkeyman for sixty dollars a year. He was carrying it away bit by bit in panniers to spread as fertilizer on the opium fields.

We stopped in Nishapur with Prince Sardar Saëd, Governor of the District. The Prince was a pleasant host whose diversions were falconry and hunting quail in a fashion new to me up till then. I went "hunting" with him a number of times in the course of three springs, and while I never managed to attain his skill, the game had distinctly sporting elements.

"The barley is just the right height," he would say; "we should have good hunting!"

Our equipment comprised a green net perhaps fifteen by ten feet with a mesh of about an inch, a small wooden whistle, and a covered basket. In a likely field where the green wheat or barley was twelve to eighteen inches high Sardar Saëd would spread the net over the top of the growing shoots. We stretched out flat on the ground behind it, half concealed amidst the stalks, and the Prince with his little wooden call would give an excellent imitation of a female quail in receptive mood.

From various parts of the field came the answering whistles of male birds, sometimes one or two, sometimes half a dozen. Sardar Saëd repeated the call two or three times; each time the answers came from nearer by. Then the *ersatz* female pretended to grow coy and the calls of the males running through the barley took an insistent tone.

"Be very quiet now!" the Prince would whisper, lying quite still. Suddenly, half rising on his rotund little belly, he would bang hard on the ground with the open palms of both hands. There would be a flutter and a bulge in the net where a startled bird tried to take flight. Like a cat the Prince pounced on it, twisting a double handful of net around it, then perhaps pounced on another. Sometimes he caught three male birds at one "cast." He rarely failed to get at least one. After four or five casts we would return home with our basket full of live quail.

The trick, aside from making a good call, was to know when the approaching birds had arrived under the net. One could not see them through the barley. I found it by no means easy to estimate just the right amount of time before springing the trap.

We reached Meshed after thirteen days, nine of which and seven nights had been spent in the kaleska on the road. From the Hill of Salutation, where the pilgrims fall to their knees in worship at the sight of the Imam Reza's golden-domed shrine and build little cairns by the roadside, we looked over the Holy City. In this, one of the most fanatical towns in all Asia, I was to make my headquarters for the next two and a half years.

Some Servants

It was not well, I was told, to try to run one's Persian household on the strict lines of Western precision or European economy. This was no idle jest. For those who attempted to do so were soon driven to the verge of insanity or assassination or both by the passive resistance of their servants. On the other hand, those who thought to preserve their peace of mind by letting their servants go unchecked ended in being shamelessly exploited and ill-served. Somewhere between the two there lay a reasonably happy medium.

Despite their foibles we became really attached to most of our household staff. Their failings were many and often extremely annoying. They would sell one out of one's house if given half a chance. Yet they provided a continuous comic relief that no funnies-strip has ever approached.

For reasons mostly beyond my control we acquired an embryonic army of them. In an establishment of some proportions it was hardly possible to get along with few. When their energies were dissipated on a variety of tasks they never finished anything they started. Those that made up for deficiencies in plumbing, trimmed lamp-wicks, washed the dogs, rolled the mud roof after each rain or cleaned leather, seldom had the mental capacity for much else. I dispensed with the usual gate-keeper through having a military guard. But we had to have a gardener and drawer of water, one or more grooms for our horses, and message-carriers since the telephone service was ineffectual or non-existent. These were in addition to the basic requirements of a cook, kitchen-boy, butler and chamber-man.

I rarely knew just how many there were in all under our roof. Several of the more exalted members of our staff kept servants of their own, "apprentices" so-called, who lived off us in ways direct or indirect. Every so often I discovered some new addition to the forces.

"Now who might that one be?" I would query. Such a one, for instance, as a wizened little old man I had noticed a few times cleaning my orderly's horse. He played most of the day in the manure, sorting it carefully into small piles as to size and quality, and saluted me precisely like an organ-grinder's monkey.

"I make a prayer, Honorable Chief, it is the groom of Ali Akbar-the-Cossack," was the response. Ali Akbar-the-Cossack was a trooper drawing the princely sum of ten dollars a month from the Administration (and on this was expected to supply his own mount), plus a small personal allowance from me. He accompanied me each day when I rode to and from my office over the cobbled streets of the town, or wherever else I might go; and when I was otherwise occupied he went with Josephine in the late afternoon or early morning to the edge of the hills.

It was not well, I was advised, for anyone in a position of importance to go about alone. There was first of all the matter of prestige to be considered. And while this may sound an affectation in Western ears, and is generally a great nuisance, yet authority is not well upheld in the East without some moderate outward show. Nor does this apply only to the East, though elsewhere it may take a different form.

There was also the fact that certain of the dispositions I had to make inevitably created malcontents. In such connection the British Vice Consul imparted one day for my information the contents of a confidential intelligence report he had just received.

"Thirty dismissed Finance employees"—dismissed by me for malfeasance, extortion and gross incompetence—"are concerned in an intrigue to 'get' the Director sometime when he is riding," went the report. "In the guise of presenting a petition they plan to pull him from his horse and then do *certain terrible things* that will make him glad to resign and leave the country."

I felt prepared to handle that occasion should it arrive, which it did not. And while happily I never met with "certain terrible things," nor even an unpleasant episode directed at me in person during all the time I was in Iran, the frequent warnings were not without some basis. In most parts of the world one who is not looking for trouble, but is prepared to meet whatever may arise, seldom encounters it in serious form. There are exceptions to this, of course, when mob passions become inflamed.

Another warning carried a slightly melodramatic touch. "Thirty-five Caucasian murderers"—five more than the initial threat to my pursuit of happiness—"have just been imported by the Bolsheviks. They are to 'remove' a number of foreigners and Persians whose presence is felt antagonistic to Bolshevik aims. Your name heads the list. It would be wise for you to increase your escort and your guard." There were actually pointed out to me several of these alleged importations. The ones I saw were unamiable-looking ruffians, in truth. I did not increase my escort, nor my guard. I was not "removed" (nor did I hear of any other foreigners who were). But I thought it flattering that my name should head the list.

There were times when we found our servants exceedingly trying. They seemed then to embody all the more irritating features of their nation. They were inconsequential, short of memory, lacking in gratitude. They lied, cheated, stole, and quarreled with one another. They reverted to highly insanitary practices when left to their own devices. And they had wonderful, long-winded excuses for each fatuous thing they did.

"I make a prayer," they would reply to any question as to why they had or had not done something, then spin an involved and fantastic tale. They vented their spleen behind our backs in uncomplimentary references to foreign dogs of unbelievers. They thought my wife slightly mad—what manservant, and we had no others, does not prefer a bachelor establishment? She on her part took them for what in effect they were: a troop of whimsical children with the latent mischief of anthropoid apes.

We demanded more continuity of effort, greater attention to detail and to cleanliness than did the average Persian household. We would not stand for the simian chatter, the usual uncouth noises in the courtyard, nor for having our repose broken every few minutes by some one of them with a question, a complaint, or a "prayer." We would not have our dishes washed in the pool, nor the water for our tea drawn from this convenient source. We were more difficult to satisfy, in some ways more insistent, than a Persian master or mistress would be. On the other hand we gave more. We gave them better wages, provided greater regularity of hours. To each upper servant we assigned a room of his own with a cot, a carpet, a table and a little lamp. This was a rare provision in any Persian household. It was a luxury they really appreciated.

Most of them had good qualities. Some were quite devoted, in their fashion. Several had real talent along certain lines, though none but Nasrullah-the-Butler could read or write, and he to no great extent.

There was Hossein, for instance, whose flair for floral decoration was a natural genius. He would arrange designs of small green leaves and varicolored petals on a dining-table set for twelve or more, from no pattern save in his own head, each arrangement different and each as charming as anything of its kind I have ever seen.

Then there was Khodadad—"God-given," a slant-eyed Berber *syce* who was as good a groom as one could desire in the field. He may have cheated me (as undoubtedly he did) but he never cheated the horses, which was far more important. And his knowledge of primitive remedies was a revelation.

With one such remedy he and a village smith caused me acute palpitation of the heart. I was riding through the mountains a full day out from my base, on a skewbald stallion that suddenly went very lame. "Mali," which means "handsome," had been shod the day before: badly, it turned out. In the late afternoon he began to favor his near forefoot. Very soon he could barely step on it. I led him the last five miles to camp at the edge of an upland village.

"I get *ahangir*," said Khodadad. The *ahangir* was the smith who did the iron-work for three or four villages—plough-tips, bullock- and donkey-shoes, and such like. Khodadad was a long time finding the *ahangir*. Together, in the dark, we pulled the shoe. It was a painful operation. Mali stood it gallantly, but in the morning he could not put his hoof to the ground. The foot was swollen to the fetlock, very hot, and evidently infected.

"*Ahangir* fix foot," said Khodadad, after our inspection. "Make all beautiful." Khodadad and the iron-smith then drilled out the nail-cavity where the infection had started. To my dismay they filled it with coarse black gunpowder, inserted a slow fuse, tamped it all in with sheep tallow, and lighted the fuse.

"*Good God!*" I cried. "You'll blow off his hoof! And black powder burns make septic wounds!" This I tried to convey in clumsy Persian to Khodadad. I was tense with consternation. "No, no!" he insisted. "Good! Very good! Make all beautiful!"

There was a loud "whoosh!" The slow-burning powder blew out in a small cloud of flame and black smoke. Mali did not seem to mind it particularly. It did a fine job of cauterization, made the foot "all beautiful" even as Khodadad had promised. The swelling went down rapidly. In twenty-four hours the horse could be led. A day later he was fit to ride. Yet I still shuddered at the memory of the treatment.

In Meshed we usually managed to make up a scratch game of polo two or three times a week, with "Tommy" Thompson, the British Military Attaché; Weldon, the Bank Manager; some Persian officers and an Indian N.C.O. of the British Consular escort. The ponies under my stable roof gradually increased in number. Khodadad made a prayer for help. Help was duly procured in the person of one Ismail, whom I appointed first assistant groom. Ismail was a handsome young man with a standard of living that made excessive demands upon a very modest salary. He therefore sought to supplement the latter in divers ways. Among others was the surreptitious sale of the manure intended for my garden.

Ali Akbar-the-Gardener loved that garden. Month by month it grew more charming under his and Josephine's tender care. He wept like a child when Consul-General Haworth's dog dug up a whole row of tulips just opening in bloom beside the pool. Ali Akbar-the-Gardener was the most honest of all our servants. Yet the more animals we added to our stables, the less manure he obtained for the garden. I made loud noises about this and forbade, under severe penalties, that so much as a single lump should be taken from the compound. The guards received instructions accordingly, but still the shortage continued.

We then had five horses, three cows, two live calves and the stuffed skin of a dead calf—since Persian cows are disinclined to give milk unless fooled into thinking it is for their legitimate offspring. Ali Akbar-the-Gardener was getting no manure at all. Ali Akbar-the-Gardener was grieved, Josephine irritated, and I began to gird myself to fight the battle of manure. I had just won the battle of milk by a strategic coup, so my morale was high. I would *not* buy manure when I was maintaining a manure factory.

"Where is it going?" I demanded with fire in my eye.

"God knows, Sahib," said the servants piously, looking up to heaven. "God alone knows!" I did not feel that the Almighty was particularly interested in the disposition of my manure.

The grooms dried part of the horse-droppings as bedding for their charges. The rest simply disappeared in some occult manner that none seemed able to explain. None, at least, until one night when I returned late, just in time to watch a shadowy something emerge from the window of a box-stall, that was the only opening from our compound to the outside save for the guarded gate. With patient effort and some ingenuity the bars of that small opening had been made removable, though still seeming secure. The shadowy thing was a long sack. It was followed by the upper half of Ismail, then by the rest of his squirming body. He dropped head foremost onto the sack which was stuffed with the precious dung. When he rose with his loot his distress was great to find me standing over him.

To such lengths would one's servants go for a few pennyworth of gain. Usually the annoyance counted more than the value of their depredations. I had the opening re-barred so that the whole wall would have to be pulled down before the bars could again be removed. Thus the battle of the manure was won.

Ismail's final fall from our household came through his abuse of my stallion Mali, which was one thing I would not tolerate. He managed then to get himself a job on the Nishapur police force, and from this was later ejected for stealing three pounds of cheese off a shopkeeper who happened to be a friend of the Chief of Police. Shortly after that episode I received a letter from Ismail penned by a Nishapuri scribe:

"Worshipful Director!" it read.

"May I be your sacrifice! I Ismail, your devoted, if before was bad am all right now. May God keep you healthy! Please inquire: nobody has served so greatly in the Police as I. Everyone is satisfied with me. Please do something that I may be sent back to Meshed, and also give me a certificate of satisfaction. May God never lessen your Shadow! . . . Ismail."

A "certificate of satisfaction," otherwise a recommendation, is a highly treasured document. Wise employers do not take on servants lacking letters; nor those with letters except after personal inquiry wherever possible, for recommendations have a good rental value and are often leased out to applicants not suitably provided with documentary evidence of their worth.

The ultimate penalty in my household for infractions of a serious nature was dismissal without a letter. With lesser misbehaviors I dealt in divers ways, meting out punishments in the manner of a regimental commander or the housemaster of a Victorian English school. These punishments included confinement to quarters for a number of days, deprivation of certain privileges, or stoppages against the miscreant's pay. To Persian temperament the last was the most awful penalty one could suffer. That the infractor might taste the bitter cup to the end and so be duly impressed by the penalty, undistracted by any suspicion that his mulcting was in some manner to our advantage, we found—on Persian advice—the most effective method was to count out the wage in full, then withhold the small amount of the fine from the outstretched palm.

"This is *yours*," I would say, holding up the coin to the light for a last, lingering glimpse. "You understand? This is *your* money," and drop it down a well. The culprit would stare after it in mute anguish as though it were his soul that had been torn from his body and dropped to the flames of hell.

They all came in for punishment of various degrees and were the better for it, as most children are the better for a chastising in their mischiefs. Against the punishments, I always gave them the choice of leaving with full pay and a letter of "recommendation" stating such virtues as they might possess but with the exact reason for dismissal. Not one ever chose the alternative—even in the very few flagrant cases when the choice rested between discharge and a formal beating to be administered by Hadi Khan, my secretary, who entered heartily into the spirit of the thing.

It was only to junior miscreants, whose dignity and prestige were not of a standing to suffer greatly, that one offered this unbenign choice. Major offenses by the more responsible ones could not be disposed of in that fashion. Such a lapse from grace, for instance, as caused Nasrullah's downfall could end only in the parting of our ways.

Nasrullah was a pious old hypocrite. Usually when we called him to some extra task he could be heard intoning prayers from the depths of his room. There would be a delay of fifteen or twenty minutes while he prayed sonorously to God-the-Merciful, the Loving-Kind; hoping that in the meantime we might forget what we had wanted. After three years in Meshed and Teheran we took Nasrullah to Shiraz. He was an excellent butler. But during my absence on the Persian Gulf he introduced a bevy of bazar harlots into the house and threw an orgiastic party of four or five days arack-drinking with allied amusements. That was the end of Nasrullah as my head butler.

Gholam Hossein had got himself involved in the matter of the harlots under Nasrullah's incitement. He, it appeared, had done the actual rounding up of the *filles de joie*. Gholam Hossein was a little man: little in stature, little in mentality and position, and no one to stand up against Nasrullah's evil genius.

"I am shocked and grieved that you who have been with me now for more than three years should blacken my house in my absence!" I said to him at the formal court of inquiry held with Hadi Khan in my garden. "O Gholam Hossein, you should burn for this, with all others of evil heart! You should at any rate follow Nasrullah away from my presence, for you have been exceedingly bad. Yet because it was he who brought you to this shame, if your heart be not black all through and you never, never will do ill again, you may stay. But you will have to eat twenty stripes from Mirza Hadi Khan."

"I make a prayer, let me eat the beating!" he cried. "And Your Honor's servant never will be bad again!"

He "ate" his beating with howls that shook the garden walls—so that I might not feel he was getting off too lightly—and he lived happily with us ever after to the end of our days in Persia, for in truth he never was bad again. Not actually bad, though sometimes a bit trying in his stupidities.

Gholam Hossein had started as the sweeper, the lowly one taking the place of plumbing in the toilets of Westerners who reside in the East. From this he advanced to be the trimmer of lamp-wicks, the polisher of leather, the stoker of wood fires, and nurse-in-ordinary to the dogs. Though faithful after his fashion in the performance of those duties, he never rose to greater heights.

No one would really have called Gholam Hossein quick-witted. Had he more than the bare embryo of a brain he might in time have progressed from being official bather of the dogs. This, among Moslems, is not esteemed a very dignified function, since they hold dogs to be unclean. Our sheepdog Marco, those times he returned from having rolled in dead camel, did not exactly belie the stigma. Yet Gholam Hossein was really fond of the dogs, and they liked him as they liked few of his race.

I had the opportunity once to time the process of reaction in the cavity that held Gholam Hossein's minute brain. It happened in Teheran, while I was Acting Treasurer-General. We had given a dinner for the Minister of Finance, the German Minister Count von der Schulenburg, and various others. The men of the party were talking over coffee and liqueurs when Gholam Hossein entered the room to put more coal on the fire.

It was mid-winter and very cold. I had told the little man beforehand in kitchen-Persian: "Gholam Hossein, every quarter-hour you put ten pieces coal on fire!" He carried out the order with tortoise-like precision. With the passage of time and under his attentions the room was getting too warm. As he went by while we were sipping our coffee I called to him: "Gholam Hossein, do *not* put more coal on fire!"

"*Bali, Sahib!*" he replied—Yes, Master! and proceeded straightway to add the prescribed ten chunks of shaley coal to the blaze. I watched him out of the corner of my eye, not wishing to disturb the conversation at table, which was reaching a particularly interesting point. There was a clock on the mantelpiece quietly ticking away the minutes.

His duty performed, Gholam Hossein retraced his steps as far as the door. There he stopped short. "Do *not* put more coal on fire!" I heard him repeat to himself. Slowly he returned to the hearth and lifted off the ten freshly-added chunks, one by one, with his bare hands.

It had taken just four and a half minutes for the counter-order to trickle through to the remote cell of his intellect.

There were numerous others. Some went with us from place to place; some we left behind when I moved to a new sector; some developed unpleasant characteristics and hurriedly departed our roof.

There was Abu Talib, our first servant and my personal valet, who rode Mali six hundred miles from Teheran to Meshed. He started from the capital as Abu Talib and arrived at Meshed as Abu Talib Khan—Abu Talib, Esquire. When things went wrong he would burst into floods of tears.

There were Meshedi Ali and Meshedi Reza, and Reza, and Ali Reza.

There were Agha Buzorg—"Big Mister," and No Rooz—"New Year," whose feelings were hurt because Josephine persisted in calling him Ramazan—"Month of Fasting."

No Rooz was one of those who developed unlovely traits and passed from the light of our presence unwept. On the day I set for his dismissal I found that he had just dropped off the brass lantern which hung from a chain in our entryway. He had been doing monkey-tricks on this for the entertainment of the guard and the grooms. His Darwinian descent was evident enough, but he was out of practice in the trees. He broke his wrist; so I had to take care of him a while longer. One could not very well turn loose an anthropoid ape with a broken wrist.

But of all the simian crew with their multiple vagaries, none was quite like Mohammad-the-Chef. He was far more than just a cook. Mohammad did everything in the *grande manière*. He was magnificent even in his mischiefs. As a cook he was one of the best I have ever known, when stirred to the full play of his talents either by difficulties on the road or by the number and importance of our guests. He was not always so stirred over preparation of the simpler repasts for two. Happily for his talents we were not much alone. There was a good deal of local entertaining, and even in the isolation of Meshed we had visitors. Once the track from Duzdab and the equally tedious track to Teheran had been made passable—after a fashion, in dry weather—for occasional motorcars, several venturesome travellers came to stop with us.

Mohammad was in his element when formal dinners brought a dozen or so of notabilities to our table. This gave scope for his imagination. He loved spectacular touches. One of his more successful efforts was built around a brace of pheasant as *pièce-de-résistance*. He had them borne into the dining room from opposite ends at the same moment, each on a platter held high by a uniformed butler. The meat lay neatly sliced around the carcasses, on which Mohammad had fixed the skins off two others; the feathers all intact, heads outstretched (on concealed wires), wings and tails spread as if the birds were soaring in to alight on the table. It was very well done. Through a side window I could see Mohammad's round moon-face peering in to watch the effect.

Effect was everything to Mohammad. He had a manner of wrapping himself in his brown *aba* with a wide sweep of his right arm that

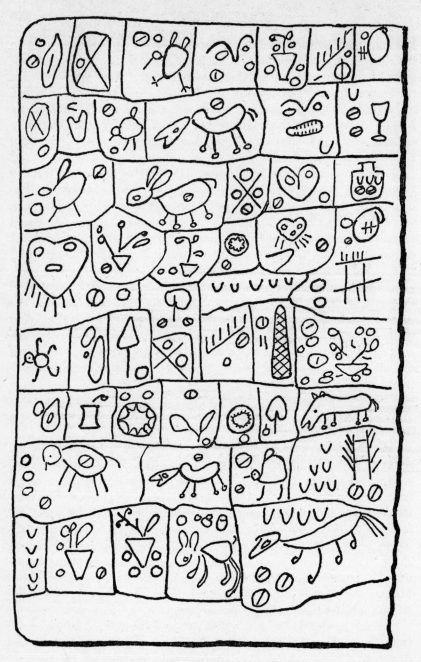

A PAGE FROM MOHAMMAD'S ACCOUNT BOOK

lent him the dignity of a Roman Senator. When improvements made the caravan routes motorable, in their way, I took Josephine along on some of my inspection trips. Then Mohammad always went with us, for he was a marvel of resource on the road. As I preferred to drive, rather than have our spinal vertebrae and the car springs cracked by Persian chauffeuring, Mohammad sat in the back, resplendent in a military coat, pink shirt and a gilt American eagle on his hat, nonchalantly taking all the salutes.

I found Mohammad in Teheran. He had been *chef* to Colonel Glerop, the Swedish second-in-command of the Gendarmerie disbanded by Reza Khan. Glerop was a noted gourmet. At the time he was living with a friend while trying to collect his back pay and travel expenses home. Mohammad, magnificent even in unemployment, sat in the cooks' club which met in a coffee-house, awaiting the grace of God in the matter of a new engagement.

He was far too superior for service in a lesser establishment than that of a high official or one of the more impressive Legations. His dignity would be blighted by lack of importance of his master. And while he waited for a seemly employment in which to display his talents, he kept in the sleeve of his *aba* a large, dry bone. This he would extract and gnaw upon at the approach of anyone who seemed disposed to call upon him for money.

"*Bi-kar!*"—workless!—he would announce without further comment, and chew at his bone. It was his signal of having declared a moratorium on his debts.

His moratoria, I came to suspect, were of a pretty permanent nature. All in all we found him an expensive luxury, though I still think he was worth it. His ideas were large, and in them his salary shaped as but a trivial beginning. The accounts he kept and grossly padded were masterpieces of imaginative design. Across their pages (for he could not read or write) marched quaintly stylized chickens, quail and partridges, eggs, fruits and nuts, vegetables, four-legged beasts of amazing shape that could be hares or lambs or gazelles; along with kitchen utensils, potted plants and other items of his purchases. None but Mohammad himself could understand those hieroglyphics. Never did he misinterpret them to his personal loss.

I think he derived as much satisfaction in outwitting us as he did from illicit gain. He had a wonderful sense of humor. When I was driven to violent protest over the excessive number of chickens, or some other article we were depicted as having consumed in vast quantities, he would sweep the whole matter away with a lordly gesture. "I will bear the loss!" he would exclaim, and start off on another line. It was nearly impossible to catch him out. But once, at least, I fooled him.

Somewhere between the milking of our three cows by Ali Akbar-the-Gardener, and our table, their yield fell off in mysterious manner. The cream disappeared. The butter acquired an unmistakably sheepy taste, which was odd as we kept no sheep. Word came to me that Mohammad had set himself up in the dairy business. He was, it appeared—indirectly, of course—purveying the richest of cow's milk, cream and butter to certain Europeans of particular taste who kept no cows; while I who did keep cows, and was as particular in *my* tastes, made futile, bellowing noises over the thin cream and sheep's butter served at my own table.

I never could discover just how it was done. We set a series of traps, supervised all the processes, measured the results, threatened the whole lot of servants with instant discharge. Yet under our very eyes the milk lessened and grew thin, the products of the cow turned in some obscure fashion into products of the fat-tailed sheep.

For a time I fought a series of losing engagements in this battle of the milk. Mohammad was sympathetic and solicitous. He had a witch-woman brought in to cast her spells upon the cows, that their yield might be to my satisfaction. She pronounced them suffering from the Evil Eye. "Their milk must be spilled upon the ground for a week," she said and then—for a consideration—she would provide for each a new blue necklet effectively charmed against the Eye's malignant influence.

"Take your witch-woman and her charms away!" I ordered, and brought into action a charm of my own, newly arrived from Europe. This was a lactometer, a small gadget that floated in milk at different depths according to the fluid density. Its calibrations showed varying degrees of richness from "Full Cream" to "Plain Water."

"Summon all the servants!" I commanded Mohammad. They formed in a large circle around the table on which stood the bowls of our watery milk and strangely processed cream. I held the lactometer to their gaping view, then tested the milk, with the results I had expected.

"This *firanghi* (foreign) machine cannot lie!" I said. "It tells me how much water has been put in the milk, how thin is the cream."

Here I expanded slightly on its prowess. "It tells me what part of the milk or cream, and of the butter, comes from my own cows, and what part comes from someone else's sheep! More than that, for it is a magical machine, it informs me"—here I looked hard at Mohammad— "who is telling me lies. It tells me the names of the evil ones who steal the milk of my cows, sell the cream to strangers, and give to me a different milk and butter that ye know I do not wish!" Mohammad was the picture of innocence and solemn dignity. "Beware! For now I know all, and if after this day the crime does not cease I shall be without mercy for the evil-doers! You have my permission to go."

The servants scuttled off. I pointed the little instrument at Mohammad. His round pink face was slashed with a grin from ear to ear. He found it a marvellous joke that I had been driven to mechanize my forces against his sleight-of-hand. He thought the lactometer incredibly funny. Yet the improbable attributes of that *firanghi* "machine" disturbed his serenity. He did not wish to put its powers of a lie-detector to the test. ("Praise be to Allah," I could feel him saying to himself, "the thing works only with milk!") And so we had no further troubles in the matter of our dairy products. Strategy and a six-inch lactometer had won the battle of the milk.

When I first engaged Mohammad it was on an arrangement I soon had reason to regret and hastily to revise. I agreed to pay him a monthly salary of twenty-three tomans (about the same then in dollars) which included three tomans for a kitchen-boy. It was a high salary for Iran in those days. We were not long established in Meshed before I was struck by the rapid overturn in our kitchen-boys.

"Why so often a new *shagird* (apprentice)?" I asked Mohammad.

"Honorable Chief, the quality of the Meshedis is as dung! I burn my time trying to train these worthless ones. Finding them unfit to serve in Your Honor's household I have then to remove them." He wasted little breath when he did remove them. I happened to overhear him get rid of one. "Begone, dog's egg!" was his delicately put advice of dismissal.

But there came a day when we heard strange and fearful lamentations rising from the stable-yard. I did not at first pay great attention to this, for a Dervish had lately been camped outside our gates. He was an unbelievably filthy Dervish with a carved black begging-bowl, an inlaid axe, and a horn. He squatted there on a leopard skin, under an inverted V of soiled tenting three feet high against my wall, and chanted loud prayers for my prosperity. So at least they began, but when I failed to requite them in a manner he thought appropriate to my station and presumed wealth, the chants changed to curses. Hideous yowls then punctured the whole of the night, interspersed with long, raucous blasts on the horn. None of this disturbed me very much, as our living-quarters were some distance from the gate. I accepted the noise outside as one of the minor tribulations of life in Meshed, until the Dervish uttered one last, all-embracing curse and departed in disgust.

And so the shrill lamentations of an early morning a few days later made no great impression on me, nor did I think particularly about this until I came home in the afternoon to find the stables half-full of wailing women. Some fell to their knees and sought to kiss my boots; from which, being of a modest disposition, I fled in confusion. The veiled figures kept up a horrid caterwauling, like keening women at a wake. There were at least twenty of them.

"What in heaven's name are these women doing in the stables?" I cried.

"They have taken refuge there," Josephine informed me. "They have come to make a prayer and they plan to stay for ever and ever until their prayer is heard. But I cannot make out what it is all about—except that it has to do with money and Mohammad. The servants seem very vague about it."

I sent for my secretary, Hadi Khan. Through the dreadful din of those women calling on God, Ali, the Imam Reza and myself to right their wrongs, it came out that they were the female relations of my ex-kitchen-boys. Mothers, sisters, aunts, wives, and one did not know what other relationship.

"Have you had ten kitchen-boys already?" asked Hadi Khan in some slight surprise.

"Good Lord, in less than ten weeks?" I exclaimed. "I really don't know; it might be. There has been rather a lot of them—Mohammad said they were all bad. I've been too busy to look into that situation very closely. What is it the women want?"

"They are asking the return of the apprentice-fees Mohammad required from them."

"Apprentice-fees?" I queried.

"Yes. They say that Mohammad—Mohammad *Khan*, maestro of all cooks—demands from each *shagird* a fee of ten tomans in advance for the honor of serving in your household under the brilliance of his instruction. The families raise or borrow the money in some way for this great opportunity; but after a few days, or a week at most, Mohammad fires the apprentice as unworthy of his efforts, keeps the fee, and of course pays no salary. The families are rather unhappy about this. Somehow they have got together over it." It sounded distinctly as though they had.

I do not usually "pass the buck" on matters that concern me, but in this case I did. "Hadi," I said, "my wife and I are going riding. We will not be back for three hours. I'm leaving this to you to fix up. When we return I don't want to find any women in my stables; but they must leave of their own free will, reasonably satisfied. You have my authority to discharge Mohammad or put him in chains if necessary, but I wish no more trouble of this kind. And hereafter I will engage and pay my kitchen-boy directly."

When we returned I found things quieter than they had been for weeks. Mohammad was the quietest of all. He had gone to bed with an illness of the head. He was in a fearful gloom for the next ten days. By then he had devised some other profit-making scheme and once again became happy.

Mohammad was really a great cook, yet I felt he had missed his vocation. He would have gone far in the realm of high finance, preferably in America from about 1925 to 1929. Even in Europe, he might have done well. He could have shown Stavisky and Kreuger a lot of things. He might then have returned to Persia and bought himself a Province, or perhaps have remained abroad and taken over all the Ritz Hotels. He might, of course, have landed in jail. It may be that is where he is now. I have had no news of him recently.

The Maidan

Our house in Meshed gave on the outer Maidan—the large, dusty common between the Arc and Bazar Gates, out beyond the earthen ramparts of the Holy City. Its southern wall flanked that square of many activities; where captured outlaws were hanged, where the battered postal wagons from Teheran and the south ended their hard journeys, and the two-mile-long camel caravans of Haji Gholam Reza

Sabzevari, the greatest merchant of Khorasan, swayed in with rhythmic beating of their bells and folded themselves jack-knife fashion to unload.

It was a spacious and well-built house. Its four connecting wings enclosed a court laid out with flower-beds around an oval pool that was long enough for a dive in the heat of summer. There were four large masters' rooms and six smaller ones, a wing of servants' quarters, gardens, and stables for our horses. There was a *hauz-khaneh*—a "cool room"—with a blue-tiled pool down its center, over which we placed our dining-table during the hot weather and ate with tasseled goldfish swimming beneath our feet, while fresh water spouted from the mouth of a stone lion's head.

The house did not face the Maidan. Persian architecture reflects the Easterner's desire for privacy. Also it is unwise to flaunt one's riches before the tax-collector or the cupidities of passers-by, wherefore the better-class Persian houses usually hide their faces or turn them inward.

Ours did both. Its colonnaded façade looked onto a delicious inner garden lower than the court, a dream of feathery poplars and flower-beds with shady paths looping a further, circular pool, enclosed by high mud walls to preserve its intimacy. A little brook appeared out of nowhere from under the wall, burbled along its edge, right-angled through patches of white and blue iris between the poplars, to disappear again into the outer garden, where lived our cows, our chickens, ducks and turkeys, a baby gazelle and sundry smaller beasts. The stable yard made yet another enclosure. On its slope the grooms spread the manure to dry in the sun for horse-bedding, and Ali-Akbar-the-Gardener quarrelled with them for sufficient with which to enrich the gardens.

A comfortable house, cool in summer, warm in winter; exceptionally well designed. It had been built by the defrauding ex-Cashier of the Internal Revenue Service with a part of the substantial sum of his defalcations. He erected two more houses in Meshed, there being a paucity of satisfactory investment in Persia for ill-gotten gain. The others were less pretentious; but all three had been confiscated. They were held now as Public Domains.

The one I took for my official abode had served successively as headquarters of the Russian troops in East Persia during the Great War, as headquarters for General Malleson of the British East Persia Cordon after the Russian forces were scattered by the Revolution of

1917, and as the Internal Revenue Offices for Khorasan. Much had to be done to make it livable after such a history, yet the result was good.

There was, of course, no plumbing, no central heating or electricity. Servants supplied the deficiencies of the first—"hot-and-cold running coolies" one would call them in China. Two huge Russian stoves built into the walls between the four principal rooms, with open fire-places throughout, kept us reasonably warm in winter. The dried fruit-wood and tamarisk brought on the backs of donkeys from distant fellings gave off an enchanting blue flame. Many oil lamps, daily trimmed, lighted the hours of darkness.

In no city of Europe or America have I lived more luxuriously than on the edge of that fanatical town of Central Asia. No house I have ever occupied has left more poignant memories of affection and content. A matter of taste, no doubt; a preference for the homely comforts of space and service and privacy to all the gadgets and modern convenience of Christendom.

The back of the servants' wing formed a blank wall along the Maidan, pierced by the single entrance to the compound. Massive wooden doors, bolted by a heavy beam, guarded the entry. A detail of a sergeant and four soldiers guarded the doors. That, at least, was its purpose. The detail, relieved fortnightly, behaved in a reasonably alert manner at times. Sometimes it did not.

There came such an occasion while Meshed was passing through one of its recurrent stages of unrest. Returning to the house earlier than usual, I found the gates wide open, the guard absent save for two men in opium-sodden slumber on the guard-room floor. This was particularly annoying because of the disturbed conditions in the town, that might at any moment flare into fanatical outburst against all "unbelievers." There were malcontents who would have been glad enough to incite an outbreak in the direction of my house.

Dismissing the servants on errands outside or to the stable yard I gathered up the five rifles from the rack. When none was looking I carried these arms to the inner garden and dropped them one by one into the farthest of our pools. Very old rifles they were. Their condition salved my conscience at such treatment of arms.

The absentee guards strolled back later in the afternoon to discover an empty rifle rack. By various artifices they managed to wake the slumberers. None had knowledge of the spiriting away of their weapons. For the next twenty-six hours that guard went through the torments of damned souls. They dared not report the disappearance of their muskets from under their very eyes while they slept or had been off visiting unmilitary haunts without permission. They could not well come to me, whose protection they were supposed to assure by strength of arms, to inquire if I had noted the removal of those arms. Nor was any such unaccountable loss of five army rifles, in an area beset with brigandage and predatory tribesmen, apt to be lightly dismissed by the Division Commander.

In their ears rang the horrid song of the bastinado; before their now sleepless eyes danced strangely distorted visions of rifles. Not their lost ones; rather the venomous grey muzzles of a firing squad. All night and all the next day the guard-room hummed with anguished chatter.

The stricken men knew not what else to do but talk. They sprang smartly enough to attention when I passed (*morituri salutamus!*) with two on duty at the barred gates where none had been the afternoon before; then reverted to their doleful argument.

The sergeant, a very feeble Non-Com, was the most abject of the lot. That two of his men had slept while the other two and himself were off in some lowly tea-house did not make a very effective alibi for the loss of the five rifles in his charge. And if any theories were held about the disappearance, these could not well be pursued in outside inquiry without at once broadcasting the news. It may have been that Mohammad-the-Cook had a theory. He looked a bit quizzically at me when I failed to make the usual inspection of the guard-room and sent him two or three times to silence the profitless chatter.

"In the room of the soldiers there is overmuch *guftigoo*"—the pleasantly suggestive Persian word for garrulity. "Go thou and make it cease," I commanded. He did so with relish, though the effect was momentary. Mohammad-the-Cook had no great love for a soldier. I suspected him of taunting the guard over their desperate predicament, which of course had become known to all the servants; but the latter were too afraid of being involved in the matter themselves to repeat it outside.

After a night and a day I relented, at least to the extent of instructing Ali-Akbar-the-Gardener to water some newly planted bulbs around the garden pool. Dipping there his sprinkler-can he discovered that he was drawing water from a submerged arsenal. He reported the matter to me in some confusion. I professed astonishment.

"Give my order to the guard," I said then. "Let them recover these weapons—doubtless hidden here and forgotten during one of the previous occupancies. They may then turn these weapons in to the Divisional Ordnance Officer." Ali-Akbar-the-Gardener had too often dipped water from that pool not to know my supposition to be nonsense. There shortly filed out of the garden and back to the guard-room a sheepish little party of soldiers trailing, like tails between their legs, five ancient, dripping muskets. But in their hearts was infinite relief.

This closed the incident so far as I was concerned. It was never afterwards mentioned in my presence, nor were the guardians of my gates again delinquent in that particular fashion. For each succeeding detail heard a story, immensely elaborated with time, of the dire fate that overwhelmed a predecessor detail which had failed in the performance of its duties. Mohammad played the leading role in the elaboration. After six months or so the story had reached a point where the offending guard had expiated its guilt in a deserted mud fort out by the edge of the foot-hills, sealed up alive into niches in the walls.

The Maidan, on most days, was a tranquil, empty square. It sprang into sudden activity when the wool caravans came in. String after string of camels with bells booming in mellow tones filled the open space, knelt and bubbled and grunted while the drovers let drop their loads; were then driven off to graze on the mountain slopes. A small army of *hamals*—porters and casual laborers—undid the great bales and fluffed out the wool for cleaning and drying in the sun after long weeks on the open road.

There were a hundred-twenty or so working in this fashion on the Maidan when Marius Kiéger sent a party of six hamals with some rolls of carpets from his office to his house. Kiéger managed the Meshed branch of the Oriental Carpet Manufacturers, Ltd. He and his wife lived about a third of a mile from us along the Toroq road. They were the only French people in Meshed, a pleasant addition to the small foreign colony.

Kiéger's hamals dumped their loads of carpets in the garden fronting his house. There they had words as usual—loud words—with the head servant over the matter of payment for their labors. The gardener and the gate-keeper joined in. And suddenly the argument flared into a shrieking row.

"Sons of burnt fathers!" they yelled at one another. "Sons of dogs!

Harlots' eggs!" and danced about, threatening to pluck out each other's eyes, to tear the beards from one another's faces. Like most Persian rows, more noise than action—until fanatical passions are stirred; but as always a great deal of noise.

The noise woke Clemka Kiéger from a siesta. She went out to see what it was about. It was, in fact, about a matter of fifteen cents, but with every appearance of an incipient massacre of her servants amidst the rose-beds and poplars of her garden. Unwisely she intervened, having but a sketchy command of the language, and was rudely met.

"Shut your mouth, unclean slut of an unbeliever!" they screamed. Clemka fled back to the house. There was a peculiarly ineffectual telephone system in Meshed, with a few dozen private installations. Kiéger had one of these in his house, another in his office in the bazar. Half hysterical, Clemka rang her husband. By an almost unprecedented chance she was connected at once.

"A pack of crazed hamals . . . in our garden . . . tearing the servants to pieces!" she cried over the wire. "I tried to quiet them . . . was horribly insulted . . . and threatened . . . just managed to escape into the house . . . they may break in any moment. . . . My God! you must hurry!"

Now the situation was unpleasant, but hardly so desperate as Clemka pictured. And, as so often happens in such minor outbursts, she had no more than hung up the telephone when the row subsided as suddenly as it had begun. The hamals took the proffered payments and scuffed off in the direction of the Maidan. Two of the servants sought refreshment, after the strife, in a tea-house near to hand. A deep calm settled over the Kiéger garden.

But Clemka's nerves had been thoroughly shaken. Certain episodes in Smyrna had left an impress of neurasthenia. Shortly she, too, departed. Madame Graux, wife of the Belgian Director of Customs, stopped off for a moment while passing by and bore her away in a droshky. There remained only the brooding gate-keeper on guard over an empty compound, where a few bales of carpets had been dumped beneath the trees.

And all this time Kiéger was running. Bare-headed, grasping a heavy walking-stick he had seized as he dashed from his office, he ran through the cavernous bazars of Meshed towards his house that was a mile or more away. Through the tortuous, covered streets in a gloom of perpetual twilight he ran, spurred on by an agony of apprehension.

The turbaned and skull-capped merchants squatting on their hams in the dark recesses of their shops followed him with insolent, heavy-lidded stares, spat lustily on the ground as he passed. Unctuous hypocrites, unhealthy, evil of heart, united only in venality and intolerance; the unholy populace of the holy city.

The hatred they hold for all unbelievers flared the fiercer against one who ran, who went hatless. In Meshed, even more than elsewhere throughout Persia, in those days, dignity permitted no rapid movement on foot, nor allowed anyone to appear in public uncovered.

All of this Kiéger sensed as he forced his way through the cluttered passages. Past haggling purchasers, past veiled women gathered in small groups before the cloth shops he ran; through little trains of laden donkeys or pack-horses, past water-carriers sprinkling the unpaved streets from goat-skin sacks. As he ran the coppersmiths stopped their hammering on half-formed vessels, the carders ceased thrumming their bows in the loosened wool. All the multiple noises of the bazar halted momentarily, and only muttered epithets, loud smacks of expectoration, sounded above the *pat-pat-pat* of his feet.

A flowing undercurrent of loathing and disdain kept feeding the flame in his own heart.

In such fashion he passed through the bazar into dusty open streets in the full heat of the summer sun, and at length came to his own house beyond the walls; to find it empty, save for a gate-keeper whose descriptive efforts of a battle successfully fought were loud but incoherent.

At that moment the *pishkhedmat*—Kiéger's head servant—returned from the tea-house to which he had repaired after the brawl. He at once assumed the attitude of the greatly-tried, faithful-unto-death guardian of his master's home and honor.

"Where have they gone?" cried Kiéger, having learned only that the hamals and his wife had departed separately, the latter in safe hands. He was fairly simmering now, what with over-exertion in the heat and a consuming rage.

"Towards the Maidan, Honorable Master!" replied the pishkhedmat, pointing dramatically.

Kiéger grabbed him by the arm and made for the Maidan. It was empty for two-thirds of its expanse; along the further edge were the hundred-twenty hamals pawing over Haji Gholam Reza's wool. As

Kiéger proceeded across the empty space a solitary figure came out of
a tea-house on the one side and headed diagonally across towards the
other. Their paths would have met somewhere about the middle.
On his back the shambling figure carried a porter's three-sided
pad.

"It's *he!*" cried the pishkhedmat. "The leader of the hamal-gang
from whose murderous attack I saved your Honor's household!"

All the pent-up rage, the accumulated fury of many months, that like
acid had been eating into Kiéger's soul, exploded in one sudden, ill-
timed gesture. Marius Kiéger was a man of medium height, powerful
in build, usually self-controlled but high-strung. I had known that
type of Frenchman well during the war. With one great bound he was
on the hamal. A prodigious swipe, and he shattered his heavy walking-
stick over the pate of the porter who at the moment summed up all his
grievances against the populace of Meshed. The man dropped like a
log. Kiéger stood over him glowering, fragments of a stick resembling
a palmetto brush in his hand.

From the ranks of hamals pawing wool on his left flank there rose
an ugly rumble. Some had watched the strange procedure. They had
seen a hatless *firanghi*—a foreigner and an infidel—in the open Maidan
fell a Moslem, a hamal such as themselves. And amongst those who
watched there was someone, a Meshedi Harry Bridges, who galvanized
the latent passions of that surly crew.

In the ticking of a few seconds the whole hundred-twenty of them
swung into motion. With loud yells and bloody murder in their hearts
they advanced across the Maidan, slowly at first, gaining momentum
as they came. Some seized stones off a pile unhappily at hand.

It happened that Kiéger's accountant, a little Greek with the
mouth-filling name of Constantinides, lived in a small house on a street
leading to the Maidan. At the moment, it being the midday period of
normal relaxation, he was trimming the rose-bushes in his garden.
From there, through a gate ajar in the wall, he observed Kiéger with his
pishkhedmat contemplating a human form that lay inert on the dusty
common. Constantinides trotted out to see what brought his chief to
stand thus in the middle of the Maidan.

As he came up to Kiéger the hamals began to advance on the run,
in a yowling mob. Kiéger was a courageous soul. He set himself to
stand off the charge. With a broken cane he faced the hundred-twenty

wool-maulers, by that time screaming for his blood. For the few tense seconds he and his two companions stood their ground their lives were worth less than the dust eddying about their feet.

But neither Constantinides nor the pishkhedmat was inclined to sell his life just then, dearly or otherwise. The two men grabbed Kiéger by the arms. "To the house of the Financial Administrator!" they screamed in Greek and Persian. "To Major Hall's house, in God's name!"

Kiéger, responsible for their unhappy situation as well as his own, let himself be rushed to the side of the Maidan where was my house, away from the charging mob now in full cry. The pishkhedmat shrieked to the guard to open the gates for the Honorable Chief-of-Carpet-Manufacturers—and quickly, in the name of Allah! By Allah's grace the gates swung open just in time. Kiéger and Constantinides dived through; the pishkhedmat fell across the sill with his head bashed open from a flung stone. Just a split-second before the spear-point of the attack reached the doors, the guards swung them to and shot the heavy bolt. Stout gates: they held against that first shock, while the thirsting hamals moiled about in search of heavier stones, ladders and a log to use as a battering-ram. Aroused now beyond any control, neither knowing nor caring whose house it might be but howling for infidels to tear apart and for loot, the crowd sought to batter down the defenses. Once mob passions are stirred they may turn murderous in a flash. And Meshed was perhaps the worst place for this in the whole of Moslem Asia.

The guard stood behind the gates with bayonets fixed.

Josephine was sitting in relaxed nudity in her tin tub, face covered with some new suggestion in the way of a beauty treatment against the harshness of the Persian climate. This time it was crushed raw cucumbers. Plans for rearrangement of certain corners of the garden occupied her thoughts. In the gentle steam of the hot bath she recalled also that she had not yet sent a message to the Kiégers to invite them for tea after polo on the morrow. Well, time enough for that later in the afternoon. And there was still an hour or so for a siesta before I would return from my office, intent on exercise. Life in Meshed was really quite pleasant . . .

There came a sudden clatter of feet to interrupt her reveries, a rude pounding on the door of the little room where we took our baths in the luxury of a portable tub, with the water nicely blended by the bath-boy to the desired temperature. These were unseemly noises in the courtyard at that hour of the afternoon.

"What does this mean?" she cried in Persian.

"*Où est Monsieur Kiéger? Mon Dieu, où est Monsieur Kiéger?*" An hysterical voice, recognizable in its Grecian slurring of French.

"How should I know?" replied Josephine. "He certainly is not here! What do you mean by disturbing me this way?" Constantinides' wailful inquiry had been a bit disconcerting to one who sat naked in her bath.

"Then he must be dead! Or he is dying; he has crawled under somewhere to expire!"

"He has *not* crawled under my bath to expire!" Josephine cried. "Go away! Hunt for Monsieur Kiéger somewhere else! I don't understand any of this, but in a moment I will come out and see what it is about!"

She sprang from the tub, slipped into a dressing-gown without stopping to dry herself off or remove the cucumber juice from her face. Outside the bathroom door she found a bloody pishkhedmat stretched out by the pool, with a mewling little Greek who ran around in circles, his face turned a nauseous green. "*Il se meurt!*" he howled. "Somewhere here he is dying! And a thousand men are now attacking this house to tear us all to pieces! God of gods, *where* is Monsieur Kiéger?"

Josephine took charge of the situation. "Constantinides, be quiet!" she ordered, shaking him vigorously. She mobilized the servants into search parties. "If Monsieur Kiéger is here we'll find him. And I *won't* have my house attacked! What is the guard doing out there?" She ran to the entry where the guard was standing with fixed bayonets behind the gates that were rocking then under the assault of a hundred-twenty infuriated hamals—probably more by this time—with bloodlust and the promise of loot urging them on.

Over the heads of the guard she brandished a pearl-handled .32-calibre revolver I had given her as an emblem of security. "If you dare let any evildoers break past those gates I myself will kill them and you as well!" she threatened. The soldiers were astounded; never had they seen such a female as this.

"Excellent Lady, we will die where we stand before anyone shall pass!" Josephine ordered two of them to the roof to guard against an attempted attack over the walls.

She ran to our telephone. This instrument rarely served any useful purpose. "The Amir Lashkar!" she demanded of the operator. And by a chance no less uncommon than that which had given Clemka Kiéger a clear line to her husband, she was immediately connected with the Division Commander.

"Oh, Excellent General," she cried in Persian, "our house is being assaulted by thousands of men with evil intent; please send your Army at once!"

The astonished Amir Lashkar promised action. He communicated first with the Police Commissariat at the Arc Gate. They were already informed about the matter. Kiéger had arrived there a moment before on the dead run. He had realized as soon as the gates of my compound swung shut behind him that he had let us in for something which could end disastrously. Without slowing up he had dashed straight through our courtyard, through the north wing into the inner garden, and with a colossal spring had scrambled over the eleven-foot mud wall at the far end. None but a powerful and desperate man could have cleared that barrier single-handed. From there he dropped into another garden whose gate opened to the road, and ran to the Commissariat, a quarter-mile beyond. The police officer in charge was a friend of Kiéger's and of mine. He happened to be drilling his company at the time. Armed with rifles they turned out at the double for the Maidan.

I sat in my office, studying petitions from oppressed villagers. Hadi Khan, my confidential secretary, interrupted the never-ending task.

"There has just come a message," he said quietly. "Your house is being attacked by a large number of men, very fanatical . . . I have ordered your horse." I always rode to and from my office, accompanied by a mounted orderly.

Ali-Akbar-the-Cossack was tightening the saddle girths in the courtyard below when I plunged down the broad stone steps. Together we galloped over the paved streets of Meshed. I had a .45 Colt automatic in my pocket; he carried his carbine unslung. People stared at us in surprise, fled to the sides away from the clattering hoofs that showered sparks off the paving stones.

We passed through the Arc Gate full out, swung left down the Toroq Road, then right-angled in a cloud of dust around the corner of a wall—into an empty Maidan. There was no sign of life, nor any sound save the echo of our galloping hoofs. Only heaps of wool, spread over the farther side. With difficulty I gained entry to my own house.

"Open at once the gates!" I shouted. "It is His Excellency the *Rais* himself!" cried Ali-Akbar-the-Cossack. Very cautiously the gates were swung open to our repeated bellowings. I pushed through the semi-circle of bayonets, then stopped short at the sight that greeted me in the courtyard.

By the pool lay Kiéger's pishkhedmat, head bandaged and all spattered with blood. Mohammad-the-Cook knelt beside him rubbing his neck with a chunk of dirty ice. On the verandah lay Constantinides stretched out in a state of collapse, muttering incoherently to himself, while Ali Akbar-the-Gardener sluiced the contents of a sprinkling can where the little Greek had been actively sick. Josephine was still in command.

She stood there in the courtyard garbed in a wet dressing-gown that had designs of white elephants on a field of blue. Her face was still smeared with crushed cucumber. In one hand she held the pearl-stocked .32-calibre pistol, in the other a lighted cigarette in a long holder. She was issuing orders in flowing if not highly grammatical Persian to fourteen armed military police who snapped to attention and saluted smartly as they trotted off to do her bidding. Their Captain moved about in the background with a broad grin on his face. He was followed by our butler bearing a tray on which were decanters, a jug of water and glasses.

Josephine barely glanced my way as I entered the courtyard. "Don't bother me just yet. I'm busy," she said over her shoulder. "I want to make absolutely sure none of the mob managed to climb over the walls."

The Police Captain circled the pool to greet me. "I think the episode may be considered over," he reported. "My men have taken a score or more of the attackers off to jail with broken heads. The rest are now being chased up along the edge of the hills." The butler approached us with the tray of drinks. Josephine was still issuing orders to the detachment.

"Your lady very kindly offered me a brandy-and-water," observed the Captain. "I hope I have your permission?"

It was not only when the wool caravans came in that the sleepy Maidan sprang into activity. Sometimes a small group of men would be seen struggling in the middle of the common with a long goose-necked pole painted in red and white stripes. That was the gibbet. It had to do with matters unconnected with the drying of wool.

Mohammad-the-Cook would then come to me in a state of pleased anticipation. "A robber is to be hanged this afternoon," he would announce. Or sometimes it might be "a very famous robber." His gratification in that case was intense.

The flat roof of the servants' quarters gave an unequalled view over the Maidan. Mohammad always placed a chair there for my comfort, though he had not been so instructed. The servants, their relations and friends, gathered on the roof of the stables. They made a sizable congregation. And usually I atttended the proceedings, not from morbid curiosity but because it interested me to watch the reactions of the populace.

Two hours or so before the time set the crowds began to gather. A detail of troops formed a circle of perhaps a hundred feet in diameter around the pole to hold back the spectators. Another smaller circle was made inside, where stood officers and witnesses, relatives of victims who had been murdered or wronged by the condemned, and various others connected with the execution. A military band added its touch of gaiety to the entertainment.

The prisoner was driven to the gibbet in a droshky. Six or seven soldiers stood upon the seats, the steps, the box of the droshky, surrounding him with fixed bayonets on all sides. His wrists were tied behind his back. Usually he had been fairly well doped with opium. He was led to a soap-box at the foot of the pole.

The crowds poured into the Maidan, packing the circle eight or ten deep. Men stood around in turbans and flowing robes, in brimless black or brown *kolas*, in tall sheepskin hats like busbies. Others circled about on horseback, on bicycles, or squatted on the seats of droshkies. There was a good sprinkling of women: townswomen in black silk or cotton coverings and black visors, village folk in grey Manchester prints and veils. Some watched along the rim behind the men. Those from the upper classes drove round and round in droshkies, peering out from beneath the leather tops like black crows in a cage. It was not permitted in Meshed that Persian women should be seen in carriages with the tops furled. Along the edge were little stands selling refreshments, candies and cigarettes, poisonous sherbets, watermelons and spitted mutton.

The Military Commander would start off the ceremony by reading a long list of crimes of which the prisoner was accused. There followed then the sentence of hanging, met by a low rumble of approbation from the crowd. The prisoner would be put upon the soap-box to make the farewell address of custom, the last apology, so to speak. A Latin could hardly have availed himself expressively of that privilege—since the man's hands were tied behind his back. But the Persian prisoner rarely failed to launch into a long, incoherent argument: how his father had been a loyal and devoted subject, his father's father before him; even as he himself, and whatever had been said of him to the contrary was intrigues and lies. But if indeed he may have been induced into evil practices, never as God was his witness would he do wrong again . . .

"*That* is true enough!" remarked the cynics in the audience, a bit bored at the lengthy effusion. The execution party by then would be showing signs of impatience.

"This is all very well," they would say to the condemned man, "but one cannot wait forever! How about cutting it short and being hanged?" Finally they would push him, still declaiming, off the box. Ankles tied together, wrists fastened behind his back, the slip-noose was dropped over his head. A Mullah gave him a last sip of water in memory of the Imam Hossein who died thirsty. Without further ceremony he was hauled slowly upwards on the rope that passed through a pulley at the end of the gooseneck. There was no drop, no blindfolding. The condemned one simply "hung by the neck until dead" of strangulation, a surprised stare upon his face.

It did not appear to be a particularly painful death. There was no struggling. The body twisted slowly round as the rope stretched, but did not writhe. The crowd showed no special emotion. After a few minutes the relations of the dead bandit's victims pronounced themselves satisfied with the blood penalty. The military band then struck up a merry tune.

The droshkies packed their peering black crows round and round the circle. The vendors of sweetmeats and sherbets cried their wares. The band marched off blaring cheerfully and the crowd gradually dispersed. There would remain only a small guard of soldiers at the foot of the pole, from which until late in the evening drooped a quiet body above an empty deal coffin.

But the executions did not always go off quite to schedule. There was an occasion when the haulers on the rope were over-energetic.

They raised the object of their attentions too fast and too high. The knot of the noose caught in the pulley. The rope broke: the chief actor fell with a heavy thump at their feet. There, after recovering his breath when the noose was released from his neck, he began to howl in sudden anguish.

"What a bore!" growled the officials. "How can we get another rope through the pulley without taking down the pole?" And that would be too long a job, what with the crowd all expectant and everything waiting.

A soldier tried to shin up the pole, but failed to reach the pulley. The masters of the ceremony sent for a ladder, while the band played a highly original rendering of "Over There" to keep the spectators entertained. The ladder finally arrived: it was too short. A small boy volunteered to clamber from the top of the ladder up onto the gooseneck, if he were to be paid a *kran*—ten cents. After some haggling over the financial details he was promised the *kran*. When he came down from having reeved the rope anew through the pulley, no *kran* was forthcoming.

"*Fardar!*" cried the officials. "Tomorrow! Come back tomorrow! We must get on with this hanging!" They chased the lad off the Maidan, his outraged howls succeeding those of the principal actor, who was now squatting glumly on his hams. It was a typically Persian scene. Then the condemned man was re-noosed and hauled very cautiously into the air.

But the struggles to reset the gibbet had not been without effect on its foundation. As the prey of a relentless justice dangled in the air for the second time, the pole swayed, then with a loud crash came down altogether.

The Military Commander was infuriated. He kicked the unfortunate prisoner—by now too dazed to howl—vigorously in the stomach. The crowd began to mutter. It was an unpropitious hanging; the fates somehow were against it. "The Evil Eye!" they murmured. It might be displeasing to God, though they knew not quite why.

"If the son of a dog won't hang, then by God we'll shoot him!" snarled the Military Commander. The prisoner was dragged over to a mud wall at the far end of the Maidan. They stood him up against its side. A firing party lined up opposite, twelve men with five different types of rifles. They fired, and the condemned man went down. But he kept thrashing around on the ground, so finally the officer in command of the firing party walked over to him. Stepping as if in an odd sort of dance he caught the prisoner's head between his feet, and standing thus fired into it seven rounds from an automatic at a range of perhaps fourteen inches. The man lay still.

The officials breathed sighs of relief. The Evil Eye had been cheated. The prestige of the military had been upheld. The guilty one had publicly atoned for his crimes of banditry.

They rolled him into the waiting coffin. The aggrieved families passed by and pronounced themselves satisfied. Then the band struck up "Over There" and they all, save only the now dead bandit, marched from the Maidan.

Shades of Upland Valleys

Within a day's ride of Meshed there were numerous upland valleys that afforded good camping at altitudes ranging from five to eight or nine thousand feet. In their cool verdure one found rest and solace from the torrid summer heat and irritations of the holy city. None was quite so enchanting as the valley of Mahal-i-Zoshk.

It had good water, always the first essential. Beautifully clear streams splashed through tortuous wooded ravines into shady pools. At those pools the wild boar came to drink as evening fell, partridges and doves and foxes throughout the day. The streams teemed with a type of trout, and up above the villages the water, delicious and refreshing, could be drunk without the usual preliminary of boiling the germs away.

Small dams diverted water from the streams into high-level irrigation ditches etched in straight lines across the sides of the hills, laboriously dug in the steep rocky slopes or built up with flat stones along their outer edges. From them little cascades tumbled at intervals down the mountainsides, forming white streaks that glinted in the sunlight against a multicolored background. Under the different effects of sun and atmosphere the mountains took on changing colors of reds and mauves and violets, more variegated than the Painted Desert.

The slopes were blanketed in flowers and flowering shrubs. Tall thistles raised pale lilac heads on long green stems; sweet smelling heather wafted its perfume to high heaven; thorns of many sorts blossomed in white and yellow and mauve. The upper ravines were billowing seas of lavender in full bloom, almost overpowering in the richness of their odor. Lower down, the air was redolent with the scent of wild mint. In no other spot on this earth have I met such a blending of fragrances as in the valley of Mahal-i-Zoshk.

As one went up the valley the walls of earth gradually gave way to stone walls, not unlike those of New England. At its head even the houses boasted walls of stone—an unusual development in Persia—but held to their flat earthen roofs, hard-baked by the sun, arranged tier upon tier; the only level spaces in the hillside villages. Upon them the women of the village performed various intimate domestic attentions on their babies, pawed over one another's hair, or rolled balls of manure to dry for fuel in the sun along with the drying fruits, mulberries and other comestibles.

Small children with bloated little stomachs helped tend big herds of goats and kids on the slopes above the villages, or splashed naked in the streams. Women milked she-goats into large copper pots. Old men, squatting in the sun, spun goat's-hair yarn on small hand spindles. Women and men together shook mulberries off the trees into sheets they held outstretched, then cooked the syrup in huge copper dishes. More men stood alongside the stream, throwing brown and black fat-tailed sheep, one by one, from a five-foot bank into a deep pool to wash them for the second shearing.

The whole life-economy of a well-favored mountain valley unrolled before us as we watched. There were lumbering operations: the valley was unusually wooded for the Persian highlands. Mostly the timber was second-growth *chenar*—plane-trees—often with five to fifteen fair-sized trees growing from the enormous stump of some giant felled years before. The cutting was uncontrolled. There are no effective forestry laws in Persia, with the inevitable result in denuded hills, erosion and drought. But in Mahal-i-Zoshk many trees had been planted, there was some natural reforestation; and both planting and reforestation seemed to have been fairly well conserved. Walnut and fruit trees were enclosed in walled gardens to protect them against the all-devouring goats; stands of poplars whose trunks had the color of white birches followed the upland contours, their shiny leaves heliographing in the sunlight; pollarded willows grew beside the watercourses, reddening the current with the swirls of their root tips. Most of the trees standing in the open, along with the walls and the roofs of houses, sported festoons of alfalfa hay twisted in ropes the thickness of a ship's hawser, drying in the sun.

Peeled plane logs were floated down the small streams to be hand-sawn into boards farther down the valley, man-handled all the way with no cant-dogs or any substitute therefor. Other logs were transported two by two into town on the backs of little donkeys that staggered under their long, inverted V's of brilliant white, the ends furrowing the ground on both sides.

Dotted over the hillsides were circular platforms of hard-beaten earth, gouged out of the slopes and built up on the lower sides like sacrificial altars. These were the threshing-floors, where pairs of bored bullocks dragged heavy log rollers with wooden teeth round and round in spiritless chase over the grain to be husked. Close by, men winnowed the chaff from the seed by tossing it down-wind in the manner practiced since man first made bread.

The Zoshkis were kindly people, hard workers, self-respecting. They came to our tent with gifts of fruit, goat cheese and walnuts. Bowing as politeness dictated, but without servility, they presented their offerings.

"We make a prayer, there are no peaches; but there be apples and apricots and the King-of-Mulberries. *Bismillah*—in the name of God!" they would offer them. All were the most delicious of their kind I have ever tasted. We purchased various supplies from the villagers at prices which were not specially inflated for the foreign interloper. Sometimes they would come with young partridges, mountain herbs, a live baby fox, or other finds and captures for sale.

Their costumes were highly colorful. Long coats of dark blue or green or faded raspberry-red were worn like kimonos over low-necked white shirts. White turbans, or green for descendants of the Prophet (there are few communities in Moslem Asia without their descendants of the Prophet), covered the men's close-cropped heads; white cummerbunds encircled their middles. They wore shoes of heavy hide soles with woven string tops, resembling the sandals of Montenegrin peasants. The most favored color combination was a tricolor of hennaed beard, white turban and blue coat.

It was in the evenings just before sunset that the valley showed its greatest charm. The fragrant smokes of ox-dung and camel-thorn hung languidly above the villages. Streamlined bee-eaters soared on translucent orange wings over the camp, whistling in low bubbly notes. A short flutter, then a long soaring glide; twisting, diving, rising again in flashes of orange and blue on set wings: to me the loveliest of all birds in the air. On the slopes behind the camp huge red-legged partridges almost as tame as chickens called back and forth across the mountainsides.

Each evening we would stretch out on camp chairs amidst the encircling shale ridges that glittered like mercury under the sunset, the lavender-scented breath of evening in our nostrils, in tranquillity and deep content.

But there had been a time when these quiet valleys, that of Zoshk and the neighboring one of Kang, were not so peaceful. It started with a blood feud between the two principal villages. From this there developed two bands of the younger men, at deadly enmity with each other, who first took to raiding the adjacent valleys and then to organized brigandage on the roads in order to provide the means for keeping up their supplies of ammunition—essentially a matter of logistics, as it were.

Brigandage and sudden death were common enough on the highways of Khorasan during the tenure of the Governor-General of that time. His own methods were a trifle subtler, but no less effective. On his return to Teheran from his post he was followed by seventeen creaking *fourgons*—springless transport wagons, each drawn by four horses. They carried the bulkier items of his extortions from the people of Khorasan.

After his departure, the Amir Lashkar—the Military Commander—at Meshed took upon himself to act as Governor-General *ad interim*. In due time this valiant officer was stirred into a show of punitive action by the continued depredations of the brigand bands from Zoshk and Kang. The ill-disciplined and worse-led force he sent out withdrew after a few indecisive skirmishes against the brigands without having captured a single member of either gang. Whereupon the Amir Lashkar sent them a message inviting the two bands to come in to Meshed and give themselves up on promise of full immunity. He swore the most solemn oath on the Koran to pardon past offenses.

"And employment under the Government will be granted all men of your villages who thus join me in preserving law and order," the Amir Lashkar pledged. "But otherwise you will in due time be annihilated!"

A few from each band accepted the conditions. They came to the Holy City. There they were well treated, comfortably lodged and given the best of food. On the strength of this the remainder trooped down from the mountains to join them. All but six of the Zóshkis gave themselves up under the repeated guaranty of immunity. These six refused to place any confidence in the sacred oath. Too well they knew the character of their countrymen.

"How would one trust the word of an Amir Lashkar?" one of those six asked me. "Where is honor found among the sons of burnt fathers?"

Early one morning twenty-six of the Amir Lashkar's guests were dragged into a caravanserai and shot without further ado. Their corpses lay in a long row on the Maidan in evidence of the Military Commander's acumen and efficiency. From a multiple red gibbet five others were hanged. They were the alleged ringleaders. Their bodies remained hanging there throughout the day and through the moonlit night, a reminder to evildoers. That same night the seventeen wagons, creaking under the Governor-General's personal loot, rolled nearer to the capital of Iran.

Only the six wary ones of Zoshk escaped the slaughter. They were still living there when first I came to the valley, quietly pursuing their lawful occupations.

"We went on a pilgrimage of expiation to Kerbela after our comrades were killed," they explained.

"And does the feud still persist between Zoshk and Kang?" I asked them.

"We no longer have any quarrel with the Kangis," they replied simply.

They were not bad people. The Zoshkis were particularly sympathetic, very polite, saluting with quiet dignity whenever we passed. But in both villages one remarked an undercurrent of sadness. They were still mourning their lost young men.

Comrade S—— Had Slanting Eyes

There was a valley where once I camped, on the Persian frontier looking across over Russian Turkestan. It was not so smiling a valley as that of Mahal-i-Zoshk. The villagers had been dreadfully buffeted by fate in many unkind forms: by earthquakes and influenza, by famine and raiding Turcoman tribes, and without respite by predatory tax collectors and sub-Governors, grasping local Khans and unrestrained troops. To all this had been added a constant difficulty over the water rights denied them by Russian agents. Though they lived on Persian territory they were kept from irrigating their lands with the water of the streams that flowed towards the Russian frontier. The Russians wished it all preserved for *their* lands across the border, and were strong enough to enforce their will.

Whilst some rain-watered crops could be grown, these were insufficient for the villagers' needs, and the various imposts against the scanty harvests left little or no surplus on which to live. The villages had been depopulated by the ceaseless visitations of the tax collector and the resultant flight of the villagers. The orchard gardens were denuded of their trees. A few wretched survivors eked out a hopeless existence by cutting and selling for firewood in Meshed what little was left of the fruit trees they once had planted; and, in utter despair, by the sale of their daughters to the Turcomani tribesmen.

They worked like beavers for incredibly little return. It was often a sixteen-mile walk from the villages to the few straggling fields that were cultivable in rain-watered crops. Dug into the hillsides around the fields were underground habitations known as *soms*, used during the periods of ploughing, of sowing and harvesting. Dismal hovels they were, dark and foul-smelling. In the center of each a slightly deeper excavation sheltered the plough-oxen, the donkeys and goats. There was peculiarly little charm to the life of a peasant on the Persian frontier below the Trans-Caspian steppes.

With the reversal of Czarist policies after the Revolution of 1917, the Soviet Government made the gesture of cancelling or modifying certain concessions and unequal treaties wrested from Persia during Czarist days. Among other adjustments at that time was a realignment of the Turkestan frontier, which Imperial Russia, for strategic reasons, had located part way down the hills overlooking Khorasan. The readjustment favored Iran, but resulted in added confusion among the frontier villages over the matter of their water rights. The little rivers flowed in all directions from irregular and broken watersheds. Some from Persian sources debouched into Russia, others rising on Russian territory poured their life-giving floods into Persia. A few doubled back and forth across the border, two or three times. Villages formerly in Turkestan but lately become Persian found their water diverted by

Russians farther upstream, while similar practices on the Persian side left Russian settlements dry. The Government administrations in both countries were bombarded with protests, besieged by deputations of petitioners.

To work out some solution, a Frontier Waters Delimitation Commission was designated by each of the countries to meet on the spot. In this matter the Russians sent as their Chief Commissioner a gentleman whose name was S——.

I came upon him when I was camping up the valley where the woeful cultivators were working the fields from their dank underground *soms*. He had arrived in that neighborhood on a tour of investigation, a little after my arrival on the same errand. Following the Persian protocol, I rode over to call formally upon him in my official capacity. He greeted me in Persian.

"Peace be upon you!" For ten or fifteen minutes we exchanged honorifics in a language in which neither of us could claim a highly polished proficiency.

"Your kindness is great!"

We made inquiries as to one another's health. "By the grace of God and Your Excellency's presence your servant is doing well," we each responded. "Since Your Excellency's advent the rains are more frequent, and the crops are yielding manyfold more than heretofore." The fulsome, stock phrases of politeness.

"My eyes light up at Your Excellency's presence!"

Servants came with the two prescribed glasses of strong, heavily-sugared tea. But these were not followed by the little cup of black coffee that usually signals the approaching end of an interview. Instead my host proposed: "May I ask if you will join me in a whisky-and-water?" This came out in faultless accent of London's Fleet Street.

"Willingly! And I am gratified to find that you speak such excellent English!" I said.

"I should speak it reasonably well," he replied. "I lived for many years in London. I was correspondent there for two Russian papers."

"You have come a long way to the little rivers of the Khorasan-Turkestan frontier!" I remarked.

"And have not you?" He laughed; an infectious laugh. "Cheerio! I hope we shall see much of one another." We finished our drinks and

I took my leave. Within the hour he returned my call. At the flap of my tent I greeted him—in Persian.

"Peace be upon you!" We repeated a few of the fulsome honorifics. We drank the two prescribed glasses of tea. And then it was my turn to inquire in English: "May I hope you will join me in a whisky-and-water?"

"Gladly!" Whereafter we exchanged no more honorifics.

He was an engaging type. But not at all Russian. I could not quite place him. He dressed and acted in every way like an Englishman; like a Londoner of a good but not highly aristocratic family, with a broad journalistic background. He had a slightly Oriental cast of feature, rather high cheek-bones, a suggestion of slanting eyes. Yet his hair was not dark, and his name seemed somewhat indefinitely northern. I put him down as perhaps a mixture of Tatar and White Russian of European stock.

We became very friendly. He was a most cooperative person, with no vapid pretensions, showing neither undue familiarity nor staid reserve. There came an evening when, over a bottle of Black Label, he told me something of his story.

"I went back to Moscow after the Revolution," he said. "Until then I had been held as of some importance in our London Press Bureau and had not been released for military service. But when the Czarist regime collapsed I found I had neither any political nor any economic reason to remain longer abroad."

He must of course be a Communist now, I assumed, or he would hardly be here in official capacity. Later on I made some indirect reference to this thought, which he chose to acknowledge.

"You are a Christian, are you not?" he asked. The question was entirely dispassionate. "Well, Christian tenets condemn working on Sunday. Today is Sunday. You have been working?" I had.

"It was necessary," I said.

"Quite so," replied S—. There seemed in those two words the suggestion of an answer to my unformed query.

He continued: "I was made some sort of Assistant Commissar. I applied myself vigorously enough. One had to. All were struggling slavishly for The Idea. In unbelievable confusion, of course. And one day I was ordered to eastern Siberia. 'A-hah!' I said to myself. 'So it has come! The end, no doubt; it is not meant that I should return from there!' But I did, as you see. I had no very unpleasant experiences in Siberia . . . and I availed myself of the opportunity to call upon my father."

"You had not seen your father for a long time?" I asked. "Was he then living in eastern Siberia?"

"I had never seen my father. He was not living in Siberia; he was in Japan. I went to Japan. I made inquiries as to where my father was living. I found he had a house outside of Kyoto. So I engaged an interpreter and asked when it might be convenient for my father to receive me. The answer came: 'Thursday afternoon at four o'clock!' "

I may have looked a trifle confused; the thought of the interpreter seemed odd.

"You see, I speak no Japanese. My father had long since forgotten all the Russian he ever knew. And though I also speak English and French and German, I realized that the Japanese are not normally good linguists, and the older ones, at least, much prefer to speak in their own tongue."

"Your father was Japanese?" I inquired.

"My father was a Japanese. He had been at one time the Japanese Envoy to the Court of St. Petersburg."

I filled two empty glasses. "It is excellent, your whisky," he remarked. "And I believe the water from your spring is sweeter than mine up yonder."

"They are both yours," I said, reverting to Persian manners.

"Thank you. . . . So I went to call upon my father, with an interpreter at my elbow. I dressed in Japanese costume, not unduly to surprise the old gentleman. At the steps I kicked off my sandals, advanced through several rooms with servants bowing low on both sides; and in stockinged feet, treading softly on the thick mats, came to an inner chamber. In its further corners several squat figures sat on the mats, draped in coverings of black silk discreetly embroidered in white crests. One of them, I knew, would be my father."

"You did not know what he looked like?" I asked.

"I had seen no picture of him taken within thirty years. A daguerreotype, I think it was, that I had seen. From behind me came a voice, the voice of my interpreter—a most punctilious guide. 'You should bow!' it said. I bowed very low, hissing in my breath. And there issued then from the far corner of the room certain words whose meaning I knew not.

"'Your Honorable Father says pray approach!' the voice of my interpreter whispered from behind my left shoulder. Without raising my head I advanced three paces and bowed low again, as I had been instructed. Again came the same words, and again the same whisper over my shoulder: 'Your Honorable Father says pray approach.' I went on three steps more, very slowly, my head still bowed. And there came then a different phrase, and from my interpreter: 'Your Honorable Father says pray be seated.' So I folded myself on my heels and raised my head, and for the first time in my life I looked upon my father."

He took a sip of whisky-and-water. "It was an odd sensation. He was a grey-haired, dignified-appearing Japanese gentleman. He asked after my health, and in a gentle, detached way, of my experiences. I told him, through the interpreter of course, a little of my life, while we sipped tea from very small cups. There was a kakemono hanging over the corner niche, a beautiful painted kakemono with a small bear crawling up a steep hill through heavy oriental foliage. The little bear was looking back over its shoulder. I assumed that the kakemono had been chosen with some reference to me. There was also a flower arrangement under it, a blossoming twig in a fine bronze vase, that was undoubtedly in my honor; but I had not the knowledge to understand it.

"Time passed and there came the whisper of that ghost-voice behind me: 'You may now take your leave.' I rose and bowed low once again, hissing my breath inwardly. Through the voice of my interpreter I wished my Honorable Father continued health and longevity. Through my interpreter he gave me assurances of his esteem and wishes for my future success. I backed and bowed myself out of the room, taking then—so soon after the first glimpse—my last look at my father."

"He may perhaps live to be a hundred years old, and you will see him again," I interposed.

"He died last year." We sat smoking quietly for a few minutes. "It was rather an unusual experience, to meet one's father in just that way for the first and only time, at the age of thirty-one; to pay one's respects through an interpreter and bow oneself out backwards. I never thought to inquire if the other squatted figures who also bowed to me were my half-brothers. Quite probably they were. Members of my family, so to speak, all of alien race, in alien surroundings. I would have liked to know my father better. He must have been a very fine man in his way.

"He was, you see, still quite youngish for an Envoy when he came to St. Petersburg. I was told he had considerable charm. And while there he became enamoured of a young lady of the Russian Court. She was also attracted by him. In those days one did not know so much of contraceptives as we do now.

"I was born a few months after his recall. For twenty-one years he sent a substantial annual remittance for my education. Then it stopped. But long before that my mother married, quite well. She was an attractive woman. I, naturally, was an inconvenient appendage. So I was sent to England to complete my education. And there I remained until after the Revolution. She and her husband both died during that episode—not very happily. I had to tell my father of that, through the interpreter, when he inquired after her health." He paused. "Life plays some odd tricks in the matter of parentage, does it not?"

And so I came to know the reason for S——'s slightly oblique eyes.

Some years later a friend of mine asked a young and very modern Japanese, who had been educated in America, what would be *his* procedure if he should return to his father's house after an absence of a quarter-century or more. (It was not stipulated that it would be the first time he and his father had ever looked on one another.) Would he approach his parent as S—— had done, in deep humility, though perhaps not through an interpreter?

"Who, I?" he said. "Why I'd call the old bozo up on the telephone and ask him for a thousand Yen!"

4 – South Persian Wanderings

On the Hamūn

The basin of Sistan, into which the River Helmand pours its life-giving floods from a distant catchment area in the Afghan massif, counts among the earliest habitations of mankind. Those parts of the basin where each spring the river deposits its rich load of silt have been irrigated and cultivated by human labor since long before the dawn of history. From the days when man first made use of domesticated animals, local herders have grazed their cows and sheep on the tender grasses at the edge of the great terminal lake called the Hamūn. Others, the most curious of all the human dwellers of the basin, have for untold generations gained their precarious livelihood by snare and net among the bulrush thickets of the lake. Without appreciable change in manners or methods, they live today, these cultivators and herders, fowlers and fishers, much as did their predecessors three millenia and more ago.

Where the once flourishing districts of Gedrosia used to exist all now is desert. Alexander the Great passed through here on his way to conquer India. Not long after his passage the Helmand shifted its course, as it has done on numerous occasions since and doubtless before. The inhabitants, wholly dependent on the river for life itself, were forced to move with it. Over the present lifeless expanses of sun-parched loam, that were the districts they abandoned, I have ridden on a surface glittering with fragments of Achemenian pottery, all baked more than twenty-two hundred years before, with not one piece of any later date.

The approach to Sistan from the Persian side is a matter not lightly to be undertaken in the annihilating climate of summer. Wind plays an important part in the life of the basin. The *Bad-o-Sad-o-bist Rūz*— the "Wind-of-One-hundred-twenty-Days"—blows on and off during four hot, cloudless months. This is no ordinary breeze. It reaches a velocity during the day of sixty to a hundred miles an hour, often for a week or more at a time, though usually diminishing at night. It is a fearsome thing to encounter on the waterless stretches that surround Sistan. In full force it blasts the very surface off the desert, and all life along with it.

The last forty-mile stretch of stony barren, from a water-hole known as Safidawa on the main East Persia caravan-route to the edge of the Hamūn, enjoys a peculiarly evil repute. Even the bleaching bones of dead camels, that form the only conspicuous marking of the caravan track, are lacking. Caravans avoid this unwholesome expanse, swept in summer by the demon wind.

About halfway across the gravelly waste I came one day in June upon traces of graves and a wind-eroded slab. These were the sole objects of note in the featureless desolation. They located the point where, during the war of 1914–18, a column of British Indian troops lost a one-sided battle with the *Bad-o-Sad-o-bist Rūz*. Caught in a relentless hail of hot black stones hurled at over a hundred miles an hour, the unfortunate Indians could move neither forward nor back. The volcanic blast shrivelled and killed their pack animals, shattered their water-containers, swiftly dissipating the contents. Gruesomely, they died within a day's forced march to safety.

I stopped to look at their forlorn little graves, so eroded by the wind as scarcely to be recognizable. The scorched desert floor cooked one's feet through heavy-soled shoes. My open car was like an oven, body and cushions blistering, even the touch of the steering wheel painful to bare hands.

"One need not wait for death to know what the fires of hell may be like!" commented Entekhabol Molk, my Persian aide. We had to keep the wind-shield closed lest the withering breath of the wind, light though it was then, should sear one's eyeballs in one's head.

"Unfit for men or animals," a British military report branded that evil track. It was no overstatement, in all truth.

From this to the tranquillity of a night passage across the Hamūn, in a flotilla of bulrush canoes poled by a swarthy crew of hereditary boatmen, made a transition that lingers in memory. When we reached Lab-i-Baring on the edge of the great, cool stretch of water, its one mud building and herders' camp of woven bulrush huts loomed like a celestial haven from the rigors of the desert. My Sistan staff and the local chieftains who had travelled out to meet me were waiting there in tents open to the breeze, now light and refreshing as it wafted over the Hamūn. Samovars sputtered in readiness for teapots; delicious *dukh*—a kind of fermented curds and whey—and other drinks hung suspended from the tent-ropes to cool by evaporation in the wind.

"Peace be upon you!" Never had that amiable salutation sounded so appropriate. The chieftains cried: "All evils will now be made right!" This was getting more ambitious. "Our eyes light up!" So went the greetings.

A brief rest followed the usual reception and inquiries after our health. The car was swathed in canvas, pegged and roped against the wind. Then tents were struck, the paraphernalia of road and camp transferred to a fleet of tiny *tūtin*—canoes made from *tūt*, the Sistan bulrush—which lay drawn up in the shallow water near the bank. We made ready to set off as the sun was sinking low over the desert behind.

My servant spread my kapok mattress atop a chunky little canoe newly built of fresh bulrushes. On this, after bathing in the sweet waters of the Hamūn, I stretched out in blissful repose, garbed in plum-colored Chinese pyjamas. There remained barely room in the stern for the dark-skinned wielder of the tamarisk pole.

The fleet started off with much crying out of instructions, in the seemingly inevitable confusion of every Eastern undertaking. Quite soon it shaped itself into an orderly array of twenty or so little craft deployed in open formation, until we came to a long lane cut through the towering bulrushes, down which the flotilla had to proceed single file. Before that the shouting had quieted down and the peace of the sunset hours was interrupted only by occasional and not unmusical queries and replies.

"Oh Habibullah, where hast thou placed the *napht?*"—the kerosene, desired for the big lamps.

"I make a prayer, it was not in my keeping: inquire of Gholam Ali!"

Melodious cries of the boat-polers floated back and forth to one another. Wholly pleasant calls issued to the refreshment boat: "Ali Reza, Ali Reza, bring thou barley-water!"—which is beer, but with its innocuous name is frequently held exempt from the Koran's interdiction against intoxicants. Then the refreshment barge would shoot up alongside the canoes of the "notables" and foaming German beer, Scotch whisky, French cognac—all brought to Sistan by camel caravan —or Persian arack would be offered by the kneeling Ali Reza and accepted according to the dictates of one's own tastes and the strength of one's religious observances.

The big kitchen barge came early into action. From off its charcoal

fires astonishing hot dishes were served on china plates, with cutlery
and napkins for the foreign dignitary. Never have I tasted a more
delectable repast nor one more admirably served. The waiters knelt in
little tūtin that made rapid darts like water-beetles from the floating
kitchen to the various units of the flotilla. Each trip was productive of
a new and delicate dish. Most of them had a heaping base of rice—
white and fluffy, or saffroned and crisped, plain or sweetened—such as
only Persian cooks know how to prepare. Spitted morsels of tender
lamb that first had been steeped in fresh lime-juice; creamy soup of
greenish herbs; chicken into whose flesh tasty condiments had been
inserted: these followed one upon another. Then came spiced meat-
balls and marvelous pilaffs, with great sheets of thin whole-wheat
bread baked on pebbles, which served the lesser lights for plates as
well as sustenance. Partridges, decidedly out of season, were produced,
with cucumber salad, sweets and desserts galore. Coffee, liqueurs and
cigarettes marked the conclusion; a veritable feast for the gods, served
in a most engaging manner.

A gentle northerly breeze, just strong enough to keep insects away,
dispensed with mosquito-nets. The servants and the tūtinran—the
polers of the canoes—pitched in after the "notables" were satiated,
cleaned out the tin-lined copper pots that were passed around, shov-
ing great gobs of food into their mouths with wide, effective thumbs.

There rose a moon nearly full and reddish gold over the bulrushes
to round out the evening, while I lay back and smoked in complete
repose, in sheer, sensual enjoyment of the scene. Crimson spots of fires
glowed along the horizon where herders in scattered encampments
were burning the reeds on the edge of the Hamūn. Countless water-
birds took off from our path to circle above us, punctuating with their
calls the snatches of song of the boatmen in lilting minor keys and
quavering half-notes—unwritten folk-songs of a little known people,
handed down through unnumbered generations.

A young man strummed a lute and sang softly to the moonlight
while the measured plunk of the poles, the dripping of water as they
were lifted, lulled me gradually to sleep. Before I closed my eyes we
had passed far into the narrow lane cut through the overhanging bulrushes. Myriads of birds, big and little, resting along the lane's edge,
stirred into mild fluttering and sleepy chirps at our passage. In the
small space of moonlit sky above us squadrons of huge dragon-flies
winged their way like airplanes in formation. With my tūtinran still

humming soft quavers over my head, fragments of thousand-years-old song whose words he himself scarcely understood, I pulled a diminutive mosquito-net across my face and dropped peacefully off to sleep.

It was dawn when we reached the Sistan side, having taken eleven hours for the crossing of roughly twenty-two miles. I rose immeasurably refreshed. The boatmen bore the "notables" on their backs through the shallow water to the gently sloping shore. On the "High Skirt of the Hamūn" horses and camels were waiting, and another camp of welcomers.

Among those who came there to greet me was one whose fine, white-bearded face had an appealing gentleness. He was the Arbab of the *Saiyads,* headman of the tūtinran and of the fowler and fisherfolk who hold in hereditary franchise exclusive rights upon the wild life of the reed-beds. With the shyness of his people he waited on one side, a little apart from all the others.

"Peace be upon you . . . my eyes light up! . . ." He fumbled with a bundle done up in home-woven cloth. "I make a prayer . . ." and with it a downy offering. The coarse parcel was filled with wild-duck feathers, the smallest and softest pluckings of breasts and bellies.

"We be now barely six hundred families—so greatly have we suffered; who are Your Excellency's servants." And in their veins flowed the purest blood in Persia. The Saiyads intermarry with no others outside their own clans.

"We are exceedingly poor. We have suffered several years of low flood during which many died, having naught to eat." Drought is the chief dread of the Saiyads, whereas the cultivators in Sistan suffer more from excess of water than from lack of it.

"This year by the grace of God and Your Excellency's presence the flood is great." In such a year, though my presence had scant to do with it, the overlapping saucer-like basins of the Hamūn fill one from the other and the vast lake becomes more than a hundred miles long. But even in a good year a Saiyad's whole annual catch of water-fowl and fish would be traded at average weight for weight against about thirty bushels of mixed wheat and barley. The Saiyads themselves eat only the stale or undisposable portions of their catch. Whatever they can dispose of they barter, needing bread for variety of sustenance but growing no grain of their own.

These are the most primitive and probably the least understood of all the peoples of Iran. Living secluded lives at the edge of the water, in rounded huts of plaited bulrush behind bulrush screens, their means of livelihood seem to keep them apart from the other elements of Sistan's self-contained population. Industrious as they are, highly skilled in their ways, a single adverse season brings the six hundred-odd families to the stark borderline of starvation.

From mid-February to mid-May they fish, in parties of six and at night, with triangular-shaped nets nine feet wide at the base. From mid-May they labor for two months at reaping and gleaning in the fields of the cultivators, drawing payment in kind—about six bushels per family, and, during the days of harvesting, for each a daily handful of green wheat or barley to parch. The next four months they pass weaving cotton cloth, repairing their nets or making new ones, plaiting mats of reeds, new huts and tūtin of bulrushes. Then from mid-November to complete the cycle in mid-February they catch water-birds with fowling nets nine yards long by five wide, woven to an inch and a half mesh. These nets they cast amongst the reeds with amazing skill, for coot by day, on dark nights for duck.

In those three months of a good season a party of six will catch from twelve to eighteen hundred birds, having a value locally of three to five cents each. The proceeds are pooled, but divided in seven parts —for with every party there goes a "dead man" who represents the tax-farmer's share. Thus each living man may earn from seven to perhaps eleven dollars for his three months' effort by day and night, to which he can add about another dollar and a half for down and feathers. All of this constitutes close to two-thirds of his annual income, since the yield from fishing is less than half that from fowling.

The life of a Saiyad is varied and picturesque, but assuredly no sinecure.

Though every Saiyad must have a small tūtin in which to get about, the monopoly of ferryage on the waters of the Hamūn and the river is hereditary in a few families. These families do no reaping nor fishing or fowling. The useful life of a bulrush craft is barely fifteen days when used on heavy duty; two to three months if employed only on fowling and fishing. It takes three to six men several hours to cut the bulrushes and fashion a raft or canoe from three cigar-shaped bundles of trimmed stalks—the middle bundle the largest, with all the stalks laid head to prow. Once I took two cars across the Hamūn on specially made tūtin propelled by eight polers each. The tūtin were produced to my order in a single day.

On occasions I went in tūtin after duck, and with some justified hope for geese and swan. Such a shoot, arranged by my good friend Shokat-ol-Molk, the hereditary *Grand Seigneur* of southeast Persia, was an elaborate affair. We would go out with many tūtin to where the Saiyads had prepared *kola* in the shallow expanses of the lake near the reed-beds.

A kola, normally speaking, is a round, brimless felt hat; but a kola in the Hamūn is a blind—a tiny atoll of silt and rushes built up by hand. Its rim projects a few inches above the surface of the water, the rushes extending high enough to cover one's head. The water, or most of it, is baled out of the kola, so that one may squat or stand in fairly dry state with gun and a vast quantity of ammunition in expectation of an enormous bag.

When the guns were all in position the duck were driven down the Hamūn over the kolas by tūtinran in the deeper water and by horsemen where the lake was shallow. Later they were driven back again by a similar party of beaters. Other tūtinran hid in the reed-beds to pick up the kill. When there was a strong wind and the duck flew low the bag was incredible in numbers and variety.

Nothing of it was wasted. The excess went to the Saiyads, who can afford no such costly means as guns and ammunition to gain their livelihood.

The earnings of the tūtinran, the barge-polers, are also pooled; and a third part goes to the tax-farmer.

"God's will is absolute," said the Arbab to me gently. "I have not to complain. Yet in very truth the burden of our taxes is not light." A poll-tax on each family, taxes on the fishing, the fowling, the feathers and down, the *tūtinrani* or ferryage—on the earnings of men who gross from unremitting labor perhaps twenty dollars a year, if it happens to be a good year: in truth, the burden is not light.

And the taxes that the cultivators and herders have to bear, the charges imposed directly or indirectly on every human and animal effort, are astronomic in quantity, incredible in burden. Not the most minute source of revenue is overlooked. By no chance does all or even the greater part of these imposts reach the central Treasury. There are the tax-collectors, the feudal headmen, the tenant-contractors of the

Government-owned domains, the tax-farmers of minor taxes, the mullahs, administrative chiefs, sub-Governors, the military, and a horde of other hangers-on to take their share. The wretched peasant pays it all, and has hardly enough left to eat for his family though he lives entirely on watermelons through the summer. In addition he has to render many days of unpaid forced labor on the dikes, the irrigation canals and the tamarisk weirs that are washed away in each annual flood.

There was a little guild of sheep-slaughterers whose imposts were recorded in seven different tax accounts. One of these was a word I did not know. It was translated for me to the best of his ability by an educated sub-collector who had, as he felt, been exiled to Sistan. The word had to do with the tax on the entrails of slaughtered sheep, exported for eventual use as sausage casings.

"Those who have paid their taxes on their bowels," the translation read. That seemed the ultimate word in taxation.

The Governor's Piano

Nasratabad, the overgrown village of domed mud houses that constitutes the provincial capital of Sistan, holds scant claim to distinction. Always isolated and inaccessible, it has remained little affected by the progress of the outside world. Not entirely unaffected, for the Governor of the province had an astonishing and flamboyant taste for western gadgets. While the rest of Sistan clung to the practices of Old Testament days, he delighted in the appliances of modernity.

Samsam-ed-Dowleh, "Swiftness-of-the-State," was a fat little man with an unabashed, childlike naïveté. He was Governor by virtue of his family connections, and unlike the usual run of his kind he was simple and unoppressive. The abject poverty of the Sistanis was not of his making.

He lived in an earthen palace surrounded by the squat adobe houses of the agglomeration that served as capital of the province. The palace enjoyed a pre-Biblical but highly efficient air-conditioning system, consisting of a pair of towers that faced into the prevailing wind, down which the hot blasts of summer passed through wetted camel-thorn into the interior and became quite cool in the process. It also boasted electric lighting of a sort—this was Samsam's pet installation—

whose feeble bulbs gave out an illusory flicker when the thing worked at all. He was immensely proud of this temperamental gadget.

He had a tennis-court, built up a good three feet above the surrounding level that became a porous bog during the rare rains. There were no side-nets, their purpose being served by a multiplicity of excessively ragged ball-boys; and the lack of width of that elevated platform made a dangerous trap for the unwary player running back after a deep drive. Samsam played with considerably greater enthusiasm than skill. It was impolitic to beat him, for to be beaten reduced him to such a state of depression as sometimes to bring tears.

"*Now* my electric-light machine will break down again tonight," he would cry. "I know it! It always does when I lose at tennis!" This it did a great deal oftener than he lost at tennis, as his opponents were usually considerate souls. The electric-light machine was an unpredictably spasmodic affair, a gasoline-driven dynamo that delivered a feeble, flickering current and kept an Indian machinist in constant employ on its repairs. It had been brought in detail from India by camel. The fuel for it was all carried on camel-back from the distant railhead.

Samsam had an orangery, a large steel-and-glass structure that looked to have been designed for a first-class public garden in India. It, too, had been imported piece by piece on the backs of camels. It contained a single orange tree bearing one pale and scraggy fruit.

He had a reception-room whose walls were almost completely covered with clocks of different shapes and sizes. French Empire clocks, cuckoo clocks, Swiss clocks with carved wooden bears following one another dispiritedly around a wooden tower; alarm-clocks, 24-hour clocks, water-clocks; a copy in miniature of London's Big Ben looking out from the perpendicular Gothic of the Houses of Parliament; lady's boudoir clocks, kitchen clocks, clocks set in seashells and in a model of the Eiffel Tower. Not one of them was running. They were all stopped at different hours, over a dozen or more years.

It was a very warm reception-room and there was something infinitely depressing about all those tired clocks with their hands held at different angles across their dead faces.

But the glory of Samsam's westernization was a grand piano. When first I saw it I inquired in amazement how on earth he had managed to bring that cumbrous instrument to Sistan.

"By boat from London to Bombay," he explained, "and by another boat from Bombay to Karachi. Then from Karachi to Quetta by railway, and by another train from Quetta to Nushki, where the Northwestern Railway of India formerly ended. And from there by camel. On its side, swung between two large camels. It was very difficult."

One would imagine so: a grand piano packed some five hundred miles across the Baluchistan desert between camels, at a speed of two miles an hour when the caravan was on the move. It had, of course, to be unloaded every day that the camels might rest and graze; to be loaded on them again every evening. And this for several weeks on end.

"You like, then, to play the piano?" I asked. "You will perhaps play for us?"

"No," said Samsam sadly. "I do not play the piano. No one plays the piano."

He was so very doleful about it I felt there must be more to the story. There was more. I heard it later from one who had been present.

In all Sistan and for many hundreds of miles in all directions there was no person who could play a piano, at the moment when Samsam decided he must have one to enliven his isolation. This did not deter him in the least. For some while after its arrival he and various friends used to thump on its keys like eager children working a new toy. Not having the vaguest conception of how to produce tunes from that huge toy with more than one finger at a time, and no very inspiriting tunes at that, they found the practice a bit cloying once the novelty had worn off. The splendid instrument graced the Governor's mud palace thereafter in vast but silent grandeur.

With the passage of time there came from India to Sistan a British Consular officer who brought with him a wife. They had ridden a great way by camel and horseback, and the lady was not at all elated when informed that they were expected to dine with the Governor the very night of their arrival. But nothing could be done about it. Samsam had heard by grapevine that the lady played the piano. For a long time he had been waiting impatiently on just such an event. He was not to be put off.

They went, and the party met in the reception-room whose walls were a morgue of dead clock-faces. Greetings having been exchanged, a ceremonial glass of tea or two hastily taken, the Governor, beaming with pleased anticipation, ushered the lady into the next room to see his piano. There it stood in all its freshly polished magnificence; probably, costs of transport taken into account, the most expensive instrument of its kind in the entire world.

"It is a beautiful piano, Excellency!" exclaimed the lady.

"You like it? You will honor us by playing it?" asked the Governor, his round moon-face quivering with pride and delight. The lady smiled bravely. She was very tired, but she seated herself on the stool and ran practised fingers over the key-board. There came forth not a sound.

The happy expressions of her audience died suddenly into looks of acute distress. She pressed on the loud pedal, thumped heavily upon the keys, to be rewarded only by a dismal clacking. The moon-face of the Governor became a picture of abject woe.

The lady rose to her feet as in a horrid dream. She opened wide the sounding board and looked within. In that painful silence one heard only the quick, panting breath of Swiftness-of-the-State. Nor was the piano destined to break the silence.

"Excellency, I am so very, very sorry!" The lady was herself almost in tears, so deep the disappointment in the eyes of her host; like a heart-breaking disaster come to a happy child. "I am afraid it cannot be played," she said gently. "You see, the piano is without hammers."

They crowded around her as she pointed. The felts, even the wood of the hammers, had been eaten off by white ants.

Wherefore the Governor mumbled his plaintive little response when I asked him if he played the piano—the grand piano that had come five hundred miles across the nearly waterless wastes of Baluchistan suspended between the flanks of camels. It seemed that the white ants would eat up the hammers faster than he could have them replaced.

"No, I do not play the piano," he told me sadly. "No one plays the piano."

There had been another though different commodity brought out from London and across the thirsty Baluchistan desert in the same manner as the Governor's piano. This made an even longer voyage by camelback, for it went on to Birjand, another hundred fifty or so miles farther north. It was a recurrent item over a considerable period and many camels were used to move it. It was beer.

During the first phase of the World War the British Indian Army established the so-called East Persia Cordon, connecting India with the Russian military operations in northeast Persia. The primary object was to prevent infiltration of enemy agents, supported by Persian tribal mercenaries, into Afghanistan and so down into India where they might create serious trouble. The Cordon also served as a skeleton line of communications which could be quickly implemented in the event of need. It operated over a peculiarly ungracious territory, sparsely populated, nearly treeless, cold and dismal in winter and hot as hell's hinges in summer. Water was scarce and generally brackish where obtainable. The few women were veiled, which probably was just as well. The British officers assigned to this uninspiring duty found little in the way of amenities of life, a pervading *ennui,* and scant chance to distinguish themselves in a military sense.

So the authorities who are constantly thinking of the warriors' welfare (or so they say) thought up a method of improving the morale of the officers and the few British other ranks—the troops were mostly Indian—isolated in their dreary exile. They approved the carriage of beer out to the headquarters of the Cordon at Birjand as mess supplies. This meant in effect that the beer had to be paid for, ex-all duties, at its basic value in London, or something in the way of three or four cents a bottle, I believe. The transport—by train, boat, more trains, and camel for the last six hundred-odd miles—was provided gratis. Had it not been, the beer on arrival in Birjand might well have been worth its weight in platinum.

It happened that Persia then produced no bottles. The source of supply was Russia, and this source, as a result of the war, had dried up. The Birjand mess was not long in discovering that the empty bottle could be sold for considerably more than the cost of the full bottle delivered in Birjand.

From this it followed that the more beer one drank the lower were one's mess bills, and that by reasonably assiduous consumption one could have a plus sign at the end of the month rather than a debit. For good British sportsmen it was not cricket to pour out the beer upon the desert. But how they learned to drink beer!

There was a Colonel of the Indian Army who visited Birjand in the course of his duties as Inspector-General, having ridden by camel the last six hundred-odd miles. He and his escort rode trotting camels which did rather better than the two miles per hour for ten hours a day of the supply train. Even so, he was not without a modest thirst when he arrived. In customary Eastern style he was met a few miles outside his objective at a pitched tent under which were hanging, wrapped in wetted shirts to evaporate in the breeze and so cool off the contents, many quart bottles of Tennant's best brew. He drank several and felt better. He then proceeded with his welcomers to the Birjand mess, where he was shown to his room. In it was a case of beer, the twelve quart bottles cooling by individual evaporation.

"Colonel," said his hosts, "you must be hot, tired and thirsty. The boy is preparing your bath. There's a little beer here which we hope is fairly cool. We didn't want to clutter up your room, but there's plenty more outside. On that table you'll find a bell. Any time you ring it the boy will bring you in a case of beer."

The basic beer unit of the Birjand mess was a case of twelve quart bottles. They could not be bothered to think in lesser terms.

Yet the transportation at no small cost of that bottled commodity round half the world served a useful purpose, which, unhappily, was not the case with the Governor's piano.

The Samsons of the Sarhad

"After the creation of the Earth was completed, God made Baluchistan from the refuse." So runs a Persian proverb. Over this refuse, during an early period, roamed the most colossal land-beast known to mankind: a rhinoceros-like beast called the "Beast of Baluchistan," estimated from its discovered bones to have stood 17 feet 9 inches at the shoulders.

In the Year of the Bull (1925) a man with rhinoceros-like wit sought to play the part of a human Beast of Baluchistan. He had the arrogance, but lacked the stature. He failed in his attempt; and it fell to my lot to rescue him from an isolated mud fort where for two weeks he had been beleaguered by infuriated Baluchi tribesmen. Their howls to tear out his heart in the course of their nightly forays had by then somewhat modified his truculence.

He was a *Sarhang*, alleged equivalent to Colonel. His name was Elishah; an inapt name, for he was not a prophet. To him there came no visions of flaming chariots in the skies, nor divine inspiration to oppose monarchic oppression. Neither did he enjoy miraculous powers to devote to the homely beneficences that had gladdened the heart of the Prophet whose honored name he bore. Sarhang Elishah failed even to recognize the unwisdom of repeating in the wilderness which God had shaped from refuse the gesture that brought lasting notoriety to Delilah the Philistine.

For unnumbered generations Baluchi men have worn their hair in long, oiled locks to their shoulders. In this they take pride, as did their ancestors before them. Sarhang Elishah undertook to cut off the hair of the Sarhad Baluchis. He actually did so in the case of two prominent chieftains, with a number of their men. This proved his own undoing.

It is a curious thing to observe the straw that breaks the camel's back. The straw in this case, that broke the backs of many camels, drove the wild tribesmen of the Sarhad into frenzied revolt, disrupted for a time the whole of southeast Iran, and strained international relations, was an unwanted hair-trimming.

I was in the basin of Sistan when Sarhang Elishah opened the drama in the highlands two hundred miles to the south. I had just returned to Nasratabad from the Band-i-Kohak—the great weir of tamarisk and stones across the river Helmand, that each year washes away in the flood and each year has to be replaced, yet is wonderfully well designed to meet the conditions of that peculiar land. For should a permanent dam be built there it might well last forever, or until eroded away by wind and sand; deserted by the river, left a dry and thankless monument to the misplaced efforts of man.

Not far from the weir Timur became Timur-i-Lang—Timur-the-Lame, or Tamerlane. In the course of an attack on Zahidan, then the capital of Sistan, he was severely wounded in the foot. The wound lamed him permanently; but he recuperated in camp amidst the tamarisks along the river's bank and returned to destroy Zahidan. From there he passed on to broader conquests that earned him the title, amongst the multitude of his followers, of "Ruler of All the World."

When I returned to the present-day capital its earthen walls and sleepy aspect were enlivened by an astonishing series of triumphal arches. These had been erected in anticipation of the visit of Sarhang Elishah when he should have finished with his tour of the highlands— the Sarhad—of Persian Baluchistan. The arches were variously constructed of mud, of steel telegraph poles left behind by the British

East Persia Cordon after the war, and wooden railway ties brought by camelback from railhead of the Northwestern Railway of India at Duzdab. They all were quaintly embellished with Persian carpets, mirrors, hurricane lanterns and glass chandeliers, tin plates and pots, and framed lithographs of Reza Khan, soon to crown himself King of Kings of Iran. The display was in no manner spontaneous, nor was it destined to be of avail. Circumstances prevented Sarhang Elishah from enjoying the triumphal entry so thoughtfully arranged by the garrison commander to flatter his Colonel's vanity.

Sarhang Elishah did not finish with the Sarhad. The Sarhad finished with Elishah.

Few regions on the globe are less felicitous than Persian Baluchistan. There are in the highland area neither towns nor villages. The burnt-up, desolate wastes are sparsely inhabited by nomadic tribes, who are among the wildest in all Asia. For only brief periods in history have they been under any effective control of the Iranian State. Until 1916 they used to fling their raids to the outskirts of Meshed, more than six hundred miles distant; striking terror amongst the villagers, making off with their flocks, carrying away their women to sell into direst slavery. The fearful repute of these raiders gave the Sarhad a name as uncouth as the region itself: Yaghistan, "Land of Outlaws."

Under the instigation of the German Consul at Kirman the tribes, during the war of 1914–18, took to convoying subversive German missions into Afghanistan and to raiding British lines of communication. Their activities became of serious concern to the General Staff in India. In 1916 an expedition under General Dyer succeeded in subduing them after fantastic adventures. Seven years later the British turned back the area to the Persians in probably the best order it had ever known.

During their temporary occupation the British managed to keep the district tranquil with two companies of Indian troops. They did this by subsidizing a few of the more reliable tribal chieftains, who on their part provided levies of irregular constabulary and guaranteed the security of the caravan tracks in or bordering upon their respective districts. The allowances paid them made it possible for the tribes, very few of whom grow enough for their own support, to dispense with raiding. It was a far cheaper and more effective way of keeping them quiet than by maintaining sufficient regular troops to the same end, under the immensely difficult conditions of climate and terrain.

In the course of little more than a year the Iranian Government had allowed the situation to slip from its grasp. Through non-payment of the promised allowances, and renewal of time-worn abuses, they revived the tribesmen's latent mistrust and hatred of everything Persian. It was a revival that boded little good for southeastern Iran.

Over the single strand of telegraph wire across the desert there came disturbing news while I was stopping with Gerald Fisher, His Britannic Majesty's Consul and Agent of the Governor-General of India, at the provincial capital of Sistan. Sarhang Elishah, so the reports said, had set the whole tinder-box of the Sarhad aflame. There was in the making an explosion that could rend the Duzdab railhead (now renamed Zahidan, after the ancient capital destroyed by Tamerlane) to little pieces, and shatter the none-too-secure foundations of Anglo-Persian amity along with it. Gerald Fisher was perturbed.

"We're in for bloody trouble," he observed gloomily. "And I *mean* bloody—a lot of people getting disemboweled and their throats slit and that sort of thing. These tribal rows go off with a bang once they start. I know 'em of old. Yet the Persian Government will not choose to understand why such a show staged on our frontiers should cause *us* concern." He was drafting a message to the Government of India asking for a concentration of troops on the British Baluchistan frontier.

"After all, whatever may be the occasion, it's *our* railway, *our* telegraph line, *our* nationals in Duzdab that are endangered. There's no limit to what may happen down there when a doltish butcher sets about hacking at sticks of dynamite. People like the Sarhadis, who've been wild and virtually independent for more than nine hundred years, cannot suddenly be dragooned, not in any case by those whom they heartily detest. And the Sarhadis are mighty unpleasant people to bedevil."

I cut short my inspection of Sistan and set forth to the Sarhad. Gerald Fisher bade me God-speed. "When the Sarhadis find out that you're practically a Persian, albeit a temporary one, they'll probably cook you in the grease of a fat-tailed sheep!" he observed cheerfully by way of farewell.

I recrossed the Hamūn in another eleven-hour trip by *tūtin*, to retrieve my car intact where it had been pegged down on the desert rim. From there, retracing our previous passage over the forty-mile stretch of stony barren to Safidawa's lone water-hole, I and my small staff proceeded south by the cheerless East Persia caravan trail another

110 miles to Duzdab. "You probably won't get through the Shamidar Pass without at least being fired on!" Gerald Fisher had cautioned me. "The crags on both sides are picketed by the rebel tribesmen."

Before entering the pass which led into the Sarhad we halted near the Mountain of the Black Chieftain, where the "Three Empires" of Iran, Afghanistan and British India meet. There, beside the only tree between the Hamūn landing and Duzdab, I helped improvise turbans for my Persian secretary, mechanic and servant. These headgear were intended to appear from a distance as unlike as possible the conventional Persian hat. The less we resembled Persian military or officialdom, the less apt we were to draw Baluchi fire.

The stunted scrub-oak under which we stopped sheltered the grave of one Sheikh Attar, an obscure holy-man buried where he had succumbed to the rigors of the desert. Only his sanctity had preserved the lone tree from being uprooted long since for fuel. Small pyramids of pebbles encircled the scored trunk; its gnarled branches were festooned with bits of cloth and string. These were the votive offerings of countless caravan drivers praying for fortunate passage across the waterless wastes on their way to Safidawa. My servant Hossein tore a strip of cloth from his shirt, gravely affixed it to the tree. "In the name of Allah!" he said, with a prayer that God should see us safely through the pass.

Under the pitiless afternoon sun the Mountain of the Black Chieftain shimmered and danced in malevolent fashion. Rising out of blood-red foothills streaked with chrome yellow, its shiny black mass gave an extraordinary effect: like a molten mountain of Inferno, or an utterly fantastic stage-setting in the wildest style of Léon Bakst. It seemed to jeer at our toilsome progress towards the pass, at an average speed of eleven miles an hour over slopes eroded like a washboard.

In the folded hills the walls of rock exuded heat as from a furnace. Yet it was a relief to get out of sight of the gibbering Black Chieftain. Hossein's prayer proved effectual. We crawled across the Shamidar Pass without incident. Trailing a long cloud of dust, we careened into Duzdab as the dung-fed smokes of evening rose above the wretched frontier station of unpoetic name: "Robbers' Water."

This curious jumping-off place, a few years before but a watering-hole of the Sarhadi brigands, then boasted a mixed population of some nine hundred souls. Its excuse for existence lay in being railhead of the single-track extension of the Northwestern Railway of India which the

British had constructed during the Great War to supply their East Persia Cordon, and had left uncompleted beyond the God-forsaken group of wells, partly brackish, lying in the middle of the desert.

The triumphal arches erected in honor of Elishah's arrival had already been dismantled. To decorate their gaunt frameworks of railway ties the garrison commander had requisitioned many bales of carpets from the local merchants in the bazar. Not very many, it was said, found their way back to the rightful owners after the dismantling. The weird little town, though outwardly calm, was intensely jumpy; bazar rumors flew thick and fast. My friend "Buggins"—officially Captain Smith, acting Vice Consul of the Government of India—awaited me on the screened verandah of his bungalow with a decanter of whisky and porous earthen water-jugs cooling by evaporation in the hot breeze.

" 'Tis the stuff," said Buggins, "to restore one's humor after the sort of trip you've had!" I did not argue the point but drank gratefully. Until well into the night we discussed the humorless exploits of Sarhang Elishah and their probable sequel. The review was not encouraging.

"What an I.Q. that fellow would score!" remarked Buggins. "He hit infallibly on the one gesture that could drive the Sarhadi clans together, turn them from sullen disaffection into rabid frenzy!" The chieftains, said Buggins, had regarded Elishah's coming in hopeful spirit. They looked to him to right their grievances, which were many, including eight months arrears of tribal allowances and an unpunished case of rape of one of their women by a Persian soldier. Family morality among the nomad Baluchis is of very high degree. Rape with them is the gravest of all crimes, in every tribe punishable by death.

"Juma Khan, Sardar of the Ismailzais, has always shown himself the most loyal and reliable of the chieftains," Buggins went on. "He came to Duzdab with a number of his men to greet Elishah, and at the same time to seek redress of his tribe's complaints. Elishah received him and his petitions with utter contempt. And then, the arrant idiot ordered the party to cut short their hair."

It was in no uncouth spirit of humor that he had done this. Elishah was as lacking in humor as the original Beast of Baluchistan. It was a gesture of authority: to make the tribal levies appear more like Persian troops, which they never had been and had no intention of being. The outraged tribesmen refused to comply with what was to them an improper and immeasurably degrading order. So Elishah commanded that Juma Khan be seized along with his small band of levies, had them forcibly shorn with horse-clippers by Persian soldiery in public, and threw them into the local jail.

Buggins poured out two nightcaps. "God-A'mighty!" he exploded, "*fancy clipping their hair!* I'd not want to play Delilah to that lot of Samsons. Why, they'd suffer emasculation as amiably!"

It developed that they had shortly escaped with their humiliation to the hills, from where they called out the whole tribe. The witless Elishah, perfectly pleased with his work, proceeded then to the isolated fortress of Khwash, where another Persian garrison was stationed. He repeated his operation on Mir Idu Khan, headman of the Reki clan of the Khwash area, and on the latter's detachment of levies. Some seventy in all were shorn. Elishah determined to make clear to the tribesmen who was master of those unfavored highlands.

His determination was short-lived. The Damani clan rose up to join the Rekis. "They chased Elishah and his garrison into the fort," said Buggins. "It's not clear whether or not they've killed him. That's all we know so far; except that the whole Sarhad is now in turmoil, all five major tribes on the warpath, swearing by the beard of the Prophet and their fathers' heads to exterminate every Persian. They've cut up a ration-and-leave party, invested the garrison at Mirjawa, and two thousand armed men with murder in their hearts were reported this afternoon concentrating on Duzdab to pillage and destroy. Some of 'em aren't so damn far away right now. Three score grazing camels were looted within two miles of the bazar today."

Buggins looked solemn. "As you know, four-fifths of the population of this comic mushroom town are British Indian traders. Probably nine-tenths of the property value is British. The entire trade of East Persia comes up over our railway to be delivered by caravan six or seven hundred miles away. Now the railway has ceased operations. Its frontier staff was evacuated last night for safety deep into British Baluchistan. I may tell you, the Government of India are very much concerned!"

That was the situation the night I reached Duzdab.

Things moved swiftly thereafter. From Sistan, Gerald Fisher managed to get in touch with the Indian Frontier Agent, who courageously remained on alone at his post at Mirjawa, fifty miles down the line from Duzdab. Over the single telegraph wire that linked Sistan, Duzdab and India across the desert, the sole line of communications left uninterrupted, Fisher spoke with the voice of the British Raj.

"I want you to get a message to Sardar Taj Mohammad Khan at all costs!" he instructed the Frontier Agent. Sardar Taj Mohammad Khan was head of the Reki tribe and the active leader of the revolt. He was believed to be in camp outside Mirjawa. "I want him told that we will most strongly resent any attack on the frontier station and will hold him strictly to account if the telegraph or the railway should be cut!"

In due course the answer came to us—Gerald Fisher by then was on his way down from Sistan. It was suave and to the point. "The Sardar states that out of his great respect for the British he will refrain from attacking Mirjawa tonight. But he calls for immediate evacuation into India of all British subjects now in Duzdab. For this purpose, and for no other, he will guarantee security of the railway."

"Hell!" commented Buggins without enthusiasm. "I've already made arrangements to evacuate the whole Indian population at a moment's notice. But an order to that effect would be the signal for a general panic and immediate looting of the bazar. We'll wait a bit for that." The Frontier Agent's message added that Reki parties were arriving on camels every few hours, and that large *lashkars* (literally "armies"; in reality armed forces of any number from fifty or so up) of Damanis, the most savage and unreliable of all the tribes, were reported heading towards Duzdab from the south. The Duzdab garrison then consisted of sixty demoralized Persian soldiers.

Gerald Fisher arrived from Sistan, having ridden down the east side of the Hamūn part way by horse and part by camel, fording the Sar-i-Shela spillway on a camel with great difficulty. He put through another message to Taj Mohammad urging a conference.

The Sardar had refused flatly to have dealings or discussions with any Persian. Under Gerald Fisher's vigorous pressure he agreed to meet us for a parley at Mirjawa. My status as a Persian official was sufficiently mitigated by my being a foreigner . . . "a kind of an Englishman," Gerald Fisher informed him. An American was nothing of which Taj Mohammad had ever heard. The Sardar gave verbal safe-conduct for our trip to Mirjawa in an effort to settle the disturbance and restore order.

We set out late that afternoon from Duzdab in a brake-van behind a white-flagged engine, accompanied only by Fisher's two Indian Attachés. Proceeding cautiously in the deepening dusk, oil lanterns playing on our flags of truce, we met Taj Mohammad with a batch of his tribesmen alongside the line some three miles north of Mirjawa. The flickering headlight picked out the folds of baggy garments and of turbans, glinted on oiled locks of hair, on rifle-barrels, sweat-streaked cheekbones and the whites of eyes. As the engine came to a halt, more and more men rose out of the dark, surrounding us with intense faces.

Gerald Fisher and I descended to greet the Sardar and his younger brother Habibullah, who then joined us in the brake-van.

"Peace be upon you!" Somehow that salutation seemed not entirely to fit the circumstances. Both men were covered, as were most of their retinue, with an amazing paraphernalia of armament. They had rifles in hand, sabers dangling at their sides, knives, revolvers and bandoliers of ammunition strung all over them. The Sardar was fat as well as heavily laden. He had to be pushed up the steep steps into the brake-van. After a further exchange of compliments we proposed going on the few miles to Mirjawa. Taj Mohammad was agreeable to the suggestion. The engine started up slowly, puffing and spattering sparks in the dark.

This move was misunderstood by the tribesmen outside. A great moan went up. They thought we were stealing their Sardar. They swarmed around us, falling over one another in clumsy attempts to get on the unfamiliar steps, surging alongside the van with a tremendous clatter of equipment, rifles waving in the air. The moan rose to an ugly snarl, punctuated by fearsome shrieks. Rifle-bolts snikkered as cartridges were chambered.

"For God's sake stop the engine!" shouted Fisher through the din. As we gathered momentum the slower or more encumbered warriors strung out on the track behind like the tail of a comet. None dared shoot for fear of killing the Sardar. At length Fisher got the driver to halt the engine. Taj Mohammad explained from the steps that he was not being abducted.

"To Mirjawa!" he ordered. "God be with you!" The tumult subsided and we proceeded on our way.

Mirjawa was in possession of strong Reki forces, armed to the teeth and extremely boastful over having driven out the Persian garrison. We moved to the verandah of the railway rest-house, surrounded by some hundred-fifty tribesmen. Their individual armament comprised a rifle, up to three revolvers, occasionally a saber, two or three long knives, two bandoliers of rifle cartridges and a belt or two of revolver cartridges. Each man was his own ammunition train.

At the outset there was a good deal of confusion and shouting, but gradually the conference quieted down to a semblance of order. Taj Mohammad was a natural born actor. He declaimed the tribal grievances with impassioned and appropriate gestures. The mortal hatred of all the tribesmen for Elishah was sufficiently evident. For the first few hours Taj Mohammad retched at every mention of that name, the tense warriors shook in paroxysms of rage and ululated shrilly.

"May dogs devour the carrion of the son-of-a-dog!" they screamed. "May the fires of hell consume the son-of-a-burnt-father!" Each comment was punctuated, as by fire-crackers, with smacking expectorations.

Non-payment of the tribal allowances and many of the abuses of the military were discussed with comparative coherence, the wild chorus howling confirmation of each point the Sardar brought up. Confiscation of rifles—most treasured possession of any Baluch—stirred deeper passions.

"At the time slave-raiding was broken up by Dyer's forces in 1916," remarked Fisher in an aside to me, "the value in the Sarhad of a prime young female slave ran to about three hundred rupees, that of a rifle to about eleven hundred."

But when the matter of the hair-clipping was raised, though none there had actually been subjected to that ignominy, they gave vent to the full force of primitive expression, burnt Elishah and all his ancestors with lurid expletives, flinging his heart to the unclean scavenger dogs. The massed *lashkar* squatting on its haunches packed every inch of space on the verandah and around the front of the rest-house. With rifles clutched upright the shaggy tribesmen swayed in unison, dark sweat-streaked faces distorted with hatred, eyes and teeth gleaming in the light of oil lanterns. It was a weird scene. One had the impression of sitting in the midst of a great pack of extremely savage wolves about to spring.

Taj Mohammad passed to the case of rape. In bitter invective he denounced the immoral habits of the Persian soldiery, culminating in this attack which Elishah had merely made the basis of further insults to the tribes. "The services of public women can be had for a few *krans* in any town of Persia!" he cried.

"It is so! It is so! It is so!" howled the chorus.

"It is *not* so among the Baluchis!" shouted Taj Mohammad. "By God, it is not!" yelled the warriors. With contemptuous disgust and realistic gesture he spoke of intercourse by the soldiers with donkeys and camels requisitioned from the tribes, and spat lustily between his feet.

"What an actor the stage missed in him!" whispered Gerald Fisher. Certainly Taj Mohammad swayed his audience through the most of that sweltering night. Yet we were all the cast of the drama, not merely its audience. Gerald Fisher played the British Raj to perfection.

"Taj Mohammad Khan," he reminded the Sardar over and again, "I most solemnly warn you against permitting the quarrels of the tribes with the Persians to endanger British lives and property!" The good British attitude of benevolent care for their nationals abroad.

"There will always be danger when the sons of dogs bare their teeth and lift their legs!" cried the Sardar.

"There will always be danger, Taj Mohammad Khan," I interposed. "But I promise to bring the true version of this matter to the knowledge of the Sardar Sipah, Reza Khan, and to use whatever influence I may have to secure prompt satisfaction for the abuses of the military. Yet if that be done you must behave loyally." My role was none too clear to the Baluchis. It was not yet wholly clear to me, since I had good reason to fear that collaboration with the British would be suspect to the Government in Teheran. I had no specific authority in a matter involving international relations, nor any assurance of being backed up in whatever action I might take. But there was a leading part in the drama I felt that I could fill, under all the circumstances, better than anyone else available; and I had to play the part as I read it.

As dawn was breaking Taj Mohammad finally accepted our good offices. With a fine flourish he affixed his seal to a document agreeing to suspend hostilities for ten days, providing no Persian troops were moved by road or rail (there was not in any case a sufficient number within striking distance to do more than aggravate the situation). If the tribes should receive redress of their grievances within that period he would renew allegiance to the Persian Government, but not otherwise.

He despatched letters by camelmen to half a dozen of the other principal chieftains urging that they observe the ten-day truce, that they should come to Mirjawa for a conference with us, but in no case to permit the escape of Elishah and his second-in-command, Major

"Brave-One-of-the-Army," from the mud fort of Khwash where they were tightly invested. This was the first intimation we had that they were still alive. The letters ended with the somewhat naïve advice: "The British Consul is slightly angry with you for creating this disorder and fighting without his permission!"

Gerald Fisher and I returned at daybreak to Duzdab where Buggins had been on alert throughout the night. The expected attackers were still in process of concentrating from the outlying districts. The Persian garrison that had abandoned Mirjawa two nights before straggled into Duzdab during the day. Some were in pretty baleful shape from heat, lack of water and fright. But they soon became aggressive, beating up innocuous Baluchi porters and camel drivers in the bazar by way of bolstering their shattered morale: whereupon all the Baluchis in Duzdab—including two of Buggins' three servants—took to the hills. This wrecked Buggins' intelligence service that was charged to bring warning of the approach of tribal forces.

As we were left without any messengers reliable enough to send out, Gerald Fisher and I drove with an Indian orderly in my car over the desert, as near as we could get to a black-tent encampment of local Baluchis behind a fold of the hills. We fought our way on foot the last few hundred yards up to the tents through a hideous pack of mongrel camp dogs. There we handed the suspicious headman three letters to be taken at once to the Ismailzai chieftains, wherever they might be. On the prompt delivery of those letters and the resultant action depended the fate of Duzdab. The effort of breaching the barricade of dogs cost us something of our dignity. It made also one of the two most lasting pictures of many sympathetic memories of Gerald Fisher—a determined officer in shorts and solar topee dancing on the slope of a red hill in the wine-colored dusk, like some modernistic Pan, stabbing at a lot of extremely unamiable sheepdogs with a flag of truce whose import they seemed to have missed. He was still blaspheming those dogs when we returned to Duzdab, after dark. Of the trip back I remember chiefly that vivid blasphemy and hundreds of little wild melons that kept shooting out from beneath our tires, skittering over the surface of the desert like phosphorescent marbles in the moonlight: hard little green melons, so bitter that not even a camel will eat them.

The other picture of him came later, when he lay naked on a camp cot with a towel across his middle, onto which dripped the slow exudations of three desert water-bags suspended from a tripod overhead. This was after the "show" was over. He lay waiting there while a bottle of champagne, wrapped in a wet shirt, cooled off a little by evaporation. The thermometer stood at 129° in the shade.

"Always carry one of these in my baggage," he said, pointing to the bottle. "It'll do us no end of good if we can only get the stuff into our mouths and not squirt it like a geyser all over the blasted desert!" We managed to catch most of it in a bucket when the cork went off with the noise of a field gun. He was quite right; it did us no end of good.

Desultory shooting crackled along the edge of town throughout the night. As far as we could make out it was only the garrison seeing things in the dark and maintaining its morale in the expenditure of ammunition. In the morning, Buggins pointed without enthusiasm to fresh defensive loopholes pierced through the mud wall of the Persian barracks.

"You will note that their *only* field of fire enfilades our living quarters," he commented acidly.

About noon advice came from Mirjawa that the Ismailzai Sardar was already on his way there to confer with us. It was astounding how such word could have been relayed so quickly; yet it was authentic. Two Rekis, the message added, would be waiting in an obscure spot a few miles away to act as our safe-conduct. They were there when I drove out to pick them up. I also received a wire from the Eastern Division Commander concurring with the proposals I had sent in an eleven-hundred word message to Meshed and Teheran. This made my position a good deal clearer. I was now confirmed as arbiter of the dispute.

Gerald Fisher left at once for Mirjawa in a locomotive. I went there in my car, over a corrugated desert trail. The car wore a string of turquoise-blue beads around its radiator-cap for protection against the Evil Eye. This I supplemented by two sizable flags of truce tied on poles alongside, together with fourteen desert water-bags. The Sarhad is no place to be caught with nothing but a string of blue beads.

I took along with me a Dodge screen-van, the only motor truck available in Duzdab, hired complete with its Sikh merchant owner-driver. As we were about to start, the Sikh lost his nerve. He refused flatly to move. Buggins, an enormous man, suddenly blew up. Tension, heat, lack of sleep, were beginning to tell on us all.

With fearful oaths in Hindustani, Arabic and English, Buggins dragged the Sikh from the van by the beard and flung him heavily to the ground. Off flew the Sikh's turban, unwinding yard after yard, exposing his shaven pate with an odd effect of nakedness. The small metal quoit all Sikhs wear in their turban as a religious emblem skipped merrily away over the desert floor, cleaving a little trail through the dust. Part of his baggy clothes caught on the hand-brake lever and remained there. He was left in curious disarray.

Buggins picked him up, again by the beard; shook him savagely till the Sikh's eyeballs bulged with the expression of a suffocated turtle.

"You will go?" inquired Buggins, an unsympathetic gleam in his eye. "You will go . . .?"

"My face!" sobbed the Sikh. "My face has been blackened!" he repeated over and over again. His feelings were very hurt, but his face had in fact been a good deal whitened by desert dust through which sweat and tears were furrowing their way to make mud-cakes in his disordered beard.

"Your face will be a very nasty green before I get through with it, if you don't go—and now!" returned Buggins tartly. He meant that. The Sikh was under no illusion about it.

The Sikh went, preferring the uncertain hazards of the Baluchis to Duzdab and Buggins. Sobbingly he retrieved various items of apparel from the dust and the hand-levers of the van. Then he crawled back onto the driver's seat. Beside him, with instructions to see that he should not break away, sat one of the Reki escort I had found waiting at the indicated spot, a peculiarly villainous-looking brigand fingering a long knife. Under that sinister stimulus the Sikh, joyless in heart and mien, performed faithfully thereafter the duties I assigned him.

Shortly before dusk we lurched up to the railway rest-house which composed Mirjawa. On the way I picked up a wounded Baluch whom my hawk-eyed escort spotted lying nearly a mile distant, dust-colored on the dusty surface of the desert. The wretched man, his leg badly broken, had been left there to die slowly in the terrific heat by a patrol of the retreating Persian garrison. Gerald Fisher was already established at Miriawa in the midst of the Reki *lashkar*. A British party under Colonel Mark Keyes arrived from the east by handcar, having flown from Quetta in three airplanes to an improvised landing-field alongside the railway some fifteen miles east. We all camped together in the rest-house. It was ghastly hot.

Peacemaking in the Wilderness

The next morning Juma Khan, Sardar of the Ismailzais, arrived at Mirjawa by camel, having ridden fast through the day and the night. He was ill and still deeply affected by the clipping of his hair; yet he made a marked impression on us all by his dignity and the temperance of his attitude. He had neither the braggadocio nor the dramatics of Taj Mohammad. He was not at all what one would have expected in the leader of a tribe of former outlaws, though his tribe had long been the best behaved in the Sarhad. In that wild area whose sparse population comprised perhaps the greatest thieves, liars and braggarts in the uncivilized world, there were two men who were dependable and sincere, upon whose word one could rely. They were Juma Khan of the Ismailzais and Mir Idu, headman of the Reki clan of Khwash. And these were the two whom Elishah had chosen first to humiliate.

As between them and Elishah, their struggles for sheer existence against his manner of upholding national sovereignty, I was troubled by no divided sympathies. My sympathies were frankly with the tribes. This did not, I think, unduly sway my judgment, but subsequent events served merely to strengthen the feeling. And while one might trust the more southerly of the Sarhad clans—the Damanis and Dizzikis— little farther than one could throw a camel by the tail, yet treachery is not the way to deal with treachery, nor are broken promises and flagrant abuse a fit substitute for effective control.

We conferred throughout the day, surrounded constantly by more than two hundred heavily armed tribesmen. Some of the lesser chieftains who had descended from the hills found Mirjawa's relentless heat in no wise to their liking. Wherefore they spent most of the day in our drinking water, or rather in the little brook that was its outflow, lying flat on their backs, fully clothed save for their armament and ammunition belts, head to foot in a long, rippling line.

The Damani chieftains declined to come down from Khwash; we were therefore forced to go to them. "Ay, but first," counselled Taj Mohammad, "there be preparations to make." He sent out his brother Habibullah at dawn the next day in my flagged Dodge van with the doleful Sikh and eight riflemen. Their orders were to fill in the booby-traps the Damanis had dug in the road against any attempt at escape by Elishah. The traps were deep pits, covered with branches brought from some oasis and camouflaged with desert earth, located where riflemen could lie concealed in commanding crevices. They made effective barriers.

Habibullah returned late the same evening: it was definitely unhealthy to circulate after dark. He had got about halfway to Khwash, he reported, having been held up continually by pickets and *lashkars* along the track; but he and his crew had filled in the booby-traps. He furthermore had relayed to the Damanis up the road, beyond the area occupied by Taj Mohammad's forces, a warning of our coming on the morrow.

While Habibullah was filling in the booby-traps, Colonel Keyes and I took a handcar to the landing-field. This—I say with feeling—is no mode of transport to be commended for traversing fifteen miles of blasted desert in a temperature of 128° in the shade, without a vestige of shade anywhere save the hot shadow of the handcar itself. We flew then in two Bristol Fighters up over Khwash to drop messages announcing our intended procedure. It was highly important that the pickets along the southern section of the track should be instructed by their chieftains to warn off other *lashkars* and wandering brigand parties from attacking us. Especially we did not wish to meet quite unprepared a big *lashkar* of Gamshadzais (a branch of the Damanis) and Dizzikis; tribes as wild and savage as any in Asia, thirsting for revenge after an unsuccessful raid on Panjgur in British Baluchistan. They had lost heavily in that repulse. Panjgur lay in Mark Keyes's territory.

"They were damn well smacked," said Keyes. "Wouldn't want 'em to return the compliment on us now!" And this they very nearly did, though more nearly on me than on him.

It was like a rebirth to get up in the cool air of eight thousand feet and above, so chill after the terrific temperatures of Mirjawa valley that I was glad enough to struggle into a heavily lined flying-suit which had been nauseating even to touch on the desert floor. We flew along the rim of Kuh-i-Taftan, the "Mountain of Sulphur," higher of the only two active volcanoes on the mainland of Asia, both of which are in Persian Baluchistan. Its thirteen thousand feet of shapely cone gleamed mauve in the afternoon sunlight, varicolored wisps of smoke trailing lazily from its sulphur-streaked crater into a cloudless sky. In time the cloudlessness of arid lands becomes oppressive. One knows there will be no cloud even the size of a man's hand in that inverted blue bowl of the sky, not today, nor tomorrow, nor for weeks and months thereafter. The smokes of Kuh-i-Taftan, sulphuric as they were, seemed friendly and refreshing; a colorful veil interposed against the merciless actinic rays that shrivelled one's skin and from which there was no other escape than the uninspiring Mirjawa rest-house.

Throttled down we glided to Khwash. This—little more than a name on a map—consisted of two mud forts about a mile apart, flanked by scattered encampments of black tents in a long upland valley, whose treeless desolation was broken by a few sparse clumps of growth near the water-holes that render it habitable. There was no activity apparent from the air. We did not fly low lest the Damanis should fire on us in the belief that these might be Persian airplanes. From sixty-five hundred feet altimetric reading, a thousand feet or so above the forts, we dropped two cannisters with long white streamers containing letters to Mir Idu and the Damani chieftains. The cannisters landed close together in the open before Mir Idu's earthen stronghold.

We circled the two forts that were in deadly warlock, one occupied by the beleaguered Persians, the other by Reki highlanders, until two men crawled out from the latter like wood-lice on the painted floor below and retrieved the message-containers. There was some rifle-fire —we could not tell whether it was aimed at us or on the message retrievers; but the lice crept back to their fort apparently intact. Then we flew home to the desert landing-field, observing several camel-mounted *lashkars* on the way, and descended to the lower regions as if gliding slowly into a furnace. If there be a Purgatory I shall doubtless go there, but the novelty of the experience will be lacking. In more ways than one will I be a hardened sinner.

We were very, very thirsty. I had noticed amidst the mass of gear carried down from Quetta by the three Bristol Fighters a large wooden case.

"Brought a lot of spare parts with you," I had commented.

"Spare parts hell!" explained one of the Flying Officers. "That's beer!"

"And what do you propose to do with it?" I inquired.

"Drink it!" he said.

"And just how, in this temperature?"

"Don't like beer?" he asked. I admitted that I did, if it could be got to my mouth in a liquid rather than a gaseous state.

"You may know a lot about this country," he remarked, a bit scornfully, "but there are *some* things it seems you don't know. How to cool beer, for instance."

So after we had landed he asked if I would like some beer. I said I would indeed, with my initial reservation. It was still 128° in the shade, and there was no shade.

"You can't even open a bottle without its going off like live steam unless you've hung it out in a wet towel to cool by evaporation," I said. "Even so it won't be very cool in a hurry. Speaking for myself, I don't much care for warm beer."

"Nor do I," said the Flying Officer. "Come and learn how it's done." He placed eight imperial quart bottles—there were four of us—in a galvanized iron bucket, half with their tops down, half with them up. They filled the bucket nicely. We walked out to where the three airplanes were pegged down to squiggly iron stakes screwed into the desert below their wings, with wood chocks placed in front of their wheels.

"*That's* the best engine," he pointed. "Turns up around seventeen-fifty on the ground." So we went to number three airplane. He held the bucket under a reserve gasoline tank, turned the tap and filled the bucket to the brim, covering the tops and upturned bottoms of the bottles of beer. Then he placed the bucket on the ground just behind the Bristol Fighter's propeller. A mechanic seized the propeller.

"Contact!" he cried.

"Contact!" The mechanic swung; the engine started. Slowly the Flying Officer ran the engine up to full r.p.m. The gasoline in the bucket evaporated in the hot slip-stream of the propeller as if it had been siphoned off. In a very few minutes the Flying Officer cut the engine. The mechanic drew out a dry bucket full of frosted bottles.

"Like it?" asked the Flying Officer. "Service, what?" I liked it. All neatly done without fuss or loss of time, on the budget of his Britannic Majesty's Air Force. In that blasted desert, so hot that it was blistering to touch any metal, we drank beer from bottles frosted like Southern mint juleps, to our immense gratification and undoubted detriment to our livers.

Next morning we started for Khwash in the two cars as the red sun climbed to torture further an already superheated world. Taj

Mohammad sat in front with me, Gerald Fisher and Keyes behind. In the Dodge van that followed, Juma Khan sat beside the melancholy Sikh. Within its cage-like body were his nephew, two of Taj Mohammad's brothers, my servant Hossein and Fisher's Indian Attaché. Both cars flew white flags on the forward corners of their canvas tops. The two Sardars carried additional flags of truce affixed to wooden staffs.

Small, well-concealed groups of Rekis picketed the road. They were strongly placed in control of narrow defiles through the rocky hills. As we approached each hidden post Taj Mohammad descended to establish contact in person. He made heavy work of clambering out of the car and back into it again, holding his rifle in his right hand, the flag of truce in his left. His corpulent body was further encumbered with knives, pistols, ammunition-belts, bandoliers and a saber that invariably caught across the door-frame. Occasionally, the latter weapon got between his legs, and once it threw him. He fell flat on his face, pitching forward with outflung hands gripping the rifle on the one side, the quaintly inconsistent white flag on the other.

"Oh, Taj Mohammad Khan!" cried Mark Keyes. "You do not thus have to seize the pastures of your father's fathers!"

After that episode I had Hossein come up from the van behind to assist Taj Mohammad in a more dignified dismounting and remounting of the unfamiliar vehicle.

The track climbed sharply to the top of the pass over the flank of the Kuh-i-Taftan. It was amazingly rough, twisting through dry torrent courses in sheer-sided, stony ravines. I was impressed by the immense difficulty of operating regular troops over this area against a determined opposition by the tribesmen, who alone knew all the watering-holes, could travel faster and subsist on far less than any regular soldiers. It was, as had been said, a naked wilderness, desolate and cruel, just as God had fashioned it from the refuse after he created the Earth.

At the edge of Taj Mohammad's territory there awaited on our arrival a swarthy lashkar led by the sons of Mir Idu and the Damani chieftains. Our messages dropped the previous day had done their purpose. The way ahead lay clear, save that it was crawling with colonies of dung-beetles. These highly unappetizing insects, dried, used to form a major part of the sustenance of captives in the heyday of Sarhad slave-raiding—those days, a few years before, when a rifle was worth around eleven hundred rupees, a prime young female slave three hundred fifty.

Three miles from the Khwash forts the chieftains awaited behind a small hill. I pried Taj Mohammad from the front seat of the car. The meeting was formal and highly picturesque. Mir Idu made an admirable impression of dignity, with the strength of character and dependability that he showed throughout the negotiations. The Damanis were as wild a lot as one might hope to see. Neither their past records nor present aspect inspired any illusions of moderation. They were seething with hatred for Elishah and all things Persian. These sentiments they restrained long enough to exchange amenities with us; while Elishah, unwitting buffoon that he was, switched the show momentarily to *opéra bouffe*.

Mir Idu had transmitted to him under a flag of truce one of the letters we had dropped the previous afternoon, advising him of our coming. There were obvious reasons, since I was under tribal safeconduct, why I could not have communicated directly with the Persian garrison. Elishah apparently thought that the uprising had collapsed and reinforcements were on the way. He sent back a reply; not an especially helpful reply under the circumstances.

"I grant no permission for any of them to come to Khwash," he wrote, "until they have submitted to me a formal application in writing and show their authority from the Central Government. And I hereby order Mir Idu Khan to inform them that I will fire upon them should they attempt to approach without my permission." This advice was not very happily received by Keyes, Fisher and myself.

"So that's *that!*" commented Keyes tersely. "Love and kisses from Elishah! A master strategist we're dealing with! Bit on the inhospitable side, though, it seems. And so he's going to fire on us, is he? Well, let's get on with it!"

"Ever try taking a trapped rat out of its trap?" asked Gerald Fisher. "It'll bite you every damned time!"

We left the Baluchis in a fearsome circle of camelry, two to a camel, behind the hill. I drove with Keyes and Fisher, and the Indian orderly clutching a flag of truce, to a point about a mile from the perimeter camp which that morning Elishah had reoccupied and bedecked with Persian flags. From there we walked, an angry little procession of four under a square of white toweling affixed to a lance.

A sentry on the wall of the fort stuck his head over the parapet as we left the car. "Stand by to repel assault party!" chirped Fisher. As we approached closer the sentry ducked from view. "Cannister and grapeshot!" Fisher cried out cheerfully. For a few moments I wondered whether the idiot Elishah would really fire on us. He was perfectly capable of it. We entered the perimeter camp without having been shot at. A dozen unkempt soldiers were lounging uneasily about. On our demand one of them conducted us to a room in the fort to see the Colonel. But no one received us.

"This is deliberate, of course," snapped Keyes after we had waited two minutes, "and I'm damned if I intend to take it!" None of us intended to take it. We walked out brusquely through the same door by which we had entered. There came a sudden change in the attitude of the soldiers. A corporal stumbled backwards in quickstep with hand fixed at salute, pleading that we remain.

"Be pleased to repose Your Honors! Be pleased to repose Your Honors!" he cried over and over again like a jammed phonograph record. "Colonel comes! Colonel comes!" We were not pleased to repose our honors until we had returned a half mile out on the plain, by no means sure we might not receive a volley from the rear. There we sat down beside a knoll to cool off inwardly as well as externally, and await developments.

"Did you ever know such an arrant blighter?" grunted Fisher.

After four or five minutes three officers and three orderlies appeared at the edge of the knoll. The officers were Colonel Elishah, tall, wooden-faced, without a trace of humor in his dull brown eyes; the Captain commanding the Khwash garrison, small, thin, pleasant-mannered; Major "Brave-One-of-the-Army," short, fat, cheery and sweating profusely. We greeted them in leisurely fashion.

"Since I knew nothing of your coming," explained Elishah, "I was resting for my nightly vigil."

Gerald Fisher gave a slight snort. "It seems he has already forgotten his ruddy message of welcome through Mir Idu last evening!"

Elishah continued with charming inconsistency. "Your rooms at the fort have been cleaned and prepared since early morning. If you will deign to bring your honorable presences to their poor hospitality . . ." When shortly we took our honorable presences elsewhere he professed grievous hurt.

It was a fatuous situation. We stood grouped there in the "blue" under a dust-streaked square of white cloth flapping listlessly from a lance-head: three Anglo-Saxons trying to save the bungling dolt Elishah, along with the surrounding areas for several hundred miles, from the conflagration he had started; six Persian military whose lives depended on what we three might do; and one nostalgic Hindu holding the white emblem of our status. In the hills around us large forces of fierce and outraged tribesmen, seeing but unseen, waited on the action of the three Anglo-Saxons. From the fort's mud wall peered anxious eyes that had looked upon the shadow of death, while their dull-witted commander strove with inane palaver further to confuse the issue.

We shook off the increasing importunities of the Persians and went back on foot to where we had left the cars, first demanding that the gates through the perimeter camp be opened for our passage. I sent the Baluchis around by camel out of range, then drove through the camp between a hastily paraded Persian guard that comprised most of the garrison. At the farther gate the three officers waited with a steaming samovar and glasses of strong tea. Earnestly they pleaded that we remain.

"It would be unsuitable for your prestige—and for ours," they cried, "for you to camp tonight with the rebel Baluchis!"

"*Your* prestige, I fear, is already too tarnished for that to matter very much," I replied. "Ours is not apt to suffer."

We gulped the tea. "Your kindness is great," we said in prescribed form. "God be with you!" and passed on to Mir Idu's fort.

The scene that night in the tribal fortress ranks among the most picturesque of my memories. Amidst Baluchis squatting in concentric circles on the hard-beaten earth floor we banqueted sumptuously on freshly slaughtered mutton, barley bread and goat-cheese. The mutton had been brought up on the hoof to the gateway, alive and protesting. As we strode with measured tread into the enclosure a warrior with bared arms, brandishing a long knife, slit its throat from ear to ear. The warm blood gurgled across our track, spattering our boots, to divert from us any possible ills of the Evil Eye.

For hours we talked while odorous preparations were carried on around us. The Damanis squatted with rifles upright in hand, shouting their resentments, rattling martial equipment in the violence of their gestures. Frantic boasting interspersed rude comments on Persian sovereignty; clamorous appeals for justice ended in bitter note.

"Where is justice to be found amongst the sons of burnt fathers? Let us kill or be killed!" cried the Sardars.

"Ay, the donkeys' sperm!" screamed the chorus of the warriors. "Ay, the Great Catamites! Let us kill or be killed!" But Mir Idu joined Juma and Taj Mohammad in support of our counsel for arbitration of the disputes.

Then came food. Horny hands dipped into the steaming mess. I was hungry and ate with pleasure until Sardar Jiand Khan, senior chieftain of the Sarhad—an incredibly old man with the head of an ancient buzzard—did me the honor to pick out the most succulent morsel from the pot and shoot it down my throat by a bony thumb. I had a glimpse of the selection as it passed into my mouth. It was an eye of the sheep. I gagged, but the morsel with its plaintive, glassy stare, slipped down. Somewhat to my surprise it stayed down, and the sounds of protest from a revolted anatomy were taken as but feeble evidence of appreciation amidst the sonorous regurgitations of the Baluchis.

We washed our sticky hands in water poured from copper pitchers by turbaned men-at-arms. Then, the debris of our feeding turned over to the lesser retainers of the Sardars, we resumed talk. It became again a drama in which the basic problems of primitive existence were being presented, and the audience, who were also the chorus, were profoundly swayed by the acting.

Several hundred men packed the courtyard of the fort. In the weird light of flaming torches their hawk-like faces, the amazing get-up of those wild nomads, seemed curiously unreal. Through the dramatics of the chiefs there ran an undercurrent of expectation that we were somehow to resolve their problems of the present. But what of the future? It was not easy to speak with much conviction of the future.

A little before daybreak the Damanis agreed to the general terms for negotiation I had worked out with the other tribes. Our next move depended on the results of a conference fixed for that morning with the officers in the Persian fort. For a few hours the curtain dropped on the play as we stretched out upon small rugs for sorely needed sleep. Neither the all-pervading odor of a goat's nest, nor a variety of little creatures sharing our primitive couches deterred us. Altitude brought unaccustomed coolness that worked wonders. We arose greatly refreshed.

Our second reception at the Persian fort was very different in tone from that of the previous day. The whole garrison of one hundred and sixty men was paraded, the officers awaiting at the gate. Yet the discussion proved no more satisfactory than on the first occasion. Elishah's egregious attempts at bluff—bald lies, when lying could be of no possible advantage—and the complete non-cooperation of the man made any coherent plan impossible. He was unable or refused to grasp his situation. Gerald Fisher yawned openly. "One could more clearly explain its predicament to a bogged camel!" he drawled.

I inquired regarding their supplies on hand. Elishah professed no concern whatever over this. "We have full rations for the garrison for more than six months," he assured me. This was patently absurd.

"Good! Then I do not have to trouble myself about any reprovisioning," I commented. The Captain commanding the garrison had a slight choking fit. A moment later he whispered in my ear: "There remain barely fifteen days' supplies at half rations!"

The voices of the British Raj sounded a growing note of boredom. I was becoming more and more irritated. As we haggled at cross purposes I would gladly have thrown Elishah to the wolves—or to the Damanis—if that would have done any good. Unfortunately it would not. But while we were getting absolutely nowhere in our discussions there suddenly appeared in the skies, remarkable in the aptness of its timing, a *deus-ex-machina* to lift the play towards its finale. Above the humorless vapidities of Elishah there arose a metallic drone. Two low-flying Bristol Fighters with the red, white and blue roundels of the Royal Air Force passed overhead. One dropped a message-container neatly in front of Mir Idu's fort, the long white streamer trailing behind like a flash of frozen lightning in the sunlight. Without waiting formal adieux we repaired at once across the lines. The Persians remained wide-eyed and agape at the barbed-wire barricade that blocked approach to their gateway.

A Reki tribesman crept out to retrieve the container. It yielded a forty-page telegram for me from the Eastern Army Commander at Meshed, relaying instructions from Reza Khan in Teheran. "You are given full authority of Amir Lashkar (Army Commander) for conducting the Sarhad negotiations," the message began. This was what I needed. It gave me effective control over the Persian force in a way I had not had as arbiter. The Sardar Sipah—soon to make himself Shah of Persia—promised that the measures I had proposed for relief of the tribal grievances and for keeping the tribes under control would be carried out. The message concluded with assurances of the Sardar Sipah's deep solicitude for the welfare of his beloved tribes. It was perhaps ungenerous to reflect a little on how this solicitude was being expressed in certain other areas.

I thereupon summoned to another conference, in the courtyard of Mir Idu's fort, all the chieftains and influential members of the clans. The Indian Attaché read the telegram to them on my behalf. In spite of their profound distrust of Persian promises, that message and the manner of its arrival impressed them.

In the open court of sun-baked clay they put their seals or thumb-prints on a preliminary treaty of non-aggression, to be further implemented after we should have worked out together the details and guaranties on both sides. It made a striking picture. The senior tribal Mullah squatted in the center, holding a huge red-bound Koran on his lap. Mir Idu read aloud the document I had drawn up with the help of the Indian Attaché as translator: after which each bearded chieftain, rifle in hand, affixed his seal to the paper; first laying his rifle on the ground as he knelt and kissed the Holy Book in the Mullah's lap, swearing by that Book a solemn oath to observe the terms of the treaty.

I returned with the Attaché to the gate of the Persian fort where the officers were standing goggle-eyed with curiosity behind the barricade. There I communicated to them the contents of the message, adding briefly that Elishah and "Brave-One-of-the-Army" should be prepared to leave within the hour for Mirjawa. "And it is further ordered," I added, "that the soldier Fateh Mohammad is to be brought out under close arrest for trial by court martial in the case of rape. The Rekis, whose clan he has dishonored, will provide his guard." The soldier Fateh Mohammad was a bilious green, though the Rekis behaved quite circumspectly.

The Sardars and other "influentials" agreed to come to Mirjawa for the definitive negotiations that might last a week or more, as we would there be in touch by wire with both Persia and India. I left the Captain, a likeable and conciliatory little man, in command of the garrison with explicit orders for keeping the peace.

In the early afternoon we set off in my two cars, followed by the two Elishah had brought up with him. One of the latter, a medium-sized truck, was packed with the Damani chieftains—a wild cargo of fearsome aspect, lightened by occasional grins as they jolted on their hams over the rough track. The screen van bore the Ismailzai and Reki headmen, with the gibbering Fateh Mohammad and his Reki guard.

About twenty miles out, in the middle of a narrow defile, we came suddenly onto the Gamshadzai *lashkar* that had been cut up during the raid on Panjgur. A swarthy brigand named Lashkaran, acting regent of the clan for the young son of its dead Sardar killed by General Dyer in 1916, was of our party but in the last of the four vehicles. There was some confusion as we halted in the dry torrent-course, surrounded by the frustrated raiders. They did not know what we were, and Mir Idu, who got out from my car to inform them, was not immediately recognized with his short hair. An impatient young man of no great intelligence took sudden aim at my head from about twelve feet away.

"Duck!" yelled Gerald Fisher from the back seat, as he and Keyes dropped into the well of the tonneau. I ducked. Mir Idu just managed to knock up the young man's rifle as he fired; the bullet whistled harmlessly through the canvas top. Lashkaran ran up from the rear, bellowing loudly. His coming saved the situation from possible complications. That was the final shot of the campaign. The revolt was over—until the next time.

My treaty needed something more than its seals and signatures to make it effective. It required good faith and strict observances of the promises embodied on the Persian side as well as on the tribal. This it did not receive. A few months later, when I was transferred to Teheran to act as Treasurer-General, I was no longer in a position to see that those promises were kept. They were not kept. It was through no failure of the tribes to observe *their* side of the agreement that they were broken.

One promise, however, I felt reasonably sure would not soon be disregarded. "The length of the hair worn by the Sarhadis," I had written into the treaty, "shall be left to their own discretion." Even another Elishah, from which may God preserve His wilderness, might hesitate to attempt to play again the role of Delilah to the Samsons of the Sarhad.

The Professor

I believe I am the only person on whom the League of Nations ever conferred a dinner-suit.

It was a very good dinner-suit, built by a London tailor famed in his special calling. Though conventional austerity gave no suggestion of any unusual background, the causes of my acquisition were not without color. They lay in the purple and red and white opium poppies of Fars, and in the unwitting devastation wrought to a great guest-palace by a venerable Italian Professor of Botany whom the League had delegated, along with certain others, to inquire into the production of opium in Iran.

Of the many visitors who came to us amidst the pale blue domes and dark cypresses of Shiraz none was quite so droll, none—happily—who left behind such smoking ruin, as Professore Cavalla. It is now several years since he has gone to join his forebears amongst the minor deities of Mediterranean mythology. Though he was wholly unlike any Persian mythological hero, his brief visit left a distinct impress on the life of southern Iran. And as the incidental cause of my sartorial distinction my "eyes light up" in Persian style over the recollection of his oddities.

Through the Professor's veins coursed the blood and vitality of Italian hillfolk. His aged sinews still flexed with the endurance of an Alpine goat. Now, having reached his threescore-and-tenth year, a passionate devotion to botany excluded all lesser things and overrode the discomforts that attended pursuit of his subject in remote and uncouth areas.

A diminutive figure, rotund of belly, a small face set in a triangular framing of narrow, pointed ears and pointed grey beard, a mischievous squint of keen blue eyes through canted pince-nez, all lent him the appearance of an aged faun. The grey remnants of his hair curled up on each side in the style of rudimentary horns. I never saw the Professor unshod, but had he withdrawn cloven hoofs from his child's size footgear one would have felt no surprise. When he talked, the sheer rapidity of his speech set his little beard awaggling much as exuberant satyrs disporting in the forests of Latium must have waggled their hirsute chins. Every look and movement confirmed the impression of an aged but naughty god of the woodlands, half man, half goat.

Down the ancient caravan track from Teheran the Professor came to us propped upright in the back seat of a 1924 Dodge sedan between his French colleague and an exhausted Persian interpreter, serenely asleep. The car carried also an Assyrian driver, a Persian apprentice-mechanic, a servant and a mass of paraphernalia. Outside it was bulwarked with baggage roped and wired along the running-boards, jammed in the angles of the fenders and swung across the rear end.

That road was old when Cyrus trod it, older yet when Alexander the Great rode on from Persepolis and left the palace of the Achemenians a smouldering wreck whose stupendous ruins flank the trail today. It had been made passable, God willing and weather permitting, to occasional motor traffic. Few modes of transport could be more shattering to the nervous system than continued bumping over that corrugated track. The unharnessed rear springs—hardly a car in Persia was provided with shock-absorbers in those days—flipped the hapless passengers between cushions and roof like popping corn over a hot fire. With full effect was one tossed whose all-up weight barely tipped the scales at 115 pounds. Yet through the agony that reduced younger and heavier men to jitters, nursing battered heads and bruised behinds, the Professor slept like a little child.

Perhaps more like a tired faun—little children may not sleep happily sitting bolt upright on a mechanized catapult. An old but cheerful satyr, fast asleep with a solar topee clamped tightly on his head. The season was young. The lovely sunlight of Persian springtime shed its warmth but softly over the tender shoots of crops and blossoming plant-life. At night the temperature dropped to chill points that made hearth-fires keenly welcome. The Professor's topee strapped under his chin behind the straggly faun's beard was neither affectation nor protection against the gentle rays of the early spring sun. It saved his brains from being bashed out against the car's roof during the steady tattoo his head beat thereon, the while he slept. In the process the helmet would be driven so tightly over his brow as to require the aid of a servant to pry it off at the journey's end, like the removal of excessively well made riding boots. From his companions I learned about his procedure on the road.

"He sleeps continuously when we are in motion," said Monsieur Cayla, his French colleague. "And no form of motion, so long as the car does not turn completely over, disturbs the serenity of his repose." It appeared that the Professor did not sleep much at night, for reasons of his own choosing. At night he had important matters to attend to. He had then to transfer his multitudinous botanical cullings each from its folded page of the London *Times* to a fresh one. Fervidly he extolled the virtues of the *Times*, though neither for its editorial policy nor its presentation of world events. His devotion to an alien newssheet was wholly material.

"The *Times*," he said, "*what* a magnificent journal! It is printed on paper of the most admirable texture for the preservation of plant specimens! Always it is the same, adapted to the plant-life of every clime. Never would I move without it!" No other periodical in his own or any language had he found quite so effective for botanical blotting paper. Wherefore he had brought to Iran, on an international inquiry into the cultivation of the opium poppy, half a truck-load of back issues of the secular bible of English gentry.

Methodically every night the Professor transferred his plants from pages that had accomplished their absorbtive duty to other pages fresh in texture, though their world news of many months before had become somewhat stale even for Persia. As his collection grew, so did his nightly task. He was extremely conscientious about it. In return for the plant-life that he carried away, he deposited large stacks of expended *Times* at each overnight stopping-point across the face of Iran.

After his return to Italy he wrote an erudite tome on Persian flora. Learned botanist though he was, he was ungrateful. He failed to mention therein the collaboration enjoyed from the publishers of the world's best known newspaper.

There was another matter that he failed to mention. Along with his official researches for the League of Nations into the practicability of curtailing the opium output of Iran, he made a careful study for his own government of the more successful methods of cultivating and processing the opium poppy. The Fascist Government, in a highly realistic attitude towards its civilizing mission in the world, felt that such a study under the aegis and expense of the League might prove extremely useful in connection with certain projects for building up opium production in the Italian colonies.

Professore Cavalla's passion for collecting plant-life brought despair to his companions of the road. Sleeping in serene comfort over surfaces that tortured the others into morose silence, the instant any halt interrupted the accustomed pitching of the car he awoke.

"*Quel phénomène!*" said Cayla, who rode with him and should know. "He wakes up each time we stop and runs away up into the mountains. *But always up into the mountains!*" Halts on the caravan track were not infrequent—for water, or that the driver might make a reconnaissance of some particularly treacherous passage through a defile; or because iron shoe-nails worn to needle sharpness, cast by countless beasts of burden over the surface of the trail, pierced motor tires with fearful precision.

Awaking each time motion ceased, the Professor would peer through the window with far-focusing blue eyes. A blink or two of his eyelids, a beatific smile suddenly illumining his little face, a softly breathed "Ah-h-h!" . . . and in a trice he was gone before his tired companions realized what he was up to. Some moments later they would discover him scampering like a hare high up the steep-sided shale hills, armed with a fistful of wee trowels and other instruments appropriate for digging out by the roots various plants growing precariously at seven thousand feet or so altitude. From the site of each captured trophy he would spot another higher up, awaiting his hand. Happy ejaculations of discovery floated in high-pitched tenor down the still air: "Ah-h-h!" . . . again and again, each succeeding cry from several hundred feet more altitude: "*Ah-h-h*" . . . "AH-H-H!"

They found only one way to get him back. Two encircling parties had painfully and pantingly to clamber the shifting slopes, outflank and surround him, drive him, protesting volubly, his hands full of plants, down to the car that had been delayed three-quarters of an hour or more by his private scientific explorations. Within two minutes of restarting he had reverted to slumber.

Thus the Professor arrived at Shiraz, and once again awoke. When he departed some ten days later Ghavam-ol-Molk, hereditary *grand seigneur* of South Persia, had lost his guest-palace, the League of Nations, the Persian Excise Department and my Administration a portion of their records, and I the greater part of my dinner clothes. The Professor lost not a single back page of the London *Times,* nor even the creases from his carefully packed suits.

The League of Nations' International Commission to inquire into opium production in Persia made an imposing array on the road. American, Italian, French and British members and secretaries formed its nucleus. Persian official attachés, experts on opium and excise, clerks, interpreters, chauffeurs, mechanics, military guards, cooks and servants rounded out its personnel. Their equipment included baggage, bedding and paraphernalia of the road, provender, water and cooking utensils, charcoal, samovars, gasoline, official records and a quarter ton of the London *Times.* With the necessary transport for all this it formed a not unimpressive caravan.

Before their arrival in Shiraz I had received a telegram from the capital asking that I take charge of the party's arrangements in South Persia, and later accompany them to Khorasan. I had only recently moved into a new "garden"—the Persian style for country house—known as *Bagh-i-Ahmediyeh,* some two miles outside the city walls. It was a very large garden, nearly a quarter of a mile long, whose heavy walls enclosed a group of three houses. One of these contained our living and guest rooms; one the kitchen, the *hauz-khaneh* or "cool room," the dining and reception rooms; and one the servants' quarters. There were in addition to our own quarters half a dozen rooms suitable for bedrooms, but we were not yet prepared for a multiplicity of guests, owing to shortage of furnishings.

Count von der Schulenburg, the German Minister, was stopping with us. So were Gladwyn Jebb and John Wickham from the British Legation. Together they about exhausted our facilities of the moment. I wired Teheran that I would play cicerone to the Commission, would be happy to put up its President and regretted that I had not suitable accommodations for the others, but for them I would arrange quarters elsewhere.

Count von der Schulenburg departed the day they arrived. His place was ceded to the President of the Commission, Frederic Delano, uncle of Franklin Roosevelt. There was neither hotel nor rest-house in Shiraz; so I had dropped my housing problem in the lap of Ghavam-ol-Molk. This amiable friend placed at my disposal for the remainder of the Commission and their entourage his gorgeous guest-palace *Mohammadiyeh,* with a corps of servants, mounted messengers, lambs, chickens, game, wines and liqueurs and other provisions for the visitors' comfort.

After three days Frederic Delano decided to go to Fasa, center of the opium culture of the Province of Fars, taking only an interpreter and a servant. He had the boundless energy of his clan, and he wished to gather his impressions first-hand. Professore Cavalla became acting President of the Commission in Shiraz. Two days later the Professor gave at Mohammadiyeh in our honor the first, and the last, formal dinner attempted by the Commission in South Persia.

It was a wintry evening. An unseasonably bitter north wind chilled us to the core as we drove in open cars with Jebb and Wickham and two servants to Mohammadiyeh. Josephine was wearing her ermine coat. Behind the earthen walls shrill howls of hungry jackal packs and hyenas broke upon the evening stillness.

In the stiff formality of flower-beds and borders, and the rather discordant blending of their colors, Mohammadiyeh's gardens reflected the influence of Ghavam's German gardener. Germanic, too, in style and effect was the solidly built mansion whose tall entrance portals swung open as we approached its marble perron.

"Be pleased to bring in Your Honors!" cried the servants of Ghavam, candle-torches in hand, bowing low before the carven doors. Into an elaborate hall we passed with slow and measured tread as gentry should who bring their honors to formal occasions in Persia. Huge red and gold foliated columns flanked a double staircase that swept in wide curves to a central landing high above. Up these flamboyant stairs recalling resplendent early steamships of the North German Lloyd we proceeded in pleasant expectancy of the good fire crackling on the hearth of the reception room above.

In all South Persia there was no other such room as this: none so spacious, its vast flat ceiling roofed with metal sheets instead of the usual mud and straw; none with such sweep of vision through enormous plate-glass windows enclosing the whole of its western side; none so costly.

"How in heaven's name," I asked Ghavam on my first visit to Mohammadiyeh, "did you manage to bring those great rectangles of plate-glass to Shiraz? What must have been your loss in breakage!" He had imported them from England, he said, by ship to Bombay and by another ship to Bushire on the Persian Gulf. From Bushire roadstead, where the British-India Line boats anchor ten miles from shore because there is no proper harbor, they were taken in little dinghies to the low alluvial shore-line, thence swung between two camels over passes of ten thousand feet altitude across the five knife-edge ridges of the Zagros Range. The Pass of the Old Woman shattered most of them; the Pass of her equally repugnant Daughter did-in nearly all the rest.

"The breakage? Oh, that may have been some eighty percent of the total shipments," said Ghavam. "I don't really know, but it cost very dear to make the room as I wanted it." I would have imagined so.

"And the grand piano?" I asked—a handsome instrument reposing inconspicuously in one corner of the huge room. "It came the same way," said Ghavam. "Over the passes, swung also between camels." In some inexplicable manner it had arrived intact.

Servants divested us of outer garments on the landing, hung them in little cupboard-like closets with sliding shutters. Doors opened; our hosts surged forth to greet us. I held back for a moment to let those doors refresh my spirit. Few works of any period have given me keener pleasure than the graceful symmetry of their decoration. Ghavam's great-grandfather had brought the artisans from India to fabricate them. Into wood whose texture was tender as the skin of a lovely woman, with grain that flowed in the patterns of an Isfahani cut-velvet, these artists of infinite taste had inserted semiprecious stones and mother-of-pearl in exquisite designs, each one different, inspired by the inlaid marbles of Delhi's Diwan-i-Khas. There were, I have reason to recall, twelve such doors giving into the great north room, the dining room and the outside verandah. I forgot temperature and the occasion of our coming as I drank in their simple beauty. Then the Professor made sibilant noises, and we advanced towards the fireplace.

During the banalities of greeting we stretched blue hands to the grateful warmth from the four-foot logs, unlimbering congealed fingers to receive the tepid gin-and-vermouth served in lieu of cocktails. The fire roared up the chimney. It struck me as dangerously overfed. I had gained some experience of the feebler points of Persian architecture, such as white-wood ceiling beams extruded nonchalantly across the upper reaches of chimney openings. But Ghavam's Number One servant, passing the second round of gin-and-vermouth, assured us that all was well.

"His Excellency the Professor," he whispered, "desired warmth. Warmth is provided. And I, Habibullah, of all men most faithful to my master Ghavam-ol-Molk, know that the superior construction of this Great House has no limitations."

So I turned my attention to the carpets of immense price covering the floor, museum pieces hanging from the walls and spread over the backs of sofas. On an inlaid table in one corner of the room were heaped the files of the Opium Commission. Above them the kindly face of King George V portrayed in Japanese silk embroidery (a portrait of staggering value, I later was told) dispassionately surveyed the scene.

In due course we went in to dinner. It was a superb repast, admirably served. Soft-footed butlers shod in white sandals of cotton string moved silently round the long table, passing succulent dishes, pouring the golden wine of Shiraz into crystal goblets. We were being offered partridges into whose delicate flesh surprising condiments had been introduced when the Number One butler whispered something to

Josephine, who at the moment was chatting fluently on the distribution of Persian flora while the Professor listened with rapt attention.

Josephine caught my eye with a signal. I excused myself and slipped to the end door. Number One butler mumbled in my ear: "I told the *Khanum*" (the *Khanum* being Josephine), "where much smoke is, there fire must be. And in big room very much smoke is making. . . ." I hurried to the reception room. It was solidly filled with smoke, glowing, acrid, rolling forth in great billows from behind which came an ominous, crackling roar.

I returned to the dinner party and proposed that we move outside. "The building is on fire," I said. Then I ordered the servants to summon all hands on the place, and commissioned Jebb to organize a bucket brigade with whatever utensils might be available. People moved swiftly to such purposes as the emergency inspired in their several temperaments. The Professor promptly disappeared and for some while was forgotten. The "Khanum" made a bee-line for her ermine coat, bore it off to momentary safety in our car on the far side of the garden. Most of the Persian servants lost their heads and ran around like waltzing mice, shouting incoherently.

I reverted to instinct and plunged in to save those precious doors, to try and drag out the irreplaceable carpets. Nothing seemed at that moment to matter quite so much. Wickham joined me, carrying a long tire-tool from his decrepit Ford. With this we developed an efficient technique. Just four motions, using the tool as a wedge and pry, wrenched hinges from jamb: one by one we dropped the twelve doors off the balcony into waiting hands below. Then together we pulled out some thirty rugs before the flaming ceiling fell in. We completely forgot George V. This was unfortunate, for the silken portrait, I learned, was among Ghavam's more treasured prizes.

In an astonishingly short space of time the whole of Mohammadiyeh was seething with people. Servants, soldiers, grooms, gardeners and tenant farmers moiled all over the place. Ghavam's brother-in-law arrived. A message about the catastrophe had been relayed to Ghavam but he declined to come himself lest his presence cause embarrassment. He knew, or so sent word, that the work of checking the conflagration was in competent hands.

Early in the proceedings two parties, one carrying a brass-and-iron bedstead, the other an enormous item of wooden furniture, crashed into headlong collision on the landing of the dual staircase. For ten minutes they blocked all movement up and down while imprecations in barrack-room Persian were generously aired.

"Sons of burnt fathers! Dogs' eggs! Whores' whelps!" they screamed at one another. "Without the brains of a sheep!"—a conservative understatement in some cases.

"You will be the *burnt* sons of twice-burnt fathers very shortly if you don't get this mess cleared at once!" I contributed.

Jebb had formed his bucket brigade. It led in a serried line from the large circular pond beyond the entrance portals, across the driveway and flower-beds and up a flimsy ladder tied together with goat's-hair rope, to the north roof. There a gallant soldier stood at the head of the line swinging an axe. He thought to chop a hole in the roof through which to pour the water. His efforts were eminently successful. While the line called alternately on God and Ali for strength, the soldier chopped himself clean through the roof down into the consuming flames.

"Good Lord!" cried Jebb. "He's dropped straight into the cauldron!" By some odd chance the soldier bounced or rolled to where the fire was less intense. We managed to pull him out from the inside, dazed and scorched but still alive.

On the balcony a group of faithful servants had formed a line of their own. They were dropping piece by piece—while iron bedsteads and wooden furniture were borne into frantic collision down the stairway—the magnificent crystal service that was the glory of Mohammadiyeh's dining room. An athletic young sergeant on the ground below was catching the items by the light of the flames. As he snatched them out of the air he passed them to attendant privates at his side. He only missed once. Then a large and heavy bowl caught him squarely on the forehead. He went down like a slaughtered ox, blood spurting over his face. Long after the attendant privates had carried him off to an improvised field ambulance the line of helpful servants on the balcony continued dropping the crystal service which shattered musically as it hit the empty walk below.

Just before the roof fell in I had seen Chester Purves, Secretary of the Commission, floating gracefully about on errands of varied importance. He was entirely unperturbed: even the blocking of the stairway failed to upset his admirable equanimity. Up to the time that he suddenly recalled the Commission's records, stacked in one corner of the reception room that was now a roaring furnace, his demeanor could not have been more tranquillizing.

"My God!" he yelled, "our files!" I was still making spurts into the near end of that huge room and felt I knew its peculiarities better than those whose energies had been otherwise applied.

"I know where they are!" I cried, and made a dash to the corner where the files were heaped under the silken image of George V, now blotted out behind the billows of smoke. As I came out bearing a portion of the records, the flaming roof-beams collapsed with the roar of an avalanche. By luck I happened to be just beyond the heaviest of the debris. I managed to roll clear of the wreckage, League records clutched in my arms, but on fire. Chester Purves, his imperturbability restored, quenched that particular fire. In the smouldering tatters of dinner clothes that still hung on me I must have made a quaint picture. Purves took note of the woeful state of my garb. It was the result of his recommendation that the League conferred upon me a new dinner-suit. "For conspicuous services rendered in the field," Purves explained. May God never lessen his shadow.

The Khanum also had not been idle. Having saved her ermine coat she applied herself effectively to rescue work. First she collected from the smoke-filled but still intact dining room Ghavam's heavily wrought solid silver service. Then Purves suddenly shouted: "Great Scott, we've forgot Archie MacLeish!" Purves was constantly remembering things forgotten.

Archie MacLeish ("Oh, West is West, and Eash is Eash, and so is Archibald MacLeish"), acting private secretary to the President of the Commission, lay in one of the lower rooms on a bed of fever which had prevented his attendance at the Professor's dinner. People ran to his room. He was wondering what the noise was all about. Archie MacLeish was rescued in style, haled forth into the night on his bed borne in the arms of many servants. There remained behind a considerable portion of his kit.

The Khanum collected as much as she could carry. She chose a suit of clothes from a wall-hook, a pair of pyjamas lying on a chair, some odd pieces of underwear, shoes, a toothbrush, shaving equipment, a grey fedora hat and the manuscript of *Streets in the Moon*. Some of these items were not easily replaceable in Shiraz. The Khanum's contribution to American literature in saving the MacLeish poems first from fire and then from water should have rated an award for a Girl Scout's good deed of the day.

Attended by Jebb, similarly laden with odd gear, she plunged forth into the night. The Khanum walks fast and invariably leaps before she looks. Intent on depositing her burden in safety from the flames, she rushed around the building where there stretched what appeared in the deceptive light of the burning wing to be a wide, circular expanse of smooth lawn.

"I'm going to put these things under that big tree on the far side of the lawn," she cried to Jebb, and straightway dashed into the waist-deep pond. Presence of mind over cold, wet matter saved the load she was carrying from a watery end. All but the hat. She held her burden aloft, while Jebb pulled her out of the water. The MacLeish hat which crowned her collection detached itself and floated away on the surface of the pool, a greyish fleck driven by the strident north wind that was helping the flames consume Mohammadiyeh.

Wet and dripping, but with rescued equipment nearly intact, she walked around the pond. Khanum and Jebb, burdens deposited, returned for more, steering a course slightly farther to the south. And all at once the Khanum found herself alone.

"Oh, Jebb!" she cried. "Oh, *J-e-bb!*" No reply, nor any trace of Jebb. This seemed very odd. Louder she called, until muffled, gurgling noises reached her apparently from far underground. Now it happens that in Persia water is scarce; so people go to infinite pains to bring it from distant mountain sources to fields and gardens that live by irrigation. This they do through underground channels. Such a channel brought water to Mohammadiyeh from over twelve miles away.

From these channels frequent vents open up to the surface of the ground above, large enough in diameter for a man to descend by a rope to clean out the course. Through one of these vents Jebb had been swallowed up. Unsuspecting, he had walked in the flickering light directly into an opening of Mohammadiyeh's water conduit and dropped some fifteen feet to a gently flowing stream underlain with two feet of mud. The Khanum, discovering the source of his subterraneous bleats, organized a rescue party. After considerable delay he was pulled by many arms, on a knotted rope, to the surface. There emerged a monkey-like figure bedraggled and outraged, blaspheming glibly through a rich coating of wet and sticky clay.

Chester Purves had come to me with a blandly inquiring face. "Where's the Professor?" he asked.

"Good God, don't tell me you've lost *him!*" I returned. "I haven't seen him since dinner. You don't suppose he went back to the big room?"

"No fear! He'll take care of himself. But we better look for him." We circled around the building in opposite directions calling loudly into the night, "*Oh, Professore Cavalla!*"

I came upon him after a longish hunt. He was quite intact. I found him kneeling amidst the trees at some distance from the house. He was not offering praise to God. He was refolding, methodically creasing, his spare suits; repacking his personal belongings in the three suitcases he had borne out from his threatened room. Of many quaint pictures of the Professor, that one is the most enduring: a little figure kneeling alone in the woods before an altar of leathern bags and orderly stacks of the London *Times,* Persian plants pressed between their pages, which he had transported single-handed and single-minded away from danger . . . kneeling in secure solitude beneath enormous pine-trees, thoughtfully rearranging his private effects.

The north wing burned itself completely out. We managed to save the remainder of the building, which mattered so very much less than the north wing. During the early morning the soldiers stole all the splendid carpets Wickham and I had rescued. The entire Commission, whose personnel, except for its President, I had, owing to limited furnishings, installed in Ghavam's guest-palace, ended up in my "garden," stretched out on the floors, covered with odd rugs, horse blankets and other makeshifts.

I was very weary, burned and wearing the scorched fragments of what once had been carefully tailored clothes. At about six A.M. I lay down to sleep. Two hours later Nasrullah, my butler, awakened me. Cursing volubly I consigned him and his whole tribe to the most unpleasant of Moslem hells. He bowed and handed me two letters. I threw them aside, yowled further epithets at the unfortunate butler and again went to sleep. When finally I awoke I found that the letters were in Ghavam's handwriting.

One was addressed to me, one to the Professor.

"I am indeed sorry," wrote Ghavam, "that owing to last night's conflagration you and your wife should not have had a good time. I desired especially to call upon you to express my regrets for the inconvenience caused you and the members of the Commission, and to thank you personally for the efforts you made to put down the fire. As unfortunately I am leaving for

Teheran in the morning I am deprived of the chances to tell you of my regrets."

Which, under all the circumstances, was surely the gesture of a *grand seigneur*.

The drear remnants of my evening clothes lay scattered beside the denuded, taped framework of my bed. At noon I went to see how the Professor was faring. In an empty room, on my mattress, our guest slept. Around him in perfect order were his suitcases, everything in them carefully folded. Alongside his pillow stretched a neat row of little trowels, polished tweezers and other implements like a surgeon's layout. Two sides of the room were built up, as though against some expected attack, with evenly aligned piles of the London *Times*.

Wassmuss of Tangistan

Among the many visitors who enlivened our Shiraz garden there was one, the former German raider Wassmuss, whose name was legend throughout South Persia. The extraordinary magnet of this man's personality had drawn thousands of fiercely independent Persian tribesmen to follow him during the first of the World Wars—in which Persia was officially neutral—for no more tangible reward than a vague promise of fuller independence. His fantastic exploits in this less-known area rivalled and in some ways exceeded those of Lawrence in Arabia. Without resources of arms or money he defied the British Empire for four years. He was one of the most remarkable characters I ever met, and his story falls among the great dramatic sagas of our time.

He came to us on several occasions in the course of a trip in 1927 away from the farm he had established at Chagodek on the desolate flats below Tangistan—the "Country of the Gorges." His gallant and devoted wife accompanied him. We later visited them at Chagodek, some twenty miles from Bushire, near the edge, but not in sight, of the Persian Gulf. There are few lonelier, more Godforsaken spots on this earth. The fires of hell would seem tepid after its eight months of summer heat. There was absolutely nothing about the place save only Wassmuss himself that could have tempted me to remain there a single hour. Yet for him that grim area had a strange and overpowering fascination.

Irma Wassmuss was the one woman of my acquaintance who I think could have stood the ghastly, disheartening existence of Chagodek. That she managed to do so undaunted reflected great credit on her, but also something of the infectious spirit of her husband. She had the charm of clear-cut sincerity, of culture and quiet courage that soon overcame a first impression of angular plainness. *He* had the greatest charm of almost anyone I ever met. He was strikingly handsome. Though barely forty-seven, his hair was pure white as a result of his four years' campaigning against the British; and he walked with a slight limp from an old knife-wound in his leg. He had clear blue eyes which from time to time glanced upwards as though in astral contemplation. He was widely read, musical, a notable linguist and a cultured and delightful companion. In addition, he was an ingenuous romanticist with an almost mystical love of South Persia.

For four years this man had made himself a nightmare to the British Empire. His name was surcharged across their situation maps in letters covering a territory the size of France. Single-handed, without military or financial support, he challenged the British Raj in the zone of its old-established influence along the Persian Gulf. He raised a strong anti-British bloc of tribesmen to attack the enemies of the Kaiser in their Middle Eastern lair. He drove the British out of Central and all of South Persia except for the ports. He carried off their Consul and colony at Shiraz, where the Vice-Consul was assassinated. Parties organized by him killed the Russian Vice-Consul and wounded the British Consul General at Isfahan, drove out the two colonies, chased the British and Russian communities from Yezd and Kirman, and captured seven branches of the British-owned Imperial Bank of Persia. He compelled the Government of India to divert to Bushire some 20,000 troops grievously needed elsewhere, and to create a further body of 11,000 men known as the South Persia Rifles. He and his colleague Niedermayer, who was operating in Afghanistan, were credited by the Kaiser with having made possible the fall of Kut-al-Amarah to the Turks—the greatest military defeat in British history in the East until Singapore—and with saving Baghdad from the British for a year.

These things he did alone, by the sheer force of a personality which formed all the sinews of war with which he had to work.

Wassmuss, before the 1914–18 phase of the World War, was German Consul at Bushire. The torrid wastes of Dashtistan and Tangistan held for him some mysterious appeal, and he on his part acquired an amazing influence over their population of predatory tribesmen. He was really devoted to those people. He loved them as perhaps none ever did before or may again; while they, inscrutably stirred before the fount of his wisdom, revered him with a loyalty theretofore unsuspected in their natures.

To this day the simplest of the tribal elements who came under his influence will greet the mention of his name in reverential awe. "You *knew* Wassmuss?" they repeat. It is as though one had known God.

He went about in Tangistani garb, wearing his hair long and living as the Tangistanis did. He spoke their idiom more eloquently than did their own religious teachers. He was an excellent horseman, and rode continually back and forth, over and over that inhospitable area, stirring the tribes to action. He had no equal in surprise marches. His contempt for danger, his resourcefulness and endurance were prodigious. Five times he was captured through betrayal or overconfidence; each time he escaped in a manner of fantastic ingenuity. And once when he was severely wounded by a knife-thrust in the leg he befriended his Kashgai assailant and swung the latter to his cause.

In the main his story is much like Lawrence's. That its *dénouement* missed the heights of the Lawrentian epic lay largely in the hand of Fate. Wassmuss set himself the harder task; nor was his the lesser measure of success until at length Fate betrayed him. He defied a far greater and more resourceful Empire than Lawrence had challenged, and did so alone and unsupported, unable even to communicate with his own people. He had neither arms nor gold with which to cement wavering loyalties—instead he was forced to seek funds from local subscribers to his cause. He had nothing but his own voice; yet this sufficed for three years and more, and still could stir the unstable tribesmen to action long after he had been reduced to an all but starving penury. And he had no Allenby to break the resistance of his enemies at the end.

If Wassmuss lacked any measure of Lawrence's eccentric genius it was not in imagination, in fortitude or resource. Nor was it in a personality which without benefit of material aids inspired even more improbable devotions than did Lawrence. While Lawrence spoke Arabic fairly fluently, he could never have passed as an Arab among Arabs. Wassmuss could and frequently did pass as a Persian. After having escaped once again from the British in 1919, he got himself engaged as a Persian gardener at the German summer Legation and remained there unsuspected until he saw fit to disclose his identity several months later.

In the absence of any tangible support he had to rely on ingenious deceptions. One of these was a fake radio-telephone contrived from a bamboo pole, a few wires, a bicycle-bell, a telephone receiver and some typewriter parts. By means of this contrivance he would "refer" on appropriate occasions directly to the Kaiser. One such conversation took place in the small garden of Haji Ahmed Khan Lari in Shiraz, adjoining the larger one I later occupied. The occasion arose when a certain wealthy resident of Shiraz showed undue restraint in contributing to Wassmuss' cause. Wassmuss "called" the Kaiser at the latter's field headquarters on the impressive but voiceless instrument. After a period of getting connected through various exchanges, Wassmuss suddenly stiffened.

"Your Majesty! Your Majesty's humble and obedient servant Wassmuss speaking from Shiraz . . ." There followed a rapid conversation in German, then a return to Persian. "*Sire,* that very man is with me at this moment before Your Majesty's Serene Presence!" Wassmuss thereupon signalled to his guest to remove his shoes in the Imperial Presence. The Kaiser, holding forth through Wassmuss and all in Persian, made mention of a shipload of gold going out to South Persia as soon as the few remaining British warships in the way had been destroyed. His Majesty spoke of the esteem he held for Wassmuss' Shirazi friend, while gently chiding the latter over his hesitancy. "And," concluded the Kaiser, "in token of Our high regard We are graciously pleased to confer on the gentleman of Shiraz the dignity of Our Order of the Red Eagle of Prussia."

The gentleman of Shiraz was awed and enraptured. He deferred no longer in the matter of pouring his riches into Wassmuss' lap. And though he, as certain others on whom the same ruse was successfully tried, was perhaps not among the best educated or more widely travelled Persians, yet it was Wassmuss' tremendous personality that carried the deception through. For to swing disaffected tribesmen into revolt with fat bags of gold, as Lawrence did, is one thing; to do so with no other resources than the inspiration of one's own voice—and to finance the movement locally as one goes—is quite another. And while Wassmuss failed in the ultimate outcome from causes beyond his control, he did in fact operate under far greater difficulties to achieve more extraordinary, if temporary, successes. Being on the unpopular and beaten side, with no "Seven Pillars of Wisdom" to further enhance his reputation, recognition of the prodigies he wrought has never been widespread.

Both men suffered bitter disenchantment in the aftermath. Both sought peace and oblivion, of a sort, in their separate fashions: Lawrence under an alias as an aircraftsman in the R.A.F., Wassmuss back in the dreadful wastes of his beloved Tangistan. Wassmuss was more of the romantic idealist. He held himself personally committed for repayment to the tribes of the sums they had advanced him or that he had promised them. This weighed on his mind as a sacred trust.

For five years he fought his Government's refusal to acquit that debt of honor. At long last they made a grant of $25,000, and with this sum Wassmuss departed once more for Bushire, accompanied by the courageous wife he had married after the war. He planned to devote the grant to a labor of love. Instead of paying it out all at once, which would have gratified only the vices of the tribes, he sought to invest it in a model farm, to transform the bleakness of the Tangistan into an area of plenty. He would then repay the Tangistanis gradually from the proceeds of the farm, the while he led those shameless highwaymen into ways of virtue and tranquillity. This project filled him with an intense fervor. The unanimous dissuasions of his friends failed completely to turn him from it.

To his project the Tangistani Sheikhs agreed; but in the end they betrayed him. The closest of his old comrades among them had died. A new crop was springing up, and even those whom he had led so successfully in his wartime raids were less amenable to his advices that they should henceforth follow the paths of peace. The simple tribesmen revered him as greatly as ever. Yet his influence with them now brought only the jealousies of their Sheikhs, and in particular of one known as Sheikh Naser of Ahmedi. This young basilisk of perfidy had just succeeded the oldest and best of Wassmuss' friends in the Tangistan.

The Sheikhs soon went back on their agreement. They intrigued against him; and the Persian Government, in the rapid growth of its anti-foreignism, supported their intrigues. What a strange anomaly and how truly Persian—the Government, in its turn, betraying one who had dedicated his post-war existence to lead those turbulent marauders into the fold of the Government's reputable subjects; betraying him in favor of the Sheikhs, whom shortly afterwards the same Government would hang, every one, for their past depredations!

Sheikh Naser and his satellites ravaged Wassmuss' plantations. They turned away his irrigating water at the time his crops depended on this for life itself. These things they did in secret, while still professing friendship. Wassmuss for long refused to believe in their duplicity. Then in concert they brought false claims to work his final and utter destruction.

It was two years before the opening of that last act in the Greek tragedy of his life that my wife and I visited him at Chagodek. We had been staying with Colonel and Mrs. Prideaux, the British Resident and his wife, in Bushire. Wassmuss was sorry that he could not call upon us at the Residency.

"As you are doubtless aware," he said, "some of the British have not forgiven me for the part I played against them during the war. I fear that Colonel Prideaux is among them." This was true. Wassmuss would not have been an acceptable visitor at the Residency.

"The man was a murderer," said Colonel Prideaux coldly. "He caused the death of many Englishmen, as well as of Persians friendly to us. And he stole our Consul in a neutral territory." Wassmuss' country, at that time, had been at war with the British, and both the British and their Russian allies had followed singular ways of respecting Persian neutrality during the war period. I found many besides myself, not a few Englishmen among them, who knew what Wassmuss had done and who did not share Colonel Prideaux's estimate of his character. Frank Prideaux had a kindly outlook by and large, but war rancors are slow to dissipate among ardent traditionalists. Under different circumstances, perhaps, he might better have appreciated Wassmuss' remarkable gifts, his gallantry and extraordinary charm.

Frank Prideaux was a stout, seriously minded official, well past the first flush of youth. He had a thin fringe of white hair around the nearly bald dome of his head. Every night, though the temperature was swelteringly hot save for the four winter months, he dressed for dinner in a black dinner-suit appropriate to the climate of England. He had a pet mongoose that spent its nights looking for snakes. The tinkling of a little bell on a collar around its neck was the cheerful, unfailing signal of its guardianship of the Residency. During the day it slept, except for two hours in the late afternoon when it would climb to the Residency roof, dive down the main drain pipe and come sailing out of the turned-up end, forty feet below, all spread out like a flying squirrel. This pastime it repeated over and over again, until dinner was announced. Then it would trot solemnly down to the Residency dining room, its little bell tinkling its arrival, and with a motion as quick as lightning leap to the arm of our host's chair and from there to the top of his head.

Without the slightest expression Frank Prideaux would solemnly eat his dinner with the mongoose, beady-eyed and acutely interested in the food, perched atop his dome. The mongoose danced continuously, swaying from side to side on that bald pate, while Colonel Prideaux quietly spooned his soup up to his mouth. Then came fish, chicken and other appetizing things. The mongoose, watching its chance, would drop like a flash to our host's shoulder, pass across Frank Prideaux's white shirt front to the other shoulder, on its way snatching from the fork that was being raised to the Resident's mouth some delectable bit of provender. Back on its shiny perch the marauder would eat its snatch with complete disregard of the controlled slap Frank Prideaux would administer to the side of his own head, being careful not to hit the little beast, and the dispassionate comment: "Damn that mongoose!" The mongoose, having finished off the item of its thievery, would chatter shrilly back at him and look for another morsel.

Chagodek, the lonely farm of Wassmuss' second unequal struggle, was a strange combination of South Persian and German style, of mud buildings around a rectangular yard all kept in German orderliness. The place was utterly without amenities. An empty vista stretched in all directions—even the immense contours of the ranges behind could rarely be seen through the heat-haze. In winter months the track to Bushire often became an impassable morass when the wind-driven waters of the Gulf backed up across a low, unprotected stretch of alluvial clay known as the Mashileh. In summer, Chagodek was like a griddle over the stoke-holes of hell. I was filled with a melancholy wonder that human beings should elect to live in such surroundings.

The infinite courage of Irma Wassmuss showed no sign of faltering. Yet one sensed something of the joy she felt in being able to talk again with people of her own mentality. She talked and talked, with never a word of complaint or self-pity, but as one who sought to quench an insatiable thirst. With loving pride they showed us their grand piano, and played it beautifully. Wassmuss led me around the farm, pointing to what he had done, to his tractors and heavy wagons.

"I once resolved," he said, "that I would drive the British forces out of South Persia to the very last unit. Well," with a whimsical smile, "I did, though not quite in the way I had expected. In those wagons and tractors I drove the last of their wartime equipment across the Mashileh—to be loaded onto boats in Bushire—and they paid me for doing it!"

Yet the forces of an inexorable Fate were too strongly arrayed against him. He waged a superhuman struggle to the very end for an ideal, as he always had done; and lost. The ideal proved the joint in his armor. Calamities of season made him vulnerable, but these he could have overcome.

"Wassmuss?" a jaundiced Persian official of Bushire spat out contemptuously at my mention of the name. "Pah! But he is nothing; he is finished! I have seen him delivering melons with his own hands in the bazar!" To that mingy little officer this was evidence enough of abject degradation. To others it might have been a token of Wassmuss' magnificent tenacity.

I managed to help Wassmuss somewhat in his relations with an ungrateful Government. I might have helped him more had I remained longer in Persia. But the treachery of the Sheikhs finished him in the end. Theirs was the mortal blow, delivered through the joint in his armor that came from his deep, mysterious love for a strange people— a people who, save for a few jealous little lordlings of the wilderness, revered him as they never had another. Hounded by those despicable Sheikhs he carried on through the final acts of the drama. The first of these was bankruptcy, which took away even the grand piano he had played for me with such happy pride. Then came a long-drawn-out fight for his honor—there was nothing else left—in the Persian courts of so-called justice, against the machinations of the Sheikhs. In this he was requited by the chicanery of a Government he had sincerely hoped to serve. In the end there remained only the bitter dregs of disillusion and despair.

His great heart at last broken, he returned to Berlin. Shattered by the perfidy of those to whose betterment he had willed his post-war existence, penniless, racked with self-reproach over his wife's futile sacrifices, he passed into a twilight of disenchantment on which the final curtain was soon rung down. A few months later, in 1931, he died, the tragic hero of a mystic love-theme that made one of the most poignant dramas of its day.

Double Camp

Our garden at Shiraz comprised an inner and an outer section. In the first a group of three houses formed irregular faces to three sides of a court that was partly paved and partly in lawn. A small brook purling through a blue-tiled channel separated the court from the flowerbeds beyond. Little wild ducks whose wings had been clipped disported in the brook or in the circular pool it fed. White pigeons fluttered down from the eaves to drink and preen at the water's edge.

The inner garden gave upon an outer nearly a quarter of a mile long, surrounded by high earthen walls. This was principally in vines: splendid vines yielding the famous wine-grapes of Shiraz; in pomegranates, sweet lemons, sour oranges, and a profusion of other fruits. Arbored paths centered on a star-shaped retreat beneath heavy shade-trees, where throughout the late spring into early summer the nightingales sang with an abandon which our guests unused to this choral intensity found disruptive of their slumbers.

Our garden lay some two miles south of town at an elevation of 5300 feet above the sea. Wherefore, though the latitude was well below that of Baghdad, the nights were seldom uncomfortable even in midsummer. A few miles farther south rose the Kuh-i-Barf, the "Mountain of Snow," in a deep cleft of which was a "snow mine." From this we got the snow that cooled our drinks throughout the summer. Each night a donkey-driver clambered up the steep path to the fissure. At its lower reaches, where the sun never struck, he loaded his beasts with the hard-packed snow and descended again before the sun rose above the encircling peaks. The snow was pure enough for internal use, which the ice of Shiraz quite definitely was not.

"Will you take snow in your drink?" we would ask our guests.

Out beyond our garden in a well-protected valley stretched some of the finest and oldest vineyards of Shiraz. Enormous vines, many of them ten inches or more in diameter at the trunks. They appear immune to the phylloxera that attacks the older vines throughout Europe. The wine is made by Armenians and Jews since religious interdictions prevent Moslems from doing so—though some of the less inhibited ones seem not to feel debarred from drinking it with relish once it is made. Too often it fails to mature well because the vintners rarely use good corks. When properly kept it is an excellent, full-bodied wine, golden-colored and delicate in flavor. It resembles certain Spanish wines, light sherry in particular, which affinity is said to be more than mere coincidence.

The story runs that a Spanish Moor some hundreds of years ago passed through Shiraz in the course of his wide-flung travels. Enchanted by the wine of the district and being a man of practical mind as well as discriminating taste, he took with him several vines from the valley where later—centuries later—my garden was to be. These he transplanted in suitable soil after his return, hard by his home in Spain. He called the spot Shiraz from the valley whence the vines had sprung. In time this became Jerez (de la Frontera) and its fame spread the whole world over from the produce of its vineyards—the wine known in French as *Xérès*; in English, sherry. The marked similarity between the wines of Shiraz and of Jerez, as in the names of the localities, tends to substantiate the story. Whether or not indisputably proven, I like to think that all the sherry in the world sprang from a vineyard that became my Shiraz garden.

I used often to ride through the valley with Josephine on a triangular course that brought us back over rolling hills, where shepherds grazed their flocks in springtime beneath the robin's-egg blue of evening skies, nowhere on this earth more delicate, nowhere more lovely. We would reach there just as a few of the myriads of stars had begun to appear—so much thicker over the Persian plateau than they ever have seemed elsewhere!—and the shepherds would be playing to themselves in the cool of the twilight.

Often we would hear the limpid notes from a reed pipe floating across the still air, and would ride up unbeknownst on some lonely disciple of the Iranian Pan tootling away to himself while his charges browsed. Squatting on his hams, pouring out his soul in pure tone under the open sky, he would express in wistful notes and quavers what he never could say in speech—all the yearnings, all the pathos of his solitary and yet not wholly discontented state. To no other audience than himself, his sheep and his goats, he piped the ageless cadences of desire; unaware of us as we sat our horses a little way off, half hidden behind a rise of ground or clump of bushes, fascinated by that guileless self-expression of a primitive spirit.

One evening, galloping homewards, we came upon a tribal encampment of half a dozen low reed tents. Josephine reined up sharply a few yards ahead of me, and I was somewhat taken aback to see a tall tribesman jump out from the foremost tent and clutch at her horse's bridle. A woman followed after him with a small bundle of rags. I saw then that they were grinning in evident delight, the man holding the bridle while the woman passed the bundle through the reins.

"What on earth are they doing?" I called.

"*Batcheh!*" cried the man—"Baby!" He pointed to the bundle and smiled broadly. "Thanks be to God, a son born to me; just a little while arrived!" It was a tiny baby perhaps three or four hours old, its wee face showing like a wrinkled crab-apple between the strips of colored rags that tightly swathed it. The woman passed the bundle once again through the reins.

"And why do you do thus?" I asked.

"Because you are the first stranger-horsemen who have come this way since he arrived," explained the proud father. "And, may it please you, in passing him so through your bridle the Evil Eye will be averted and he shall gain strength and good fortune, *Inshallah*—if God wills. *Bali*—yes. That you be notables and also foreigners I can see: wherefore—*Inshallah!*—great strength and fortune will come to my son!"

"*Inshallah!*" I responded.

If God so wills I heartily hope that strength and good fortune attend one nomadic *batcheh* of southern Iran (he should be nineteen years old now) whose godparents, in a manner of speaking, we are.

Shiraz was a grand center for sport. There were many sorts of duck, geese, snipe and other waterfowl in the marshes that in wet weather took on the dignity of a lake. There were quail and sand-grouse in the bottoms; pheasant, bustard, and two kinds of partridges along the slopes. Wild boar, foxes, a long-tailed yellowish wildcat and quantities of gazelle roamed the valleys. There were wild asses a little farther east, and large flocks of ibex and moufflon in the surrounding hills within easy reach.

I could leave my garden after an early breakfast, get a splendid day's shooting and be back by tea-time. Sometimes we stalked our game. Sometimes a sweeping drive would be arranged, usually by

Ghavam-ol-Molk. With him I went out often, and one could wish for no more engaging companion. He was a keen sportsman, a hard rider and an excellent all-around shot. He did things in the *grande manière*. The first drive he staged in my honor had a Maharajaesque touch to it, and the results were spectacular.

Ghavam sent out sixty men to start two hours before sunset and make a slow drive through the night. They could cover somewhat better than sixteen miles before we arrived, he told me.

Four of us, with several attendants, left in two cars at a quarter before six in the morning. We motored for an hour to about 7000 feet, where a marquee had been set up and horses waited in readiness. We were served hot tea in the tent. Then we rode, with a horse-holder each, to between eight and nine thousand feet, climbing on foot the final half mile, which was very steep. On a saddle of ridge whose pommel and cantle were two Alpine peaks we took our positions behind low piles of rocks, seventy yards or so apart. The saddle fell away in a sheer cliff on the farther side.

I had scarcely got settled in my stony lair when I caught a signal from Ghavam, stretched out in the next position on my left. We had been in place less than five minutes. The nearest part of the drive must have been fully an hour away.

"*LOOK!*" said Ghavam with voiceless mouth, his round brown eyes bulging. I stared at the slope opposite. More than sixty ibex were strolling calmly down the side of the peak, browsing as they came. It was an amazing sight. I watched them for perhaps fifteen minutes while they moved nearer, yard by yard. They were not at all perturbed. I chose my head—a magnificent specimen. Then, just beyond effective range, they turned and went slowly over the edge of the pommel. Ghavam and I ran to the cliff hoping they might swing back, but they did not. They disappeared down the face of the precipice, where we could not have recovered the trophy even if we had got a lucky shot, and we saw them no more.

"What a pity!" said Ghavam. "I never saw so big a flock of ibex! And now perhaps we shall see nothing more all day." We did, though. Half an hour later a flock of moufflon appeared over the same shoulder of the peak facing us. There were thirty-eight or forty, several with splendid heads. They browsed towards us much as the ibex had done, but this lot did not turn aside. They did just the contrary. When they approached within range Ghavam whistled to stiffen them into attention, fired, and the whole flock, less one, charged straight down across our positions.

It was tremendously exciting. We stood up, firing with rifles as they came, with guns loaded in buckshot as they plunged past in gigantic leaps, with rifles again while they rocketed up the reverse slope of the cantle flinging the loose stones behind them. In no sport have I ever felt greater elation than in that moment, facing the frenzied charge of twoscore wild sheep. One hurtled over my shoulder not eight feet away—so close that I ducked. Two or three others sailed past at perhaps double that distance. We killed seven in all, five of them with good heads, with only three of our guns in action. The fourth gun down the slope never got a shot.

"By the ninety-and-nine names of Allah, that was close doing!" cried Ghavam. He was as excited as a schoolboy. When the smoke of battle cleared we rode back to the tent, every horse but one with a moufflon slung under its belly. It was not yet ten o'clock in the morning.

From the ancient province of Fars came the name of Persia—now officially supplanted by the more native style of Iran. The *f* and *p* were from early times interchangeable: Fars or Pars, Farsi or Parsi for a person of that province. Hence the *Persis* of the Greeks, and its derivatives *la Perse* in French, Persia in English. Hence also the Parsees of Bombay, the descendants of Zoroastrian refugees who fled from persecution after the Moslem conquest of Fars.

Among its varied population some are of the purest Aryan descent in all Iran. They are good people in most cases, where they have not been corrupted by the hypocrisy and evil ways of the towns. Certain of the non-migratory tribes along the fringe of the Gulf are held to be pre-Aryan, survivals of the original Turanian occupiers of the land who were pushed off the plateau by the Aryans from the northeast. And there are other nomadic tribes, of yet different lineages, whose life routine was then the most picturesque of any of the diverse habitants of Iran.

The greatest of these were the Kashgai. Traditional deadly enemies of the Khamseh, they were Turki tribes of Transcaspian origin, probably from Kashgar. They overran the western part of the province as the Khamseh overran the eastern, covering an enormous area in their spring and autumn migrations. From near sea-level on the slopes (the *garmsir,* or hot region) of the Gulf where they made their winter quarters, they wended their way across the serrated immensity of the Zagros range over passes that reach 10,400 feet, to summer pastures close to that altitude up to four hundred miles away.

I administered the Kashgais directly, with a mobile branch Agency travelling with them on their treks. They totaled then but a fraction of the immense horde they once had been. Their more than 60,000 families in 1870 had been decimated by famine, by epidemics of influenza and governmental malevolence, reduced by permanent migration elsewhere of many families as a result. Yet, even so reduced, the tidal wave and reflux of that host across the four parallel ranges of the Zagros massif into the upland valleys beyond, and the Bakhtiari farther west in Luristan, were—before the nomadic tribes were broken up by Reza Shah—the most spectacular recurrent mass migrations of this world. They made an amazing procession, particularly during the up-trek in springtime when close upon a hundred thousand souls with perhaps a million animals poured through the narrow passes, and every single female of generative powers was pregnant.

Women heavy with expectant life rode slow mares bulging with foal, last year's colt capering beside each rotund mare, last year's infant tied upon the back of each pregnant mother, with another of a previous year balanced in front of each lap.

Older boys and girls drove the flocks of sheep and goats in front, forming a screen behind them to pick up the new-born lambs and kids as they were dropped. These they deposited two by two in panniers slung across the backs of donkeys, until each plaited rim was filled with a row of tiny, bobbing heads.

She-camels in foal, she-donkeys in foal veered from side to side beneath their burdens. Colts of the Kashgai breed known as the Gulf Arab, small but sturdy and highly esteemed, gallivanted all over the open valleys in squealing groups of mischief. Baby camels, fuzzy and awkward, sprawled along like four-legged ostriches; one rather expected them to lie flat and stretch their silly necks on the earthen floor at the slightest fright. The more mature donkeys and camels moved at their various paces under their loads of camp paraphernalia. Some of them bore folded looms on which hung partly finished tribal carpets. The looms were set up at each halt that the women and girls might knot a few rows in ancient patterns carried only in their heads; to be packed up again for the forward move.

Men of rank and substance—the officers and senior N.C.O.'s, for this was in its way like a military formation—rode on stallions. Other men and women and youths—the old soldiers and raw recruits—tramped along on foot driving the animals, all in an appearance of utter confusion. Yet every one had his assigned task.

If that incredible trek may have appeared ragged and haphazard, it was nevertheless one of the most amazingly organized mass movements in existence. There were no written orders, nor more than a scattered handful of men in the whole tribe who could have read them had there been any. Yet across the desolate mountain region where sweet water is scarce and far between, over the few practicable passages of the inhospitable Country of the Gorges, they moved in their thousands without blocking each other, with their hundreds of thousands of animals to be fed and watered as they went.

Each tribe (for numerous lesser units composed the major grouping called the Kashgai), each subdivision, each family, knew by hundreds of years of tradition just where to camp, just how to time their movements at a sheep's pace from water-hole to water-hole. Just when, though seasons would vary greatly from year to year, to catch the fresh grasses of spring as they begin to tint the slopes and upland valleys in a gradually ascending wave of tender color. And yet not to overlap one another, nor lack forage or water—except in the dreadful years of drought and famine. That was the really astounding part of it all.

I have watched, fascinated, for hours on end while a subtribe forded a torrent that lay across its path in one of the majestic upland gorges of Tangistan. With loud yells and lusty imprecations, men on foot drove the laden camels and horses and mules through water swirling belly-deep while other men and women floundered along behind the beasts of burden, hanging to their tails. The pregnant women, feet drawn high, balanced themselves on their swollen mares, each holding a couple of children and a basketful of new-born kids and lambs above the flood. All the sad little donkeys veered away from the brink of the flow, were prodded and pushed by squads of boys through the racing freshet which as often as not swept the lot off their feet and carried them struggling two or three hundred yards downstream. And the flocks that crowded the water's edge kept up one shrill, continuous bleat as more men methodically threw sheep and goats—hundreds upon hundreds of them—into the torrent, to be caught by a weir of youths stretched across another shoal below.

Sometimes, on the official tours I had frequently to make away from the two or three roads that were in a manner passable by automobile, I would go with a double camp. This, when properly arranged, is to me the utmost luxury in travel.

The first stage would never be a long one. "There are bound to be delays in getting off," my Persian assistants advised. A basic truth, in the East. "Nor is it well," they pointed out, "to go so far the first day that one cannot conveniently send back mounted men to pick up the things one has forgotten."

So we would start in the early afternoon and ride twelve or fourteen miles to where a camp had been set up beside a shady spring or mountain brook. All told, what with an escort of twenty or more riflemen, we would form no mean cavalcade. The riflemen were not purely for show. In the mountains there were robber bands, and these think twice before they attack an armed force that they do not greatly outnumber.

During the night the second camp would pass through, continuing into the morning on its way to the camping ground for the second night. After I departed in the morning the first camp would be broken and would proceed at leisurely pace to wherever I had elected to spend the third night.

Thus in unhurried fashion the two camps alternated, each with its own furnishings, pack animals, cooks, servants and armed guard. Every evening we came to a properly prepared camp, without being limited to the distance a single baggage train traveling at two miles an hour could cover during the day. There was none of the fuss of making and striking camp when one was weary from a long day, or in a hurry to get off in the morning. The system was flexible enough for all purposes. Should the occasion arise I had only to send a mounted messenger to change the destination of the baggage train. And its comforts completely spoiled one for other manners of progress.

I would arrive in the late afternoon, having covered up to fifty miles on horseback with two or three relays laid out. I would have inspected the situation of several villages and perhaps a subtribe or two, have received masses of petitions and listened to long and involved tales of calamity, oppression and intrigue. I would be hot, tired, thirsty. And as I rode up to the camp all physical cares of the moment would slough away.

"Peace be with you!" breathed the bowing servants. A groom sprang forth to lead away my horse. Half a dozen steps took me to a folding rookie chair set up beneath the open tent-flap in the shade of a clump of trees. Gratefully slumping into the chair I would stretch out first my right leg, then the left. A bearer knelt to pull off my boots, loosen the breech-cuffs, place soft Persian slippers on my feet. After a moment or two I would reach out a hand to the left. It fell upon a pipe ready to smoke lying on a folding table, and as I lifted it a servant approached from behind with a lighted match. I reached out a hand to the right: my fingers closed around a glass of whisky and cool water that appeared suddenly like a magic growth on the canvas top of another small table. Without having uttered one word I would lean back in the repose of evening and breath deep content.

Just after the last gulp of whisky-and-water was drained, but never before, there would come the quiet announcement: "Honorable Chief, bath is ready."

I would then move slowly to the double-walled back of the tent that enclosed the bath-dressing room, doing what from early youth I had often wanted to do but had found few appropriate occasions—divesting myself of my clothes as I went, casting them in airy unconcern behind me. I would step from the last item of apparel into the canvas-and-rubber tub flanked by pails of water of just the right temperature, with a short-handled dipper to serve in lieu of a shower. A bearer gathered up my discarded effects in detail. From a pole suspended on the side of the dressing-annex my clean linen and pongee or tweeds hung in the order in which I liked to put them on. Refreshed and in excellent humor I would return to my chair.

Entekhabol Molk, my senior assistant, would join me then, having freshened up in his own manner in his separate tent. From that point our procedure depended on the circumstance of locale. When we were camped in 'the blue' we discussed the events of the day over more whisky-and-water that sprang like an Indian conjurer's rosebush from the canvas table, until dinner was served at our usual late hour. Entekhabol Molk was an admirable collaborator. He was one of the most honorable of men in the standards of any country, sound and conscientious, and with a pleasantly Anglicized taste for whisky-and-water when off duty. But when we halted beside a village or tribal encampment there would always be a large concourse of petitioners awaiting.

"Let them be heard!" I would announce, the signal for the tent to
be thrown open in durbar. The chief suppliants, the mullahs, village
headmen or tribal chieftains, would be invited to squat upon a narrow
carpet facing my chair; other 'notables' and grey-beards on two similar
carpets spread at either side; the mass of lesser fry on the ground
before the tent. The solemn honorifics of politeness had first to be
exchanged. After these died away I would listen to the cries of an
anguished people for the justice of which they had heard the name
but had never known.

"Nay, but we be grievously oppressed! Here all is ruin, all is woe!
Half our families have fled in their despair; we who remain have to
bear the double burden. We starve, yet everything we have is taken
from us. We are driven to sell our daughters, to leave our homes, or
else to die! All, all is ruin!"

"Ay, ay!" the rocking chorus wailed in lamentation. "It is true! It
is true! As God is witness, it is true!"

It *was* true, much of it, and a mournful commentary on the malefi-
cence of man, as on the fatuity of a system whose certain end was to
render productive areas into desert. There were, of course, cases of
exaggeration stirred up by 'intrigue.' Often the issue was highly confusing. But for the most part the suppliants were like little children.
They could understand only the things they saw before their faces, and
not all of those.

"Why," they asked, "when our landlords take three-fifths of our
harvest as their share, and for taxes and interest on advances and
many other charges, do yet other collectors come with guns and say
we have paid not enough; so they take away half or more of what
remains and leave us not sufficient to eat? And others again, and yet
others, who beat us then because we have nothing?" A moaning choral
of despair rose with the words of the leaders.

"And why do the military each year come to seize our older men
for soldiers, or so they say, and shut them in a cellar while the force
lives upon our village until we sell our animals and the ornaments of
our women, and our fruit-trees for firewood, to buy our greybeards
off?"

"Ay," they cried, "and the Governor sends his armed men with an
order for the arrest of one whose name is Hassan, or Hossein or Ali—
nay, but we be many of such name in our village!—and each of us so

named shall be taken away to jail and beaten unless he can raise the ten tomans" (ten dollars, no small amount to an Iranian villager) "that may prove he is not the Hassan or Hossein or Ali wanted!"

They could not seem to understand why a depopulated village should have to pay the same taxes as when it had comprised three times as many families—and pay these several times over each year; nor why they must pay taxes on dead animals, on uprooted fruit-trees, on various other things they did not have or do.

All these things and many more they failed to understand, for they were simple people.

And I who understood only too well was filled with a vast pity at the hopelessness of their lot. For though one might do one's best to right their grievances, it could be little more than a momentary palliative in the endless cycle of oppression and abuse. The responsibilities of decision were not light in themselves. Any that I might take and then find impossible of fulfilment would weaken the prestige on which all decisions depended, and with it my utility. Conflicting pressures in Teheran made the support that might be expected from the capital nebulous at best. One could not very well build up the country's revenues by suspending in large part the basic taxation on the productivity of the land, and even had I done so the wretched peasants would have been exploited just the same. But it was depressing to feel that my most thoughtful verdicts stood little chance of enduring beyond my own authority to enforce them.

Those tormented children of the soil looked to me somehow to cure their ills with a written word that should serve as a magic formula. And the fallibility of the formula and the magic, as time would pass, left me heavy-hearted for the future of my wards.

On an autumn afternoon we rode across a broad plain, and by one of the most spectacular approaches to any habitation on this earth came to the village of Dashtak. The trail meandered close to a detached, sheer-sided rock that rises perhaps two thousand feet clear from the floor of the plain, which is itself over five thousand feet in altitude. Slapped up against this giants' anvil is a little village of no importance; but in it lived a family of mountaineers who alone among all men possessed the secret of scaling the great butte.

"O, Honorable Director!" cried the *Kadkhoda* of Dashtak, the headman of the district, who had ridden out to meet us, "there are no other people on the earth who know how to climb that mountain! And now you shall see how it is done." He had arranged for three of the family to make the climb for my enlightenment. We watched them from our horses as they crept lizard-like up the sheer side of the rock, carrying little loads of camel-thorn from which at various points they lit torches to show their progress. With strong Zeiss glasses I could see almost nothing in the way of hand- or footholds. It was an incredible performance.

"And has no one outside that family ever tried to scale the mountain?" I asked. The Kadkhoda shook his freshly hennaed curls that fringed an absurd little inverted cooking-pot of a hat. "None save those with the inherited skill and knowledge from numberless generations could possibly do it," he said. Seated on his wooden saddle from which hung two great wool tassels, with an iron ring around his horse's lower lip, he looked the living replica of a bas-relief of one of the Sassanian kings.

At the end of the plain we came through a stand of *baneh* trees, all scarlet in autumn coloring, onto a wall of rock fifteen hundred feet high. Up its face the path climbed in short zigzags to a V-shaped gap some five hundred feet deep at the top. I have never seen a pass like it. Three cascades fell through the V down to the plain below, where stood a little mill of vine-covered boulders and a few rice-fields surrounded by colored willows and wild oaks. The cascades had cut strange formations in the rock, whose whole face was pock-marked with caves. Countless pigeons kept flying out, wheeling, fluttering back into the eroded chutes. The opening of the V stood out against a background of dark-toothed mountains, with the sun etching the trail in molten silver on the rock-face of many mouths. Over it all for one last, improbable touch, a rainbow centered on the V, framing the whole picture like a fantastic Valkyrian stage-set on a heroic scale.

"May God preserve us!" cried Entekhabol Molk. "Can we get the animals up there?" The Kadkhoda clattered on ahead. "*Bali!* Yes!" he called. "Follow me!"

The trail mounted almost vertically upwards in flights of steep steps cut in the solid rock. The steps were often more than two feet high, worn smooth by generations of naked feet, deeply indented by innumerable hoofs and spread over with powdered manure. We dismounted. It was a difficult enough climb on foot. For the loaded animals it must have been a heart-break at the end of a hard day.

Slipping, striking sparks, jumping like goats and frequently falling, they managed in some manner to reach the top.

In places the track almost disappeared. Now and then it crept through galleries in the caves; elsewhere over artificial ledges built precariously of loose boulders. After a thousand-foot ascent up the face of the wall the trail entered the V formed in the nearly perpendicular stratification. There was still another five-hundred-foot climb to where the village lay amidst stands of yellow walnut and scarlet plane trees. Tier upon tier of flat-roofed mud houses stood backed against a still higher, circular wall of mountains around an arc of more than 280 degrees.

"The ampitheatre of the giants!" I whispered to Entekhabol Molk. He could only nod, with wonder in his eyes. The scene fairly took away what little breath one had left after that astonishing ascent.

Women holding overgarments of grey check or red across their faces watched from the flat roofs as we passed between walls topped by dried bulrushes. A large crowd of respectful villagers, with a sprinkling of white-turbaned mullahs and blue-turbaned *Sayids,* waited before the house of the Kadkhoda to greet our arrival. In front of it, as we approached, three men held down the sacrificial sheep from whose suddenly slit throat the blood spattered across our track to avert the Evil Eye.

Men plodded wearily up the stepped paths, bearing loads of wood or camel-thorn on their backs. Small children peeked around corners and out of dark and fusty interiors. Animal-bells toned a mellow chorus to the voice of a muezzin singing into the sunset: "God is great! I bear witness there is no other god than God! Come ye to prayer!"

The sunset faded and fires sprang up in the dusk. Pleasant smokes and odors of evening rose in the still air as we proceeded to the roof of the Kadkhoda's house where I was to hold durbar. There also, before I had a chance to stay the sacrifice, another protesting sheep had its throat slit over the mud floor. Fortunately no part of a sacrificial sheep, save only its blood, is ever wasted.

"Our ancestors owned this village," stated the Kadkhoda after the usual preliminaries. "And here be the documents that prove it." Yet a few years earlier the Finance Minister had claimed it as *khalesseh—* public domain—and for certain considerations that did not appear in the files had turned it over to one Taj Khanum. "A city-woman we had never even seen!" cried the greybeards. "Soldiers came to enforce the order. And one of them was killed, but it was an accident . . . as God is our witness it was an accident! Wherefore they threw all our men into a cave and took everything we had."

The soldiers absolutely stripped the village. Eleven thousand dollars was the amount wrung from those unhappy peasants. "We had to cut down our fruit-trees," the Kadkhoda explained. "With everything of our possessions we had not yet enough to meet the payment demanded." Which payment, for some whimsical reason, was then announced by the Ministry of Finance as the price of repurchase of the village from Taj Khanum by the villagers. Whimsical in true Persian style: for Taj Khanum did not get the money—the Commander of the Southern Division got the bulk of it; and the Dashtakis did not get the village that was theirs twice over. Still alluding to it as public domains, the Ministry had then leased it out complete with its peasants to the highest bidder, who was yet another absentee landlord now yammering for my support.

On the Kadkhoda's mud roof splashed with the blood of a sacrificial sheep I cut that particular Gordian knot. Whether it would stay cut was another matter. I could scarcely hope that it would do so for long. For Dashtak was a naturally rich village, and the hands of greed start refashioning the cut knot as soon as the saber is withdrawn.

I would like to think that my efforts expended there and elsewhere were not wholly without avail: that one may have left the diverse multitude of things one touched a shade better for having touched them, may have helped relieve—if only for the moment—the distresses of an ancient and withal a likeable people. For the Dashtakis and their kind were good people, and that mountain village in its extraordinary setting was for me the real Persia.

The Persia of magnificent contrasts, a land of surging expanses, of melancholy grandeur overpowering in the immensity of natural upheaval. A land of sudden and unexpected beauty, breath-taking in its delicacy of tone. A land whose strips of verdure tucked in the folds of barren hills seem greener, the robin's-egg blue of evening skies more exquisite, the breath of lavender-scented uplands fresher, than perhaps anywhere else on this world.

The Persia of ancient dignity and Old World manners, of simple and kindly villagers dreadfully tormented by others of their countrymen too often neither kindly nor simple: the Persia I had grown to love and which I left with infinite regret.

5 – Europa Infelix

The Pen and the Rake

After we left Persia there came an interlude passed amidst the yellow broom and slanting cypresses of Provence; not in the touristy section along the Riviera, but west of Marseille in a *manoir* overlooking the Etang de Berre. That broad lagoon with its Roman relics around the rim was then on the way to become one of the world's great international air-traffic junctions. Yet it had lost little of its primitive charm in the process.

Across it, at the outlet where a canalized channel connects with the Golfe du Lion, lay the little fishing village of Martigues. Here came artists in the summer to paint in its colorful setting of weathered lichen-grown stone, brown nets and tinted sails. Here, too, an artist of gastronomy named Pascal served the most perfect *bouillabaisse* one could ever hope to taste; the fish of various sizes and types and hues taken still alive and wiggling from a barrel aboard an ancient smack tied up before his restaurant, the flavoring such as none in Marseille could equal.

"*Moi!*" announced Pascal, throwing out his chest, "I make the best *bouillabaisse* in the world!" And he did.

The manoir we occupied stood upon the slope between the Etang and the sheer cliff of Vitrolles that rose like a saffron-colored flame behind. The slopes were cultivated in wheat and barley, in truck gardens and olive orchards and vineyards—especially in vineyards. Field stretched after varicolored field, edged by rows of cypresses all leaning southeast; oblique screens of cypresses that made windbreaks against the harsh blast of the mistral. In early summer the sown rectangles turned into rippling carpets of red poppies and blue cornflowers.

Our manoir was named La Croix Route. Even in Marseille, twenty-four kilometers away, few made sense out of that combination. "But no!" they would say when I gave it as my address. "That cannot be! You mean, perhaps, *La Croix Rouge?*"

"I do *not* mean *La Croix Rouge,*" I would explain each time in wearied tone. "I mean *La Croix Route*. That is its name. It was not I who gave it. *Route* is Provençal; one should know that here? It means

341

brisée. La Croix Route—the Broken Cross." Even then they would shake their heads, insisting it could not be.

"Impossible! One does not say such a salad!" But yes, one did.

Stretched out behind the manor-house lay our broken cross. Flowers pushed pert little faces through its openwork tracery. A great wrought-iron affair, it had been snapped off its stone pediment by the mistral years before and never re-erected.

From Martigues there came to our service in the manor-house one Firmin Marius and his wife Nance. Firmin was his family name; a highly respected and substantial family of Martigues fisher-folk. He always put that name first, before his given one, in the manner of the French official records kept of every personal event from birth till burial. Firmin Marius was a retired fisherman. He never had been a servant.

He first appeared to serve at our table resplendent in blue turtle-neck sweater, purplish coat, and mauve cap atop. From his breast pocket projected a pipe, black and befouled from many years of stoking with tobacco that would slay a goat. He moved with the roll of the sea.

Even in the Provençal simplicity of our establishment the cap was a bit incongruous, bobbing around the dining-room against a background of Louis XV panelling. We eased him with gentle suggestion out of that accessory, to which he was deeply attached. The sea-roll I would not have changed for the most perfectly trained butler in all Europe. Not, that is, at La Croix Route.

"*La femme*," he called Nance. She was a dark-eyed Italian very ample in the waist, and officially our cook. Firmin would never admit that such was man's function where there was a woman on hand.

"The *cuisine*: it is for the woman to do that!" he stated with finality. He was in fact protecting her reputation as a cook. He himself always prepared the fish that was the usual *pièce de résistance*, supervised and added the final touches to the sauces. He was, bar none, the best fish cook I ever knew.

Each day our fish rolled up the hill from Marignan in a tiny box of a wagon, announced by the tinkling of a little bell. The wagon, an incredibly ancient vehicle, was pulled at two miles an hour by a twenty-eight-year-old pony, totally blind and lame all around. The hunched-up female who drove it had long passed threescore and ten.

She had not a single tooth in her head. Wonderful fish in endless variety she brought, fresh from the sea.

But there came an evening when we returned late from Marseille. It was just our dinner hour. The table had not been set, nor was Firmin out to meet us. I discovered him slumped in a chair at one end of the kitchen table, his head bowed on his hands. Nance sat hunched-up at the other end. They looked utterly dejected. There was no sign of preparation on the stove, nor on the table.

"Firmin," I asked, "what can be the matter? Why is dinner not yet started?"

"There is nothing," he replied in a voice that was as a sigh from the tomb.

"Nothing! But why?" Our cupboards were reasonably well stocked.

"*La poissonière*—the fishwoman—she did not come."

"But surely we have other things to eat?"

"*Mon Dieu!* And what good? There is no fish!"

Firmin simply could not grasp the idea of preparing a dinner when there was no fish. In the British Army I had under me for nearly two years an Irish subaltern who, in his way, was like that. But *he* could not face a meal—any meal—without potatoes.

We never grew tired of fish at La Croix Route, what with its amazing variety and Firmin's superb preparation of it and his splendid sauces. We had other things, of course. But to Firmin those did not count for much.

One evening when the music of our phonograph struck some responsive chord in their Provençal hearts we saw Nance and Mélie shyly dancing a kind of square-dance on the terrace outside. They were rather like a pair of performing she-bears, broad-beamed in flounced skirts and multiple petticoats, shuffling heavy, misshapen shoes over the red tiles. Embarrassed as schoolgirls they were, when they found us watching them through the window.

Mélie was the wife of Séraphin, the farmer. She must have been uncommonly pretty in her youth, well more than half a century before. Even under the devastating hand of time and hard work her features remained good. Through skin as wrinkled and weather-beaten as walrus-hide her face was still vivacious. She was bent half over from the years of toil and from rheumatism.

They had, Séraphin and Mélie, the dignity of the land; as Firmin had the self-reliance and reserve of the sea. They lived in a tiny room, without light, off a pitiful little kitchen. For furniture they possessed a bed, a small deal table, one chair and a broken stool. But whenever we brought them a present of a bottle of port, or a jar of honey, or a small knicknack from Marseille, they invariably made a return gesture the next day. It might be a dish of berries, or a few vegetables, or a melon. Never did they fail to return some offering in the same simplicity of manner with which they had accepted ours.

Neither of them could read or write. They lived on the land. When there was a purchase to make, Mélie tramped the three miles down to Marignan, the three miles back again up the hill. She had never been in an automobile. I could not induce her to get into ours. Once she almost reached the point of risking it, but not quite.

"*Merci, merci Monsieur!*" she cried. "That will be for another day!" The other day never came.

When we left we presented her with a slop-pail as a parting gift. Mélie said she had wanted a slop-pail all her life, and would rather have that than any other of the several cumbersome articles of housekeeping we gave away.

Each morning she trudged down to the fields carrying some implement of toil. It might be a hoe or a sickle; when Séraphin went out with his scythe it would be a rake. Long, long hours later she plodded back, weary, bent, yet always cheerful. Past the grove of splendid pines she clambered, past the edge of the *terrasse anglaise* where sometimes I might be writing in the shade of the grape arbor. She would see me there writing, and wave her rake from below the terrace.

"One returns!" she would cry out cheerily. "You write?" Then, holding aloft the rake: "*Ça! Ça c'est la plume de nous autres!*"

That's the pen of us others!

For the fortunate ones able to wield a pen as effectively as Mélie her rake over the poppy-reddened fields of Provence, how full could be the satisfaction of a day's work done!

Fire in the Queen's Bedchamber

The Orient Express wound slowly across the Romanian plain through a billowing yellow sea of maize and wheat dotted with islands of dark green woods. Tall well-sweeps rose here and there like bea-

cons above the tasseled corn, marking open spaces where cattle and
sheep and tight little troops of white geese gathered around the water-
holes. This was rich land of rarely failing harvest, along whose rutted
tracks the shod hoofs of oxen shuffled in leisurely tempo.

At the Bucarest station all was bustle. Two smartly dressed officers
approached the *wagon-lit,* saluted, and turned a squad of porters onto
my bags.

"*Bien arrivé!*" they cried. "General Gorsky's compliments! He awaits
you in your hotel." At hideous pace we were whirled to the Athénée-
Palace through a surging traffic of droshkies and American motorcars.

Major General Alexandre Gorsky, Inspector-General of Romanian
aviation, extended his cordial welcome across cups of Turkish coffee.

"All arrangements have been made," he announced. "All our information is available to you. You shall see everything of our situation."
In truth I was shown during the next two weeks about all that one not
wholly untrained observer could well assimilate. The scope of General
Gorsky's ideas was large, as were the reports he had received of the
unlimited resources, in those frantic days of 1929, behind the group
I represented.

"In half an hour we shall see the Minister of Defense," he continued.
"You have just the time to change." From then on one's changes were
frequent and diversified. Not knowing exactly what I might be in for
I had brought pongee coats and flannel trousers for the plains, where
the heat of late summer can sometimes be oppressive, tweeds for the
mountains, conventional short black coat and striped grey trousers for
official calls, dinner-coat and full dress for evening formalities. All of
them I used, but they were not enough.

The Minister of Defense was most affable. On that first morning I
learned something of what was expected from my visit. It included a
fairly comprehensive remodeling of the Romanian military establishment, the equipping of a greatly increased Air Force, and the development of an air-postal network. There were flying and ground schools
to be established, and extensive construction of airdromes, hangars,
repair centers, barracks, officers' clubs and divers other items. By the
second or third morning of discussion the financing involved had
rounded to the tidy sum of forty-four million dollars. Even in the
joyous pre-October days of 1929 I could not feel that my principals
would be wholly enchanted by the opportunity. A few weeks later
when the Wall Street crash had come I knew exceedingly well that

they would not. But General Gorsky and the Defense Minister were firm in the conviction of the feasibility of their program.

General Alexandre Gorsky was an interesting and an agreeable companion. He wore well, and left one with the first impression of a sincere and honorable man. A trifle optimistic in fiscal matters perhaps; but so were rather many of my own compatriots at that same time.

General Gorsky put a little Farman three-place cabin plane at my disposal, with an Air Force Captain who was his personal pilot. At first view the Captain's long, highly polished fingernails seemed a trifle disconcerting. Like the long nails of a Chinese mandarin, I presumed they were to show that he never worked on his equipment with his own hands. But he really was an excellent if somewhat temperamental pilot.

"My mistress prefers them like this," he observed later with regard to his nails. "She feels it makes me more tigerish!"

In the little Farman I was flown all over Romania inspecting airdromes and sites for airdromes, factories, projected air routes and other locations the General wished that I should see. We struck off to the north into the Bukovina which prior to the peace treaties had been Austrian crown land; over the Carpathians to the Transylvanian provinces that formerly were part of Hungary's thousand-year dominion; into Bessarabia which had been Russian. After several such trips General Gorsky informed me one morning that we would leave in the afternoon for Constantza, spend the night at the Officers' Club there and fly next day to lunch with Queen Marie at Balçik, her summer-palace on the Black Sea.

I told him I would be ready; then, as an afterthought, asked what I ought to wear.

"A morning-coat, of course," said the General briefly.

"I thought so," I cheeped. "That's the one thing I didn't bring with me. A short black coat would not do?"

"A *short* coat to lunch with the Queen?" He was so taken aback that I did not further pursue this line of thought. I rushed around to my friend Rives Childs, the American Vice-Consul. "Can you lend me a morning-coat to wear to lunch tomorrow at Balçik?" I pleaded. Rives could, but our figures were not quite alike. His was shorter and a good bit stouter. The coat, when I slipped it on, emphasized the difference.

I gulped down the glass of old *ţuica* he proffered, and fled to a tailor. By dint of bribery and dire threats I drove the protesting Jew to drop the work he had in hand, tear the coat apart, let down the sleeves, take in the waist and refashion it within the hour—all in such way that it could be restored to its original state two days later. It was in no manner of speaking a signal success as a fit, and the extended cuffs of quite another shade than the rest of the sleeve lent the whole garment an odd tone of faded green. But it was a morning-coat. Thus equipped I flew with General Gorsky to Constantza in a furious rain-storm at thirty feet above the level plain. Our Captain-pilot pulled up steeply to clear the Danube dikes.

In the morning we proceeded to Balçik. There was no airdrome nearby, but a moderately flat field bordering a cliff over the Black Sea offered landing space of a sort. The General had arranged by telephone with the Queen's A.D.C. for a smudge to be lighted on the field as a beacon.

It was a stormy day with a strong off-shore wind and occasional slanting rain-squalls. The Captain chose to fly a short way inland to avoid the danger of drifting out to sea. The slow little Farman was not an ideal plane in which to find oneself over the Black Sea with half a gale blowing off the cliff-bound coast.

It was not an ideal plane in several other respects. The seat had been designed for two quite narrow passengers, and General Gorsky was no sylph. The Gnome-Rhone engine lubricated lavishly on castor oil. This day it threw out such quantities that the pilot could see nothing out of the forward window. Wherefore he kept one side window open, through which poured thick fumes saturated with globules of oil freshened by occasional douches of rain.

In France, during the first phase of the World War, I had grown rather to like the familiar smell of castor oil used in our rotary and radial engines. But that was in open aircraft. It was all very different squashed inside a closed cabin, wearing a borrowed morning-coat on one's way to see a Queen. The weather was warm when we took off so I had packed away my overcoat where it could not be got at in flight. There was hardly room for it in any event, with Gorsky in the seat. Since oil and water do not mix, the front of my garb took on a peculiar dappled appearance. So did my derby hat. The General had excused me from wearing a topper.

Flying low, we saw neither coast-line nor smudge nor any other conspicuous feature breaking the flat, alluvial landscape. The rich plains were yellow with corn, and great piles of grain were being threshed on circular threshing floors by troops of four to six horses in line abreast, each troop hitched to a fluted stone like a section of Corinthian column, trotting round and round as in a circus ring. The little villages were made up of very small oblong cottages with sloping wooden or thatched roofs. Piles of straw bigger than the cottages were being accumulated for the winter forage. Some of the farmhouses were white, with red peppers picturesquely hanging on their walls. There was a sprinkling of lemon-yellow watermelons; and as always around the water-holes, marked by their tall well-sweeps, were brown and white sheep, brown cattle, white geese and white oxen.

Yet there was little to differentiate one village from another. After a time General Gorsky began to show signs of nervousness.

"We should have seen the fire before this," he announced to the pilot. "I think you have passed Balçik."

"We have not yet come there, my General," called the Captain. "Our ground-speed is low; we are making very much drift." General Gorsky studied his map. There was nothing in view by which we could check our course.

"I tell you we have gone past it!" he shouted, leaning forward. I could feel the side of the plane bulge between the longerons. As long as *those* hold . . . I thought to myself.

The Captain turned around in his seat. He waved his arms. I watched, fascinated, the flashing of his long, polished fingernails. He seized the map, stabbed it with a forefinger like the spur of a fighting-cock. "My General, we are *there!* We are *there!* We are *there!!*"

The nose of the plane was slowly rising, the air-speed indicator dropping off. I began to take an interest in our immediate destination. It seemed a poor solution to spin into the ground even if we were too far south. The Captain whirled around in his seat and with a sharp "m-yah!" slapped the stick forward, then whirled back again, waving his arms. He was a true Latin: he could say nothing without his hands. Had there been any sun he might have heliographed with his finger-tips.

"My General! We have not yet reached Balçik! This wind holds us back; we move more slowly than you figure! In five minutes we should be there! We are less than five kilometers from the coast—you would not wish me to carry you out to sea in this storm?" The nose of the plane was rising again.

"M-yah!" cried the Captain, and slapped forward the stick.

"*You* are flying the plane!" the General shouted. "But you might as well land us in the Black Sea as in Bulgaria, and that's what you're going to do if we keep on this way!" The Bulgarians were at that time not kindly disposed towards the Romanian military regime. The General was in uniform, as was the Captain; the Farman belonged to the Air Force. I happened to recall that my passport was deposited in Bucarest. And we were still heading southwest.

General Gorsky suddenly exploded. "Holy Virgin Mother of Jesus!" he bellowed. "You and your sacred five minutes! I tell you we're over the Bulgarian frontier now! In the name of God, turn around! Go back at once! In another minute we may be shot down, or have to land, and we might be interned here for a year!"

"M-yah!" cried the Captain, and pulled the plane around.

General Gorsky was right. We had been over the Bulgarian frontier. (After the 1940 territorial adjustment, Balçik itself fell in Bulgaria.) With ten minutes of flying we came to the limestone cliffs that give the name of "silver coast" to this area, bore then due north and shortly sighted the fire burning in the middle of a small field. The Captain swung around in his seat with arms outstretched, bowing almost to the floor of the plane.

"My General! A thousand apologies! You were right and I am a fool! I miscalculated! You are far better at finding your way than I am, my General!"

"Exactly," said Gorsky, his good humor restored. "I knew you were wrong." He turned to me with a gratified smile. "I have been here often before," he remarked. "I do not lose my way." I remembered having been told that he was an old and intimate friend of the Queen.

We circled for a landing over the edge of a high cliff that fell sheer to the sea, rolled between a flock of sheep and the brushwood fire, and came to a halt a little before the end of the field which was marked by a row of telephone poles. It was a very nice landing, but I felt no regret that we had not to make it in the reverse direction. A waiting Ford bore us away, down the bumpy road to Queen Marie's little palace at the edge of Balçik bay. The palace was a pleasant building in the Turkish style—Balçik village is predominantly Turkish in aspect—with white stucco walls, deep verandahs, a minaret and a splendid outlook over the sea. It had a fine park with magnificent flowers, a pergola of limestone columns and arches, and a waterfall. Here I took stock of myself—a depressing review. My clothes were damp, spotted and smelling strongly of cooked castor oil. In trying to improve the matter I managed with the well-meant help of others to make it a good deal worse.

For half an hour palace attendants worked on my personal appearance. A valet attempted to remove the stains with cleaning fluid. The result was disastrous. Instead of a spatter of smallish spots there was a complete overlay of large oily circles which gave a singularly dissolute effect. The original odor remained, enhanced now by another quite as unlovely. I felt very distressed about all this.

One of the attendants then had a bright thought of his own. He rushed up and before I could stay his hand he sprayed me all over with attar of roses from a silver atomizer. It made an incredibly fearful combination. I tottered out to the pergola for a few minutes in the forlorn hope that some part of it might dissipate on the open breezes. Some of it perhaps did, but not enough. Trailing a blended aroma of castor oil, cleaning fluid and strong scent, an abashed leopard conscious of his spots, I forged slowly in to meet the Queen.

Her Majesty was good enough to show no surprise, whatever she may have felt. I made some passing reference to a castor-oil bath in the plane and let it go at that. She expressed her pleasure at my coming to Romania. "I am delighted," she added, "to hear that you are so enthusiastic over Gorsky's program. I am very deeply interested in my Air Force."

"I have always been an admirer of ambitious effort, Your Majesty," I replied, and in the tenuous state of my morale wondered if that were a graceful evasion of her opening remark. After luncheon we discussed the Gorsky program at some length. The Queen was intelligently inquisitive, well informed, and no less optimistic than Gorsky. She never alluded to any other sovereign authority than herself: "My Air Force . . . My people . . ." And she assured me that the love of her people for their Queen would bring them to adopt any measure, accept any sacrifices for the national welfare, of which she might approve.

We sat down nine to an informal luncheon: Queen Marie, Gorsky and I, the Captain, two Chamberlains and three other officers, with an empty chair for the Princess Ileana. The conversation was carried on in Romanian, French, English and German. The Queen wore a white blouse embroidered Romanian fashion in red and blue, and a plaited skirt. She had a white ropy thing in her hair; and around her neck a band—which may have been to hide telltale lines. But she looked very handsome and was in excellent form.

She placed General Gorsky on her right. I sat on her left, with the empty place for the Princess Ileana on my other side. The dining room was spacious and the long table bore a multitude of glasses, silver and native faïence on a cloth of Romanian embroidery—a gay and cheerful ensemble.

"My daughter Ileana is moving her little boat to a better mooring for this wind," the Queen told me. "When she does that I never know what time she will be back. I am glad you like my refuge by the sea."

"It is charming, Your Majesty," I said.

"I adore it. I have such a reposeful feeling here." One could readily believe that repose might be a welcome break from time to time in the hectic rounds of her life. Yet though the situation and the palace itself were reposeful, I wondered if anything that had to do with the Romanian royal family, or indeed with Romania, could ever come under that designation.

"But last night was not entirely restful," she continued. "We had here a minor *contretemps*—oh, luckily, nothing serious! At the moment we are a little crowded for accommodations in Balçik, so Ileana is sharing my bedroom." I had heard that Carol's wife, the unhappy Helen of Greece, was staying there, but she did not put in an appearance.

"My daughter Ileana is really a charming companion," continued Queen Marie. "She has, however, one unpleasant habit. She talks in her sleep. I have never been able to cure her of it. Last night she was particularly garrulous. Twice I awoke to her prattle: the second time I could not again get to sleep. I lay there thinking of many things. But she rambled on louder than ever, interrupting even my thoughts. 'This,' I mused, 'is really too tiresome!' I sat up in bed and threw a pillow at her. 'Ileana, be quiet!' I called. It had no effect. 'I shall have to get up and shake the girl,' I said to myself. And then I noticed a strange glow in the corner of the room."

The butler passed fresh sterlet from the Black Sea, and the *sommelier* filled our glasses with an agreeable Romanian white wine. The Queen, despite her English birth, was a keen advocate of Romanian products. It had sometimes been alleged, not too kindly, that she tended rather to overdo her cultivation of the products of the Romanian Staff College.

"At first," the Queen went on, "I thought the glow was some weird reflection from outside. I wondered what it could possibly be, for there was no moon. Then I heard a crackle. 'Aha,' I said aloud, 'we are on fire!' I went over to Ileana's bed and shook her vigorously. 'Stop that chatter and get up at once!' I cried in her ear. 'The room is on fire!' Ileana got up, still half asleep. 'Look there!' I called. The side of the room was burning between the fireplace and the outer corner, flames slowly licking up the walls. It had started, evidently, from a defective flue. 'I don't want to rouse the household,' I said to Ileana. 'They'll get excited and tear everything to pieces.'

"You know how servants are," the Queen explained to me. I did know, having once lived in Persia.

"Wide awake now," Queen Marie went on, "Ileana ran to the door. 'I'm going to get my crew!' she called back. 'The military guard here is too beastly stupid to be of any use!' "

The tale was interrupted as the Princess Ileana herself came in to lunch. She wore the uniform of a Romanian Naval Lieutenant. She was soaking wet, her hair in damp curls above a wet and freckled face.

"I moved my boat!" she announced in triumph. "It was very rough; we were almost blown out to sea. One of my crew was washed overboard, but we managed to pull him back with a rope. Then we had trouble getting ashore." She dripped in little puddles as she sat beside me. I began to feel less self-conscious of my own attire.

"We were talking of the fire last night," said the Queen. "And how you went off in your nightgown to fetch your crew and naval guard because the soldiers guarding *me* were too stupid to put out a fire!"

"*Stupid?*" burst out Ileana. "They are as stupid as oxen! When I ran out they stopped me. 'I am the Princess Ileana!' I cried. 'I am going for my naval men because the palace is on fire!' They simply gaped. 'It is not possible,' they said. 'You cannot be the Princess Ileana. The Princess Ileana would not come out at this hour of night in such a costume as that! And we see no fire.' 'My God!' I cried. 'I wouldn't come out at all if we were not about to burn up and if I thought *you* had sense enough not to throw oil on it!' and I ran on through them."

The Queen proceeded: "I waited, and the room grew very warm. I had a lot of my best potted plants in there. I feared they would spoil. So I moved them all out onto the verandah, two by two. I had just got the last ones outside when Ileana came back on the run with her naval men."

It was an entertaining picture, I thought: Queen Marie in her nightgown moving her potted plants two by two out onto the verandah away from the heat of her burning bedchamber.

"And then?" I asked.

"Why, then they put out the fire. It had not done a great amount of damage. Only to one corner of the room, and above the fire-place. Oh yes, there was also a small hole in the roof. Not bad, we could still sleep there. But the night was quite cold. So," concluded Queen Marie, "before returning to bed I moved all my potted plants back into the room again."

Queen Marie, though very influential, had at that time no official voice in the rule of Romania. There was a Council of three Regents to handle the affairs of State during the minority of Carol's son Mihail. In December 1925 Carol had renounced all his rights as Crown Prince and had left the country for good with the red-haired Magda Lupescu, following certain family and public objections to this lady's influence and his behavior. After King Ferdinand's death in 1927 the youthful Mihail succeeded to the throne. Framed photographs of his somewhat pudgy features faced one in every governmental office, every shop, hotel and station.

I returned to Romania a year later. Carol had also returned and had become King in place of his son. In a well-engineered *coup d'état*, abetted by a group of officers who felt that their military merit was more apt to be recognized under his aegis than under that of the regents, he flew from Paris to Bucarest and assumed the crown. Hastily the rather surly stare of Mihail from the framed photographs, in replica on stamps and coins and bank-notes, gave way to the self-assured gaze of His Majesty King Carol II in the latest uniform of his devising.

"Designing new uniforms for himself is the King's second favorite pastime," I was told in Bucarest. "He has quite a flair for it."

I sat in King Carol's entourage at Baneasa airport when the Italian Air Force's aerobatic team put on a performance for the Romanian Air Force. They were extremely good, from any standard. They gave an exhibition of team stunt flying that I have never seen surpassed. But there was one touch of Italian martial spirit I observed with a certain interest.

The team was composed of seven pilots—five sergeants, and two Lieutenants who flew as the wingmen. They first came across the field barrel-rolling in line abreast, their wing-tips almost touching. All their stunts were remarkable displays of precision flying, and one that they did I have not seen before or since. Again in close line abreast they dived at the field, then pulled straight up into a massed stall and slid back side by side on their tails, very little space separating their wing tips. The noses of the planes dropped in unison; at about seventy-five feet above the ground they had regained flying speed, and zoomed up over our heads in the pattern of a spreading leaf.

It was a difficult and dangerous manœuvre, beautifully executed and perfectly timed. What I also observed about it was that after the initial dive on the field there were only five who carried out the balance of the stunt. These were the five sergeants. The two officers pulled out and faded away after the dive. The expendability of sergeants on that particular trick, I heard, ran rather high.

Some while later I demonstrated an American training plane to King Carol at Braşov. He had been much impressed by the Italian stunt team. I on my part was considerably impressed by the preparations for His Majesty's viewing of the sturdy but unromantic trainer. Those responsible for the arrangements had set up a red marquee supported on gilded poles, trimmed with golden tassels and gold embroidered crowns, with *CR* (Carolus Rex) *II* in flowing gold script beneath the crowns. Under this was a dais surrounded by three steps, all carpeted in red; and on the dais stood a large gilt-and-brocaded chair with the royal insignia embroidered on its back.

In due course King Carol arrived driving a robin's-egg-blue front-wheel-drive Cord phaeton. He was wearing the new blue uniform of Commander-in-Chief of the Romanian Air Force which he had recently designed, somewhat along the lines of the R.A.F. dress uniform but more elaborate. The uniform set off his tall figure effectively. He was handsome in his way, though a sensuous mouth weakened his face. General Gorsky and two other officers were with him, and more officers followed in another car. The King was in excellent humor. He took his seat on the field throne, the officers standing on the steps below the dais according to their rank and relative importance. General Gorsky was on the top step at the right of the King, who from time to time would say: "Gorsky! What do you think about that?" as some technical point came up in the discussion. The General replied quietly and precisely, but I gathered the impression that he preferred Queen Marie's manner of consulting him to that of King Carol.

The demonstration of a single training plane cannot very easily be made dramatic. Doubtless the King better enjoyed watching a number of units in formation sliding downwards on their tails. Nevertheless he showed keen interest and asked a good many pertinent questions. Before he left he invited me to call upon him in his summer palace at Sinaia two or three days later.

A little before the appointed hour I was informed that His Majesty, unhappily, was indisposed. His Majesty was still indisposed the next day when he was to have opened Parliament, but had to postpone this ceremony because, as the press reports said, of a light attack of mumps. But I had it on impeccable authority that what he was really suffering from was a not so light attack of Nicky. Prince Nicholas, Carol's younger brother, had been criticized by the King for having let his affections stray into pastures where the eligible lambs were not of royal stock. This, from Carol, seemed to Nicky to come with exceedingly bad grace. In the ensuing argument Prince Nicholas, who was something of a boxer, punched the King heartily on the nose and the eye and also kicked him in the groin. He was dissuaded with difficulty by several of the King's attendants from further mayhem on his royal brother.

In due course Nicholas married the girl of his affections, who was not of royal blood, without the King's permission. As a consequence he was forced to renounce his rights and leave the country. In September 1940 Carol in his turn departed his homeland, still accompanied by the faithful Magda Lupescu, having been forced by pressure of the pro-Axis Iron Guard (and this was to his credit) to abdicate in favor of Mihail, who thus regained the throne he had previously lost to his father.

There was never a dull moment among the Romanian royal family.

There Was No Peace

Several protracted periods of European strife are lumped chronologically by the historians, since further breakdown merely tends to confuse the issues. Such, among others, were The Hundred Years' War, and The Thirty Years' War. The simplification of reference does not mean that armed struggle was continuous throughout those periods. It means that during them there was no lasting or effective peace.

The Great War that broke out in 1914 did not end with the Armistice of 1918. There were peace treaties, but for five years or more a series of violent semidetached wars continued to enliven a large part of the European scene and considerable sections of Asia. For a brief time thereafter—until a renewal of hostilities came in 1931 from the East—there was a breathing spell of a sort during which armed encounters were sporadic and mostly localized. But there was no real peace. The so-called "World War II," though the alignment differed somewhat from the first phase, was essentially a continuation of the unfinished Great War of 1914–18.

In the interim between the two phases I wandered extensively over the intransigent face of Europe and Asia, by airplane and automobile, boat and train, horse, camel and canoe. I talked with the nationals of many States, of all sorts and walks of life. Certainly the great bulk of the people, even in the defeated nations, did not want war. But they thought about it deeply and the fear of it underlay their thinking. How to avoid it, and yet preserve their national and economic integrity. How to retain the political independence, in some cases the territorial gains, acquired in 1919 and after. How, on the part of certain broken Powers and deprivileged classes, to retrieve their losses. How to meet the impact of new ideologies whose implications were not clearly understood, and so the more feared.

The upsurge of nationalistic and racial megalomania was one not insignificant effect of the war's first phase which, along with fostering the growth of dictators in many areas, led rapidly to its second. In some countries government officials were forbidden, and non-officials were afraid, to talk to "foreigners" except through the controlled medium of State appointees.

Little nationalist wars of "self-determination" sundering long-established ties of interdependence, tribal revolts and wars to suppress the tribes, class wars, wars over irredentist fever-spots, for restoration of the far-flung boundaries of classical or mediæval kingdoms, for commercial and political advantage: each made its contribution to disunity and to the ultimate disruption of national life over a large part of Europe and Asia.

In America we tacked through this period of global storm warnings in a haze of geographic complacency, following the treacherous lodestar of economic nationalism and fortuity.

I went to Turkey not long after Mustafa Kemal Pasha, working almost without mechanical aids to reshape his country from the complete wreckage of the Ottoman Empire, had in ten days driven the numerically superior and better-equipped Greek Army some two hundred miles into the sea from its attempted conquest of Anatolia. Of the widespread crop of dictators that sprang from the Great War's first phase, he was in many ways the most remarkable.

On the negative side, his faults were manifold. He was utterly ruthless—he could hardly have been otherwise and have built a self-reliant republic, though by no means a democracy, from the shambles of the Ottoman débâcle. He was without morals in the accepted sense of the term, and could sometimes be very unpleasant. He condemned his best friend to death without batting an eyelash, though in this he was not lacking justification. He was one of the most assiduous two-fisted drinkers of his time. Yet his accomplishments were prodigious.

He drove out the Sultan and abolished both the Sultanate and the Caliphate. He defied the victorious Allies and forced them to withdraw from Constantinople—which he then renamed Istanbul—and eastern Thrace. He built a vast new capital, Ankara, around an ancient citadel in the middle of Anatolia and made the reluctant Turks like it. Besides driving the Greeks into the sea (and thereby writing *finis* to Lloyd George's premiership of Britain, since the lion-maned Welshman had supported their Anatolian venture), he caused the Italians to quit the rich province of Adana, the "Southern California of Turkey," which they had occupied and had every intention to hold. He smashed the brigand chieftains who held sway in the fastnesses of the Taurus, and broke the power of the reactionary Moslem clergy. All this he did, at least in the beginning, practically without tools, with little else than his own genius and the stamina of the over-strained Anatolian peasant-soldiers.

A few tools he made. One of his early collaborators was the pint-sized Colonel Ali Bey, an ordnance officer whom I knew well. Mustafa Kemal called Ali Bey while the Greeks were driving towards Ankara. The Inter-Allied Commission of Control had destroyed a part of what little remained of Turkish armament after the Armistice. But Anatolia is a large area and there were many unrevealed caches of ammunition; and at inland points guns of divers origins and calibers had been rendered unusable, or so the Commission thought, merely by removing their breech-blocks and throwing them into the Marmara.

"You will make breech-blocks for those guns!" said Mustafa Kemal to Ali Bey.

"Yes, sir!" replied Ali Bey, who had at his disposal neither steel nor machine tools. But there was something in Mustafa Kemal's gray-green eyes that discouraged argument. Like wolves' eyes, they glinted coldly in the half-light of the grim, grey caserne on the slope of Ankara.

"I made them," said Ali Bey quite simply. "I found a supply of railway axles, left by the Germans on the Anatolian section of the 'Berlin-Baghdad' railway. I thought they must be good steel—couldn't test them. I shaped the breech-blocks in a hand forge and trimmed them with hand tools. It wasn't easy," averred Ali Bey. One could imagine it was not.

"When they were finished the Gazi asked me if the guns would fire," continued Ali Bey. "I told him that the breech-blocks fitted and I was confident the guns would fire once. Couldn't guarantee them after that. But they fired all right, and with them and the determination of our soldiers we threw the Greeks out of Anatolia."

The Anatolian peasant soldier is a remarkable type. Pure Tatar backbone of his nation, inured to hardship, sober, peaceful and trustworthy, he is self-reliant and hospitable at home. Strongly independent, he is surprisingly subject to discipline by those in authority. A British General who knew Turkey well once summarized the mentality of the Turkish soldier.

"Give a company of 'em a batch of Armenian babies to watch over," he said, "and they'll care for those babies as if they were their own. They'll split up their own blankets to keep 'em warm, share their own bread with them and try to get some goat's milk to go with it. Grinning, sort of sheepish about it all, but infinitely gentle. Then comes an order from their authoritative commander to bayonet the babies, and bayoneted stolidly every baby will be. The soldiers don't much like this, but an order is an order and conscience doesn't come into the matter."

Though his prestige was unlimited and his personal power absolute, Mustafa Kemal built no structure to perpetuate the latter as Reza Shah had done, nor any material wealth that did not revert at his death, by his own wish, to the State. He discarded his honorific title of Gazi—"The Conqueror"—along with the dignity of Pasha, and took the family name of Atatürk—"Father of the Turks." He abolished the fez as being a headdress that differentiated the Turk from the peoples of the West, whereat there was a surge of purple caps and strange Vienna-made felt hats to the fore. He changed the orthography of the Turkish language from the beautiful, but difficult, flowing script to Latin characters that more people could learn to read and write. He forced the violently opposed Moslem clergy to call the prayers in Turkish instead of in Arabic, and had the Koran translated into the vernacular that the people might themselves understand the Moslem Word of God instead of depending on a self-perpetuating class of clerics to interpret it. He broke the clergy's entrenched privilege of defining Islamic law—the sole base of Turkish justice up to that time—by adapting a form of the Swiss civil code to Turkish needs. And he abolished polygamy, despite the Prophet Mohammad's specific assurance that man could be blessed with four wives.

This limitation on divine tolerance raised no great dissent in the towns, where a multiplicity of wives had long been found an economic liability as well as disruptive to one's peace of mind. But on the farms it was otherwise.

"How," asked a well-to-do Anatolian farmer, standing on a hill and with a broad sweep of his arm pointing to his rolling acres, "can I ever cultivate all that land with only one wife?"

I sat one night at dinner in the Turküvaz (Turquoise) Restaurant which was subsidized by Mustafa Kemal (he liked it for itself and for the *cachet* of Western modernity it lent to Istanbul) and was served by waitresses all alleged to be Russian princesses. Most of these young ladies had a Russian background of sorts and several were not unpleasant to look at, though some, one suspected, sprang from no greater distance than a modest taxi ride from the Turküvaz. One ate very well there, and the Hungarian orchestra played with charm and discretion.

My dinner partner was Hungarian. She was extremely good-looking and danced the tango most gracefully. She was dancing with a young man who had acquired his Latin rhythm at its source, when the Gazi walked in with a small entourage (chosen, it was said, largely for their relative immunity to alcohol). They sat at a long table not far from where I was dining. The Gazi was in a civilian suit. He was shorter than all but one of the others of his party. His thinning hair, brushed straight back, was blond, betokening his Macedonian ancestry. I saw his unfathomable grey-green eyes fix upon and follow my dinner partner, tangoing with the young man.

A little later, when the dance was over and my friend was seated beside me, at the moment surreptitiously passing bits of fish through the open transom behind us to eight or ten of Istanbul's population of undernourished cats, a Turkish officer approached from the Gazi's table. He clicked his heels and said in French: "His Excellency the Gazi-Pasha invites you and your lady to join his party."

"His Excellency is very kind," I said.

"He also invites the gentleman who danced the last dance with this lady," added the Conqueror's envoy.

We repaired to the Gazi's table. He was affable and talked to us in French, though in Turkish to his companions. He urged us, and them, to an immoderate consumption of French champagne, brandy and Scotch whisky, while he himself drank arack neat, in tumblerfuls. He seemed to take great pleasure, though his expression rarely varied, in watching my dinner guest and the lithe exponent of Latin rhythm dance the tango. He had them do it over and over again for nearly four hours. The weary orchestra was permitted to play no other type of music in all that time save one Hungarian tzigane. The Gazi's insistence was not unpleasant, yet it was not to be refused. Before the night had finished I suspected that my lady was regretting ever having learned to tango. The young man had wilted visibly.

By about five-thirty in the morning the Gazi himself was visibly wilting. The arack, a drink with all the gentleness of white mule, was beginning to have its effect. He had been drinking steadily for over six hours, and I had no knowledge of how much longer. He never eased the kick of his white mule with any water.

When he was finally assisted out by two of his coterie (it seemed they applied themselves in relays to the task of keeping pace with his potations, else none could have afforded very steady support), we also departed. It was not possible to take one's leave before the Gazi.

I escorted my friend to her apartment in a hotel not very far away. She was pretty fatigued. Not too fatigued, however, to tote a large paper bag full of remnants of food salvaged from the Conqueror's table which she dispensed to some two hundred mewling cats that intercepted us from the smelly, cobbled back streets of Pera.

In no part of the world is there a more delightful stretch of water and land than the Bosporus. Winding between the steep, palace-studded shores of Europe and Asia, the overflow of the Black Sea pours in constantly shifting fresh-water currents to the Marmara and the Mediterranean, returning in part on a counter-current of colder, saline water flowing deep below the surface. Through here the Argonauts tacked and rowed in search of the Golden Fleece. Dolphins play amongst the square-sailed and lateen-rigged *caiques* that sweep down from the Black Sea with the sunlight flashing on their canvas, and snort in the moonlight at the watchers on the banks. By day the Lost Souls fly ceaselessly up and down, down and up, between the Black Sea and the Marmara, a few inches above the surface.

The Lost Souls are in the shape of small white-bellied, sooty-backed sea-birds. Lesser shearwater, the ornithologists call them. But the people of the Bosporus aver that they are the spirits of the excess wives and slaves and concubines of the Sultan's Seraglio who in years gone by were thrown into the Bosporus when their charms palled or they became unduly troublesome. Condemned to perpetual searching they fly back and forth over the Bosporus, past the palace walls of their favor and their fall, up and down without respite or repose. In tight formations, by groups of a dozen to sixty or more, they ply their way; swerving to avoid the ships and rowboats and the dolphins playing in the channel, never seeming to alight nor to rest save for the holding of a few beats of their wings as they glide close above the surface.

It is said that they sleep on the unstaid bosom of the Black Sea. I have scarcely ever seen one otherwise than in motion. The few exceptions perhaps were not Lost Souls. For some Bosporus people hold that the souls of honest oarsmen also take this form and join the Lost Souls in their incessant flight.

"Nay," they maintain, "but these be the souls of the good boatmen whom Death has taken and allowed to return to the water they loved so well." Honest boatmen are few and far between. The evil ones who have passed on are presumably rowing with Charon on the turbid Styx.

Across the Bosporus at Haidar Pasha stands the German-built, or at least designed, Asiatic terminus of their long-projected "Berlin-Baghdad" Railway, the spinal cord of the *"Drang nach Osten."* The building is a dour, grey pseudo-Renaissance structure with purple windows—a final touch of Germanic gloom. It has, under a hangar-like cover, five platforms from one of which the evening express to Ankara sets forth. The evening express to Ankara takes sixteen hours, laboriously clambering up into the Anatolian plateau.

I spent a good many months in Turkey over a five-year period negotiating and laying out an airline for the Turkish Government, together with an attempt at re-equipment of the Turkish Air Force. Mustafa Kemal and his collaborators had created from the remnants of the

"Sick Man of Europe" a strong influence for peace and progress in the Near East. But they were only too aware that peace and unprepared-ness do not march together. They were also indisposed to permit the airlines of foreign powers to fly over Anatolia.

The airline between Istanbul and Ankara, when finally established, took two hours instead of the sixteen by train. During the protracted period of getting it into being I had frequently to go to Ankara by rail. Most of Istanbul's business tycoons and local government officials then regarded a visit to Ankara as tantamount to exile in the desert. They spent no more time there than was absolutely essential for their con-tracts and arrangements with the Ministerial authorities. Mostly the same people made the trip over and over again, returning, when pos-sible, the next night, and I got to know or at least to recognize the majority of that troop of unenthusiastic travellers who took the evening "express" from Haidar Pasha.

To make sure of catching it one had to take a ferry from Galata that left one gangling on the platform for nearly an hour before the express shuffled off. There was a later ferry, but when the winds and the currents were adverse this often missed the train. In the amiable Eastern style the wives and mistresses and friends of the departing passengers came over to wish their relations and beloved ones God-speed on the fearsome, if not wholly novel, venture into the wilderness of Anatolia. Most of these well-wishers I also came to know by sight.

But one evening on the platform I saw a new face. My Turkish colleague, who had been purchasing a bottle of arack, not obtainable on the train, rejoined me.

"Who is that?" I asked, pointing to a tall, dark-faced figure with greying, crinkly hair. He was dressed in a well-cut if somewhat worn frock coat, and around him were more people than surrounded anyone else on the platform. They were paying him more deference, and I noticed that many kissed his hand and bowed rather more lowly than he returned their bows. Some looked to be Pashas of the previous regime.

"You do not know?" said my friend in surprise. "Why, that is the former Chief Eunuch of the Sultan's Seraglio!" It seemed that I was to run into ex-Chief Eunuchs all over the place.

"And why so much deference to him now," I inquired, "when the Sultanate has been abolished and the Seraglio is a museum?"

"Ah, but he was a great man in his day," said my friend. "He had charge of all the Sultan's womenfolk. There were eight thousand or more, with all the female slaves, concubines, servants, and so on. He had the equivalent rank of Grand Vizier, and what was most important of all he had the ear of the Sultan. Moreover, he was a very honorable man. You have doubtless noted that most of those about him are carry-overs from the old regime. They remember him not only for his great influence, but for his courtesy and helpfulness in taking their petitions to the Sultan."

"And what is he doing now?" I asked.

"Ah, *now*," said my friend, "he is the principal midwife of Istanbul!"

Despite the younger Turks' passion for modernity, the older ones hold to their prejudice against male doctors entering female quarters. But who could be more acceptable in his post-war profession than the former Chief Eunuch who had full charge of the Sultan's eight thousand or so women, who when his delicate and responsible job blew up under the impact of Mustafa Kemal took a refresher course in modern midwifery, and was happily remembered by his contemporaries for his unfailing courtesy and helpfulness?

In 1930 I led a "mission" of four airplanes around Europe. We visited some twenty countries, omitting only Spain, Portugal, Italy and Albania. Jimmy Doolittle (lately Lieutenant General), "Uncle Joe" Cannon (now Lieutenant General), and Jim Parker (lately Major General, and lost in the Pacific) were the prima donnas. I am fond of Jimmy Doolittle and have the highest regard for his technical ability. But in that year I would as soon have led a carload of live red monkeys around Europe as Jimmy.

We started off in Greece. I had a personal letter from a mutual friend to Venizelos, then the Prime Minister, who promised to attend our demonstration of aerial prowess. He did not attend, and my last interview with him lacked cordiality.

The Greeks, like all the others in eastern Europe, were afraid for their security, and with reason, though they had abandoned all aggressive intent after Mustafa Kemal indicated to their then leaders the error of their ways in Anatolia. They were building up an Air Force and an air transport line, and were much interested in American aircraft. Mr. Zannos, the Air Minister, was particularly amicable. He had a very pleasant aide, Captain Averoff, a handsome young Greek with a Russian name and an English education.

Our four aircraft were assembled in quick order by our two hard-working mechanics. The demonstration was set for a Tuesday, at Tatoi. On the Sunday we went out to a picnic in the Temple of Minerva at Sunion on Cape Colonna. All, that is, except Jimmy Doolittle. He was not in his best humor. Also, he said, he wanted to check his compass on the rose at Tatoi airfield.

That evening on returning I sensed that something had happened in Athens. Before I learned what it was I ran into Captain Averoff in the bar of the Grande Bretagne. He was waiting for me. He offered me a drink with unrevealing nonchalance. There were lighted candles in the Grande Bretagne bar; the electricity seemed not to be functioning.

"Lights not working?" I inquired casually.

"No," said Averoff. "They've gone out in this quarter of town." Then he remarked: "The Air Minister would like to see you."

"Oh?" I queried. "Tomorrow morning?"

"Tonight," said Averoff, "at your early convenience." I may have looked mildly surprised but Captain Averoff added nothing for my enlightenment.

We went together to Mr. Zannos's office. The Air Minister was working late for a Sunday in Greece, I thought. He proffered me a cigarette.

"I believe you have been away from Athens all day," said Mr. Zannos.

"Yes, I was at Sunion," I affirmed.

"A pleasant spot," said Mr. Zannos. "Major Doolittle did not go with you?"

"No, he stayed at Tatoi," I said. "He had work to do on his airplane."

"Oh, yes," murmured Mr. Zannos. Then: "You know, I am sure, that we have a strict regulation forbidding anyone to fly over Athens lower than a thousand meters. Was Major Doolittle aware of this regulation?"

"He was informed of it," I said.

"It seems to have slipped his mind this afternoon. You have heard about the incident?" I had not. "Well," continued Mr. Zannos, "after having checked his compass on Tatoi airfield, I am told, he then re-checked it by flying up and down our principal avenue in Athens just below the treetops. Your 'Hawk' has a very powerful engine." (It had, for those days: 600 h.p.) "The blast from its short exhaust stacks and propeller blew out quite a lot of windows on one side as he flew up the avenue, and on the other side as he flew back down again. The roar—which is considerable, you know—frightened all the horses. There are many on the avenue on a Sunday afternoon. They all ran away, upsetting their carriages and throwing out the passengers. Some got tangled up with trees and electric light poles, or went through shop display windows. There was a good deal of confusion, as you may imagine, and a certain amount of damage. Several wires came down, and part of this district is without light as a result. The people have been rather upset."

I voiced my distress and deep regret, assuring the Air Minister that we would make atonement for the damage wrought and any other amends that he might feel appropriate. This sort of occurrence was one of the penalties, I added, of touring with a prima donna.

"Don't take it too much to heart," Mr. Zannos said sympathetically. "*I* understand. We have them too. But I'm afraid you will have to see the Prime Minister tomorrow. Frankly, he is not exactly pleased."

The next morning I called upon Mr. Venizelos at Kafissia, in a hotel where he spent the warm days of Athenian summer. He received me in a small room, seated by a window which I had to face, in a black suit and a black skull-cap which accentuated his venerable, carefully trimmed white beard. His thin white hands moved restlessly on his knees. The episode had not amused him, and he said as much. That was about all he did say. I explained the affair as best I could, with what I thought were suitable apologies and the assurance of honorable amends, ending in much the same vein that I had followed with Mr. Zannos. I added that I hoped the Premier would not feel prejudiced against our intended demonstration of American aeronautical development. He uttered not a word. Perhaps his mind was on the pact he was then negotiating with Turkey. I bowed myself out of the room with his cold, unresponsive eyes looking fixedly at the wall.

When I saw Jimmy Doolittle later in the day I said: "I've been fed crow and don't much like the dish. I hope not to have to repeat it."

"Well, I had to check my compass, didn't I?" replied Jimmy.

On the outskirts of Athens in temporary barracks and camps, as also outside Saloniki and other locations in Greece, were more than one and a half millions of Greek refugees, many of them from areas where their ancestors had been established since the sixth century before Christ. The majority of them had fled from Anatolia and eastern Thrace when the Turkish forces drove the Greek Army out of Asia

Minor in 1922. The rest were the Grecian element of the compulsory exchange of minority populations set up by the Turko-Greek Convention of 1923. In all of Turkey save only the former capital of Istanbul not a Greek remained resident, including areas on the Black and Aegean Seas where they had been located for over twenty-five centuries. On the other side, some half million Turkish Moslems were transferred from Greece, Macedonia and western Thrace to Turkey in the general reshuffling of races.

This was probably the most remarkable exchange of populations ever effected up to that time. It was hard on the individuals concerned and necessitated considerable international financial assistance in compensations and resettlement. But it worked. Where before there had been constant political turbulence due to racial and religious antipathies, there is now nearly complete homogeneity. It forms an interesting precedent for what is perhaps the only solution for tranquillity in certain of the more explosive sections of central and eastern Europe.

We gave many rides to V.I.P.'s (Very Important Persons) in all the countries of our tour around Europe. "Uncle Joe" Cannon, one of the world's smoothest pilots and the least temperamental of our prima donnas, did most of these personally conducted flights. At Sofia he took up the somewhat dissolute Prince Cyril (liquidated fourteen years later for collaborationism as one of the three Regents of the State), and his sister Eudoxie. Their brother King Boris was away at the time, attending the funeral of a friend who had recently been murdered.

From the Ankara race course Uncle Joe took up the Turkish Premier Ismet Pasha, later to be President Ismet Inönü, successor to Kemal Atatürk. The hero of the Turkish counterattack against the Greeks on the Sakarya River and diplomatic victor of the Lausanne Conference was accompanied by his wife and two young sons, all jammed onto the narrow seat of our little passenger plane. Ismet, small in stature and a bit deaf, was quite elated at making his first flight. None of them had ever been in the air before and they decided to die together rather than separately, should Fate so ordain. The Ankara race course with its 3000-foot altitude was on the short side for a low-powered "puddle jumper" carrying two passengers—albeit small ones—beyond its normal complement. But they came back from their flight over the ancient citadel and modern buildings of the sprawling new capital enthusiastically air-minded, the elder son, then about ten, loudly demanding that papa immediately acquire an airplane of just that type for family use.

At Vienna, Uncle Joe took up President Miklas of Austria for that amiable gentleman's first venture in the air. The President was short but stoutly built. He wore a black morning-suit and derby hat. When he and his aide of even more generous proportions sat down together in the little plane, after some levering on my part, I saw the fabric sides bulge above the longerons. Yet he was so pleased with the flight over Vienna and the Wiener Wald that he later sent Uncle Joe a silver medal embossed with the President's cherubic likeness and the date of his aerial baptism.

Many other notables we took up for their first bird's-eye view of the world as it was then. Of them all, the most enchanted and most enchanting was the daughter of the Estonian Chief of Staff. Uncle Joe also drew her, being our official "taker-upper," though there was some slight argument over this at the time. She was a lovely, lithe young creature with blonde tresses and as graceful as a deer. She desired acrobatics. The General, her father, had no objections and told me that nothing had ever fazed her yet, so I sent her up in our open-cockpit training plane, adjusting the safety-belt, parachute, helmet and goggles to her slim figure and flowing locks. After twenty minutes of vigorous aerobatics she came down radiant, pleading for more. Even the usually undemonstrative Uncle Joe, senior flying instructor in the United States Army Air Force's advanced pursuit school, was impressed.

"She's quite a gal," he said. "I twisted her and I looped her, stalled her, spun her, snapped and barrelled her. Ran out of tricks while she was signalling me to do something more. I'd have flown her on her back if I hadn't felt that she probably would slip through the belt and forget to pull the 'chute rip-cord." Appreciatively, she presented Uncle Joe with her red beret as a memento.

That evening the Chief of Staff gave us a party. We sat out of doors in a walled garden and consumed vodka and mulled Burgundy and many excellently prepared dishes, for Estonian cooking is very good indeed. The walls were high and narrow, with several gaps through which passed sizable footpaths. Around the top of the wall the General's daughter ran with sure-footed grace, sailing over the six-foot gaps like a gazelle. Springing lightly down she led me by the hand, followed by the rest of the party like a pack of hounds in full chase, through a large bonfire burning in the center of the garden. With the leap of a springbok she plunged through the middle of the flames, and I beside her, for it was St. Johan's Eve and in Estonia on St. Johan's Eve people celebrate by jumping through bonfires.

"I should have flown her on her back," Uncle Joe remarked dryly. "If she slipped out of the belt and forgot to pull the rip-cord I bet she'd have come down all right, 'chute or no 'chute!"

We flew across the Gulf of Finland to Helsinki, landing on an improvised strip amidst the pine trees of the small island of Santahamina. The harbor was gay with small sailing craft. The landing-field was far from ideal but there was then no other. Several Finnish Air Force officers squatted along the edge of the strip, signalling with their hands as we came down. After we had pegged out the planes we were taken to the Yacht Club and drank schnapps out of cups.

Finland, like the United States, was in the throes of prohibition. It worked there in about the same way as with us. One drank strong alcohol in tea-cups, one drank out of sight in private rooms, one paid exorbitant prices to bootleggers for uncertain products, but one drank —probably a good deal more than if drinking had been completely legal.

One evening I went with Major Halaama, Air Force engineer officer, to watch the test of an anti-aircraft searchlight. During the test the operator swept the indented shore-line and picked out a motor-boat proceeding at moderate speed. The light played full on the motor-boat for several seconds.

"Don't keep it on that boat so long!" Halaama cried to the operator. "You'll make him nervous!" Then in an aside to me: "That's one of our best bootleggers!" There was a fast decoy boat that the Coast Guard patrol always chased, Halaama said. While the patrol hounded this well-known and unladen quarry the little put-puts by the dozen would run in amidst the islands and land their cargoes of liquor unimpeded. It sounded not unlike the procedure in the enlightened United States.

I returned in mid-winter to Helsinki to observe the tests of a new Finnish military aircraft powered by a Wright "Cyclone" engine. The plane had been built on a small island in the harbor, then solidly enclosed in ice. The temperature was 26° below zero Fahrenheit when I went out to it on a sled propelled by a Gnome-Rhone rotary aviation engine, a relic of the World War's first phase, with a wooden air-screw.

There was no windshield and the sled did sixty miles an hour. That was the coldest ride I ever hope to take.

The Finnish Chief of Staff and twenty or so of the highest officers of the General Staff and the Air Force came out to witness the test. They made quite an impressive group in their long military greatcoats and heavy fur collars. The new plane stood in the open, as the shop where it was built would not house it once the wings were mounted. The engine was very cold. So was everything else except the mechanics grinding away at the inertia starter. The engine would not start. It had not been run since it had left the factory some six months before. We later learned that the Finns had not removed the "gunk"—a thick, anti-corrosion sludge with which the engine had been liberally smeared inside. Under the circumstances it was remarkable that it ever did start. After an hour's effort at winding up the starter, warming the oil, priming, and then doing this all over and over again, it coughed a couple of times. The sound brought the General Staff from a small shack where there was a wood-burning stove and several bottles of bootleg schnapps. But nothing else happened for a long while.

The General Staff were standing behind the plane, examining some feature of the tail structure, when the engine suddenly started off with a hiccoughing roar. It ran just long enough to cover them completely, their fine greatcoats and fur collars, their fur caps and fur gloves, their faces and their moustaches, with a thick layer of warm, treacly, blackish gunk. They all dived into the frozen snow, but it was too late. The engine then caught fire. This we managed to put out. Some of the wiring was damaged. It was decided that it was not an auspicious day for a test, so we all repaired to the warm shack and polished off the schnapps. I never saw such a bedraggled General Staff. They took rueful stock of the state of their garments, but were quite sporting about the affair.

The next day the plane flew successfully, using skis, over to another island where there was a hangar. The General Staff were not on hand to see it take off.

On this trip I left Helsinki aboard a ship that all but filled the narrow channel, which was kept open by the constant passage of ice-breakers. Under the port regulations we nevertheless had to have a pilot. When we were opposite a lighthouse on a little frozen island, about a mile abeam, the pilot left us. He simply stepped off the ladder and walked away, his dark figure and small handbag outlined against the ice. It reminded me of a silly piece of doggerel from my youth: "Oh, Mr. Captain, stop the ship; I want to get off and walk!" This was the pilot's last trip of the season. Our vessel was the last one out of Helsinki that winter before the whole Gulf of Finland froze over solidly and even the ice-breakers could not get through.

At Budapest the "Flying Mission" was met by Butler Wright, the American Minister, with his whole staff; "Nicky" Horthy, the Regent's son, representing his father, and a large gathering of high officials of the Army and various government departments. The following day Admiral Horthy, the Regent, came out in full uniform to watch our demonstration from a red-carpeted platform, along with almost everyone of importance in Budapest.

There was no pattern of any kind in the arrangements for our reception by the various American Embassies and Legations concerned. Some of the Chiefs of Mission, like Butler Wright, could not have done more for us. They recognized the flight for what it was—a demonstration of American progress in the vastly important and growing field of aviation. Some could not well have done less. The State Department left it to the individual envoys to act as each might see fit, and the range of what they deemed fit was infinite.

From Budapest I subsequently had a letter from a Hungarian inventor who desired to interest me in a device of his design. Very many inventors sought to interest me in the products of their brains, but this was one of the more entertaining descriptions of these brain-children that I received. It is quoted exactly as written.

1931 vi/20 Budapest

Dear Sir:
    Beg to call up your attention for a special safety mechanical instrument, wich is asure and stop the flying machine to fall down. How this instrument are working, the folloving writting certificate explain, what certificate vas giw out imder the Budapest Josef Scientific University's opinion.
Writting certificate:—Triangle shaped dropingumbrella, wich is when folded izey to put on the upper body, behind the pilot sett. This umbrella could be filled in two side. Namely that place on the body, where the vings are come out roght 8 left side 1-1 botle filled with Helium gas .150. Athmospher, get place. This helium will fill the umbrella and open wery quikly.

In case any trouble happen on the machine,—on the mech.
board has a button; when that button puled,—the two helium
bottle valveopened, /from the valve to the umbrella true, a pipe
lead the helium!/ The pressed gas puffed the umbrella, while
openself and liftingself over the whole machine, and stop to fall
the aeroplane, and put them straight Falling conditions. The
pressed helium gas work sure and servequik opening. the folder
work are the same, like the dropingumbrella.

The umbrella holder guide beetven the central body and the
back vings employed; and the machine become under the umbrella—mean! the umbrella cover the machine in case the machine vaobling.

Now My Dear Sir !

If. you are interesting about—how this instrument are vorking
and if you Sir, like a original draving! Kindly send your worthy
ansver, and Y will mail you one at soon.

I'm wery truly yours,

*   *   *   *   *

Throughout the whole continent of Europe the picture was taking
its pernicious shape. The upsurge of nationalism, the obvious preparations and growing truculence in Germany, the inability of countries to
agree upon a common course in the common interest, the inability of
the people in most of the countries to trim their own sails towards any
mutual objective, all made part of the sorrowful crazy-quilt. There was
no real peace; and as year followed year it became ever more apparent
that the temporary respite in world-wide hostilities was on the wane.
The great mass of the people of a continent that had only recently
been ravaged by war, who ardently desired no more of it, were gravely
alarmed by the portents of further war which any reasonably experienced observer could not help but see. Yet they were unable to get
together to halt the trend. And the governments of the countries that
least desired any renewed test at arms, including the United States,
failed to take effective measures either to prevent it or to prepare
adequately for it. In the light of what has followed it is not surprising
that a good many Europeans have lost faith in a system of government
that proved so inept in solving the most acute problem of the pre-
atomic age.

I left Europe shortly before the Spanish civil war offered a preview of things to come. When I next returned the whole face of it had changed.

Odyssey of a Retread

In April, 1941, I returned to active duty with our armed forces. This time, though temporarily as it turned out, it was in the Navy, as the Army Air Corps showed little interest in "retreads" when I first sought reappointment in that branch of the service. At six o'clock in the evening of 21 May—a remarkably fine evening for an often foggy coast—I took off from San Francisco, having flown across the continent, bound for the Near East.

It was the maiden flight of the new model 314-A Clipper, as well as the first commercial flight across the Pacific to Singapore. We dropped the Golden Gate behind in the blaze of the dipping sun, and from ten miles out sped smoothly at 10,000 feet above an unbroken layer of cumulus that glistened in the sunset like the frozen wastes of the Antarctic. The steward served cocktails, whisky-and-soda, and an excellent dinner. At 8:20 in the morning, refreshed by sound sleep in a comfortable bunk, and having shaved with an electric razor which was part of the washroom equipment, I debarked at Pearl Harbor. It was an odd sensation, this flight of 14 hours 20 minutes, most of it while one slept, after earlier trips by boat in five or six days during which the passengers unpacked their wardrobe trunks, got themselves engaged and perhaps disengaged, and pursued their various fashions of whiling away the time.

We laid over in Honolulu for twenty-four hours: pleasant hours, crowded with color, that I passed with the Bill Jardines. The flowers, flowering trees, shrubs and vines were at their best; the little Japanese-Hawaiian girls looked freshly attractive. We swam on the far side of the island, where I picked up a glass fishing-net float that had drifted from Japan, a minor portent, it may have been. In the evening Bill's capable and charming wife cooked a steak whose equal has rarely come off any broiler, which we ate on the verandah of their house up on the hillside overlooking the town and the harbor, with a myriad lights twinkling down below.

The next day I flew to Midway over a deep blue sea dotted with fluffy white clouds and small white wave crests. As we cleared Pearl

Harbor the whole Pacific battle fleet was coming in from manœuvres. Six or seven battleships in line astern churned white wakes directly below, with destroyers laying smoke screens and formations of aircraft flying high, flying low, zooming off the carriers and diving as at an imaginary enemy. I wondered then if that concentration at an island base thick with Japanese was a good idea. Six months and two weeks later it seemed not to have been a good idea.

A few minutes farther out we flew over a Japanese vessel. The Rising Sun showed brightly from her staff. "Release bombs!" cried Colonel Wang of the Chinese Air Force, one of our passengers. We had no bombs, and in that day one gravely exchanged courtesies with vessels flying the Japanese emblem. But Colonel Wang was not a neutral. His mind harbored no courtesies for the Japanese flag.

The two tiny atolls, Midway and Wake, that at the outset made trans-Pacific flying possible, look from the air like thin, varicolored doughnuts on a field of lapis lazuli. Their abrasive sand of powdered coral glints like ivory in the sunlight. On it grows green vegetation of grasses and low trees, and around the ivory rim of the beaches runs a narrow line of sparkling white, formed by the breaking wavelets of the ocean. The center of the doughnut is a shallow lagoon of delicate greenish-blue in fascinating contrast to the deep Mediterranean blue beyond the rim, with purple streaks of coral heads rising just below the surface.

The lagoons, though shallow, are deep enough for flying boats after a path has been cleared by blasting the coral heads. There were two squadrons of PBY's on the lagoon at Midway and two thousand men turning the atoll into an air base where before, save for the P.A.A. landing pier and inn, had been only a cable station. But for me, a casual traveller headed towards the Near East, the chief interest of Midway was its bird life. There were millions of birds, of a considerable variety of species. Among them the greatest in number were the goonies.

The goonies are the most entertaining, and the goofiest, birds in the entire world. Only another gooney can tell the sex of a gooney. In the spring they fly down from the Aleutian Islands, though it seems not definitely known from just where they take off. The males arrive first and wait on the beach for the females. The law of supply and demand is met in due course, but the earliest batches of female arrivals are greeted with extreme effusiveness. The proposals are made with a wholly ridiculous form of dance.

After this expectantly awaited honeymoon the female lays one eight-inch egg in the sand or under a bush, and from this a fuzzy brown chick is hatched. The chick doesn't move but just sits and sits, is fed by its mother, and grows and grows. In time the mother departs. The poor chick, its brown fuzz mostly worn off its white feathers by then and nearly full-grown, is left to fend for itself. Its body is too heavy for its wings and it doesn't know how to fly. It walks with the utmost clumsiness, but finally crawls up a bank and throws itself off. It falls on its head, gets up in a daze and tries again. After several trials it hits on the right idea, runs down the bank into the wind and so manages to launch itself in the air. Once air-borne it performs easily and well.

The adult birds are so tame that they will hardly get out of one's way. They walk bent over, with a curious swaying motion like the old-style detective in a nineteenth-century melodrama. They run a long way into the wind to take off from the ground, and now and then fail, but in the air they bank and swoop most gracefully.

On the ground they go about in little groups of twos and threes, sometimes up to five. From time to time they bow to one another, raise their long beaks straight in the air, bow again, touch beaks, do a little shadow fencing and dance, facing each other or arrayed in a solemn circle. The great majority are white: handsome, clean, and sleek-looking. The black variety are scavengers. They are the gentlest, the most unsuspecting, and the most ridiculous birds imaginable.

Alas, the poor gooney! He is one of the casualties of the War. Dangerous near the ground to low-flying aircraft because of his great size, he is being eliminated. On Eastern Island of the Midway atoll, where the runway was being built, sixty thousand goonies had been clubbed to death by the Marines, with many more to go. The Marines, to their credit, hated this task. On the main or western island the birds had up till then been spared, though it was by no means certain that the respite would be other than temporary.

The driver of the reconnaissance car in which I made an inspection of the defense project with Colonel Pepper, the Marine Corps Commander on Midway, was careful to avoid the chicks that squatted in the deep tracks in the sand and would not budge. They had been told by their mothers not to move and they didn't. We straddled them and, the car's clearance being high, left them still squatting, considerably bewildered but unscathed. But the highly paid civilian drivers of the contractor's trucks working on the defense project could not be bothered to avoid the squatting chicks, and I saw a good many fuzzy little carcasses that had been run over and squashed.

Besides the goonies, terns of all kinds literally covered the ground at night. They would barely move as one walked among them. One type, the Balting tern, was particularly striking, with big black eyes, black bill and legs, and pure white body. They are called "love terns" on the atoll, as they always go in pairs.

At Wake there were some birds, in normal quantities, but no goonies. Eighty-odd years ago a German boat was wrecked on the atoll and the rats and descendants of the rats that escaped the wreck ate the goonies' eggs, so the goonies now avoid this atoll. The eight human survivors of the wreck, including two women, rowed 1508 miles in an open boat to Guam (probably a good deal more unless they went dead straight), a feat scarcely inferior to that of Captain Bligh of H.M.S. *Bounty*. All that remains on Wake Island of their venture is a rusty anchor and many small but inquisitive rats.

I was eating a papaya at 9000 feet between Midway and Wake above a dead-calm sea, deep blue and dotted with purple cloud-shadows of the fluffy white cumuli just below us, when we crossed the mystic international date-line and shifted painlessly from Saturday to Sunday. A few minutes later we passed, at about 300 yards off our port side, at the same altitude, the *China Clipper* winging eastwardly from Hong Kong to San Francisco. It was an impressive demonstration of navigational precision that brought those two wee specks, travelling in opposite directions at 160 miles an hour, together at that given point in the middle of the 8000-mile span of the Pacific Ocean to Manila.

That evening I swam in the turquoise-blue water of Wake Island's lagoon, clear as crystal and of ideal temperature. There were big sharks lunging hungrily outside. The sharks could not get in, but on the atoll was a crippled fisherman whose calf had been bitten off by a shark as he waded in a foot or so depth along the rim to cast his net.

Guam, different from the atolls, is a green island, hilly and lush with tropical vegetation. I drove to Agana, sixteen miles from the landing, to call on the Governor, Captain McMillan, U.S.N. It was a pretty drive, with fine views over the sea through coconut palms and breadfruit and "walking trees," amidst nipa-thatched houses on stilts and carabao shambling in the cornfields. The "walking trees" grow from a tangle of high, exposed roots that reach continually farther out, and gradually the tree moves on in search of fresher pastures.

We stopped for a night in Manila, from whose torrid heat, where the air was absolutely dead at 4:00 A.M.—or more exactly from Cavite some twenty miles out—we made the first passenger flight to Singapore. Skirting the coast of North Borneo and Sarawak, with the 13,750-foot peak of Kinabalu dominating our flank, we listened to a speech by President Roosevelt. The continual sending of position messages interfered with his voice, but when it came through he might have been one of the eight of us in the control cabin instead of someone on the opposite side of the world.

In Singapore, at Raffles Hotel, I renewed memories of twelve and twenty-nine years before. Raffles had not changed a bit nor had its fine, hot curries. There were Australian and New Zealand troops in and around Singapore, and a few barbed-wire entanglements and machine-gun emplacements, but the tempo of life on the whole appeared not to have undergone any great change due to the war in the west. Ethnologically, which one sometimes forgets, Singapore is a Chinese city, with a smatter of Malays and Indians, a thin façade of British, and a general leaven of all the races of the East. The sprawling, red-tiled town is prettily set off by flame-of-the-forest, frangipani and other brilliantly blooming trees, but its stickiness is wearing. Yet we danced nightly at Raffles, and one evening I went with a party to the "New World" and danced with the Chinese taxi dancers. They were very circumspect, but had good figures, pretty little hands and feet, and danced very well.

I talked at length with Air Marshal Sir Robert Brook-Popham, Commander-in-Chief, Far East, whom I had known when I was Air Attaché in London. He was considerably criticized for the deficiencies of the Singapore, Malayan and Burmese defenses, and was later relieved. The defense preparations, aside from the big Naval Base, were not inspiring. But I had the impression that Brook-Popham appreciated the situation better than some of those higher up who criticized him later, and that he received scant help in his efforts to correct it.

I also ran into Joe Gody, my flight mechanic of the European flying tour of eleven years before. He was now Wright engine expert for the Brewster fighters we had sent to the R.A.F. in Malaya. These were

obsolescent aircraft and in no striking number, though that was perhaps inevitable with the demands in more urgent theatres of operations.
Joe Gody complained sourly of the red tape and the length of time it
took to get anything accomplished in Malaya.

From Singapore I proceeded in the K.L.M. plane *Wielewaal*
("Golden Oriole") along the western edge of Johore State and thence
to Medan in Sumatra. The Sultan of Johore at the age of sixty-seven
had recently taken unto himself his third wife, after divorcing his second, a Scotchwoman. He grew so heartily to dislike the latter that he
abandoned the palace where he had lived with her, built a new one,
and gave up drinking Scotch whisky, of which he was extremely fond.
Now he would drink only American rye.

On the Malayan side of the Strait the coast is edged with sandy
beaches, the water near them yellow from the river-borne silt. Farther
out a lovely light-green strip shades into the solid blue of the deep:
dotted with conventionalized bamboo-stake fish traps, in zigzags or
shaped like arrow heads, very distinctive from above. The low, deeply
indented Sumatran coast is an even grey-blue of mangrove islands and
of littoral built up by the mangroves that germinate new roots in the
air. These drop off, take root in the mud, and by collecting more mud
washed down from the highlands make new land, grow new roots
which in their turn drop off, and so ever press forward upon the sea.

At Medan we were put up in the Hotel de Boer where I had
stopped twenty-nine years before. With Captain Smirnoff of the *Wielewaal*, a remarkable ex-Russian Dutchman and excellent airman, and a
thirty-year-old Indian princess, the Maharaj Kumari Lalita Rani Devi
of Burdwan, very decorative in her Indian costume, I did my part in
consuming considerable quantities of Martini cocktails, champagne,
rijs taffel and brandy, over which we discussed the social problems of
India until well into the steamy tropic night. The Princess Lalita's
marriage at the age of fifteen-and-a-half had not been a success, and
her commentary on some of the ancient practices of her people and on
her private life was uninhibited and diverting. She was returning home
after a three-month "vacation" at Bandoeng.

We flew next day to Penang, thence across the narrow isthmus and
up the robin's-egg-blue Gulf of Siam, spotted with purple cloud shadows
that looked just like islands. Some *were* islands, the only visual difference being that these had narrow rims of white sand which the cloud

shadows had not. Bangkok, sprawling on the banks of its muddy, meandering river, spattered with grey and gold and white pagodas, was entirely surrounded by flooded paddy-fields as far as the eye could reach. The fields made an infinite repetition of irregular rectangles in variegated shades of yellow, brown and green; a vast mosaic of abstract decoration. In the rectangles were fat little dots of shiny grey: water buffaloes wallowing in the fields they soon would plow. Small thatched houses hiding in trees on tiny green islands here and there broke the endless pattern of flooded earth.

In the loops of the river a large number of ships were lying at anchor. I wondered how many of them were Japanese.

We did not stop long enough to let me refresh my memories of Bangkok of a dozen years before, but kept on over the paddy-fields, the jungle, and the silt-laden Andaman Sea to Rangoon. There I went with the Princess Lalita to the Shwe Dagon. Barefooted we clambered up the long steps and around the platform where the Buddhist worshippers knelt and intoned prayers to candlelighted Buddhas beneath the golden glory of the greatest of pagodas. As elsewhere in Burma the younger feminine worshippers in their gaily colored silks were wholly enchanting; dainty butterflies flitting around the graceful spire as though around an eternal flame.

The monsoon broke as we left Rangoon. From there to Jodhpur, two-thirds the way across India (1840 miles done in one day), there were thick black clouds from which the rain beat in sheets upon the leaden water already covering the fields below.

We halted to refuel at Akyab. Up to this point it might have seemed a prophetic trip, since every place at which I touched from Midway to Calcutta was lost to our Oriental enemy a few months thereafter. Midway and Pearl Harbor, the other two stops from San Francisco, were to be the locale of not insignificant "incidents." Six months later one would have been hard put to repeat this trip, or any very extensive part of it, for a considerable time to come.

At Dumdum, the airport of Calcutta (where "dumdum" bullets originated), I regretfully ceded the agreeable companionship of the Princess Lalita. The trip across India was exceedingly rough. As we proceeded up the Persian Gulf the ground stops were hot as hell's hinges—Jiwasi, a refueling point scraped on the nothingness of the British Baluchistan coast; Sharja, rallying place of Arab brigands in

Trucial Oman; Bahrein Island, center of the Gulf pearl fisheries, with
the highest known humidity of any spot on the earth's surface. The
devastating summer heat of the last is now tempered—indoors—by the
air conditioning of the California Texas Petroleum Company's installation.

The empty wastes of the Arabian mainland opposite Bahrein are
among the most uninviting portions of the world. Waterless and barren, too ill-favored to support life over much of their extent, they are
insufferable in the merciless heat of summer. I therefore heard with
amazement a California Texas official remark casually that he was
going across to Jiddah, on the Red Sea, in the next few days, not by
air but on the ground.

"Oh, it's not at all bad," he explained. "I go in an air-conditioned
trailer. Dumps of gasoline and other supplies have been laid down
along the route. I read the latest magazines and smoke my favorite
brand of Havana cigars. Every now and then I push an electric bell
and my white-coated Arab servant brings me an iced whisky-and-soda.
Sometimes I vary this with Martinis." The picture changes fast these
days.

At Basrah the reputed air conditioning of the airport hotel was
functioning only in the bar. The bar was perhaps thirty-five degrees
cooler than anywhere else; so cool, comparatively, that one's teeth
chattered on entering it sopping wet from the saturated heat outside,
and liberal portions of whisky were indicated to stave off pneumonia.
Then after one became adjusted to its temperature there was a natural
reluctance to plunge forth into the furnace beyond the bar. That bar,
still amply stocked in those days, had a somewhat repressive effect on
complete sobriety.

I was headed for Turkey, but until our arrival at Basrah neither I
nor anyone with whom I consulted had the least idea of how I was
going to get there. All Iraq was in turbulence from the German-
fostered uprising of Rashid Ali and his pro-Axis cohorts. At the Habbaniya airfield, fifty-five miles west of Baghdad, some three hundred
British and twelve hundred native levies, with a modest number of
ancient training planes, had been surrounded for four weeks by twelve
to fifteen thousand Iraqi regulars with tanks, modern fighter aircraft
(some of them American-made), and guns mounted on the escarpment
which edged the field and frowned down upon the cantonment. The
Iraqis could have rushed it and annihilated the defenders in a single

night, but held off in the hope of capturing it without suffering casualties.

In the Basrah bar I learned that Habbaniya had just been freed, the Iraqi Army badly drubbed by the R.A.F. operating from Trans-Jordan and elsewhere along the fringe, the Rashidi uprising falling apart; but that Baghdad was seething with riots, now chiefly against the Jews, and the surrounding desert areas were infested with Arab marauders on the rampage for loot. All communications were cut as far as the Turkish frontier.

Captain Smirnoff rightly felt disinclined to risk his aircraft in a landing at Baghdad. I found the Air Officer Commanding R.A.F. outside the bar. He rarely entered that haven, he said, lest it prove too great a strain on his devotion to duty to leave it when duty called. With him I arranged that the *Wielewaal* should land at Habbaniya to drop me off—the first non-R.A.F. plane to touch wheels there since the start of the disturbance. This required a bit of handling, he said, as they would probably shoot at us unless warned. He undertook to communicate the warning and authorization to land there by highest priority, "Urgent," radio message.

We took off in the steaming dark at 4:00 A.M., and at 6:00 circled Habbaniya as instructed. Captain Smirnoff had no red flares, which were part of the recognition procedure laid down for friendly aircraft coming in to that field, but we managed to land without being fired on. We had not been expected. Smirnoff, in his convincing way, said "fill her up" to an R.A.F. corporal, who, without comment, filled the tanks with high-octane fuel. During that process I checked my total of 17,965 miles in ten flying days from New York, an average of just on eighteen hundred miles a day. Smirnoff then took off for Gaza and I was left talking to a sergeant about the siege.

"Silly buggers," he said dispassionately of the Iraqi besiegers. "They was clean around us, with their guns at point-blank range on that there bloody escarpment. They could 'ave pickled the lot of us if they'd struck."

An hour and a half later the Urgent radio message of the night before came through from Basrah, advising of my coming and requesting that the *Wielewaal* should not be fired on.

The senior R.A.F. Staff Officer assigned a car to take me into Baghdad, along with two British refugees from Mosul and an enormous dog of one of them. The dog was as big as an Iraqi cow, and I saved his life by agreeing to take him. There was no other means of transporting him nor any food for his maintenance, so he otherwise would have been shot.

Armed patrols were circulating through Baghdad, and machine guns commanded the main intersections on Rashid Street. Except for these and the sound of an occasional shot the town was quiet. The previous day the Iraqi Army had turned on the rioters and mowed down a good number, which had tended to slow things up. The riots were serious while they lasted. There had been rape, mutilation and murder, with about a thousand casualties between the Jews and rioters together, and extensive sacking of shops and houses marked in advance under the eyes of the police. Some Jewish women and girls were raped first and then thrown from the roofs. Yet a number of Jews were saved from the rioters by the Arabs. All this was an aftermath of the collapse of Rashid Ali's insurrection.

The Rashidis sprung their *coup d'état* on the date originally set by the Germans, but the Germans had been thrown off schedule by about a month, owing to their campaign in Greece and Crete. Had they not, the fate of Iraq might well have been different and the situation in the Middle East even more tenuous than it was. When the collapse came Rashid Ali fled to Teheran, taking with him the Grand Mufti of Jerusalem and £175,000 from the Iraqi Treasury. The Iraqi frontier post relieved him of the money, and the Iranian post took the party's arms and armored vehicles, but let Rashid Ali and the Mufti pass.

I stopped five days in Baghdad with Paul Knabenshue, the American Minister. There was then no way to get out in the direction I was heading. And two days in advance of the event, which took place at 0330 hours on 8 June, I learned from the British Ambassador that the British and Free French were going to strike in Syria, which would doubtless close, for some time at least, that avenue of approach to my destination.

Paul Knabenshue's conduct throughout the insurrection was splendid. On the morning of the *coup d'état*, when he was in pyjamas, shaving, a wide-eyed servant announced that the Regent was below. Half-shaved, he pulled on some clothes and rushed down, to find the Regent also in pyjamas. The Regent had just managed to escape through one door of the palace, thanks to a trusty chauffeur, as the Rashidis were coming in by another door to seize him.

Paul Knabenshue drove his wife out to Habbaniya in his car, with a Legation dragoman and an American flag. Mrs. Knabenshue sat in back. At her feet was a bundle wrapped in a rug. The bundle was the Regent. At the long, narrow bridge over the Euphrates they were held up by a Rashidi guard, who passed them but looked a bit inquisitive. Just then a donkey laden with camel-thorn entered the far end of the bridge. Paul Knabenshue decided not to risk waiting, lest the guard's curiosity lead him to look under the rug. The car lunged ahead, raced across the bridge and hit the donkey smack in the rear when the little beast swung suddenly around, catapulting donkey and load clear off the bridge. The car was then in the clear, as the Rashidis had not yet crossed the river, and the Regent was allowed to come up for air. From Habbaniya the R.A.F. flew the Regent to Transjordan, Mrs. Knabenshue to Basrah.

Paul Knabenshue returned and organized the Legation for a state of siege. He took in 170 British and Americans from the area of the American Legation—mostly British (the British Embassy was on the other side of the Tigris and rather far away), several of whom were still there when I arrived; and sheltered them for five weeks behind barricaded and sand-bagged gates and windows. They were encircled by Rashidi soldiers and military police, their communications cut, and a cannon was mounted at point-blank range of about fifty yards. The Rashidi Foreign Minister sent a message to Knabenshue that the Legation would be bombed within an hour unless he ceded his British refugees. This he refused to do without proper assurances for their safety, which were not forthcoming. The Government, however, thought better of the bombing.

To the Government's demand that he dismiss his Iraqi servants he acceded. The refugees pitched in to run the camp. Bankers and doctors cleaned floors and did the laundry; a judge did the ironing; a young British girl who was the governess of the six-year-old King did a most excellent job of running the mess in four shifts (food supplies were permitted to be brought in from day to day). They had a considerable armament of rifles, shotguns and revolvers and were prepared to stand off any sort of mob, though hardly a concerted attack by the Army. The American flag flew day and night from the staff.

They dug latrines in the garden, kept the swimming-pool filled with emergency drinking water, operated a machine shop in the cellar, made glasses and candlesticks by cutting beer bottles in half and fashioning handles from brass strip, maintained a bar (one beer before lunch, two tots of whisky in the evening), published a daily sheet called *Knabenews,* put on theatrical efforts and concerts, and all told, made a very good show of it under the circumstances.

The British in Baghdad could not speak too highly of Paul Knaben-shue. His prompt and effective action undoubtedly saved many people from indignity, assault and probable death. After the frequent occasions in which Americans have sought refuge in British Embassies and Legations, it was gratifying to find an American Minister returning the British gesture in kind, and doing it extremely well.

I took the first train from Baghdad to Mosul—the first out of Baghdad in any direction since the disturbance stopped all transportation services. The carriage was riddled by bomb splinters, and the three Englishmen who accompanied me and I ate our picnic dinners with loaded revolvers by our sides, and later slept on them. For the countryside was extremely insecure, with wandering tribesmen armed from Syria, and parties of disbanded but armed Iraqi soldiery, all out for loot.

Finch, the British Consul at Mosul, I had last seen when I stayed with him in Kermanshah fourteen years before. He, with ninety-five others, including seventeen American well drillers, missionaries and engineers, had been interned for thirty days in the small Consulate without any news of the outside world, since the Iraqis had removed their radios. The Iraqi military guard were unamiable, and by about the third week the ninety-six cramped internees were not too happy. Finch did not dilate upon this, but remarked that the grace said by the missionaries over the bad, often spoiled food and the language of the well drillers sometimes made an odd blend.

All the houses of foreigners had been thoroughly looted. Mosul town was not very safe because a young R.A.F. pilot, flying over to bomb the German Messerschmitts on the airfield a few days before, had let go at the upturned faces of a considerable group of people standing in front of a coffee house. He got seventy-five of them, all Moslems, and the episode had not been well received by the remainder of the population.

When I went into the bazar in a car with two British co-travellers we took an Arab police escort. The Englishmen were smoking peculiarly vile cigars called "Morning Glories," and the effect of these, on top of the lurching of the car, suddenly turned the Arab a nauseous green. We stopped and pulled him from the car, with Captain Corry of the Iraq Police shouting at him in Arabic: "Face into the wind! Face into the wind!" But it was too late. The guardian of our safety tottered towards a wall, stumbling over his rifle, and there retched with dreadful groans for full five minutes. He was not much good as an escort after that, but we propped him up in the seat, resting the muzzle of his rifle through the open window, in which manner he continued to serve his purpose though scarcely conscious.

By chance (for the railway west of Mosul had been out since the R.A.F. had blown a little bridge in northeast Syria) I discovered the Taurus Express standing in the Mosul station with steam up. The bridge had just been repaired, and the train turned out to be a special for the evacuation of Minister Gabrielli and seventeen other members of the Italian Legation Staff, expelled from Baghdad and on their way to Italy under diplomatic *sauf-conduits*.

I had rather expected that I might have to ride a mule, with an armed escort, through the Kurdish hills to the nearest point in Turkey where perhaps I could get a car to take me to Diyarbekir on the Anatolian railway, a trip involving considerable complications. The Italians had not yet arrived when I discovered their special train all steamed up. They came by motor from Kirkuk with three armored cars as escort. When they did arrive, dirty, hot and tired, they found me ensconced, with the connivance of the *Chef du Train* and well barricaded with baggage, in the center compartment of the one *Wagon-lits*. There was a lot of talk, with gestures, in Italian, French and Arabic, bearing on the insufficiency of accommodations, which I tranquilly disregarded. Eventually the train chugged off. Forty-seven hours later I arrived in Ankara, having skirted northern Syria without undue difficulty, and after a few days continued on to Istanbul.

The Pearl of the Bosporus was an interesting spot to be in just at that time. Astride the crossroads between the Balkans and the Middle East, the Mediterranean and Black Seas, Istanbul was the best listening post in Europe and western Asia. It was also the breeding ground *par excellence* of rumors. Rumors sprang fully armed like Pallas from the brow of Zeus; littler ones grew and flourished as the rose tree of an Indian fakir. All of them came "straight from the horse's mouth." It was among the oddities of Istanbul that there were more horses' mouths than horses.

Istanbul was the mingling place of an extraordinary collection of nationalities. It always has been, but the circumstances of the war accentuated this. Voyagers of all kinds, some of them on *bona fide* business or governmental missions, others less unequivocal, all of them potential sources of information, came from almost every country of Europe and much of Asia, despite the difficulties of transportation and visas. Evacuees and diplomatic staffs whose missions had abruptly terminated poured through in both directions: Axis and satellite nationals from Syria, Russia, Iran and Afghanistan heading west; more than eleven hundred Russians, in one mass exodus from Axis and Axis-occupied countries, wending homeward eastwardly by circuitous routes.

De Gaullist escapees from German-held areas, on their way to join the Fighting French, passed Vichy-French returning to the aegis of the "senile Marshal." Jewish refugees from Romania, without passports or authorized destinations, tried in grim desperation to escape through the Straits in fantastically overpacked, unseaworthy little craft. One of these, the *Struma,* grossing 262 tons, was turned back after having been held for seven weeks in the roadstead opposite the massive white marble palace of Dolma Bahçe. Just outside the mouth of the Bosporus she foundered, and of her 769 passengers there was one survivor.

In the roadstead swung jauntily at anchor the shapely white bulks of the *Basarabia* and *Transilvania,* prides of the Romanian merchant fleet; the *Svanetia,* luxury liner of the U.S.S.R.; and the Turkish President's yacht *Savarona,* formerly belonging to an American lady and probably the most sumptuously fitted craft of her type in the world. Around them, taking on or discharging cargoes or just waiting their chances, were a sizable though varying collection of other vessels flying the Romanian, Greek, Bulgarian, Russian, German, British, Hungarian, Italian and Turkish flags; all, save the Turks, in preparation for unannounced dashes north or south through the blockades of mines, submarines, destroyers and aircraft maintained by both conflicting sides.

Up and down the Bosporus and out into the Marmara, in summer, the Embassy and Naval Attachés' launches of the four principal European belligerents flaunted the colors of their respective nations. Often the Hammer-and-Sickle of the Soviet launch, or the white ensign of the British *Macook* or *Bluejacket* would pass by Baron Franz von Papen's German speedster flying an enormous, blatant swastika flag and three swastika pennants with the Nazi buzzard spread-winged upon them, followed by the Italian launch sprouting Fascist flags and pennants all over it, like a beribboned poodle trailing its mistress.

The American Embassy also had a launch, the *Hiawatha,* but it was seldom used.

All the belligerents maintained huge intelligence staffs, disguised in various ways. Most of the personnel were known by sight to one another. On several occasions I lunched or dined at the Park Hotel with a party of British and Americans, while at the table on one side sat Ludwig Moyzisch, Chief of the German Gestapo in Turkey (formerly Chief of Staff to Seyss-Inquart in Austria) amidst a group of his collaborators; on the other side sat a gathering of Italian intelligence officers, and behind us a table full of Japanese. From time to time one of us would drop an "indiscreet" remark in audible tone, feeling certain that it would be picked up, and would watch for the effect.

Turkey was a neutral enclave completely encircled by territories under belligerent occupation. The neutrality was nervous and artificial. The Turks on the whole inclined to our side, but they were realists and had not been unobservant of the fate of other Balkan States that had been forced to take a decision and disintegrated gallantly, without effectual support. Yet most well-informed Turks realized that Turkey would cease to exist as an independent nation should the Axis win.

Into that curious atmosphere the enigmatic figure of Franz von Papen fitted perfectly. He was the suavest and the ablest of the diplomats in Turkey. He repeatedly assured the Turks that there would be no act of aggression on Germany's part as long as he remained at his post. Consequently, whenever he went to Berlin or elsewhere in Nazi-held Europe, the Turkish high officials and foreign observers were on the *qui vive* for signs of an impending Axis attack. His infrequent absences were also watched to see if by chance one of them might end in his liquidation. For von Papen, though not many people would trust him farther than one could throw a water buffalo by the tail, was no dyed-in-the-wool Nazi. There were plenty of high-ranking Party members, including von Ribbentrop's sister in the German Embassy at Ankara, who earnestly desired his ruin.

He strove incessantly to destroy British and Allied power in the Middle East. Through the German Embassy's "Oriental Department" in Istanbul he planned revolts of pro-Axis elements in Syria, Lebanon, Palestine, Iraq, Iran and Afghanistan to coincide with a German drive on Turkey and the Near East.

That the Axis did not strike in this area after Crete, instead of invading Russia, was perhaps one of the vital strategical errors of the war. The Turks would have resisted any passage of their territory. But the British were too hard pressed in too many places to have afforded immediate or effective support. The German military machine, then in its mechanized flower, could probably have swept through Turkey in twenty days, or have by-passed and isolated the Anatolian plateau. Had Franz von Papen's program been followed instead of the Russian gamble, it seems clear that the German thrust must have captured the oil fields of Iraq and Iran, at least interdicting the Suez Canal, as well as controlling the access to the Black Sea. In that event, the subsequent complexion of the war could have been very different.

I went up the Black Sea to the Russian border by Batum aboard one of the Turkish coastwise vessels that crept from open roadstead to open roadstead, close inshore and only by daylight because of mines and torpedoes, beneath the rugged splendor of the Anatolian highlands. The decks, on the outward trip, were jammed with Turkish soldiers; with sheep during the return. There was no difference in the manner or the tightness of their packing, save that the sheep came aboard three at a time, hoisted by their front legs, and the soldiers kept a small circle cleared wherein one or two would dance squatting Circassian dances for hours on end to the music of a single-stringed guitar held downward from the hip.

There was also little difference in the odors wafted from those tightly packed decks, and that little was in favor of the sheep. I recalled a British story from the 1914–18 phase of the war, about certain bets—the British will bet on practically anything—placed on the relative power of the odor of an Anatolian goat versus a Turkish prisoner of war. A judge with a sense of smell deemed appropriate to the task was duly appointed. The goat was led in first; the judge fainted. Then the Turkish soldier was brought in, and the goat fainted.

The Turkish Government and most Turks who lived in the area of the Straits were acutely sensitive to the threat of Russian domination from the north. They were largely pro-United Nations, but the fact of Russia having fortuitously become one of these did not increase Turkish enthusiasm for the United Nations' cause. It was of interest, therefore, to find that along the southeastern Black Sea coast, facing and contiguous to Russia, the bulk of the population had not that feeling.

They hated the Germans, whom they knew from 1914–18 associations. *"Alleman"* (German) was an opprobrious term on the Turkish Black Sea coast. But the Russians who had occupied that coast as enemies had conducted themselves in such a manner that the Circassian Turks retained no unpleasant memories of the occupation or the occupiers.

Shortly before their German-engendered declarations of war on us I went into Bulgaria and Romania. It was interesting to be among the German invaders—"protectors" in these States, blatant and dictatorial in their field uniforms—to see the German signposts of direction for motor transport, tanks, hospitalization and a multitude of other arms and services plastered all over Sofia and Bucarest. I sat amidst the protectors as they consumed the fat and the cream and the wines of their unhappy satellites, who even then, though *sub rosa,* were beginning to evince their acute dislike of their masters.

It was interesting to meet one's secret contacts in the dark of the blackouts—and no blackout I have seen was more impenetrable than that of Bucarest—by whistled tune and whispered word of recognition from a disembodied voice, then be guided by the arm to an unseen vehicle and driven tortuously to a secret rendezvous, listening for the sound of wheels, horses' hoofs or footsteps before one entered. How the driver ever sensed where he was going was beyond my understanding. If he could see anything in the India-ink opaqueness he had missed his vocation. He should have been a night fighter pilot. All driving lights were blacked out save for a little blue square the size and luminosity of a lump of sugar dipped in bluing. There were no other lights anywhere. Like Columbus, I did not know where I was going when I was on my way, I did not know where I was when I had arrived, and I did not know where I had been when I returned.

The Romanians were apathetic about the war. To be on the same side as Hungary had, for them, a grim absurdity. They were afraid of Russia. Many were not averse to a Hitlerian treatment of the Jews. But, except for a Fascist few, there was no enthusiasm for their German overlords.

At the end of September 1942 I returned by air across Africa to the United States, thus completing an aerial circuit of the world, save for the short link between Habbaniya and Gaza, for my fourth circumnavigation. The air-ferry route, which had played no small part in the turning back of Rommel, was now running full blast. Each intermediate field across the Anglo-Egyptian Sudan, French Equatorial Africa, Nigeria and the Gold Coast was dotted with aircraft of many types being ferried in a continuous stream to join the fray, with a few crashed and burnt ones that would never get there. The route followed a median line through the area marked on African maps "Region of Greatest Heat."

At Maidugari, in Nigeria, there was a young Polish pilot in the R.A.F. who had just been retrieved from the desert after fantastic adventures. His feet were in pretty bad shape, but his Polish imperturbability remained unshaken.

He had been wingman of a ferry flight of Spitfires when his engine suddenly "conked" and let him down over the flooded Lake Chad area. Apparently no one in the formation saw him drop out. He managed with considerable luck to set the Spitfire on the only patch of yellow, and therefore dry, ground anywhere in sight in a wilderness of swampy green. He stayed there for five days, firing four of his five flares, but no one appeared. His emergency provisions, though consumed with Spartan restraint, were running out; he was fighting a losing battle with the man-eating swamp mosquitoes, and he saw no future in sticking to his little patch of dryish land.

So he set forth across some of the most difficult going in Africa, from hummock to hummock, sometimes swimming, threading his way through dank jungle growth for days and days without being able to see anything beyond a few yards' distance. His feet swelled and his water-logged boots shrank, cutting off the circulation, so he abandoned his boots; in two days his feet were like raw, fly-blown legs of mutton.

There were snakes and crocodiles and hippopotami and elephants, but what all but finished him off were the mosquitoes. The heat by day was bad, though bearable in the swampy areas. At night he hung himself in the branches of trees, as the mosquitoes were a little less deadly above than on the ground, but sleep was well-nigh impossible. He drank the stinking swamp water and ate twigs and leaves and grasses. He killed one water beast—I think it was a small crocodile—with his last flare and a sharp stick, and ate it raw as he had no way of making a fire.

One day he came upon a sprawling native village. But an old man, who seemed to be a slave, limped out and warned him away. The old man spoke a few words of French. The men-folk of the village were away on a foray, he said; they were very bad men and if they should return and find the Pole they would surely eat him, for they were cannibals. The Pole thought he would make pretty poor eating in the then state of his being, but the old man seemed sincere, so the Pole hobbled on. The old man gave him a little food which undoubtedly saved his life, and indicated the general direction of the nearest settlement where people were not cannibals.

The Pole lost all sense of time. His feet were in such condition that he had to alternate hobbling with crawling on his hands and knees. In this fashion he came upon a jungle trail.

As he moved down the trail he was overtaken by a long file of black men bearing spears, shotguns, blowpipes, umbrellas, fans and honorific symbols. There was a large black man being carried in a chair. He wore a white topee above flowing but not very copious raiment. Beside him were footmen to fan him and protect him from the sun, and behind his chair walked his wives. There was another chair in which rode another and younger personage who it appeared was the older man's son. A lot more warriors brought up the rear.

The Pole did not much care by then whether he was to be eaten or not. But the big black man turned out to be the principal tribal chieftain of the district, an enlightened gentleman who eschewed human flesh. He also spoke a little French. After a formal exchange of introductions the Pole was placed in the second chair and thus proceeded to a distant village. He was fed, nursed and brought back to life, given two shiny black wives, and in due course ceremoniously accompanied the chieftain, swung in a chair and surrounded by attendants to all his needs, another ten days' journey to a point where he was picked up by jeep and taken to Maidugari.

He found there that it had been seven weeks since he went down in the Spitfire.

Clambering into a bucket-seated C-47 after it has stood for a couple of hours in the African sun, and then climbing to nine or ten thousand feet, is a test of one's resistance to pneumonia. The temperature inside the cabin on the ground was incredibly awful; before taking off one would be as wet as if dipped in a hot spring. I carried a spare shirt and a pull-over in my musette bag. At 3000 feet I removed my wet shirt and hung it up to dry; at 5000 I put on the dry one, at 8000 the pull-over. This I reversed on the way down, and so kept reasonably comfortable.

After touching at Ascension Island, where the wing tips of the C-54 used for the transatlantic flight appeared to be just missing both side walls of the landing strip blasted across the rugged island, I continued from Natal in another C-47 with a leopard cub, one medium-sized and seventeen small monkeys, and a bunch of overpaid, underdisciplined, as yet unmilitarized ferry pilots returning home. Of the lot, the leopard cub and the monkeys (though by the third day one could sense that there were monkeys aboard) were the best behaved. The larger monkey needed a bit of exercise from time to time, and would come gallivanting forward to the pilot's cockpit and tweak at the instrument settings. This the Captain of the ship reproved mildly; he had far more trouble with the ferry pilots.

At Borinquen in Puerto Rico the medium-sized monkey escaped into the uppermost reaches of a very large hangar. It took seven men with three extension ladders and several fire-extinguishers some four hours to retrieve her (it was a she-monkey). The rest of us not involved in the chase still preferred the monkeys to the ferry pilots.

One of the ferry pilots had got lost among the fleshpots of Georgetown, British Guiana, the night before, and failed to show up for the 4:00 A.M. take-off. So at Borinquen we made up his weight in good Puerto Rican rum at $10.00 a case.

Shortly after returning to Washington I transferred back to the Army Air Corps. This involved complications and a certain accuracy in timing, since by then an interim period as a civilian, even for a few hours, precluded being recommissioned in the A.A.F.

I was informed that probably none before me had sworn in as a senior officer in the Army while wearing Naval officer's uniform.

Return to Europe

After ten months with the Combined Chiefs of Staff at Washington I attended the "Quadrant" Conference between President Roosevelt and Prime Minister Churchill in Canada during September 1942. The bulk of the large American military and naval delegation proceeded by special train from Washington's Union Station to an unknown destination under the alias of "Abraham." It occurred to some of us with a modest knowledge of American continental history that Wolfe had fought Montcalm on the Plains of Abraham just outside the walls of Quebec. By way of encouragement along this line of thought, Annex No. 1 to our secret orders informed us that the Chateau Frontenac had been allocated to the exclusive use of the American and British delegations. We were, therefore, not wholly astounded to find ourselves approaching Quebec the following morning.

Annex No. 1 vouchsafed the further information that the Frontenac Room was reserved for senior officers and senior civilian delegates, where refreshments would be "provided"; while in another room, set apart for junior officers and civilian personnel, "drinks can be purchased." The senior officers, putting together these two items, arrived at a gratifying conclusion. Our guess proved correct, though there was just enough uncertainty on the subject to add a sporting zest to our evening relaxations. The chits we signed for our "refreshments" added up to tidy totals when sizable international groups forgathered for informal conference. But they did not bounce back. The Canadian Government's hospitality could not well have been more lavish or better done. We were not even allowed to pay for our laundry. The food was superb. To the British who came straight from London's drastic limitations the multiplicity and range of delectable dishes were a revelation and a godsend.

By and large the Conference carried on in a spirit of friendly and harmonious collaboration. Some of us, both British and American, had been warned, jokingly yet as one might be put on one's guard on entering a poker game against a group of hard-boiled and well-heeled players, not to accept anything less than Dominion status for our respective nations. We laughed over this together in the intimacies of the Frontenac Room. Differences in viewpoint existed, of course, particularly concerning some phases of the long-range conduct of operations in the China-Burma-India theatre. These were threshed out in lengthy committee meetings and gatherings.

People worked until late at night preparing relevant data for the next day's meetings. The logistics lads had the toughest job: I had only to rub a crystal ball and produce such things as the Japanese air reaction to contemplated operations twelve or eighteen months hence. Strange contraptions were solemnly considered, including an unsinkable aircraft carrier of vast dimensions made of ice and pulp. Inevitably, not everyone was completely happy over the scrapping of favored plans prepared through months of tedious effort, the drastic modification of others, the subordination of offensive activities in one part of the world to those deemed more immediately vital in another, the delicate questions of inter-Allied command. But on the whole the far-reaching military decisions arrived at in the First Quebec Conference reflected much credit on those who took them.

The conferees were guarded by antiaircraft batteries mounted on the Plains of Abraham, and by towering, resplendent Canadian "Mounties" scattered about the entry and through the halls of the Chateau Frontenac. There was a petite Wac pfc. on her first venture outside the confines of the United States whom I never saw, off duty, accompanied by less than seven six-foot-two troopers in bright scarlet uniforms. She was the most closely guarded person at the Conference, far more so than the President or Mr. Churchill. It may, of course, have been that the Mounties deemed it prudent to guard her against one another.

There was also a Second Lieutenant Wac on our delegation. She was slim and a good dancer, and went on the overnight boat-trip up the Saguenay River which the Canadians arranged for the combined staffs. I saw her dance successively that evening with General George Marshall, Field Marshal Sir John Dill, Admiral Lord Louis Mountbatten and Rear Admiral "Savvy" Cook.

The most picturesque of all the figures at the Conference was a British officer who came by the *Queen Mary* with Winston Churchill. He wore a dull brown, zippered Teddy Bear sort of battle dress without insignia except for the stars and crown of a Brigadier and a single ribbon with two rosettes that was the triple D.S.O. He was introduced at first as Brigadier Douglas, but by the second day, after his introducers had several times fallen into such lapses as, "Do you know Brigadier Wingate—I mean Douglas?" he emerged as Wingate. He was the organizer and leader of the "deep penetration groups" that had performed phenomenal feats throughout large areas of Japanese-held Burma.

Brigadier—later Major General—Wingate was a remarkable combination of a highly convincing realist with an almost mystic intuition of the enemy's mentality and reactions. He had a natural bent for jungle warfare, which he first employed with conspicuous success against the Italians in Ethiopia. When he entered the dining room of the Chateau Frontenac he walked with a curious gliding motion, peering keenly from side to side under his low-hanging, thick brown hair like a jungle animal taking stock of its surroundings. As he went to conferences in other rooms of the hotel he moved through the long corridors as though he were infiltrating behind the Japanese lines. It was a natural movement or one long acquired; not, I think, in any way an affectation.

Wingate had flown from Burma to London and had been delayed *en route* by weather. On his arrival he learned that the *Queen Mary*, with Winston Churchill and the Prime Minister's conference staff aboard, was to sail the next morning from Glasgow. So he had to take a night train which passed, though some distance apart, the night express from Edinburgh on which his wife was travelling to meet him in London. They had not seen each other in over three years.

The Prime Minister heard about this and ordered that Mrs. Wingate should be taken from her train and be rushed in the middle of the night across country to Glasgow. She was aboard the *Queen Mary* when Wingate came up the gangway in the morning. At Mr. Churchill's invitation she remained aboard. She was the only official wife, save for Mrs. Churchill, at the Conference. Mrs. Wingate was slim and dark-haired, with very pale skin. When she followed her husband into the dining room in a white semi-evening gown it was as though he were reconnoitering a passage for an improbable but unperturbed refugee through a potentially hostile jungle.

Wingate gave an interesting estimate of Japanese military reactions. "Take a Japanese unit, say a Division," he said, "and put it in a tight spot. The Japanese higher command states that the enemy will attack with superior forces, from a certain direction and using such and such tactics. The Division is told to stand its ground to the last man, though in view of the enemy's superior strength it is likely that the whole Division will be annihilated. And the Division, for the honor of the Emperor and the glory of its traditions, will do just that.

"Then take the same Division," he continued, "in the same place, under the same conditions, told the same thing. But the enemy doesn't do what he was supposed to. He attacks from another direction, in a different way, using quite different tactics. The whole Division loses its head, becomes confused, puts up an ineffectual resistance and doesn't even stand its ground." In Burma, and I think elsewhere, this happened a number of times, though it took imagination and good leadership to trick the little men into confusion.

Wingate told me of an occasion when he was leading one of his six "deep penetration groups" through the Burmese jungle far behind the Japanese lines. His men, save for some Burmese tribesmen, were by no means jungle-trained fighters. Some were British navvies drawn from the Calcutta docks, hastily trained and equipped in India. They crossed the Irrawaddy in a fanciful passage and slipped through the jungle to the edge of a small town that was a railway and road intersection. This place had often been bombed by Allied aircraft, though only by daylight. So the Japanese garrison, who didn't like being bombed, used to spend most of the day in the jungle. Burmese servitors prepared and cooked their evening meal, and when, as dusk approached, it was ready they would notify the Japanese by ringing a gong made of a triangle of railway rail.

The Burmese told this to Wingate when he arrived with his small force a little before the Japanese chow was prepared. He knew that he could summon the garrison from the forest by beating on the gong, and ambush them as they came in unsuspecting. But he did not do this. Instead he and his men ate the Japs' supper, instructed the Burmese not to ring the gong, and silently filtered away.

"That confused 'em," said Wingate, "more than anything we could do. I didn't particularly want a fight just then. When they finally came in, wondering why the gong hadn't rung, and discovered that their supper had been eaten and we had passed on, they didn't know what to make of it. The Burmese exaggerated our strength, and the Japs stood around hissing in their breath and saying, 'That, what mean?' It wasn't in the book. Their discomfiture lasted a long while and affected Jap morale over a good part of central Burma. I was informed about all this later. They don't appreciate mysteries."

Wingate's "deep penetration" groups were one of the things most enthusiastically approved and supported by the Conference. His death in an airplane accident some months later in Burma brought to an untimely end the brilliant and picturesque career of an officer who, in addition to the other military qualities he possessed, had a keen imagination.

After the Quebec Conference I flew over to London for three weeks' temporary duty at the Air Ministry, flew back to Washington for three weeks, and again to England for permanent duty as Assistant Chief of Staff (A-2) of the Ninth Air Force, which had been transferred from the Middle East and was being reformed as the Tactical Air Force for the invasion.

During the first of these trips the blitz returned to London. After a number of raidless months there was an alert nearly every night, with enemy bombers over the Greater London area on a good many of them. The warning of the "banshee"—the alert—resounded in every quarter of the vast city, frequently more than once during the nights in the dark of the moon when the enemy bombers were less easily picked up by R.A.F. night fighters. The millions who listened to its wail carried on with their duties, continued to eat their late dinners with a slightly forced nonchalance, cursed the interrupters of their rest and turned over, or descended with cold distaste into the shelters or the Underground, according to their temperaments and circumstances. The wardens and fire fighters and rescue squads strapped on their steel hats and went to their assigned posts, though they may have had little sleep the night before. The "ack-ack's" shattering roar, the expended flak coming down like metallic hail, the *"whoosh-whoosh"* of the rocket batteries in Hyde Park flinging their sizzling greeting through the crisscross of the searchlights were ample to rouse them if they drowsed.

By the half-light of morning further grim scars, some still smouldering, added to the voids and gutted shells of buildings of the city Hitler had promised to rub out.

Whoever designed the "banshee" turned out a masterpiece of sinister tone. It was not a terrifying sound, but it drove home a malignant implication. Very many people have heard the banshee in London and elsewhere in England, hundreds upon hundreds of thousands of them a great many times. For many thousands it was among the last sounds they ever heard. Those who have not heard it missed the high symbol of unity and understanding between soldier and civilian in Britain; a unity based on sharing the common danger of death and dislocation and acute discomfort, on mutual respect for stoicism in the face of violent enemy action, which the happier inhabitants of a community *at* but not *in* war, as was the United States, can never fully appreciate.

There was no class consciousness or distinction in British fortitude, just as there was no part of the United Kingdom nor any facet of British life not drastically affected by the war.

A thick autumnal fog lent its dour grimness to the days—the so-short days that made a feeble start at about nine and died out by four o'clock, merging almost imperceptibly into the long, blacked-out nights whose opaque density under the fog had an unfathomable unreality. The blackouts of Bucarest and, later, on the Anzio beachhead were as complete in their blackness, when the sky was dark, as man could well devise. In those, one simply could not see. But in the London blackout-*cum*-fog one had the sense of being enshrouded. It was as if a thick black tent had quietly collapsed over everything, with no available exit.

If there was no raid one could flash an electric torch intermittently downward, provided its brightness was dimmed by a couple of sheets of tissue paper or, more usually, their equivalent from the toilet. But this served no better end, when the fog was down, than possibly to reveal the edge of the pavement without suggestion as to its destination. Walking any distance in the London blackness on those foggy nights which began in mid-afternoon was a test of one's sense of direction, of one's luck and perseverance.

Several times, though I was no stranger to London town, I found myself with little more idea of where I was than a transplanted mollusc. Off the main thoroughfares like Oxford and Regent Streets and Piccadilly one met few persons on a thick night. Two or three times, when I attempted afoot to find an address that I thought I should be able to locate, I barged into some unseen individual who knew where *he* was and set me, for a while, on the correct course. But mostly I felt my way along depopulated streets, which never seemed to be the right ones or to lead in any consecutive direction, with about the same assurance I would have had groping through an unexplored cavern in a mountain of black basalt.

There were busses, the Underground, and a modest number of taxis driven by ancient hackmen who had been disillusioned soon after birth. Travel by bus at night was complicated by a number of things, including the probability that after a long and dreary wait you couldn't get on it—it was already packed. If you did, it was the wrong bus, or you got off at the wrong place. The Underground operated until midnight, if one could locate a station. Occasionally, after futilely stabbing about in the dark, I would reach a station to find that the last train had departed and the only signs of life were some scores or perhaps hundreds of people stretched out for the night in its cheerless security.

A taxi, or rather a small slice of a taxi, could often be had at one of the larger hotels if time was no object. The driver, of course, had to be agreeable to one's proposed destination. For the return, the probability of finding a vehicle was about equivalent to that of drawing a horse in the Irish Sweep.

On the clearer nights—there were some—one could see two or three yards and make one's way about with a good deal more certainty. Then a downward flashing torch would reveal, along the dark reaches of the Bayswater Road and many other parts of London, certain evidences of Anglo-American amity. By the walls and stone balustrades; in re-entrant angles and entryways, were many pairs of shod feet, always two by two. One male pair and one female pair, usually facing each other, and sometimes the female pair would be uplifted on its toes. Above the feet were bodies, male and female, pressed tightly together; and nine times out of ten the male body was that of an American soldier.

There were other characteristics of the London scene by day. Barrage balloons at rest poked their snouts from the midst of the trees in green parks and squares like water buffaloes in their wallows, under the widespread surveillance of perhaps a hundred of their kind floating fatly in the sky. The cement tanks of "static water," built in a multitude of places such as by the side of Westminster Abbey and in empty spaces where large buildings formerly had stood, were grim reminders of the disastrous fires in the early days of the blitz when sufficient water to fight with was not available.

The array of British uniforms worn by a multiplicity of nationals, many of whom spoke little or no English, carrying their identification on their left shoulders in little patches labeled from "Norway" to "Italy" with nearly all the nations in between, visualized a part of what the "United Nations" comprised. The extent of the buildings requisitioned for headquarter and staff activities of the United States forces gave a foretaste of what the American invasion of England was to be. In certain sectors such as Grosvenor Square the American occupation had taken over the great majority of the houses and the oval park in the center where motor transport was garaged under the trees. From this sprang the apt travesty on a currently popular song—"A Nightingale Was Heard in Berkeley Square," rendered as "An Englishman Was Heard in Grosvenor Square." The one seemed hardly more improbable than the other.

These things and many others encountered by day and by night were the background against which the quiet resolution of the people of London and of all Britain stood out in the greatness of a spirit that, undaunted, uncomplaining, unbragging, had maintained a mass resistance never surpassed in history.

The Ninth was building up to be the world's largest Air Force. At the time of the invasion it comprised approximately 174,000 officers and men, with medium and light bombers, fighters and fighter-bombers, photo reconnaissance, troop carriers and gliders, cooperating directly with and covering the ground forces. The Eighth, the Strategic Air Force, did the high-altitude heavy bombing of enemy industrial targets and distant military centers. Together with the R.A.F. and the Air Forces operating out of Italy they were credited by von Rundstedt and other German high commanders, whom we captured later, with having been the basic cause of the Wehrmacht's disruption and collapse in the west.

Until the invasion the Ninth had no ground forces with which to cooperate, except in exercises on the Devon coast. Our efforts were directed primarily at pounding enemy airfields, railway marshalling yards, suspicious constructions intended to serve as launching sites for V-bombs and rockets, and other installations in France and the Low Countries. This in itself was no small program.

Major—later Lieutenant—General Lewis H. Brereton commanded the Ninth. I had relieved "Louie" in three successive commands in France during the summer of 1918, and later was Assistant Military Attaché for Aviation at the American Embassy in London when he held a similar detail in Paris. He had changed little in the interim. Short, aggressive, frequently irascible, he had a mind as keen as a razor and often as cutting. He "knew his stuff" and was lightning swift in his strategical and tactical appreciations; but he was not always very diplomatic, largely because he did not make the effort to be. In relaxation he was a gay and amusing companion. He loved *bons mots* and was adept in producing them. There was an occasion when one of his senior staff officers expressed apprehension over a personnel request the "old man" proposed to make which several of the staff viewed with concern. Louie glared at him in cold displeasure.

"When I need a Colonel to run the Ninth Air Force I may call on you," he snapped, "and again I may not!"

"General, I'm only trying to keep you from what some of us feel could prove a mistake. You *have* made a few of that sort, you know," said the Colonel.

"Well, I hope you're not going to turn out to be one of them!" retorted Louie and, pleased with that sally, immediately fell into an excellent humor.

Louie Brereton's incessant mobility sometimes was the despair of his staff. But he did a splendid job, with the aid of several highly capable subordinate commanders, in organizing and directing a most effective force for paralyzing enemy resistance.

England was turning rapidly into a vast airfield. France, Belgium and Holland were becoming a proving ground for tactical air operations; while the heavies of the Eighth kept on pounding the enemy's strategical centers. One of the disadvantages of cross-Channel air operations was that when our targets were clear our bases were very apt to be weathered in, or vice versa. Even flying between headquarters and some of our many fields, though they were so located as to be as nearly fog-free as possible, was often attended by long delays. Sometimes I would go by jeep, and here again one's schedule was fortuitous, especially when one didn't know the road. Directions from local inhabitants were usually wrong and at best not easy to follow, though they nearly always ended with, "You cahn't miss it!"

One foul evening, after I had been creeping over a winding road in the dark and fog with blackout lights the size of lumps of sugar not even throwing to the hedge on the near side of the road, I reached a straggling village. A venerable inhabitant emerged from an unseen pub and helped set me on my way.

"You goes over the 'ill and takes the left fork across the common," he said. "Then you turns right where the church used to be, and right again at the second public house on the left—that's the King's 'Ead. You cahn't miss it!" The hell I cahn't, I thought and was right.

Our manual on deflection firing from medium bombers was entitled "You Can't Miss It!" It was easier to hit an Me-109 than one's way in the dark from local directions.

In March 1944 I proceeded on temporary duty to the Italian front, and flew out in a B-17. From the tip of Cornwall we struck southwestwardly across the Bay of Biscay beneath a 500-foot ceiling, seeing only the leaden water below (there were apt to be Hun patrols above) until we picked up Cap Finisterre in Spain. Then, in the first cloudless sky

I had seen in four months, we skirted Portugal and dropped into Gibraltar in the early afternoon.

The contrast in those few hours between war-gripped, foggy England and The Rock gave an odd feeling of unreality. In the soft sunlight beautifully bright oranges, tangerines, lemons and bananas, all but impossible to obtain in England, were being sold everywhere from small roadside stands and pushcarts and by innumerable grocers. The shops were well stocked with edibles, tinned and otherwise. Good Spanish wines, sherry, brandy, English gin and even Scotch whisky were to be had at reasonable prices. There was no blackout. That evening "Bruce" Freeland and I watched the searchlights playing on the ships in the roadstead, the lights of Algeciras gleaming from across the bay through the palms and pines. From our window in the Rock Hotel we looked down upon the brilliantly lighted Naval base and at the riding lights of the ships anchored in the moon-path beyond. There was not even a blackout curtain. It seemed that there must be something wrong with the picture—it couldn't *really* be that way.

In the morning, after dodging Spanish Morocco, we chased our shadow over the chocolate-colored soil of the rich farmlands of Algeria, the green basins, the treeless brown and red rolling hills, and little rivers—dry in summer but now full to the brim with clay-colored torrent—looping their way to the sea. Large fields of grain, of vineyards, of very orderly orchards, stretched out protected from the winds by tight rows of poplars, cypresses and eucalyptus. Rambling adobe-colored Arab villages interspersed new French villages whose cheerful white walls and red tiled roofs were neat but uninteresting in their American checkerboard lines. The aspect from the air of that well-developed part of Algeria was prosperous and smiling.

"Them A-rabs," commented our navigator after we took off from Maison Blanche, "are the goddamnedest thieves in the entire world! Why, one of 'em got into the tent of our bombardier and stole his pants —he had 'em rolled up under his head—without ever waking him up!" The navigator was matching coins and bills of various nationality, including an Alexander-the-Great piece, over the drift sight with a spare flight officer. The navigator eventually got them all, leaving the flight officer penniless as we headed towards Bizerte.

The variegated sea was flecked with small patches of white foam like whipped cream. Robin's-egg blue streaked the darker blue of the depths, over the shallows and where the silt-laden rivers debouched;

and there were purple patches from the shadows of the clouds. White sea-birds drifting sideways in the wind made tiny dots, distinguishable from the foam-crests they sailed across. The plane's shadow kept a little ahead, like an outrider, not quite so deep purple as the shadows of the clouds.

Tunis was weathered in, so we by-passed it, and in due time picked up the salt pans of Stagone island: each rectangle a different shade from white to a tender green, backed by whimsical windmills. The pumice-colored town of Trapani, hooking out to sea, dropped behind. Then there was nothing save the tousled Mediterranean, until Vesuvius's languid smoke-plume led us over green fields and pollarded willows draped with trellised vines to the cluttered landing field of Pomigliano, whose buildings had been razed by Allied bombs topped off with German dynamite.

That night in Naples was enlivened by the furious roar of ack-ack, the crash of heavy bombs close around us (it was the only destructive raid the Germans threw against the city), and things seemed more natural. They seemed still more natural a day later going up to the battle of Cassino, for there I sloughed off twenty-nine years and save for a few minor discrepancies was transported back to Flanders in 1915.

The road followed a narrow valley between medium-sized ranges, with bigger mountains beyond. There was an almost solid line of traffic going out, a not quite so solid line of empties—except for the loaded ambulances—coming back: trucks, jeeps, command cars, desert wagons, guns, tanks, motorcycles, scout cars, signal cars, bulldozers, pontoons on wheels and all the other varied panoply of attack. Many of the trucks were taking troops up to the line—New Zealanders, British, Americans white and colored, French, French Africans, Indians, Poles. Alongside the road were ammunition, engineer and other supply dumps, field hospitals, parks of all sorts of armored and other vehicles, tents under olive trees and on the sides of hills; and everywhere mess, debris and wastage. All the villages and farms were devastated, yet there were some civilians working in the fields close behind the lines. Every bridge was blown, with temporary structures of wood or by-passes around; and off to the sides vehicles were struggling in knee-deep mud. Guns of many calibers barked from distances down to fifteen feet from our heads, their flashes sparkling across the hillsides and torn valleys like fireflies on a summer evening.

The scenes, the spirit, the smells, the atmosphere were almost identical with Flanders in 1915–17; except that in Flanders there were no snow-covered mountains or olive groves, and here there were no swollen bodies of dead horses covered with chloride of lime. There used to be a lot of those in the earlier phase of the war in Europe. They saddened me then, and I detested the stench and the inflated entrails coiling out behind. But now I somehow missed that familiar part of the wreckage of warfare.

The Battle of Cassino was, in its essential respects, 1915–17 style—blasting one's way with human bodies for a few yards of gain through incredibly bad fighting country where the defense had nearly all the advantage. "Uncle Joe" Cannon's medium bombers did a perfect job of demolition on the town itself, but the craters filled with water and held up our tanks, which also were unable to get around over the flooded fields. I was in the eastern end of the town—we held about three-quarters of it then—when a New Zealand tank came back through the dense smoke screen, a fantastic sight, all white and covered over with rubble, chunks of concrete, plaster and mortar like a brontosaurus that had gone beserk in a cement mill. I later saw the sole survivor of a company of Germans which had been annihilated by the previous day's bombing. He had gone completely cuckoo.

There was a good deal of disappointment that the German resistance at Cassino should be so strong after the plastering inflicted on that unhappy little town from the air. But the terrain greatly aided the defense, and some of the senior air officers were not particularly impressed by the over-all strategy, which seemed generally unimaginative. "Uncle Joe" Cannon was among them.

I had not seen "Uncle Joe" since we flew around Europe together in 1930. He was a Captain in those days. Now he wore two stars—soon would receive a third—and was heavier by quite a few pounds, but otherwise he was the same quiet, sound and genial officer he had been on that tour. He was proud of his Twelfth Air Force and especially of the 42nd Wing, which did a beautiful job at Cassino and which he considered the keenest outfit of medium bombers in the world. I met him in the incredible pink palace at Caserta that housed practically all the high Allied headquarters in Italy, with marble-topped gilt console tables holding the files under frescoed ceilings and corporals typing on golden desks from gilt and tapestried chairs. General Eaker's Mediterranean Allied Air Force offices were half a mile or so away in the same building, and his mess and quarters, where I spent a few nights, were in the beautiful "English Garden" beyond the marble and stucco watercourse fringed with ornate marble statues.

When the Battle of Cassino bogged down in temporary stalemate I flew up to the Anzio beachhead. And here I was taken back to the Ypres salient in 1915. The landing strip, port and whole beachhead were under spasmodic daily shell-fire and nightly bombing. VI Corps command post at Nettuno seemed curiously familiar, though I had not been there before, in its catacomb of wine cellars deep in the subsoil reached by a long flight of steps, spread through many zigzagging passages on various levels, each office in a separate recess. Miles of electric light and telephone wires were strung overhead; pin-up girls shared the hewn earthen walls with maps, charts and aerial photos.

I slept in another wine cellar deep underground, furnished with carved wash-hand stands, commodes and night tables from smashed buildings, some framed prints on the walls, and a fifty-gallon urinal can which was not very regularly emptied. There were two feeble electric lights. A wood-burning stove with a very long pipe kept the place filled with acrid smoke. Slimy ooze, unpleasant to touch, covered the walls two inches deep. The first night a kindly Colonel gave me a slug of the worst gin I have ever tasted. But I slept well and each morning awoke thinking I was in Ypres.

Outside, on cloudy nights, the darkness was complete. *No* lights were permitted, not even a match. Moving about the narrow, tortuous streets with their roughly filled shell holes was tricky after dark, even if shell-fire flashes occasionally helped. Forward of the Divisional Command Posts, on most of the roads, movement was permitted only at night, since the roads were under enemy observation.

"Ducks" scuttled in to the beach by day with loads from the ships outside—sometimes between geysers from enemy shells exploding in the water—, waddled ashore and careened off on the roads towards the forward dumps. From the jetty Negro truck drivers with staring white eyeballs drove hell-for-leather over a route not highly esteemed for its tranquillity. There was a short-cut past a frequently shelled corner where the black cat insignia of a British unit had been painted, with a pointing arrow. It was a quicker way out of the worst of the shelling, but no Negro would take it because of that black cat.

The roads were pitted and either exceedingly dusty or muddy as buffalo wallows. They were marked with a multitude of signs: "No

halting on road"—"No passing"—"No lights at night"—"No stopping"—
"Keep 50 yds apart for safety"—"Look out for wire," and so on. Other
signs urged the use of the prophylactic stations (a few civilians were
still living in shacks and huts over the battle area), and a series of four
did so in doggerel: "Private Joe Doaks"—"A Happy Lad Was He"—
"Forgot To Take His Pro"—"Now He Has V.D."

One night a patrol went out on our right between the lines, which
were there fairly far apart because of flooding. Seven men returned
together. About an hour later the eighth came back across the canal
that marked our forward position. When interrogated he said he had
nothing special to report but would like a shot of "Pro."

In the forward area many of the senior officers, as well as those on
Air Support Control, radar and similar activities, lived and had their
offices in dug-in, sandbagged trailers, though in most parts of the
beachhead water was so near the surface that it was difficult to dig in
except on slight elevations. The 45th Division Artillery Officer, Brigadier General McLain, had his trailer in a wood. Alongside it was a
large shell hole from a German 170 mm. that burst there two nights
before. The hole was half filled with water seepage. "Yesterday morning when I looked out," General McLain chuckled, "I found the Chap-
lain baptizing a soldier in it!"

Impromptu meetings on the battlefield sometimes have a fantastic
fortuity to them. I was in a Fighter Control trailer one day when a
Canadian Flying Officer in a white sweater came in. The American
Lieutenant in charge of the trailer recognized him at once as a classmate of his at Princeton whom he had not seen for five years.

"Good God! Where'd you drop from, Hank?" cried the Lieutenant.

Hank pointed straight up. "The sky," he said laconically. "Knocked
down by ack-ack. Just baled out of a Spit and landed alongside of you
here. I sure am glad to see you!"

The little Cub liaison planes did fine work on the beachhead, as
elsewhere. Flying back and forth at about twelve hundred feet they
did practically all the visual reconnaissance for the Divisions, adjusted
artillery fire and took oblique photos of enemy terrain. They were
warned of the approach of enemy fighters and then would take refuge
over "isles of safety" formed of dug-in half-tracks and trucks mounting
machine guns which could set up a box barrage around them. They
looked distinctly out of place, pottering nonchalantly around at about
eighty miles an hour over our lines, but probably no queerer than the

jeep I used with a stuffed, antlered reindeer head lashed in front in lieu of the wire-cutting beak.

One thing was generally admitted on the beachhead: the whole beachhead, and most everybody on it, would have been lost on 19 February had it not been for air support—fighter-bombers close in and light and medium bombers farther out. Airmen sometimes overstate their case by claiming the ability to do everything alone. But one may safely predict that there will be more change in the pattern of warfare when the next outbreak comes than there was between 1918 and 1944, and that the predominance of air power will inevitably be accentuated, along with long-range atomic projectiles, which may then destroy what is left of the world.

I flew back to Naples in the late afternoon of 22 March to find Vesuvius erupting dirty grey clouds up to twenty thousand feet. The Capodochino airfield, as usual, was encircled by three to four rows of closely packed aircraft of many different types, with one which had belly-landed lying prone in the middle, and ruggedly individualistic pilots taking off in several directions at the same time. We had to circle for ten minutes before getting down. In Naples I found my former billet occupied in strength by the 340th Bomber Group, whose baggage was all covered with black volcanic ash. They were refugees from the vicinity of Pompeii.

"The worst calamity since Pearl Harbor!" one of them moaned. For the first time in history a Bomber Group had been bombed out by a mountain. The eruption had hit them at two o'clock that morning on their field above the ruins of Pompeii. It came in a thick black downpour of volcanic cinders interspersed with glowing red-hot bits the size of golf balls, which piled up two feet deep on their aircraft and landing strip. They could not take off, and in the débâcle ninety B-25's were so badly damaged as to necessitate base repair. The control surfaces and plexiglass were completely ruined. Many of the young men of the combat and ground crews had visited the ruins of Pompeii a few miles farther down the slope and observed the devastation of 79 A.D. Few if any had ever seen a volcano before they camped on the slopes of Vesuvius. That they felt a certain emotion when in the middle of the night the mountain suddenly erupted on their heads is understandable.

Bruce Freeland and I went out the next day to the site of the disaster, but on this first attempt we could not find the field. We got thoroughly tangled up in a dense black rain of cinders that rattled on our command car like buckshot on a greenhouse. We could not make over three miles an hour through this, as it was impossible to see two feet even in the path of the headlights. When we finally broke out of it the twenty-thousand-foot cloud of cinders rising over Vesuvius piled blackly menacing against a background of white cumulus. There were fiery streaks down the side of the mountain, with great billows of red flame, and lightning flashed continually across the black spewings from the crater.

A few days later we found the field, a scene of grey desolation eighteen to twenty-four inches deep in volcanic ash. The Group head-quarters building had partly caved in and a nearby village was gradu-ally uncovering itself from its unwanted garment of penitence. Bull-dozers and scrapers had cleared a by-pass road, leaving four-foot banks of ash on either side. The olive groves were grey and stricken, the trees heavily powdered and the ground blanketed under a desolate mantle. Peasants were laboring mightily by hand to upturn the soil in the fields, for if a heavy rain should come the ash would set like cement and nothing could grow, whereas if it were turned under before the rain fell it would enrich the soil.

Twelve thousand civilians had been evacuated from the stricken villages—in many cases forcibly, for they clung to their scant posses-sions. But some remained who toiled with desperate intensity to save their land. The spring vegetables that mean so much to Italian sus-tenance had gone. The vine crop which produces the well-known Lacrima Christi was ruined, but if the ash could be worked under before the rain, next year's wine might be excellent.

On another scarp of the mountain we came to the village of San Sebastiano. This had been cut in two by a long river of lava fifty feet high and up to a quarter of a mile wide. One half of the village was intact: not even a layer of volcanic dust had settled on it, for the wind was the other way. The half that lay in the path of the flow had been blotted out without leaving a trace of what was there before, save where some house stood across the edge of the flow, and, like the village itself, half of it remained scarcely damaged and the other half was gone.

The slowly moving lava river had split around San Sebastiano's old church, which stood on a spur of the hill, most of the flow passing to the left; but the dome had collapsed under the impact and the edifice stood gaunt and broken, partly covered on its upper side by the hissing black river of eruption. Where the flow made an impassable road block across the main street little children were offering to barter

chunks of pure sulphur, dug from between the lumps of lava, for "cara-
mella" or cigarettes. But farther down the slope people with silver
crucifixes in their hands knelt as they faced the molten head of the flow,
still sluggishly creeping forward, and prayed for a divine miracle to
divert its course from a threatened village, house or orchard. Like an
enormous, fairy-tale black caterpillar with searing, fiery breath it
wound its slow and ponderous way across the landscape, shrivelling
and obliterating everything it touched in its path of death.

Naples was dilapidated, exceedingly unkempt and grossly over-
crowded. Such restaurants as remained open were out of bounds to
troops, ostensibly because of the typhus epidemic. Soldiers of a multitude of nationalities moved in all directions without order or formation
or any apparent fraternity with one another. Uniformed noncombatants
were impressive in their infinite variety and in sheer mass. Hordes of
civilians milled aimlessly about the streets at all hours of the day.
There were signs which warned those who cared to take note, in almost
every district, of the prevalence of particularly virulent types of vene-
real disease. The black market was rampant.

"Those great, ornate black hearses like oval goldfish bowls on
wheels," said one officer who was in a position to know, "with heavily
carved black pillars and a splendid coffin covered with flowers, followed by marchers on foot bearing silver crosses and a lot of black-
garbed mourners driving in a long line of carriages—you see dozens of
'em every day. Well, about half of the coffins are full of stuff being
transported to the black market. Checking 'em is a bit delicate as *some*
of the funerals are genuine and the families don't exactly welcome
having the casket laid open for inspection."

Through all the sordidness and squalor there gleamed those touches
of color that, with its superb physical setting, have always been the
charm of Naples. On some of the narrow, stepped streets which run
steeply uphill the projecting balconies in tiers bring the tops of the
house fronts almost together. The houses seem to lean towards one
another in friendly gesture, all but making an arcade of the street
below. Through the narrow gap left between their upper stories the
springtime sun filters down in shafts of gold that strike the stands of
fresh spring flowers at the bottom, the ascending tiers of booths with
their pyramids of oranges and lemons and red apples lighting each
dim passage in spots of jewelled brilliance.

From Naples I flew over to the eastern front, then back and across to Elmas Field on the edge of Lake Cagliari in Sardinia. This was head-quarters of the 42nd Bomb Wing, which "Uncle Joe" Cannon considered the best in the world. From my own experience there were not many better.

Medium-bombing conditions in central Italy and in northwestern France and the Low Countries were by no means identical. We who operated out of England had worse weather to contend with, especially at our bases. We had to get our altitude before leaving the English coast because only the narrow Channel separated us from the enemy's flak; and this tended to reduce our range. The enemy flak and air opposition were more heavily concentrated in northwestern Europe than in Italy. Despite the adverse conditions, our bombing was pretty good and steadily getting better, but in smacking small targets right on the nose it would be hard to surpass the precision work of the 42nd Bomb Wing.

I went with them on a mission whose object was to knock out a railway bridge between Arezzo and Florence. The bridge was only 230 feet long and 32 feet wide, a tiny and almost imperceptible target from 8500 feet altitude. Two squadrons of B-26 Marauders of the 320th Bomb Group—the Group that had done the bombing of Cassino—took off at noon from Decimomannu Field, about fifteen miles from Elmas, to carry out this task. (Marauders taxying to their take-off look like a long line of trained seals following one another with their flippers—the high tail fin of the B-26—held aloft; while Fortresses assembling before dawn on an English field resemble a file of elephants moving trunk-to-tail.)

We took off three at a time, which was not done with Marauders, as far as I know, anywhere else in the world, and saved about six minutes forming in the air. The formation of the two squadrons, each with three four-plane elements in tight defensive position, required only eight minutes. In England, with thirty-six-plane formations and our altitude to gain, it took an hour.

After covering the length of Sardinia and the coast of Corsica to Borgo, where our escort of twenty-six Spitfires made rendezvous, we crossed the Ligurian Sea and made landfall in Italy at 9000 feet over the mouth of the Ombrone River (crossing into north-ern France we would have been at 14,000 feet). It was a twenty-six-minute flight from the coast to the target, the last eight min-utes being on the straight bombing run. A bombing run of this length would have been sheer suicide in France, where even forty

seconds invited catastrophe. But on this target no flak had been pre-
dicted, and we met none, so the bombardiers could take their time.
The four planes on the median line used Norden sights; the others
bombed on the leaders.

We dropped ninety-one 1000-pound bombs (one wing ship was
too far out to bomb and one bomb hung up) on the target that looked
like a thin hair without color or feature. The bomb bursts opened up
like dingy black cauliflowers, soon blotting out the target. The pattern
was perfect and the strike attack photos showed both approaches plastered and at least two direct hits on the 32-foot-wide bridge. That was
Precision bombing with a capital P.

On the way back I recognized at a distance the mediæval towers of
San Gimignano, the "perfect" hill town, that I had not seen for thirty-
three years. Two Me-109's dived out of the sun and made a pass, then
high-tailed it for Florence. We saw no other enemy aircraft. The lack
of opposition was not typical of the area as a whole. There were many
"happy valleys" where the flak was dense. Had we been forced to take
an alternate target of shipping in Livorno harbor, owing to our primary
being covered, there would have been flak aplenty.

We landed two at a time, four hours and twenty-five minutes after
the take-off. One more railway bridge was gone. The disruption of the
enemy's rail communications north of Rome by bombing bridges and
marshalling yards resulted in the complete rail isolation of the fighting
front from its source of supply. The effect of this was shortly evident.
It was to be still more evident in France.

From Sardinia I flew back to England and the maze of final preparations for the invasion.

The Far Shore

> "I am a part of all that I have met,
> Yet all experience is an arch wherethro'
> Gleams that untravel'd world whose margin fades
> Forever and forever when I move."

The two most stupendous spectacles wrought by the hand of man
that I have witnessed were both in war. They occurred no great way
apart geographically. They were twenty-seven years apart in time.

The first was in June 1917 in Flanders, just before the dawn zero hour in the Battle of Messines Ridge. The massed British artillery on the 17,000-yard front was enough to make a solid line of cannon hub-to-hub for the whole length, had the guns been so placed. For ten days they had fired incessantly. During the last few hours before the attack they fired as fast as they could load. It was impossible to distinguish any individual fire or explosion in the continuous roar. Up on Mont Kemal, along whose lower slope our forces were poised for the attack, the intensity of the flashes, like streaks of white-hot metal spluttering through the dark, brought a strange elation.

Ten seconds before zero hour nineteen deep mines laid under the German lines were fired: 450 tons of ammonol in the greatest man-made explosion in the history of the world up to that time. The blinding spouts of light were such as might attend the world's final disruption. Their concussion shook the north of England. To those of us waiting for the attack it was only a heavier shock in the ceaseless earthquake from the guns. But the sight of it was something that can never fade in the memory of one who saw it.

The second and in some ways more extraordinary spectacle was the view from the air of the Normandy invasion in June 1944. This greatest amphibious operation in the world's history was a fantastic thing to look upon in its integration of an infinite number of normally disconnected parts, backed by countless thousands of other parts whose efforts kept the lethal flow pouring through the narrow abrasions in the enemy's defenses.

The converging lines of more vessels of more different types than had ever before been assembled churned their way grimly from far scattered ports of embarkation through the mine-swept lanes in a greyish sea. Among them many ancient hulks plodded for the last time under their own power on a one-way trip to an honorable end—a massed *hara-kiri* by dynamite in which they blew out their stomachs and quietly sank in line astern off the beaches as blockships for the artificial harbors. Oddly shaped contraptions were towed by tugs at a speed of three knots: the concrete caissons for those harbors, each mounting its own ack-ack defenses atop.

Ships of every shape and size from battle-wagons to launches moved in solemn procession to the four invasion beaches with the relentless urge of salmon heading towards their favored rivers to spawn. Just off the beaches many of them did spawn, and multitudes of young zigzagged and serpentined over the surface, churning white trails behind them. From the air these scurrying specks gave the impression of a lot of rather obscene water-beetles scuttling in the general direction of something on which they could feed. When they reached the shore they crawled out, and some joined the thin lines of jeeps and trucks and half-tracks winding into the interior where the smokes of battle mounted in multiple shades of grey and brown, white, yellow, black and red—from the bursts of naval gunfire, from burning ammunition dumps and tanks, from landing craft on the beaches, and burning Norman villages and farms over half the Cotentin peninsula.

The movement over the crowded beaches seemed less confused from the air than on the ground, since the lines of flow were more obvious and made clearer patterns. Long threads of men like ants wound slowly inland; little clusters of other ants waited on the slopes and in the shelter of the cliffs. Along the shore the beached LST's with their opened doors gave the illusion of great crocodiles lying on the sand, half in, half out of the water, with jaws agape from which they spewed smallish, rectangular objects on wheels that waddled away across the beach.

Offshore where "Mulberry A"—the artificial port for the American beachhead—was being assembled, the air view was confusing, and day by day became more so with the row of sunken blockships protruding from the water, the growing line of cement caissons that served as a sea wall, the great steel floats beyond, and the floating piers, bridges and causeways connecting with the shore; besides the masses of ships that lay in the transport area and behind the protection of the "Gooseberries"—the breakwaters—as these grew. To and fro amongst them, streaking the surface in all directions in straight and curving lines of white foam, the little water-beetles scuttled merrily on their appropriate occasions.

Near the shore several battleships and cruisers fired sundering charges on the scattered German defense works. Some of these concrete installations of formidable depth and solidity were reduced to impotency of action in fairly short order, though their deep chambers remained intact. A venerable battle-wagon bristling with ack-ack served as port control office and antiaircraft defense center. Almost all of the ships, including the sunken blockships and concrete caissons, flew their own barrage balloons which flecked the sky like jellyfish in a summer sea. Over it all, the Allied air cover in black and white invasion markings seethed spitefully at different altitudes, looking for a Luftwaffe that offered surprisingly little serious opposition.

In such an operation not all things go off perfectly. Inevitably confusion crops up. Landings were made in the wrong places: some companies were separated by several miles from the rest of their organizations. Certain units lost their equipment. Our low-flying patrols and bomber missions carrying out their tasks under the prevailing low ceiling were shot at lustily by our own warships and Allied merchant vessels, despite all recognition signals, if they approached below 3000 feet. The weather being what it was—with 3000 feet often the maximum ceiling—and given the multiplicity of our missions, such approaches were not in all cases possible to avoid. The high-speed launches of the R.A.F. Air-Sea Rescue Service, which had performed miracles in picking up thousands of British and American airmen forced to "ditch" in the Channel, fished three of our pilots out of the "drink" in one day, and a fourth managed to swim ashore, all downed by ack-ack fire from Allied ships. A liaison officer aboard one of the Naval command vessels pointed out with acrid humor in a radio message that gunners of the mercantile marine were paid overtime for their efforts beyond eight hours daily, which efforts, he stressed, were mostly devoted to shooting at our own aircraft.

All branches of the service made errors of commission and of judgment. The wonder was that the coordination worked as admirably as it did.

Against the grim realities of invasion odd flashes of humor played like summer lightning across a darkling sky. It is one of the saving graces that men's minds, keyed to the stark business of killing or being killed, react as they do to the touches of comedy which unexpectedly crop up in these humorless matters.

One of my advance parties landed on D-plus-two after various misadventures. Their LST was damaged by an enemy mine and lurched ashore at five in the afternoon instead of five-thirty in the morning, on a section of beach some distance from their intended point of debarkation. Their start was hardly propitious, but they had their comic relief with them.

This was in the shape of a tall, rawboned Major with a deep and penetrating voice, whose task was to establish advanced headquarters for Ninth Air Force on the Far Shore in the vicinity of Omaha Beach.

He began his unwitting relief of the tension in the early-morning dark as the packed landing ship wallowed through a restless sea. Gathering the air personnel around his force of three waterproofed jeeps, he made a brief address.

"We're shortly going into something we don't know anything about!" he boomed in his deep voice, pointing dramatically through the flashing dark which all eyes had been straining to penetrate. "We don't know how we're going to come out, or how many of us will get through. I'm not a religious man, but I think we should do something to prepare ourselves. I think we ought to say a prayer!"

"Okay, Mike," (that was not his name) the others assented. "Suppose you lead it." They knelt around the three jeeps while Mike started to intone the Lord's Prayer. He rather fumbled the beginning, which put the others off. After a dozen or so words he stuck. Someone prompted him and he went on, soon stuck again. There was a moment's silence; then the deep boom of Mike's voice. "For God's sake, somebody *say* something!" he bellowed. That effectively broke up the prayer.

Mike was firmly opposed to anyone's having food, even hot coffee, just before the landing. The others took a dim view of this. "In a short while," roared Mike, "we may all be struggling in cold, wet water! It's a dangerous thing, I tell you, to plunge straight into cold water on a full stomach!" He was outranked by three of my officers and overruled, which was just as well, since the LST ran into trouble and drifted all but helplessly for the next twelve hours. But Mike's warning was not wholly inapt, as far as he personally was concerned.

The LST finally grounded. Mike had collected his own small party in the three jeeps, which formed the vanguard of the other vehicles aboard. The jeeps' hoods were down; the upright extensions of the exhaust pipes smote the air above their folded windshields. Mike was alone in the first jeep, which was otherwise laden with musette bags and miscellaneous gear. As the ramp went down he raised his right arm with his fist clenched. The only thing lacking was a cavalry saber in his upraised hand.

"Here we *go!*" he roared. "Come on, boys, FOLLOW ME!" and drove the jeep off the ramp into twelve feet of water. There was a large *glug* as it disappeared, and two or three spreading, concentric rings on the surface of the sea. Then, one by one, there floated up several items of loose equipment; and finally Mike, tin-hatted, pistol in belt, emerged blowing like a porpoise and set forth to swim ashore.

It appeared that the LST had grounded on a narrow sandbar with deep water beyond. The crew had the devil's own time changing position so that the rest of the keyed-up invaders could debark with their equipment. It was five days before the jeep was salvaged. I drove it afterwards. It had no horn or lights and the engine would not idle, but otherwise it was intact.

Just before landing, the party had observed with some astonishment that the surface of the sea along the beach was covered with expended rubber articles designed for use as prophylactic safeguards and contraceptives. The breaking waves tossed these about, thousands upon thousands of white spots, distinctive among the foam flecks.

"My God!" cried one of the party. "What sort of an invasion is this? Looks like the boys who came ashore yesterday were mighty amiably received!" One of my officers had landed twice in the Mediterranean and knew the answer. The troops had encased the muzzles of their rifles, carbines, pistols, machine guns and other weapons as well as their wrist watches, money, photographs and so on in these convenient protectors as a guard against the salt water during the voyage and the landing. Before they hit the beach they stripped off the rubber items from their weapons and threw them into the sea. The effect as one followed along later was prodigious.

My party finally got ashore and made their way with some difficulty to Grandcamp-les-Bains. They dossed down that night in a moderately intact house whose grounds on both sides were sown with unremoved mines. During the night the bellowing voice of Mike was heard above the din of the ack-ack. He was stamping about, beating on the walls and the floors with the butt of his carbine.

"Turn out at once!" he shouted. "Everybody turn out! Bring your side-arms, carbines, whatever you've got. There are five of 'em!"

"Five of *what*, Mike?" inquired Joe Mahar, one of three Lieutenant Colonels in my advanced party, in a tone one might use to a querulous child.

"How the hell do *I* know?" roared Mike. "*I* haven't seen 'em!"

They were, it came out, five flares which had been dropped above the Grandcamp beach by low-flying enemy aircraft. The ack-ack was roaring mightily over the matter. Our air personnel, armed only with pistols and carbines, hemmed in by mines and very apt to be shot at in the dark by our own highly nervous sentries, were not wholly clear just what they could do about it. But Mike continued bellowing for them all to turn out.

Mike did not remain long at Ninth Air Force advanced headquarters. In some ways this was a pity. There is nothing like a little unintended buffoonery to lighten the tension of warfare.

The Far Shore was a curious kaleidoscope of movement fanning out from the toeholds on the beaches, not as yet very deeply established. Interspersed amidst the moiling flow were dead spots of tranquillity, scarcely affected by the advent of the Martian hosts. To some of the simpler Norman peasants we must indeed have appeared like warriors from Mars. We landed from the air by night on silent wings, we dropped from the air holding great white umbrellas, we crawled out of the sea in the bellies of amphibian monsters that snorted their way inland over the beaches, we ran up and down the roads in boats on wheels, we rained devastation from the air and the sea and the land upon their villages, towns and farms.

I did not go across by sea and so missed that amphibious experience, but I would not willingly have forgone the view of the assault from the air. I landed by aircraft back of Omaha Beach as soon as our hard-driving and efficient Air Engineers had laid out our first metal landing strip in incredibly few days' time. The beaches, the landing strip and the roads along the coast seethed with mechanized life in weird and uncouth shapes, with toiling men amidst heterogeneous dumps of supplies and equipment, of wreckage and wastage being shoved about by bulldozers or left to rust or crumple where it lay. "Rat race," and "our can of worms," were expressions that went for many things, but were peculiarly apt for the beachheads. Yet during the five-day storm that wrecked the Omaha "Gooseberry" I ran up the road close to Cherbourg, days before we captured the town, as fast as the departed Mike's dunked jeep would go, and met with scarcely any traffic interference at all. It showed what the beaches meant in the continuing supply of the invasion, and what a serious storm could do to disrupt the supply. Ninth Air Force troop carriers and transports were then flying ammunition across the Channel for our artillery.

The by-passed spots of tranquillity, like obscurely marked isles of safety in the traffic of a city, were often deceptive. Beneath the poppies the fields were strewn with mines; death lurked in the quiet hedgerows. Sinister signs with black skull-and-crossbones and the words "ACHTUNG! MINEN!" and sometimes a French sub-line *"Attention! Mines!"* were all over the place. On one particularly virulent MINEN sign on the edge of a mine-strewn field, some Frenchman had scrawled in pencil, "*Merde pour Minen*"—a not politely translatable intimation of contempt. Though their presence did not always mean that mines had actually been laid in the fields and ditches they covered with their warning, the reverse was equally true.

In the Sainte Mère Eglise area the little fields were spattered with the naked skeletons of gliders whose skins had been stripped off by passing troops and local peasantry to serve as shelter, or for souvenirs. Many lay upended, overturned, broken-winged, where they had run into the unyielding hedgerows. There are few less felicitous terrains on which to bring a glider down at night, save on glaciers and Himalayan upheavals, than this sector of Normandy. The more open and so more obvious fields were mostly planted with anti-glider stakes. Modern warfare is rarely fought under friendly conditions of climate and terrain.

There was a narrow road down which I drove a jeep where an Afro-American engineer company had taken refuge in the hedgerows because a considerable intensity of enemy artillery fire was detracting from the road's natural charm. The ditches had been cleared of mines. The double row of shiny black faces with round white eyeballs peering out of the hedges had a curious appearance of aborigines grimacing from an African jungle. But the blowpipes of these aborigines were M-1-30 carbines. I was not greatly disturbed by the enemy shelling, but I felt a bit uneasy about those M-1-30 blowpipes protruding from the hedges below pair after pair of large white eyeballs set in ovals of black. Yet no lethal dart came in my direction.

Soon after I first landed I talked with a middle-aged Norman farmer standing in the ruin of what had been a fine old grey-stone farm. He gave me the V sign. "So you have come!" he said simply, and his sweeping gesture embraced the steadily pyramiding number of tens of thousands of men of foreign persuasion surging over the fair face of Normandy, along with the wreckage of his ancient domain. "Pay attention in that field—it's mined," he remarked, as if saying that there was poison ivy in it. He spotted my *Croix de Guerre* ribbon with one outreaching finger, and nodded solemnly. "So you know us!" he said. "I fought in the last war. I was wounded in the vicinity of Nancy."

"So was I," I said, "though lightly."

"I not so lightly. Good luck!" said he, and returned to his salvaging operations in the debris.

Nearby a Normandy cow stared mournfully across the skull-and-crossbones of an "*Achtung! Minen!*" sign at the bloated body of one of its kin that lay with legs upraised in mute and final protest. There were many bloated bodies of Normandy cattle spattered over the landscape, though a substantial number of survivors grazed unconcernedly in the torn fields. The defunct mostly had not been mined; they had been "liberated."

It was said of the Normans that they were not notably effusive over our efforts for their liberation. Stories of Frenchwomen sniping at our troops went the rounds, as inevitably happens under these circumstances. To the best of my knowledge—and I had some facilities for checking the substance of such tales—there was not an authenticated case of the sort, save perhaps for two women of no very high background married to German soldiers, who were forced to shoot under threat of prompt and unhappy severance of their relations with this world. There were many instances of local inhabitants taking grave risks to aid our progress.

The Normans are a dour people, reticent and suspicious, with none of the volatility of the more central and southerly French. But they are substantial, hard-working and independent, and their substance derives from the soil and the sea. The Allies freed them from the indignity of foreign occupation, which on the Cotentin peninsula had been less oppressive than in many other sections, for the primary reason that this peninsula seemed to our higher strategists to offer the most favorable approach for the destruction of the German Army. We devastated their ancient towns, their charming villages and farms, in the process; in some instances for no more permanent advantage than to create "road blocks" which might delay German military movements for a few hours. We made a shambles of their transportation system, and left them hungry in a land of plenty because distribution depends on transportation, and military priorities for our own advancing forces absorbed all efforts at repair.

A good deal of the destruction could not well be avoided under military necessity; some of it was accomplished by the Germans in retreat. But the net result of "liberation" was that the Normans were left far worse off than they had been under the German occupation. There was even a nonfraternization order applied in some areas such as Grandcamp-les-Bains, which served to further mutual suspicions. Our Naval authorities refused for several weeks after D-day, on the grounds of security, to permit the Norman fishermen to leave port and resume fishing—their sole means of livelihood as well as a valuable source of food supply for many others. And we were critical because the people of the peninsula did not all dance for joy, like Potemkin's villagers during the passage of Catherine the Great, over our advent.

The military command in its purely military objectives handled the complex problems of coordinated attack as effectively as ever in history. The planning and the conduct of any coordinated effort to prevent military victory in Europe from degenerating into social disaster among the people we professed to be liberating—and Normandy, as a rich agricultural province, was far better off than many of the "liberated" areas—were fatuously unimaginative and inept.

Passing through the small towns and villages, where our bulldozers were busily ploughing a way in the debris, many a venerable Norman turned from digging in the ruins of everything of permanence that life had held for him to give me the V sign, then turned back to try to salvage from the rubble some bit of wood, or metal or crockery a few inches long, to carry away in a broken baby carriage.

With three of my officers I reconnoitred a valley about twenty kilometers southeast of Cherbourg, a few days before we captured the town, to try to estimate the effects of a combined strike of heavy, medium and dive bombers on the German positions there. Our advanced elements had been pulled back some 1400 yards just prior to the bombing, but the positions were not very clear. We may have been a bit far out, as some of our Thunderbolts were strafing at about fifty feet altitude over the trees behind us.

We went back up on the ridge for a better view and cruised along this in a jeep. Arthur ("Michel") Roseborough, one of my Lieut. Colonels who had come over with Mike on D-plus-two, pointed out that we had improved our position to the extent that we were now in full view of the Germans on the other side of the narrow valley. This was true, but there appeared to be some compensating advantages. A few hundred yards along the ridge we were accosted by three husky, blue-smocked peasants who said that there was a wounded American soldier in a manoir back down in the valley—and would we like to pick him up? I turned the jeep around and the three Normans clambered aboard. I heard some demurs from my companions. "This may be a trap!" one of them said.

The Normans led us down a narrow road through thickish woods. We did not see a single person. I heard the snicker of bolts as my three officers chambered cartridges in their carbines. Each one covered a Norman. The bombing had finished. "We ought to be just about in the German lines by now," Michel observed. But I did not believe it was a trap.

We eventually turned right through an avenue of broken trees and came to a manoir which had a protecting barricade of tree trunks. There was no one about, but considerable evidence of very recent German occupation. "Don't like the looks of this!" said Michel. My other two officers didn't much fancy it either. I led the way into a wing indicated by the Normans, followed by the others, all with carbines at the ready. Inside the closed door was a small room and in this were three women, a young boy and the wounded soldier whom we were seeking. The women had bound the soldier's leg with strips of undergarments. It had been pretty badly torn by mortar fire, but they had done an excellent field job of cleaning and bandaging it. He had been hit nearby shortly after the Germans had retired from the place the previous night. Two of the women had brought him in. He was thin, dark, spoke bad Spanish, and turned out to be a Mexican from southern California.

They had offered him Calvados to drink, which he stoutly refused. In this he was wiser than we. After we loaded him into the jeep to take him to some field ambulance we shook hands all around and congratulated the Normans on their work. I gave them some K-rations which was all we had with us, and they brought out a bottle of Calvados and one cracked glass. The Calvados must have been all of five weeks old. We were pressed to drink a full tumbler each. It went down like flaming nitroglycerine.

"*Jee*-sus!" said Michel with tears pouring from his eyes. "I *told* you we shouldn't have come here!"

Normans, both of the organized Underground and others, did a great deal to assist our fliers downed in German-held territory to escape capture and filter back through the lines. A considerable number succeeded in getting out this way; others were concealed, fed and sheltered until our troops had overrun the places where they were hidden.

Throughout France the Underground—the Resistance—accomplished one of the miracles of the war in bringing out to safety across France and the Pyrenees, under the very noses of the Gestapo, thousands of Allied pilots and air crews who had been forced to bail out over western Europe. The organization, the gallantry and determination were amazing, as were the results achieved. Our young men were passed along from one point to another, personally conducted, fed, clothed in civilian clothes, provided with phony papers, given medical care, and finally guided over uncharted (and exceedingly rough) passes in the Pyrenees, by a large fraternity of nameless persons whose lives were at stake if they were caught. The casualties among this fraternity were very high. Often there were delays in moving our young men, which made them nervous, because whole sectors of the system had been destroyed by the Germans, their personnel tortured and killed. But they were reborn from their own ashes and in due course started functioning again.

During the three months before D-Day we were receiving returnees in England, who had come out this way, at an average rate of three a day—two Americans and one from the R.A.F. I talked with a good many of our lads who had come out quickly or had especially interesting stories, and saw reports on most of the others. Of those with whom I talked I asked certain questions, including one as to how long it was from the time they "hit the silk" (bailed out) until they were in the hands of "organized friends." Brief refuge afforded by people not in the organization and who had not passed them on did not count. The last two to whom I put this question gave an insight into the growing efficiency of the organization.

The first replied: "Oh, about forty seconds!" The second said: "Why, sir, I can't exactly say. I saw someone on a bicycle pedalling like hell below me as I went down. I thought he might be a German and tried to slip away from him, but he was there when I hit the ground. He turned out to be a French boy about fifteen years old. He could speak a few words of English. He took my parachute and hid it under a sort of haycock. Then he hid me in a ditch and pulled a bunch of brambles over me. He gave me a little bottle of red wine and a chunk of bread, told me to stay where I was and not to budge. After that he pedalled off and in the evening when it was dusk a man came and took me away. So I was really in the hands of 'organized friends' before I even hit the ground."

When our planes passed overhead, and there were air battles or much flak, young lads would cruise around on bicycles, watching for parachutes. If they saw any open up, the boys nearest would sprint to where these were dropping and seek to intercept and hide the airmen before the Germans got them. This was a late refinement of the organization. It only worked in certain instances, of course, but the system as a whole was amazingly effective. A large number of Americans and British, their parents, wives and sweethearts, have a personal reason to be exceedingly grateful to the Underground.

The second phase of the World War was one in which weird and wondrous contraptions played an extraordinary part. The full story of those we used, and of some which the Germans had in preparation, is slowly coming out. It was the grace of Providence that many of the German conceptions were not technically ready to launch before we smashed the *Wehrmacht* and overran their launching sites and production centers.

I examined an installation at Sottevaste, some twenty-four kilometers south of Cherbourg, just after our ground forces had uncovered it. It was a colossal affair of excavation and reinforced concrete in a valley below the little hill town of Brix. It was more than half a square mile in area, with some emplacements 100 feet deep. Two thousand laborers of perhaps a dozen nationalities in the Todt organization had been working there for ten months, and the project was not half completed.

We had bombed the place, but not intensively. Rigid priorities called for visitations on other installations nearer completion, though of lesser scope, and there were plenty of these. Our spasmodic bombing of Sottevaste had delayed progress and depressed the morale of the Todt staff, the people of Brix told me, but the effect on the enormously thick concrete works had not greatly altered the physical outlay.

The plan was not entirely clear, but it was undoubtedly intended as a launching site for much larger rocket projectiles—V-3's or beyond—than those turned loose up to the end of active hostilities. It was not likely that two thousand men would be employed for such a length of time, with the enormous expenditure in concrete and other materials, unless the German High Command believed that the device which it was intended to launch from here was well on its way to perfection and large-scale production. The Todt staff told the people of Brix that the installation was for a remote-controlled, electro-chemical "super-cannon" that would completely wipe out the British Isles. But it did not appear to be oriented on the British Isles. It seemed rather to point at New York.

We had in the Ninth Air Force one very different type of contraption that would have seemed equally improbable a few years back. This was a night photographic apparatus which, combined with a gadget known as a "Gee-box," enabled us to take pin-point or overlapping strip photos on the darkest nights far back of the enemy's lines, at any desired altitude and with amazing precision, from an aircraft whose crew saw nothing of the area they were photographing nor any feature on the ground from the time they left their field in England until they returned. The photographic apparatus had been devised by Dr. H. E. Edgerton of M.I.T. I had it brought up from Italy, together with Dr. Edgerton, who had been testing it there, and for the first eleven nights from D-minus-one the only night photographs we got of the invasion area were taken by this one apparatus—which was the only one of its kind in existence. All of these photographs were taken at between 400 and 800 feet altitude. The ceiling during that period was never high enough to use flash-bulbs, whose utility was limited in other respects as well.

Night photography was important in showing up enemy traffic movements, which, because of our bombing, were largely confined to the hours of darkness. We could pin-point a road intersection or run a strip down a road with such accuracy and clarity that one could spot a dachshund in the photo and tell which foot it had lifted, if there had been a dachshund on the road. On the twelfth night we lost the plane. It never came back, nor was there any report on it or on the crew, one of whom was our senior Gee-box instructor. Dr. Edgerton built a new apparatus in an amazingly short time from bits and pieces picked up all over England. Later more aircraft were so equipped and did yeoman service during our battling into Germany.

On D-plus-thirty I was hit in the course of a forward reconnaissance on the ground at La Haye du Puits. The situation was "confused." Our troops had entered the edge of the little town the previous day but had been driven out that night during stiff fighting. There was no "line" properly speaking. No one knew exactly where our advanced elements were at.

Captain Leo Goldsmith and Lieutenant Robert Crane were with

me. We had not seen a soul in some while. There was a good deal of rifle, machine-gun and machine-pistol firing, and the place was being shelled, though we could not tell by whom. We could see the railway crossing and station of La Haye du Puits about 150 yards down the road. This spot was presumably in enemy hands.

We started back to where I had left our jeep hidden under a hedge. After a few steps something connected with my right knee. It hurt like the devil but did not knock me down. It didn't feel at all like a bullet. It felt as if Babe Ruth had swung a home run on my knee with a bronze bat. But it was a bullet all right, from a Schmeitzer machine-pistol, and it went clean through my knee-cap. I heard the shot, among others of the same kind. There is no mistaking the flat bark of a Schmeitzer. The bullet was protruding from the inner side of my knee, loosely held by the skin. I could have cut it out with a penknife.

I let myself down on one haunch, and observed that I was alone. I also noted that I was making a perfect sitting target for being polished off. There was a little building nearby, a sort of roofed-over sheep-pen. I heard Leo Goldsmith's voice calling me from there. Using my carbine as a crutch I got up and hobbled over to this small refuge. The door was open. It was dark and evil-smelling inside. There were German overcoats scattered about the earthen floor. On one of these Bobby Crane lay stretched out with his left calf mangled by another Schmeitzer bullet. Leo Goldsmith had not been hit.

It was not an inspiring place. I had no desire to be collared by the Huns, and two of us were not in very good shape to do anything spectacular. After Leo had dressed Bobby Crane's wound and mine I decided to make a break for the jeep. The wooden door, swung outward on leather hinges towards La Haye du Puits, would at least partly conceal us from view from that direction as we sneaked along the wall of the sheep-pen. I tested our chances in a one-legged hobble; Leo and Bobby were to follow on their three legs if I got around the corner of the building without being potted. There was a fair amount of shooting but we made it, and the three-legs beat me to the jeep. Leo levered us aboard, bucked the jeep around; we took the corner in the opposite direction like a badly scared jackrabbit. I recall making a futile protest. "It's no good turning us over!" I cried. "We're not eggs— or if we are we're cracked eggs!" He did not turn us over, which reflected well on the innate stability of the jeep. We bounded rearwards a mile or so to a regimental collecting company station, seeing not a living person on the way, and from there Bobby and I were taken on a series of jolting ambulance jaunts to the 91st Evacuation Hospital outside of Ste. Mère Eglise. I was operated on in a tent that night and was flown to England in a Ninth Air Force transport the next day. Leo brought me half a bottle of cognac that I had left behind. This helped quite a bit.

It is salutary for the soul to spend some while, but not too long, in a hospital as one of a large fraternity of combat casualties whose wounds cover the whole varied and unamiable range of weapons of modern warfare. There is inspiration in the spirit of most of the men who have been knocked out in battle. Once on the road to recovery they gripe over every conceivable thing, but on the whole they take their own misadventures cheerfully. In my ward the more lightly wounded, with a few exceptions, wanted to return to their units in action. Even the badly maimed often felt that they had been luckier than many others around them. There were some, of course, who had not been lucky in any manner of speaking.

The human wastage of warfare is not alone evidenced in shattered bodies. Fate plays some odd tricks in the matter of timing. One young officer I met in hospital told me that he had been training for four years; during the last two, intensively for an invasion of Europe. He had never been in action until he landed on Omaha Beach on D-Day. He lasted just forty seconds before he was knocked out for good, as far as the war was concerned, by an 88 mm. shell.

The surgical treatment in the American hospitals of my experience, and in the experience of nearly all others with whom I have talked, was marvelous. Our nurses did a splendid job. One waxes rather less enthusiastic over some phases of the administrative end. For seven weeks in the 192nd U. S. General Hospital at Cirencester in Gloucestershire I was less appetizingly fed than during any equivalent period I have spent anywhere in the world. There were four dietitians in that hospital. The food was perfectly good U. S. Army rations. The cooks also were American: I think they probably had been concrete mixers in civil life. But all in all we were very well cared for by the medical branch.

There is no more bitterness, so far as I can judge, in a hospital of combat casualties than elsewhere. But one is led inevitably to reflect on the whole tragic scheme of things that under the guise of national destiny has reduced Europe, once the nucleus and pride of our civilization, as well as much of Asia, to ruins and lasting misery. I have yet to hear a satisfactory definition of civilization, but I cannot feel that its final expression is either in plumbing or in the development of bigger and more effective weapons of destruction. Whatever it may be, it seems destined for self-immolation unless the forces that have been unleashed can be controlled through some form of world federation. And to this end a resurgence of rabid nationalism and constant stressing of national sovereignty would hardly appear to be the path.

I am glad to have known the world as it was before the impact of the "scientific age" changed it unbelievably in my brief span of time. Many of the changes fill me with acute sorrow. The disappearance of so much that was beautiful, mellowed by age and loving care, of so much that was gracious in human relationship, is for me a personal loss. I do not feel especially happy over many of the substitutes for these things in an age of material tastes. What the immediate future is likely to bring in the way of other changes I find it difficult to look to with unmixed enthusiasm.

Yet my purpose holds, for I hitched my wagon to a restless star too early in life now to watch the world revolve from a detached and static point.

> "........ *for my purpose holds*
> *To sail beyond the sunset, and the baths*
> *Of all the western stars, until I die.*"

Index

427